Debates in Geography E

Debates in Geography Education encourages student and practising teachers to engage with and reflect on key issues, concepts and debates in their specialist subject teaching. It aims to enable geography teachers to reach their own informed judgements and argue their point of view with deeper theoretical knowledge and understanding.

Expert editors and contributors provide a balance of experience and perspectives and offer international, historical and policy contexts, evidence-informed classroom debates and a glimpse of the subject's expanding horizons.

Debates considered include:

- what constitutes knowledge in geography?
- constructing the curriculum
- how do we link assessment to making progress in geography?
- the contribution of fieldwork and outdoor experiences
- technology and media
- how we use Geographical Information
- how geography contributes to 'global learning'
- sustainable development and geography education.

The comprehensive, rigorous coverage of these key issues, together with carefully annotated selected further reading, reflective questions and a range of specific web-based resources, will help support and shape your own research and writing. *Debates in Geography Education* is a source of knowledge, experience and debate that will be essential reading for all students studying at Masters level, practising teachers who want to develop a better understanding of the issues that shape their practice, and Education Studies students considering in-depth subject teaching.

David Lambert was Chief Executive of the Geographical Association from 2002 to 2012 and is now Professor of Geography Education at the Institute of Education, University of London, UK. He is the author of a wide range of books, including *Teaching School Subjects I1–19: Geography* and *Learning to Teach Geography in the Secondary School, 2nd edition*, both published by Routledge.

Mark Jones is a PGCE Geography Tutor and Senior Lecturer in Education at the University of the West of England, Bristol, UK. He is engaged in research into secondary curriculum development, innovation and building sustainable geography networks in Bristol and the south-west region.

Debates in Subject Teaching Series

Series edited by: Susan Capel, Jon Davison, James Arthur, John Moss

The **Debates in Subject Teaching Series** is a sequel to the popular **Issues in Subject Teaching Series**, originally published by Routledge between 1999 and 2003. Each title presents high-quality material, specially commissioned to stimulate teachers engaged in initial training, continuing professional development and Masters level study to think more deeply about their practice, and link research and evidence to what they have observed in schools. By providing up-to-date, comprehensive coverage the titles in the **Debates in Subject Teaching Series** support teachers in reaching their own informed judgements, enabling them to discuss and argue their point of view with deeper theoretical knowledge and understanding.

Titles in the series:

Debates in History Teaching
Edited by Ian Davies

Debates in English Teaching
Edited by Jon Davison, Caroline Daly and John Moss

Debates in Religious Education
Edited by Philip Barnes

Debates in Citizenship Education
Edited by James Arthur and Hilary Cremin

Debates in Art and Design Education
Edited by Lesley Burgess and Nicholas Addison

Debates in Music Teaching
Edited by Chris Philpott and Gary Spruce

Debates in Physical Education
Edited by Susan Capel and Margaret Whitehead

Debates in Geography Education
Edited by David Lambert and Mark Jones

Debates in Geography Education

Edited by David Lambert and Mark Jones

Routledge
Taylor & Francis Group

LONDON AND NEW YORK

First published 2013
by Routledge
2 Park Square, Milton Park, Abingdon, Oxon OX14 4RN

Simultaneously published in the USA and Canada
by Routledge
711 Third Avenue, New York, NY 10017

Routledge is an imprint of the Taylor & Francis Group, an informa business

British Library Cataloguing in Publication Data
A catalogue record for this book is available from the British Library

Library of Congress Cataloging-in-Publication Data
Debates in geography education / edited by David Lambert and Mark
Jones.
    p. cm. — (The debates in subject teaching series)
Includes index.
ISBN 978-0-415-68778-2 (hardback) — ISBN 978-0-415-68779-9 (pbk)
— ISBN 978-0-203-13661-4 (ebk) 1. Geography—Study and teaching I.
Lambert, David, 1952- II. Jones, Mark.
G73.D283 2013
910.71—dc23   2012024057

ISBN: 978-0-415-68778-2 (hbk)
ISBN: 978-0-415-68779-9 (pbk)
ISBN: 978-0-203-13661-4 (ebk)

Typeset in Galliard
by Cenveo Publisher Services

Printed and bound by CPI Group (UK) Ltd, Croydon, CR0 4YY

Contents

Abbreviations

AB	Awarding Bodies
AEB	Associated Examining Board
AfL	Assessment for Learning
APG	Action Plan for Geography
BPRS	Best Practice Research Scholarship Programme
BTEC	Business and Technician Education Council
CAFOD	Catholic Agency for Overseas Development
CAL	Computer Assisted Learning
CARE	Christian Action Research and Education
CASE	Cognitive Acceleration in Science Education project
CPD	Continuing Professional Development
CSE	Certificate of Secondary Education
DCSF	Department for Children, Schools and Families
DEA	Development Education Association
DES	Department of Education and Science
DfE	Department for Education
DfEE	Department for Education and Employment
DfES	Department for Education and Skills
DfID	Department for International Development
Ebacc	English Baccalaureat
ECM	Every Child Matters
EfS	education for sustainability
ESD	Education for Sustainable Development
Esri	Environmental Systems Research Institute
GA	Geographical Association
GEReCo	Geography Education Research Collective
GIS	Geographic Information Systems
GNC	Geography National Curriculum
GNVQ	General National Vocational Qualification
GTCE	General Teaching Council for England
GTT	Geography Teaching Today

GYSL	'Geography for the Young School Leaver'
HEI	Higher Education Institutions
HMCI	Her Majesty's Chief Inspector (English and Welsh Schools)
HMI	Her Majesty's Inspectorate
HMSO	Her Majesty's Stationery Office
ICT	information and communication technology
ITE	initial teacher education
ITT	initial teacher training
IBG	Institute of British Geographers
JMB	Joint Matriculation Board
KS	Key Stage
LEDC	Less Economically Developed Countries
MEDC	More Economically Developed Countries
MGH	'Making Geography Happen'
NEAB	Northern Examinations and Assessment Board
NPQH	National Professional Qualification for Headship
NSS	National Student Survey
OCR	Oxford Cambridge and RSA Examinations
Ofsted	Office for Standards in Education
PGCE	Postgraduate Certificate in Education
PLTS	personal, learning and thinking skills
POS	programme of study
PPGIS	public participatory GIS
Pre-U	Pre-university
QCA	Qualifications and Curriculum Authority
QCDA	Qualifications and Curriculum Development Agency
RGS	Royal Geographical Society
RSA	Royal Society for the Encouragement of Arts, Manufactures and Commerce
SCAA	Schools Curriculum and Assessment Authority
SAT	Standard Assessment Task
SCIP	School Curriculum Industry Partnership
SEAL	social and emotional aspects of learning
SLN	Staffordshire Learning Network
SOLO	Structure of Observed Learning Outcomes
TCK	Technological Content Knowledge
TPACK	Technological Pedagogical Content Knowledge
TPK	Technological Pedagogical Knowledge
TVEI	Technical and Vocational Education Initiative
UNCED	United Nations Conference on the Environment and Development
UNESCO	United Nations Educational, Scientific and Cultural Organisation
USP	unique selling point
VCE	Vocational Certificates of Education

VGI	volunteered geographical information
VLE	virtual learning environment
VOIP	Voice over Internet Protocol
WCED	World Commission on Environment and Development
WJEC	Welsh Joint Education Committee
YPG	'Young People's Geographies'

Contributors

Mary Biddulph is Lecturer in Geography Education at the University of Nottingham and is a member of the Centre for Research in Schools and Communities. She has written widely on the subject of young people's geographies, student agency and curriculum development in geography and with Roger Firth (Oxford) led the Young People's Geographies project. Mary was editor of *Teaching Geography* 2009–12.

Clare Brooks is Senior Lecturer in Geography Education at the Institute of Education, University of London. A former London secondary school teacher, and Subject Leader for the Geography PGCE, Clare's interests are in teacher development and knowledge. She was Programme Leader for the MA in Geography Education at the Institute until 2012 and edited *Studying PGCE Geography at M Level* published by Routledge. She is currently leading the introduction of a new international Masters Degree: the MA Education.

Graham Butt is Professor of Education at Oxford Brookes University and Chair of the Geography Education Research Collective (GEReCo). Graham's research is predominantly in the field of geography education, although he has also published on teacher workload, modernisation and assessment. In 2011 he edited *Geography, Education and the Future*, a collection of research-based chapters offering perspectives on the changing relationship between geography and geography education.

Gemma Collins is Lecturer in Geography Education at the University of Birmingham. A former secondary school teacher, Gemma is now a teacher trainer. She has also worked with the Ministry of Education in Tanzania, in the areas of curriculum, pedagogy and CPD for teachers.

Bob Digby taught for 24 years in three schools in Leeds and London, and for 11 years as a Geography Education Tutor at Sheffield, Manchester and Brunel Universities. He is Principal Examiner for one of Edexcel's GCSE Geography specifications, and author of many school textbooks and journal articles. Bob serves as President of the Geographical Association (2012–13).

Mary Fargher is Lecturer in Geography Education at the Institute of Education, University of London. A former secondary school teacher and head of department, she works in initial teacher education and is the geography lead tutor for

Teach First. Her PhD research was on the role of GIS in teaching and learning of place in school geography.

Jane Ferretti taught geography in secondary schools in Sheffield until 2003 and is now at the University of Sheffield where she is responsible for the Geography PGCE and also works on Master's courses. She is an active member of the Geographical Association and sits on both the Publications Committee and the Editorial group for *Teaching Geography*. She edited *Meeting the Needs of Your Most Able Pupils: Geography* and has written for *Teaching Geography*.

Roger Firth is a Lecturer and Fellow of St Anne's College at the University of Oxford. A former secondary school teacher, he has worked at Nottingham Trent University and Nottingham University. He has written widely on geography in education, Education for Sustainable Development (ESD), the school curriculum and the Young People's Geographies project. His most recent research interests are subject knowledge and the school curriculum and subject pedagogy.

David Gardner is a part-time Lecturer for the PGCE Geography at Goldsmiths University and the Open University. He was formerly geography adviser at the QCDA from 2005 until the organisation was abolished in 2011. A former secondary school teacher and deputy head teacher, David has written a range of geography textbooks and guides for Key Stage 3 and GCSE.

Duncan Hawley is Senior Lecturer and PGCE Tutor in Secondary Geography at Swansea School of Education, Swansea Metropolitan University. He taught geography and geology in a range of secondary schools and in a field studies centre. He is the current Chair of the Physical Geography special interest group of the Geographical Association and a former Chair of the Earth Science Teachers' Association.

John Hopkin began his teaching career in Birmingham, teaching in a variety of comprehensive schools before becoming School Effectiveness Adviser with a wide range of responsibilities. John is a long-standing member and past President of the Geographical Association (2010–11). His particular interests include the teaching of places in geography, curriculum planning and assessment, and he is author and editor of a range of successful textbooks, websites and other resources.

Mark Jones is Senior Lecturer in Geography Education at the University of the West of England, Bristol where he teaches on undergraduate, postgraduate and Masters programmes. A former curriculum leader with 18 years' teaching experience in secondary schools in Bristol and South Gloucestershire, he now leads the PGCE Secondary Geography course. His research and publications focus on student participation, cross-curricular creativity, and connecting university and school geography.

Alan Kinder has worked in geographical education for over 20 years as a geography teacher, curriculum leader, field studies officer, local authority adviser, and as a trainer and consultant. He is the author of a wide range of professional

articles on geography and curriculum materials. Alan is a long-standing member of the Geographical Association and a recent chair of its Education Committee (2009–12). In 2012 he was appointed Chief Executive of the GA.

David Lambert is Professor of Geography Education at the Institute of Education, University of London and was Chief Executive of the Geographical Association from 2002 to 2012. A former secondary school teacher and teacher trainer, he has written widely on geography in education, citizenship, assessment and the curriculum. His most recent book was co-authored with John Morgan in 2010, *Teaching Geography 11–18: A Conceptual Approach.*

John Lyon is currently Programme Manager at the Geographical Association (GA) and formally an assistant head at a large 11–18 comprehensive school in Rotherham. He is a Chartered Geographer, taught geography for almost 30 years and has an NPQH qualification. He is now responsible for the leadership and management of the GA's programme of support for teachers' professional development, including funded projects and the development of the Secondary Geography Quality Mark.

Fran Martin is Senior Lecturer in Education at the University of Exeter. Her PhD investigated PGCE primary students' conceptions of geography, pedagogy and epistemology, leading to her description of primary geography as 'Ethnogeography'. Fran was president of the Geographical Association from 2011 to 2012, and is a member of the *Primary Geography* editorial board. Fran's other research interests are in development education and intercultural learning.

David Mitchell is Lecturer in Geography Education at the Institute of Education, University of London. A former school teacher, he is now a geography teacher, educator and researcher, and subject leader for the geography PGCE. He has written on geography education and in 2009 he edited *Living Geography: Exciting Futures for Teachers and Students.*

John Morgan is Professor of Education at the University of Auckland. Before that, he worked in geography education at the University of Bristol and Institute of Education, University of London, where he was a Reader in Geography Education. His most recent book is *Teaching Secondary Geography as if the Planet Matters* published by Routledge in 2011. He is a member of the Editorial Collective of *Geography* for the GA.

Alan Parkinson is a teacher, curriculum developer and author. He spent three years working as Secondary Curriculum Development Leader for the Geographical Association after 20 years as a secondary geography teacher. He is currently a freelance geographer, working on numerous projects for publishers and other organisations. He is a founder member of the Geography Collective, creators of *Mission:Explore*, and a prominent blogger and social networker.

Charles Rawding is Senior Lecturer in Geography Education at Edge Hill University, Lancashire. Prior to becoming involved in teacher training, he was

Head of Geography in a large comprehensive school on Humberside. He has written widely on curriculum innovation in geography. His most recent publication in 2010 was the three-volume series: *Contemporary Approaches to Geography*. He currently chairs the Teacher Education special interest group for the GA.

Maggie Smith was until 2012 Lecturer in Education at the Open University, where she was the subject leader for geography on the PGCE course. She also chaired the PGCE Masters module, and was academic coordinator for the teacher education strand of the Open University EdD programme. Maggie has been a long-standing, active member of the GA, particularly contributing to the ESD and Citizenship special interest group.

Alex Standish was until 2012 Associate Professor of Geography at Western Connecticut State University. Previously, he taught in primary, secondary and special needs schools in the south of England. He has been researching geography education and global change, as revealed in his latest book *The False Promise of Global Learning: Why Education Needs Boundaries* (2012). In 2012 he was appointed Lecturer in Geography Education at the Institute of Education, University of London.

Liz Taylor is Lecturer in Geography Education at the University of Cambridge, where she coordinates the Geography PGCE course and supervises at Masters and PhD level. Liz taught geography for eight years in a large comprehensive school and her research interests include young people's understanding of distant place. She authored *Re-presenting Geography* for Chris Kington Publishing and has served on the editorial board for *Teaching Geography*.

Paul Weeden was Lecturer in Geography Education at the University of Birmingham from 1999 until he retired in 2010, and at the University of Bristol from 1993 to 1999. Previously he was a secondary school teacher and an advisory teacher. He is secretary of the Assessment and Examinations special interest group of the Geographical Association and has written on geography and assessment.

Phil Wood is Lecturer in Education at the University of Leicester and currently teaches on both initial teacher education and Masters courses. His main interests focus on learning innovation, developed through various action research projects with local schools.

Introduction to the series

This book, *Debates in Geography Education*, is one of a series of books entitled *Debates in Subject Teaching*. The series has been designed to engage with a wide range of debates related to subject teaching. Unquestionably, debates vary among the subjects, but may include, for example, issues that:

- impact on Initial Teacher Education in the subject;
- are addressed in the classroom through the teaching of the subject;
- are related to the content of the subject and its definition;
- are related to subject pedagogy;
- are connected with the relationship between the subject and broader educational aims and objectives in society, and the philosophy and sociology of education;
- are related to the development of the subject and its future in the twenty-first century.

Consequently, each book presents key debates that subject teachers should understand, reflect on and engage in as part of their professional development. Chapters have been designed to highlight major questions, and to consider the evidence from research and practice in order to find possible answers. Some subject books or chapters offer at least one solution or a view of the ways forward, whereas others provide alternative views and leave readers to identify their own solution or view of the ways forward. The editors expect readers will want to pursue the issues raised, and so chapters include questions for further debate and suggestions for further reading. Debates covered in the series will provide the basis for discussion in university subject seminars or as topics for assignments or classroom research. The books have been written for all those with a professional interest in their subject, and, in particular: student teachers learning to teach the subject in secondary or primary school; newly qualified teachers; teachers undertaking study at Masters level; teachers with a subject coordination or leadership role, and those preparing for such responsibility; as well as mentors, university tutors, CPD organisers and advisers of the aforementioned groups.

Books in the series have a cross-phase dimension, because the editors believe that it is important for teachers in the primary, secondary and post-16 phases to

look at subject teaching holistically, particularly in order to provide for continuity and progression, but also to increase their understanding of how children and young people learn. The balance of chapters that have a cross-phase relevance varies according to the issues relevant to different subjects. However, no matter where the emphasis is, the authors have drawn out the relevance of their topic to the whole of each book's intended audience.

Because of the range of the series, both in terms of the issues covered and its cross-phase concern, each book is an edited collection. Editors have commissioned new writing from experts on particular issues, who, collectively, represent many different perspectives on subject teaching. Readers should not expect a book in this series to cover the entire range of debates relevant to the subject, or to offer a completely unified view of subject teaching, or that every debate will be dealt with discretely, or that all aspects of a debate will be covered. Part of what each book in this series offers to readers is the opportunity to explore the inter-relationships between positions in debates and, indeed, among the debates themselves, by identifying the overlapping concerns and competing arguments that are woven through the text.

The editors are aware that many initiatives in subject teaching continue to originate from the centre, and that teachers have decreasing control of subject content, pedagogy and assessment strategies. The editors strongly believe that for teaching to remain properly a vocation and a profession, teachers must be invited to be part of a creative and critical dialogue about subject teaching, and should be encouraged to reflect, criticise, problem-solve and innovate. This series is intended to provide teachers with a stimulus for democratic involvement in the development of the discourse of subject teaching.

Susan Capel, Jon Davison, James Arthur and John Moss

December 2010

Introduction

Geography education, questions and choices

David Lambert and Mark Jones

> Debating is out of fashion because of a widespread assumption that, if you challenge people's beliefs, opinions or arguments, this could damage their self-esteem, or worse.
>
> (Hayes, 2004, p. 1)

> In the absence of an institutional basis for debate, parents, teachers and the public at large must do what they can. One recourse is to write books ... but for this to be effective it must grow from a renewed habit of debate, in schools, higher and further education and particularly in places where teachers are trained and educated.
>
> (Burgess, 2004, p. 217)

Introduction

This book provides readers with essential reading to inform their discussions, debates and decision-making on important themes within geography education. It outlines some key debates written by individuals who share a serious commitment to the continued development of geography in the school curriculum. The emphasis is geography in the secondary school, but we are careful to include chapters from primary education and perspectives of geography in Higher Education to emphasise the need for debate within but also across these phases of education.

The ethos guiding the development of this book is to provide a collective response to what Dennis Hayes (2004) has called a 'culture of compliance' (p. 3) where informed debate in schools has become marginalised and 'out of fashion' (ibid, p. 1). Authors have avoided polemics and instead offer narratives and explanatory accounts aiming to deepen our understanding of important debates in contemporary geography education in the UK. The authors drawn together for this volume are from a wide variety of backgrounds: some practising teachers, some recently practising teachers who have now become teacher educators; researchers in the field of geography education; tutors of Masters courses – again in the field of geography education; independent and freelance consultants

and authors of geography education materials; and finally more than one employee of the Geographical Association (GA).

In this chapter we provide you with an overview, reminding you of the rich legacy of debates in geography education and highlight current concerns. Supporting this is what we hope is a useful summary of the policy setting (Figure 0.1 on pages 3–4). It is, we argue, important to understand and acknowledge 'where we have come from' in these debates.

The book as a whole is organised into three main parts: policy debates, 'classroom' debates (concerning curriculum and pedagogy) and subject debates. Sometimes the purpose of a chapter is to inform – to ensure that some fault lines and conflicts in the field are properly anchored and located in policy and historical perspective. Sometimes the purpose is to provoke, or at least to stimulate, thought and reflection. The former may encourage us to see that things are not always what they seem (and that things come around!), whilst the latter may impel us to re-examine current orthodoxies and habitual practices.

CONTEXTS FOR GEOGRAPHY TEACHING: PROMISE AND CONSTRAINT

First, we have invited three chapters that take on what we have called 'policy debates'. These set the scene and describe the broad circumstances in which teachers work. In our intensely busy professional lives it is sometimes difficult to discern these policy debates beyond the self-evident fact that politicians and ministers in particular appear compelled to 'meddle' and change things around, as if to keep us on our toes. Whilst there may indeed be some truth in this, for change is a constant state for anyone working in the public sector, it should not conceal the fact that there are profound challenges that face the policy makers: how to raise levels of educational participation and achievement amongst the youth of a wealthy post-industrial nation; how to encourage appropriate pedagogy – and content – in an information-rich society; how to organise education in the context of a globalised neoliberal economy; and, above all, how to decide what to teach children in a world which *we now know for sure* is threatened in terms of its human occupation (see Morgan, 2011) – at least as a habitat for more than seven billion human beings for whom the good life is usually equated with consumption on a western capitalist model. Each of these mega issues, but particularly the latter, concern geography educators.

None of the chapters in Part One directly addresses the full scope of these challenges. The objective is, more modestly, to set out the policy choices that have been taken over the years in order to give the present some form of lineage. Together, they help us understand where we have come from and where we may be going. Policy choices are always controversial, often with winners and losers. We believe that teachers should be expected to take a view on such matters, because although we have to operate within a system, one that the democratically elected politicians have made for us, this does not mean that we

1970	Schools Council secondary school geography projects announced: *Geography for the Young School Leaver* ('Avery Hill') and *Geography 14–18* ('Bristol')
1976	Prime Minister James Callaghan stimulates the 'great debate' in his Ruskin College speech Schools Council A level Project announced *Geography 16–19 Project* (London)
1977	(DES) *Educating our Children* (DES) *Education in Schools: consultative document* (HMI), (DES) *Curriculum 11–16 Working Papers* Geographical Association (GA) response to these documents: e.g. see *Teaching Geography* 3, (2)
1978	(DES) *The Teaching of Ideas in Geography* (HMI 'Matters for Discussion' series)
1979	Conservative Government takes Office
1980	(DES) *A View of the Curriculum* (DES) *A Framework for the School Curriculum* GA Response: e.g. see *Geography*, 65 (3)
1981	(DES) *Geography in the School Curriculum 11–16* (HMI), (DES) *The School Curriculum*
1985	(DES) *Better Schools* (HMI) (DES) Curriculum Matters No 2 – Curriculum from 5–16
1986	(HMI) (DES) Curriculum Matters No 7 – Geography from 5–16
1987	(DES) The National Curriculum 5–16: a consultation document GA response: *Bailey and Binns* (eds.) *A Case for Geography* Sheffield: GA
1988	Education Reform Act (geography becomes a 'foundation subject' – compulsory for 5–16-year-olds)
1989	(DES) *National Curriculum: From Policy to Practice.*
1990	(DES) *Geography National Curriculum Working Group Final Report*
1991	(DES) Geography in the National Curriculum (England) (1st version) (SEAC) Geography in the National Curriculum: Non-statutory guidance for teachers.
1992	(CCW) Inset activities for National Curriculum Geography (CFAS) National Curriculum Standard Assessment Tasks (SATs). Geography pilot in 41 schools: students sit two 1 hour papers, tiered entry at levels 1–3; 3–5; 5–7 and 7–10)
1993	(CFAS) Evaluation KS3 Geography Pilot Tests (SEAC) Pupils' Work Assessed Geography KS3 (Ofsted) Geography: Key Stages 1, 2 and 3. Report on the first year (1991–1992). (SCAA) Final Report: The National Curriculum and its Assessment (known as the Dearing report) – recommendation for geography to become optional at KS4
1994	KS3 Geography SATs did not proceed.
1995	(DFE) Geography in the National Curriculum (2nd version) (Ofsted) *Geography: A review of inspection findings 1993/94*
1996	(SCAA) *Consistency in Teacher Assessment: Exemplification of Standards KS3.* (SCAA) *Key Stage 3 Optional Tests and Tasks: Geography*
1997	Labour Government takes Office (SCAA) *Geography and the use of language: Key Stage 3*
1998	(QCA) *Geographical enquiry at Key Stages 1–3:* Discussion Paper No. 3 Geography and history suspended from the primary curriculum for one year, to allow schools to focus fully on the numeracy and literacy strategies.

Figure 0.1 Key events and official publications. The policy setting for geography education in England and Wales 1970–2012.

1999	(DfEE/QCA) Primary Geography National Curriculum
	(DfEE/QCA) Geography: The National Curriculum for England Key Stages 1–3 (3rd version)
2000	(Ofsted) subject reports 1998/99 Primary Standards in Geography (HMI)
	(QCA/DfEE) Geography: A scheme of work for key stage 3
	(ACCAC) Cwricwlwm Cymru 2000
2001	(DfES) *Schools – achieving success*
	(Ofsted) subject reports 1999/2000 *Primary Geography; Secondary Geography*
	(Estyn) *Good Practice in Geography*
2002	National Curriculum in Action website launched
	(DfES) *KS3 National Strategy: Literacy in Geography*
	(DfES) *KS3 National Strategy: Access and Engagement in geography: Teaching pupils for whom English is an Additional Language.*
	(Ofsted) Subject reports 2000/01 *Geography in primary schools; Geography in secondary schools*
2003	(DfES) *14–19: Opportunity and Excellence*
	(Ofsted) Subject reports 2001/02 *Geography in primary schools; Geography in secondary schools*
2004	(DfES) *Five Year Strategy for Children*
	(DfES) *Every Child Matters: Change for Children*
	(DfES) *KS3 National Strategy: Literacy and learning in geography*
	(DfES) *KS3 National Strategy: ICT across the curriculum: ICT in geography*
	(Ofsted) Subject reports 2002/03 *Geography in primary schools* (HMI 1998) and *Geography in secondary schools* (HMI 1985)
2005	(DfES) *Higher standards, Better Schools for all*
	(DfES) *KS3 National Strategy Leading in Learning: exemplification in Geography*
	(Ofsted) Annual report 2004/05 *Geography in primary schools* and *Geography in secondary schools* (last in series)
2006	DfES (Department for Education and Skills) renamed the DCSF (Department for Children, Schools and Families)
	(GA/RGS) 'Action Plan for Geography' launched
2007	(DCSF) *Children's Plan: Building Brighter Futures*
	(QCA) Geography National Curriculum (4th version – for KS3 only)
2008	(Ofsted) Subject report *Geography in schools: changing practice.*
	(GA/RGS) 'Action Plan for Geography' funded for a further three years
2009	(GA) *Manifesto: A Different View.*
	(DCELLS) *Geography in the National Curriculum for Wales Key Stage 2–3*
	Cambridge Primary Review
	Independent Review of the Primary Curriculum Final Report
	Geography Assessing Pupil Progress (APP) materials in trial schools
2010	Coalition Government takes office.
	DCSF renamed DfE (Department for Education)
	Wolf Review on vocational education.
	(DfE) The Importance of Teaching: Schools White paper
2011	(GA/RGS) Action Plan for Geography ends.
	(GA) Geography Curriculum Consultation Report
	(Ofsted) subject report *Geography: Learning to make a world of difference*
	Introduction of the English Baccalaureate
	National Strategies website closed
	QCDA abolished (bringing an end to over 40 continuous years of a curriculum body (starting with the Schools Council in the 1960s)
	(DfE) Expert Panel Report: Framework for the National Curriculum
2012	(GA) *National Curriculum Proposals* published for consultation
	GCSE reform announced
2013	(DfE) proposals published following consultation
2014	First teaching of revised National Curriculum

Figure 0.1 (Continued).

simply 'obey orders'. Teachers, arguably more than any other professional group, need to do their work *responsibly*, which means with a sense of moral purpose. This is why we argue that teachers of geography need two things: a concept of geography and, equally important, a concept of education (see Lambert, 2009 for an elaboration of this argument). There is a sense in which these matters override policy debates.

One of the consequences of accepting that school teaching occupies such a moral space is that it demands reasoning on the part of the teacher. That is to say, we should not expect teachers to behave habitually, as compliant techno-crats – delivering the curriculum and fulfilling Ofsted 'requirements' or whatever – without subjecting this activity to some questioning. Thus, it is now *de rigueur* to conceptualise learning to teach as a critically reflective process, demanding the explicit articulation of theoretical frameworks which guide or shape class-room practices. Although not without its critics, this approach has become commonplace and a sort of modern orthodoxy. But it has in some ways, ironi-cally, undermined a core value of the teacher – at least in the secondary school. This is the value of subject specialism and the belief that young people can be inspired, dig deep and be 'initiated' into intellectual enquiry and the world of ideas. Education under this rubric cannot be reduced to reflecting on the effectiveness of teaching, just as learning cannot be reduced to the acquisition of a neutral set of generic 'skills'. The problem with reflective practice is that it can leave us very much trapped with such a stripped-down concept of educa-tion and an attitude to the subject that it is nothing more than a vehicle for 'teaching and learning'. This is why, in conceiving this book we decided to have Part Three devoted to debates to do with the subject. We are saying that to be a teacher of course one needs to 'know stuff': after all, teachers need something to teach. But much more important than this, one also needs a reasonably clear but dynamic grasp of what used to be called the 'spirit and purpose' of geography (Wooldridge and East, 1951). In their 2010 book, Lambert and Morgan have attempted a detailed discussion of the fluid and complex conceptual territory of geography: they argue that geography teachers need to intellectually engage with this – and resist the temptation to impose a firm and fixed view of school geography, as if the wider discipline itself were frozen (or indeed as if the world itself were now fully understood!). In this volume, *Charles Rawding* takes up this debate emphasising his personal views on the need for geography teachers to be current. The potential for school and uni-versity geographers to redefine school geography and promote currency is a theme taken up by *Graham Butt* and *Gemma Collins*.

Thus, a key debate which had assumed increased urgency in the early years of the century and has not abated since is the very role of the subject specialism in 'excellent teaching'. All agree with the virtues of subject knowledge. Thus, for example, Charles Clarke as Secretary of State for Education published a consultation document in 2003 extolling the virtues of subject specialism (DfES, 2003). So did Michael Gove seven years later in the coalition's White Paper

The Importance of Teaching (DFE, 2010). It is what ministers do. But despite exhortation, and the establishment of the importance of subject knowledge in the teaching standards, it is astonishing how little attention headteachers pay to subject leadership in schools. It is astonishing how little attention Ofsted really pays to the quality of the subject teaching as distinct from general teaching skills. And, moving closer to home, it is also surprising how difficult it is to persuade new teachers of geography that a set of atlases (or interactive maps on a tablet?) may be considered to be an essential resource for teaching geography. Margaret Roberts recently has been eloquent in elaborating on what we might see as the strange disappearance of geography from the planning of geography lessons (Roberts, 2010, 2011). In the meantime Alex Standish (2011) has accused – we think rather harshly, but he has a point – geography teachers in England of turning their backs on the subject discipline. This echoes the measured and penetrating analysis of Bill Marsden (1997) 'on taking the geography out of geography education'.

Perhaps the main reason for what appears tantamount to a collapse of confidence in subject identity of secondary school teachers of geography is the steady erosion of infrastructure to nourish and support subject specialist teachers and curriculum development. Despite the warm ministerial words, and in some cases more than that, such as the five year Action Plan for Geography (2006–11),[1] the fact is that local authorities, emptied of geography advisers/geography expertise, are now virtually irrelevant when it comes to nurturing, supporting and challenging geography teachers, and Ofsted is so distant and punitive in its outlook that it cannot be taken seriously as a source of professional nourishment. In addition, teacher education departments in universities have been systematically undermined by governments for twenty years now, driven by the belief that teacher training is best done in school. This is a form of anti-intellectualism wrapped up in beguiling talk of a mature and responsible profession being able to take 'ownership' of training; but such a view disregards almost totally the need for any professional group to make and remake the knowledge that defines it. In schools, which are intensely practically oriented places, often very inward-looking and with constant, urgent 'busy-ness' to attend to, it is very difficult indeed to do this, *especially* in the field of subject knowledge development.

COMMUNITY RESPONSE: FURTHERING THE LEARNING AND TEACHING OF GEOGRAPHY

The Geographical Association (GA) is the leading professional subject association for geography teachers with 6000 members and strong links with the academic discipline. One of the GA's key roles is to offer leadership for school geography, particularly during periods of rapid policy change in education. It has always done so through creative engagement with both teachers and policy makers. The leadership activity of the GA can thus be seen as a community response to the

changing policy environment: it is where subject meets policy maker. It is now well established that the GA played a key role in helping establish the place of geography in the first national curriculum, made statutory in the Education Reform Act of 1988 (see accounts in Rawling, 2001; Walford, 2001). A crucial moment was the process leading to the publication of Bailey and Binns' *A Case for Geography* in 1986, which still repays reading today. It is interesting that much of Part One of this book hinges around this 'moment': *Fran Martin, John Hopkin* and *David Gardner* focus on primary, Key Stage 3 (KS3) and the post-14 settings respectively. They all bring us up to date but they all write to a greater or lesser extent in the shadow of 1988 (see figure 0.1, pages 3–4).

As these chapters make clear, the policy environment in the 21st-century has become ever more relentless in the pace and frequency of change. The GA has attempted to respond to this swirling tempest in various ways. It did so by recognising that there were certain discernible trends and shifts. Thus, the publication in 2009 of the GA's manifesto: *A Different View*[2] recognised that:

- Teaching had (by 2009) become re-professionalised in a manner that valued technical competence above all else;
- With the narrow focus on exam performance and effective delivery, 'curriculum thinking' (driven by broad goals and moral purpose) had been undermined;
- Pedagogy and curriculum had become blurred: the 'curriculum problem' (what to teach) became subservient to enhancing the 'student experience' through 'personalisation';
- Skills and competences, oriented to 'building learning power' and 'learning to learn', dominated the innovation and change discourse in schools often at the expense of rigorous subject development; and
- Questions of curriculum deliberation (the idea of curriculum as a 'complicated conversation' about what to teach) were noticeable mainly by their absence.

The main purposes of the manifesto were first to say something grand, unifying and a little provocative about the idea of geography in the schools and through this to reignite the idea of curriculum thinking with geography teachers. It is debatable whether a campaign such as this has direct impact, mainly *because* it appears to set up a challenge to the dominant discourse of the day. It is not designed to make teachers' work 'easier'. On the other hand, what it represents is a highly positive encounter and a step towards expressing the role of 'traditional subject knowledge' in a 21st-century curriculum. In itself, the manifesto is no curriculum, but it manages to establish some principles upon which modern school geography may be articulated. For this reason it is an important component of debates in geography education in the UK. A number of chapters in this book refer to the manifesto. Some others, such as *Mary Biddulph* on curriculum making and *Roger Firth* on knowledge, take the debates considerably further.

By 2011, when the GA published its 'national curriculum consultation',[3] the policy context had changed with a change of government. No longer fighting for its life, as we see in Part One of this book, the need now was to address political pressures that although ostensibly supportive of geography appeared to limit its definition to a narrow form of 'cultural literacy' (Hirsch, 1987). Nevertheless, the 2010 White Paper *The Importance of Teaching* heralded:

- a radical departure from the (new labour) orthodoxy of skills, competences and 'personalisation';
- a revised national curriculum to state 'core' and 'essential' knowledge in traditional established subjects;
- more emphasis on effort and motivation, and whole cohort achievement, rather than differentiation (personalisation) by 'ability'. This alludes to an eastern, Confucian model of education rather than western model based on individualism and was a relatively unremarked point in the government's expert panel report on the national curriculum published in December 2011.

(DfE, 2011)

The main purposes of the GA's consultation were therefore somewhat different from the manifesto. A key audience was still geography teachers, and the emphasis was still to engage them with the significance of 'bringing knowledge back in' to school geography.[4] But at the same time it was also to find a way to embrace a Hirschian notion of 'core knowledge' ('extensive' factual geographical knowledge) together with deeper, intensive conceptual and procedural knowledge. Crucially, it was also meant to persuade policy makers that a 'better school geography' could be identified and achieved through the community of geography teachers as represented by the GA. The 2011 geography curriculum consultation in this sense was far more political than the manifesto. Its contents can be taken from the GA's website, but in summary it provided:

- A strong statement of geography's curriculum purposes, through building and developing young people's 'capabilities' (their 'functionings' and human agency based on world knowledge, conceptual understanding and capacity to apply intellectual and other skills critically and productively: see Lambert 2011).
- A simple knowledge taxonomy, introducing Knowledge 1, Knowledge 2 and Knowledge 3 (similar, but not identical to GCSE 'assessment objectives' AO1, AO2 and AO3; broadly knowledge, understanding and skills).
- A first draft simple curriculum 'framework' based on Place, Space and Environment and Geographic Tools.
- Broad brush statements of learning expectations at 11 years, 14 years and 16 years.[5]

DEBATES FOR THE FUTURE

The GA's 2011 geography curriculum consultation raised debate on a number of significant issues in geography education, and this book tackles these and several more besides. The consultation report identified three in particular.

Distinguishing curriculum from pedagogy: To what extent is there a clear sense of what a national curriculum document is for, and what such an instrument can and cannot do? The main curriculum question is *what* shall be taught, and it is evident that this question can easily be submerged by questions of pedagogy – on *how* the teaching and learning is enacted. This binary distinction is important, but also in some ways false, for in many ways what is taught is partly determined by how educational transactions are conducted. Several chapters open up this debate, such as those by *Roger Firth* and *Mary Biddulph* already cited above on knowledge and 'curriculum making' respectively, plus *Mark Jones* on personalisation and *Jane Ferretti* who opens up a debate on pedagogy.

Defining the school subject: Is it possible for the geography curriculum to offer a clearer definition of the subject's goals and purposes? It may be easier said than done, but to what extent can a geography curriculum '… based on concepts, principles, fundamental operations and key knowledge … lead to learning processes which are more focused on deep learning (fewer topics pursued to greater depth) …' (Oates, 2010, p. 17)? Again, *Jones* and *Ferretti* contribute to this discussion, and this is added to by *Phil Wood* who focuses on skills and *Clare Brooks* who looks at concepts. An important aspect of this debate is picked up by *Duncan Hawley* whose chapter is on physical geography. The somewhat weakened state of physical geography in some schools is the cause of considerable concern if we argue for synthesis across both the natural and social sciences to be key in establishing geography's 'unique selling point' (USP) in the curriculum. For many, one of *the* defining features of geography in education is fieldwork, and *Alan Kinder* addresses the continuing significance of doing geography in the real world, despite issues of cost, inconvenience and perceived dangers that conspire against taking children out of the classroom.

Getting the level of detail right: To what extent does the understandable desire for water-tight definition of the subject, implying something much more fine-grained than goals and purposes mentioned above, carry major risk? Experience from the 1991 national curriculum, which resulted in 184 'statement(s) of attainment' for geography alone, has indicated that too much detail limits and constrains teachers, and encourages superficial 'coverage'. On the other hand, too little detail can become abstract, relatively meaningless and too permissive: a concern with the 2007 Key Stage 3 (KS3) national curriculum for geography, which was very light on prescribed content, was that geography in some secondary schools has become dangerously ill-defined, a point picked up in this volume by *John Morgan* and in a different way amplified by *Liz Taylor*, who asks what it means to make progress in learning geography. In other secondary schools we recognise that too little detail was also seen positively as

'increased flexibility' resulting in a period of curriculum renewal at KS3.[6] *Bob Digby*, in the context of public examinations, also tackles the issue of 'coverage' and depth intersecting with *David Gardner's* discussion of the rather too cosy relationship between the devising of syllabuses and specifications, the writing of tests and examinations, and the production of 'authorised' (and highly profitable) textbooks. In a rather different context, *David Mitchell* explores the scope – and need – for geography teachers to teach controversial issues, which is not always encouraged if the syllabus or specification is perceived to be 'content heavy'.

In debating school geography we are surely correct in stressing curriculum and pedagogy in the context of policy shifts and the wider subject discipline. There are several broader debates to add to this kernel of professional concerns. Perhaps the greatest of these – indeed, the elephant in the room – is assessment. In addition to the examinations-oriented chapters mentioned in the previous paragraph, *Paul Weeden* opens up geography assessment debates providing a way in to this topic and reminding us that assessment is important and is there to be used – and abused. But there are a number of others, broadly falling into two groups: to do with technology and the wider social purposes of geography in education. With regard to the former, *Mary Fargher* opens up debate about the place of geographic information (GI) in the school geography curriculum, while *Alan Parkinson* explores the role of information communication technology and social media – not least in the context of professional formation and nourishment. These discussions are of course significant. Geography without technology is about as imaginable as history without documents: technology enables us the map the world, to (re)present it and communicate it. Indeed, it is a usable and accurate myth that the GA was established in 1893 for the very reason of using the leading technology of the day (heavy glass lantern slides) to communicate geography for educative purposes.

As we have mentioned, one of the enduring debates in school geography centres on its purposes and how the subject is justified in the school curriculum. There are reasons why geographers find it harder to make a cut-and-dried case for its inclusion – in comparison say with mathematics, chemistry or even history. On the one hand, the case for geography is so blindingly obvious it sounds banal, as with Michael Palin's appeal as President of the RGS in 2008:

> You can travel the seas, poles and deserts and see nothing. To really understand the world you need to get under the skin of the people and places. In other words, learn about geography. I can't imagine a subject more relevant in schools. We'd all be lost without it.

On the other hand, Michael Young's (2011) challenge is remarkably difficult to dispatch – at least with any measure of agreement amongst geographers:

> It is the importance of its concepts in the lives of young learners that gives geography its crucial role in the curriculum. If geographers cannot make

these arguments, then it is difficult for us non-geographers to make the case for geography and to argue that in making it voluntary from the age of 14 we are in danger of undermining the next generation's future.

(pp. 182–3)

It is partly for these reasons that geographers in education have been arguably more suggestive than most of the need to show 'relevance'. No collection of essays on geography education would be complete without addressing this concern and we invited three chapters to open up these debates. Thus, *John Lyon* tackles the world of work and the notion of 'applied' studies in geography; *Alex Standish* and *Maggie Smith* take on two major cross-cutting themes, namely global citizenship and sustainable development respectively. These chapters provide rich context for the central debate that runs through this book, namely the nature and 'definition' of the discreet subject discipline, geography, and its educational value. Michael Young, and the government, require a harder-edged response than 'geography is everywhere' and other slogans that try to say so much, but in fact tell us little.

Conclusion

In their book *The Spirit and Purpose of Geography*, Wooldridge and East (1951) begin their concluding chapter with the following:

Geography begins only when geographers begin writing it.

(p. 171)

This statement signifies the important relationship between the discipline and those who learn, teach and research geography. The chapters in this book cover key debates in *geography* education and all the chapters have been written by *geographers*, a term which can sometimes be hidden within specialisms such as environmentalist, meteorologist or urban designer or subsumed within the generic roles of student, teacher, educationist or researcher. The interview question that many teachers have been asked – 'are you a teacher of your subject or a teacher of children?' – may not appear too demanding superficially, but it should provoke: it should provoke consideration of what it means to be a teacher of geography in the 21st-century. Just as Michael Young challenges us to make an argument for the subject, we should be able to debate what it means to be a geographer whether as a geography student, teacher, educator or researcher. Thus we invite the reader to consider this as they engage with the different debates concerning *geography* – the subject.

By 'writing it' (geography), we renew critical engagement with the nature and purpose of the subject. We keep under consideration its representation in different educational contexts and on-going challenges, presented as policy and played out in practice. But *writing* comes with different audiences and purposes

in mind; using many different genres and communicated through a variety of media and increasingly via new technologies. This volume and other recent contributions to geography education (e.g. Lambert and Morgan, 2010; Butt, 2011; Morgan, 2011) signal an urgency for renewed engagement from those in geography education with the disciplines of geography. Having these books is all well and good but, as Dennis Hayes (2004) reminds us, what counts also is in the *reading* of books. Producing a book is fine. But its success depends on 'how many people take up the arguments presented ... and develop or challenge them' (p. 5). We hope that reading some or all of the chapters in this volume will inform your writing – whether it is an essay or school policy, journal or magazine article, blog post or tweet, for this adds further to the quality of debate whether face to face or virtually. Returning to Wooldridge and East, perhaps geography only begins when geographers start *debating* it (again)? Debate, however, needs to be informed and we hope that the chapters in this volume provide at least some ways in.

Notes

1   The Action Plan for Geography was jointly and equally led by the GA and the Royal Geographical Society (RGS) (with the Institute of British Geographers (IBG)). The evaluation report can be read and downloaded at http://www.geography.org.uk/projects/actionplanforgeography/ It was financed by the government, instigated by schools' minister Stephen Twigg and brought into full fruition by his successor Andrew Adonis.

2   This can be explored at www.geography.org.uk/adifferentview. Its main contents are:

  i. Geography, the curriculum resource
  ii. Thinking geographically
  iii. Living geography
  iv. Young people's geography
  v. Exploration and enquiry
  vi. The real world and 'fieldwork'
  vii. Curriculum making.

The manifesto was published in the form of a printed booklet, plus website including downloadable images, lesson plans and videos.

3   The consultation and its report, plus several important supporting documents and many lengthy comments from teachers can be seen on www.geography.org.uk/getinvolved/geographycurriculumconsultation. This can be seen as part of a process by which the GA hopes to influence policy makers directly in the formation (and support) of a 'better school geography'.

4   This phrase references Young (2008).

5   NB: the GA's proposals argued for compulsory geography to 16 – as in the original national curriculum introduced in 1991. A key difference between 2011 and then is that in many schools KS3 is reduced to two years. The expert panel (DfE, 2011) recommended formalising this so that KS4, the GCSE years, was extended to three years enabling compulsory history and geography to 16 years.

6   As part of the APG, a series of well-attended regional conferences, teacher CPD events and new schemes of works hosted on the 'Geography Teaching Today' (GTT)

website supported teachers in 'curriculum making' at KS3. All materials from the GTT website can now be found on the GA and the RGS (with IBG) websites.

Key readings

1. Morgan, J. (2011) *Teaching Secondary Geography as if the Planet Matters*, Oxford: David Fulton. John Morgan's thought-provoking book examines the important relationship between society and nature, at the time when we are beginning to formally recognise the 'Anthropocene' (the geological era during which time human activity has impacted on physical systems, especially climate). It is specifically addressed to geography teachers, for while climate change and biome destruction are familiar 'environmental issues' taught in schools, Morgan suggests current curriculum approaches may actually inhibit young people's understanding of the causes of environmental problems. The book is an essential read for teachers seeking to adopt more theoretically informed approaches to developing in young people a more critical environmental awareness.
2. Marsden, W. (1997) 'On taking the geography out of geography education; some historical pointers', *Geography*, 82 (3), 241–52. This is an important article and a precursor of the critical stance taken by Alex Standish (2009; forthcoming) and others on the undermining of geographical subject knowledge in the school curriculum. Marsden shows that historically the disciplines (including geography) are important in education, not least to guard against indoctrination and government meddling. But he also shows that subjects are always under threat from other priorities, including those of progressive educationists (who would integrate subjects) and 'good causes' such as environmentalism and citizenship.

References

Bailey, P. and Binns, T. (1986) *A Case for Geography*, Sheffield: Geographical Association.

Burgess, T. (2004) 'What are the key debates in education?' in D. Hayes (ed.), *The Routledge Guide to Key Educational Debates in Education*. London and New York: Routledge.

Butt, G. (ed.) (2011) *Geography, Education and the Future*. London: Continuum.

Department for Education (DfE) (2011) *The Framework for the National Curriculum: a report by the expert panel for the national curriculum review*. Available from: www.education.gov.uk/publications/standard/publicationDetail/Page1/DFE-00135-2011 [Accessed 2 January 2012].

Department for Education and Skills (DfES) (2003) *Subject Specialisms: a consultation document*. London: DfES.

Hayes, D. (ed.) (2004) *The Routledge Guide to Key Educational Debates in Education*. London and New York: Routledge.

Hirsch, E.D. (ed.) (1987) *Cultural Literacy: What every American needs to know*. Boston, MA: Houghton Mifflin Company.

Lambert, D. (2009) *Geography in Education: Lost in the post?* A professorial inaugural lecture, London: Institute of Education.

Lambert, D. (2011) 'Reframing school geography: A capability approach' in G. Butt (ed.), *Geography, Education and the Future*. London: Continuum.

Lambert, D. and Morgan, J. (2010) *Teaching Geography 11–18: A Conceptual Approach*. Maidenhead: Open University Press.

Marsden, W. (1997) 'On taking the geography out of geography education; some historical pointers', *Geography*, 82 (3), 241–52.

Morgan, J. (2011) *Teaching Secondary Geography as if the Planet Matters*. Oxford: David Fulton.

Oates, T. (2010) *Could Do Better: Using international comparisons to refine the National Curriculum in England*. Cambridge: Cambridge Assessment.

Palin, M. (2007) 'Celebrating the action plan for geography' in *GA Magazine*, No 8, 22–3.

Rawling, E. (2001) *Changing the Subject: The impact of national policy on school geography 1980–2000*. Sheffield: Geographical Association.

Roberts, M. (2010) 'Where's the geography? Reflections on being an external examiner', *Teaching Geography*, 35 (3), 112–13.

Roberts, M. (2011) *What Makes a Geography Lesson Good?* Available from: http://www.geography.org.uk/projects/makinggeographyhappen/teachertips/ [Accessed 20 March 2012].

Standish, A. (2009) *Global Perspectives in the Geography Curriculum: Reviewing the moral case for geography*, London: Routledge.

Standish, A. (2011) Comment on the GA's national curriculum consultation made at 15:49 on 03/10/11: http://www.geography.org.uk/getinvolved/geographycurriculumconsultation/feedback/ [Accessed 2 March 2012].

Standish, A. (forthcoming) *The False Promise of Global Learning: Why Education Needs Boundaries*. New York: Continuum.

Walford, R. (2001) *Geography in British Schools 1850–2000*. London: Woburn Press.

Wooldridge, S.W. and East, W.G. (1951) *The Spirit and Purpose of Geography*. London: Hutchinson.

Young, M. (2008) *Bringing Knowledge Back In*, London: Routledge.

Young, M. (2011) 'Discussion to Part 3', in G. Butt (ed.), *Geography, Education and the Future*. London: Continuum.

Part I

Policy Debates

Chapter 1

What is geography's place in the primary school curriculum?

Fran Martin

> [There is] a muddled discourse about subjects, knowledge and skills which infects the entire debate about curriculum, needlessly polarises discussion of how it might be organised, parodies knowledge and undervalues its place in education and inflates the undeniably important notion of a skill to a point where it too becomes meaningless.
>
> (Alexander, 2010, p. 252)

Introduction

When I began teaching in 1980 there was no such thing as a National Curriculum. Although this gave great freedom to teachers, it also meant that primary pupils' curriculum diet was very hit and miss. If a teacher loved geography as I did, and saw its relevance in primary pupils' education, then it was included. However, as HMI reports of the time showed (DES, 1978), in too many primary schools geography did not appear explicitly on the curriculum at all. The inclusion of geography as a statutory subject in the National Curriculum therefore brought the advent of what was, in some senses, the best of times for geography. However, the curriculum as defined by policy documents and the curriculum as it is articulated in schools are two different things and may go some way to explaining why, in the two decades that have followed, and despite its statutory status, geography has not had a stable place in the primary curriculum.

In this chapter, geography's 'place' in the primary curriculum is interpreted in three interconnected ways: the first concerns geography's *status*, the second concerns the *nature* of geography, and the third concerns geography's *relevance* as a contribution to primary pupils' education. Each of these will be discussed in turn, focusing on a 20-year period, 1991–2011, during which time successive governments have introduced a number of curriculum changes. At each point of change there have been debates about the nature and relevance of geography within the discipline and at political and societal levels. How those debates have been played out in the context of the primary school requires some understanding of the nature of primary education.

An important feature of primary schools is that, for the most part, pupils are taught the whole curriculum by their class teacher. This is significant for a number of reasons.

- Not only does geography have to find a place in the primary curriculum as a whole, but it also has to find a place in each class teacher's mind as being worthy of inclusion.
- As research by Catling et al. (2007) has shown, if geography is to find a place alongside all other subjects, it has to be seen as *relevant* by primary school headteachers and senior management teams, as well as by individual teachers.
- However, the majority of primary headteachers and class teachers are not geography specialists and so their *image* of the subject may be one that is outdated and seen to lack relevance in terms of its contribution to primary pupils' education.
- Because primary teachers are not geography teachers, but teachers of geography, they have difficulty interpreting the *nature* of geography as expressed in the National Curriculum orders.
- This makes geography's place (and the place of other foundation subjects) more vulnerable and subject to variations in the *status* accorded to it at local levels, no matter what status it is accorded nationally.

As such, primary schools provide a very different context to that of secondary schools. Thus any discussion of the debates surrounding geography's place in the primary curriculum cannot take place without reference to the curriculum as a whole, or without reference to the distinction between subjects and the curriculum, particularly since there is a subject hierarchy in primary schools that is a direct legacy of the Victorian emphasis on the 'three Rs' (Alexander, 2004).

GEOGRAPHY'S STATUS IN THE PRIMARY SCHOOL CURRICULUM

Following the Education Act of 1989, when the first orders of the Geography National Curriculum (GNC) appeared in 1991 the subject gained a legal status that required it to be taught at Key Stages 1 (KS1, 5–7-year-olds) and 2 (KS2, 7–11-year-olds). The National Curriculum was divided into core (English, maths and science) and foundation subjects (the remainder of the curriculum). Time allocations for each subject has not been a statutory matter, but during the first review of the NC led by Sir Ron Dearing in 1994–95, time management was identified as a major problem (Foley and Janinkoun, 1996). The review teams were given guidance of 36 hours per year at KS1 (or 4½% of curriculum time) and 45 hours per year at KS2 (or 5% of curriculum time), figures subsequently reinforced in non-statutory guidance provided by the Schools Curriculum and Assessment Authority (SCAA, 1995). If 4–5% of curriculum time was given to each foundation subject, this left approximately 65% for the core subjects,

conveying a clear message to primary teachers about which subjects were more important and deserved more of a place in the curriculum. Although there was a revision of the original orders (DfES, 1995) and a substantial reworking (DfEE/ QCA, 1999), both remain legacies of the 1991 orders. As such, primary teachers continue to work from a GNC that is outdated (Rawling, 2001, p. 83), and inappropriate as the basis for education in the 21st-century (Alexander, 2004).

Nevertheless, during the period 1991–98 evidence from annual Ofsted reports shows a steady rise in geography's place in primary classrooms, accompanied by a similar rise in the quality of geography teaching. In the early 1990s Ofsted noted '... Geography teaching now took place in every school, and the judgements were that geography was satisfactory, if not well taught, in very nearly every primary school' (Catling et al., 2007, p. 118).

Further evidence of an increase in geography's status in primary schools comes from the Geographical Association. Table 1.1 shows a sharp rise in primary membership (based on numbers subscribing to *Primary Geographer*, the GA journal for primary schools) following the introduction of the statutory programmes of study (DfE, 1991), with numbers peaking in 1997.

The picture looked rosy in 1997 but then, in January 1998, the National Literacy and Numeracy Strategies for primary schools were introduced and marked what many have seen as a catastrophic period for foundation subjects (Ofsted, 2002; Galton et al., 2002; Alexander, 2004; Catling et al., 2007). To enable teachers to concentrate on implementing the National Strategies, David Blunkett (Secretary of State for Education at the time) removed primary schools' obligation to teach the specified content of the non-core subjects.

Since then, many schools have all but given up on the original 1988 National Curriculum notion of children's absolute entitlement to a genuinely broad curriculum in which the arts and humanities are treated with no less seriousness – even if with rather less time – than literacy and numeracy (Alexander, 2004, p. 23).

Table 1.1 Primary membership of the Geographical Association 1991–2011

	Total PG	Total GA members	Total PG members as %
1991	4025	9672	42
1992	5303	10391	51
1993	5867	10955	54
1997	6001	11573	52
1998	5348	10728	50
1999	4723	9923	48
2000	4238	9360	45
2009	2024	5975	34
2010	1924	5665	34
2011	1750	5517	32

Source: GA, 2011a.

While a direct causal link is not possible to make, Table 1.1 shows that from 1998 primary membership of the GA entered into a period of steady decline to levels below that of 1991, a phenomenon also found in other subject associations. In 2000, with the introduction of a significantly revised National Curriculum (DfEE/QCA, 1999) the requirement to teach all subjects of the primary curriculum was reinstated. However, as indicated above, this did not appear to make a difference to the declining fortunes of primary geography. Further evidence from a longitudinal study of primary schools shows that 'geography's allocation of curriculum time [fell] from 5.6% in 1996/97 to 4.1% in 2003/04, a reduction of some 27%' (Catling et al., 2007, p. 122). In addition, Ofsted reports from 1996/97 to 2004/5 show that geography was consistently at the bottom of tables showing the quality of teaching and pupils' achievements.

A further factor affecting the status of foundation subjects in the primary curriculum has been that of assessment. From 1993, core subjects have been tested at national level at ages seven and eleven years through Standard Assessment Tasks (SATs). Rawling (2001) argues that when Labour came to power in 1997 there was a shift in emphasis from curriculum input (the programmes of study) to curriculum output (in the form of targets, league tables and national reporting). SATs results became part of the Ofsted framework for inspection of primary schools, with schools being judged on the relationship between their SATs results and national targets. Although value-added measures were applied from 2002 to allow fairer comparisons to be made between schools with different pupil intakes (DfE, 2011), the stakes inherent in SATs results and school league tables were so great that the overall result was a further narrowing of the curriculum and less space for the foundation subjects.

Concerns about this and increases in primary teachers' workload led to the National Union of Teachers commissioning research into primary teachers' working lives. In 2002 the report (Galton et al., 2002) showed that, along with music, geography was now the least taught subject in primary schools (Table 1.2).

As teachers interviewed at the time said,

> It feels all the time as if you're rushing to cover this huge curriculum that you've been told to deliver and it doesn't end up being balanced because of the pressure on literacy and numeracy, which comes from the pressure for results so they're not getting sufficient time on the other subjects.
> Too often the subjects like art, and history and geography and the subjects that children really enjoy, and P.E. are squeezed out.
>
> (Galton et al., 2002, p. 38)

The evidence presents a dismal picture, but while this is a reflection of the national situation, there were great local variations. Catling et al. (2007) and Ofsted (2008, 11) note that there have been significant advances in both the presence and quality of primary geography. Thus provision seems to have become polarised between circumstances found in a very good minority of schools and

Table 1.2 Curriculum time in selected subjects in primary schools (%)

	% of curriculum time at KS1	% of curriculum time at KS2
English	25	26
Maths	21.5	22.5
Science	8.6	9.3
Geography	3.9	4.5
Music	3.5	3.4

those in too many schools where geography has been squeezed out altogether. The question arises about why it was that primary geography suffered more than any other subject in this environment. Geography educators broadly agree that this is because primary teachers, as non-specialists, tend to have limited subject knowledge and lack confidence in interpreting the geography curriculum as expressed through the National Curriculum orders (Martin, 2005; Woodhouse, 2006; Iwaskow, 2006; Catling et al., 2007; Morley, 2010). In primary schools there is thus a problem of perception, not only of the relevance of geography, but also of the nature of the subject and its potential.

THE NATURE OF GEOGRAPHY IN THE PRIMARY CURRICULUM

From the moment the idea of a National Curriculum was introduced in 1988, there have been debates about the nature and purpose of geography in the curriculum. Figure 1.1 shows the views of specialist geography communities as represented through universities and the Geographical Association on the right, and the Geography National Curriculum (GNC) as an interpretation of those views in the centre, with the public and primary teachers' and pupils' perceptions of the subject on the left. Lines A–B and C–D represent a disconnection between the GNC and both the subject specialist and the generalist communities on either side. As a member of the NC geography working group and then geography subject leader at the Qualifications and Curriculum Authority (QCA), Rawling (2001) gives an insider perspective on the political debates that were raging at the time. Her analysis of the ideologies underpinning the content of the GNC showed that whilst the emphasis changed from one version to another, they were largely cultural restorationist in nature and ceased to reflect advances in geography made at university level. This created a disconnection between academic geography and the GNC. Figure 1.1 shows a loose connection between the GA and GNC views because the GA has worked closely with QCA and thus had some (albeit limited) opportunities to influence the curriculum. However, there is no similar loose connection between the GNC and primary teachers' conceptions because there is evidence that primary teachers' images of geography show far

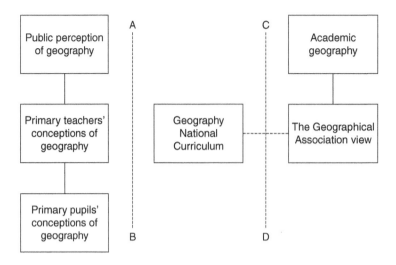

Figure 1.1 Connections and disconnections between different views of geography

greater similarities with the public 'popular' view (as exemplified by the archetypal geography quiz question) than they do with the more conceptual GNC, and it seems that these generalist views are passed on to their pupils.

Research conducted with primary student teachers at the beginning of their training consistently shows that the majority hold a largely knowledge-based image of the subject and make little reference to enquiry, fieldwork skills or conceptual understanding (Catling, 2004; Martin, 2005; Morley, 2010). This is similar to the public, media-driven view of geography that focuses on an encyclopaedic factual knowledge of geographical features and their locations. The problem is that the GNC, as an interpretation of geography the subject, acts as a mediator between public, everyday views and specialist views, and this is particularly problematic for primary teachers. In a paper prepared for the coalition government, Tim Oates (2010) makes a distinction among content (key propositional knowledge), concepts (organising concepts, principles and fundamental operations) and contexts (experiential, everyday and social knowledge) on the one hand, and between the National Curriculum and the curriculum in its entirety on the other. He argues that when context dominates, as has been the case in revisions of the National Curriculum, too much emphasis is placed on pedagogy and experience, and when content dominates the subject is imposed on learners in ways that are not motivating or meaningful. Oates goes on to state that there is a need for all three, but that the National Curriculum restrict itself to specifying content, while teachers should identify those contexts that are meaningful to their pupils and that could act as 'the curriculum vehicle for concept-based and knowledge-based National Curriculum content' (Oates, 2010, p. 8).

When this analysis is applied to the current primary geography national curriculum (DfEE/QCA, 1999), it reveals that it contains a mixture of content (both concepts and prepositional knowledge) and context (pedagogic approaches) without being transparent as to which is which. As Alexander has observed, there is a 'muddled language of "subjects", "skills" and "knowledge" which confounds sensible curriculum debate' (2010, p. 252). This presents a huge challenge for generalist primary teachers who struggle to confidently reinterpret the implicit understandings and ways of seeing the world that the GNC represents. Evidence suggests (Catling, 2006; Martin, 2008a) that student teachers have an image of geography that is largely knowledge-based which acts as a filter when they try to interpret the GNC, with the result that their teaching may emphasise those aspects that match their image (content) and pay less attention to those aspects that don't match their image (enquiry learning, the conceptual framework). Geography provision for generalist primary trainee teachers on PGCE courses is between 6 and 12 hours (Catling, 2006), making it hard for primary geography educators to expand these limited images.

Once qualified, the curriculum divide discussed earlier has affected subject-based Continuing Professional Development (CPD) which has focused on the core subjects and ICT (Galton et al., 2007; Ofsted, 2008, 2011). With further lack of access to CPD in geography, there is evidence that Newly Qualified Teachers' gradual developing expertise in primary pedagogy leads them to downgrade the role of knowledge (Martin, 2005, 2008a). As their pedagogical repertoire increases, they become more confident about selection of curriculum contexts; enquiry and issues-based learning may therefore become more common practice, but the organising concepts and fundamental principles of the subject are lacking as is, on occasion, essential knowledge.

This was noted by Ofsted, who observed that 'weaknesses in teachers' subject knowledge often led to their teaching being limited to the development of pupils' geographical enquiry skills' (2008, p. 11), and that as primary schools moved towards a more topic-based, integrated approach to the curriculum, 'the subject was often peripheral ... or there was too great a focus on skills, rather than on knowledge and understanding' (Ofsted, 2011, p. 19). Further research by Catling (2001) showed that year 6 primary pupils' definitions of geography, ten years after the introduction of the GNC, emphasised the use of maps and an awareness of and knowledge about the world and countries, broadly reflecting a public perception of the subject. It is important that children develop a strong locational knowledge, but if this is developed without the organising, conceptual framework then there is a danger that such knowledge can decay over time.

Pupils should emerge from schooling with large bodies of knowledge ... but the critical issue is this: organising concepts and principles are crucial to the acquisition and retention of this knowledge.

(Oates, 2010, p. 9)

With little time given to geography during primary Initial Teacher Training (Catling, 2006), and few opportunities for Continuing Professional Development once qualified (Ofsted, 2011), it is a challenge to see how primary teachers can improve their subject knowledge. Ongoing concerns of this nature led to the government funding a five-year programme delivered by the Geographical Association and the Royal Geographical Society, the Action Plan for Geography (2006–11). As part of the APG, the GA promoted a vibrant, dynamic view of geography as one that recognises the importance of real-world learning, values children's own experiences, and emphasises the importance of thinking geographically through the use of key concepts (GA, 2009). This vision underpinned the work with 1200 primary schools and has left a legacy that is continuing to support primary teachers through the Primary Quality Mark and a national network of geography champions. The success of the APG is evident in Ofsted reports showing that the quality of teaching and pupils' progress is beginning to improve and that where standards are high this is often due to the school being involved in the APG (Ofsted, 2008, 2011). However, the most recent Ofsted report suggests that while quality has improved, 'there was marked polarisation in the quality of teaching and learning as well as the geography curriculum in the primary schools visited' (Ofsted; 2011, p. 6). The APG has been very effective where primary schools and teachers have been reached, but there are approximately 17,000 primary schools in England so only 7% have had access to this high-quality work (GA, 2011b).

To return to the point made at the beginning of this chapter, primary school teachers are generalist teachers of geography, and within a generalist tradition they are asked to 'think about, plan and teach the curriculum as a whole' (Alexander, 2010, p. 254). In the case of geography, as for many other subjects, primary teachers' perception is that they are being asked to act outside their experience (Martin, 2005, 2008b). To many primary teachers, debates about the nature of geography education are therefore less relevant than debates about the nature and purpose of primary education and the primary curriculum as a whole. Currently the broader primary context is such that geography seems to have suffered more than any other subject from a lack of understanding of its nature, which in turn affects whether it is perceived as relevant or not. In the next section I will consider how more recent debates about the primary education have affected geography's perceived relevance in the curriculum.

THE RELEVANCE OF GEOGRAPHY IN THE PRIMARY CURRICULUM

A further development since the mid 2000s has been the move in primary schools away from discrete subjects and towards a more integrated curriculum. Schools, supported by comments from Ofsted (2005, 2008), began to work in more cross-curricular ways, developing what has become known as the 'creative curriculum' (Burgess, 2007). Burgess offers some ways forward for schools

wishing to develop a creative curriculum based on commonalities noted in the four schools in his study:

> All four schools explicitly put learning to learn above what was learnt. There was a universal emphasis on *skills before content*. The staff believed that it was not what you did that was important but the way you did it, that children had to be equipped with the skills and the ability to apply them in different situations.
>
> (Burgess, 2007, p. 17, italics in original)

This is a prime example of the sort of debate that has arisen over the primary curriculum. It is one in which different aspects of the curriculum, teaching and learning are set up in what Alexander has called false dichotomies: knowledge *or* skills, teaching *or* learning. A polarised discourse about the curriculum positions alternative views as discrete and oppositional and 'can mean that time is spent justifying a position rather than purposefully developing the curriculum' (Swift, 2010). For the majority of primary teachers an integrated, creative curriculum designed to develop critical and reflective thinking, and transferable skills is very appealing; it does not require them to grapple with the conceptual and organisational territory that each subject represents. In the case of geography, there is evidence that this leads to a focus on process (enquiry and life skills) and context (well-being, sustainable behaviours), while content in the form of knowledge and understanding needed for pupils to make their own decisions is lost.

Clearly it is not feasible to expect primary teachers to develop high levels of subject expertise in all ten subjects that they currently are expected to teach. Alexander proposes the notion of curriculum capacity as an alternative to expertise. Curriculum capacity is the ability to 'move with ease around the conceptual and organisational territory that each subject represents' (Alexander, 2010, p. 254) without needing to have the levels of expertise of a subject specialist. In this view, such capacity would enable teachers to be more flexible and confident in their interpretation of a National Curriculum, in other words, to be more creative in how they make connections between content and contexts in the best interests of their learners. The final section will discuss my work with Simon Catling (Catling and Martin, 2011) that explores how Alexander's notion of capacity might be developed in the context of primary geography.

CONCLUSIONS: THE FUTURE FOR GEOGRAPHY IN THE PRIMARY CURRICULUM

We are currently going through another period of curriculum change. We do not know what the place of geography in the new primary curriculum will be, but whatever happens it seems as if the new curriculum will be based on specifying core knowledge for those subjects that are statutory (curriculum content) and will give

schools freedom to devise a percentage of their curriculum locally (curriculum contexts) (DfE, 2010). However, in light of the debates discussed above, whether the geography has a place in a statutory curriculum or not, the more pressing matter affecting whether it has a place in the curriculum in reality concerns primary teachers' perceptions of the nature and relevance of the subject. How can the subject be conceptualised so that they perceive themselves with the capacity to work creatively with whatever curriculum emerges over the next two to three years? I have proposed a new paradigm for primary geography (Martin, 2006, 2008b) that draws on teachers' and pupils' everyday geographies. With others (Catling and Martin, 2011), I have explored what this might mean for how knowledge is understood, and the need for primary teachers to connect pupils' knowledge productively with knowledge beyond the 'everyday'. Teachers have everyday experiences of subjects, but not an understanding of the key concepts that underpin them. What they need is a subject specialist to share with them the narrative (organising conceptual framework) of subjects, so that they can use their own personal experience to make better sense of those subjects and then decide which aspects of the academic subject (outside their experience) they might then teach. This would also support pedagogical reasoning, deciding which activity was appropriate at which point and in which order – what Tim Oates (2010) refers to as curriculum coherence.

In this chapter, I have identified three areas of debate that help us to consider what place geography has in the primary school curriculum. The first set of debates concern the space afforded it in the curriculum and how much time it is given in comparison with other subjects; the second set of debates concern different perspectives on the nature of geography education, which in turn affect the third area of debate concerning the relevance of geography in the primary curriculum. Due to the nature of primary education, and the politically driven overemphasis on the core subjects, primary geography has found itself in a 'Catch 22' situation. It is a subject that is not well understood outside the geography community; primary student teachers come to their training with a limited and outdated view of what the subject has to offer; but due to the curriculum divide there are limited opportunities within ITE courses to change these views so teachers enter the profession lacking subject knowledge and confidence; teachers therefore struggle to see the relevance of the subject, and either avoid teaching it, or teach it in such a way that does not enthuse their pupils.

Thus the relationships between knowledge and the curriculum in the primary context are significantly different from those in the secondary school context. Taking these into account would seem to be important in generating meaningful 'transition' work between KS2 and KS3.

Acknowledgement

I am grateful to the comments of Di Swift on an earlier draft that helped me to organise my ideas more coherently.

Key readings

1. Catling, S. and Martin, F. (2011) 'Contesting powerful knowledge: The primary geography curriculum as an articulation between academic and children's (ethno-) geographies', *Curriculum Journal*, 22 (3), 317–15.

    Catling and Martin discuss the idea of ethno-geographies in relation to academic geographies and, drawing on the work of Paulo Freire and Michael Young, examine the claims that each makes to be a form of powerful knowledge. The authors propose that ethno-geographies, rather than being encountered as in some way deficient and in need of replacing by academic disciplined knowledge, could 'be brought into dialogue as a democratic partner in the mutual interplay of learning' (Catling and Martin, 2011, p. 332).

2. Young, M. (2011) 'The future of education in a knowledge society: The radical case for a subject-based curriculum', *Journal of the Pacific Circle Consortium for Education*, 22 (1), 21–32. Michael Young argues that if we are to give the importance of education in a knowledge society any serious meaning, we need to make the question of knowledge our central concern and this involves developing a knowledge-led and subject-led, and not, as much current orthodoxy assumes, a learner-led approach to the curriculum. He explores what this means for the curriculum, subjects and the purpose of schooling.

References

Alexander, R.J. (2004) 'Still no pedagogy? Principle, pragmatism and compliance in primary education', *Cambridge Journal of Education*, 34 (1), 7–33.

Alexander, R.J. (ed.) (2010) *Children, Their World, Their Education*. London: Routledge.

Burgess, T. (2007) 'Lifting the lid on the creative curriculum: How leaders have released creativity in their schools through curriculum ownership. National College for School Leadership, Available from: www.ncsl.org.uk [Accessed November 13, 2011].

Catling, S. (2001) 'English primary schoolchildren's definitions of geography', *International Research in Geographical and Environmental Education*, 10 (4), 363–78.

Catling, S. (2004) 'An understanding of geography: The perspectives of English primary trainee teachers', *GeoJournal*, 60, 149–58.

Catling, S. (2006) *Plus or Minus One point Five Percent: Geography provision for generalist primary trainee teachers on PGCE courses – a report*. Oxford: Westminster Institute of Education, Oxford Brookes University.

Catling, S., Bowles, R., Halocha, J., Martin, F., and Rawlings, S. (2007) 'The state of geography in English primary schools', *Geography*, 92 (2), 118–36.

Catling, S. and Martin, F. (2011) 'Contesting *powerful knowledge*: The primary geography curriculum as an articulation between academic and children's (ethno-) geographies', *Curriculum Journal*, 22 (3), 317–15.

Department of Education and Science (DES) (1978) *Primary Education in England*. London: HMSO.

Department of Education and Science (DES) (1991) Geography in the National Curriculum (*England*). London: HMSO.

Department for Education (DfE) (2010) Schools White Paper *The Importance of Teaching*. London: HMSO.

Department for Education (DfE) (2011) 2002 KS1 – KS2 Value Added Pilot Available from: www.education.gov.uk/performancetables/vap_02.shtml [Accessed 9 December 2011].

Department for Education and Employment/Qualifications and Curriculum Authority (DfEE/QCA) (1999) *The National Curriculum for England: Geography*. London: DfEE/QCA.

Department for Education and Skills (DfES) (1995) *Geography in the National Curriculum (England)*. London: HMSO.

Foley, M. and Janinkoun, J. (1996) *The Really Practical Guide to Primary Geography*, 2nd edn. Cheltenham: Nelson Thornes.

Galton, M. and MacBeath, J. with Page, C. and Steward, C. (2002) A Life in teaching: The impact of change on teachers' working lives. A report commissioned by the National Union of Teachers.

Geographical Association (GA) (2009) *A Different View: A manifesto from the Geographical Association*. Sheffield: Geographical Association.

Geographical Association (GA) (2011a) Membership numbers, personal communication.

Geographical Association (GA) (2011b) *The Action Plan for Geography 2006–2011, Final Report and Evaluation*. Sheffield: Geographical Association.

Iwaskow, L. (2006) 'Learning to make a difference', *Primary Geographer,* 61, 22–4.

Martin, F. (2005) 'The relationship between beginning teachers' prior conceptions of geography, knowledge and pedagogy and their development as teachers of primary geography', Unpublished PhD Thesis, University of Coventry.

Martin, F. (2006) *Teaching Geography in Primary Schools: Learning to Live in the World*. Cambridge: Chris Kington Publishing.

Martin, F. (2008a) 'Knowledge bases for effective teaching: Beginning teachers' development as teachers of primary geography', *International Research in Geographical and Environmental Education*, 17 (1), 13–39.

Martin, F. (2008b) 'Ethnogeography: Towards a liberatory geography education', *Children's Geographies*, 6 (4), 437–50.

Morley, E. (2010) 'Learning to be primary geography educators'. Thesis submitted in part fulfilment of the MA (Ed.): Professional Enquiry at the University of Winchester.

Oates, T. (2010) *Could do better: Using international comparisons to refine the National Curriculum in England*. Cambridge: Cambridge Assessment.

Ofsted (2002) *The Curriculum in Successful Primary Schools*. London: Ofsted.

Ofsted (2005) *The Annual Report of Her Majesty's Chief Inspector of Schools 2004/05*, London: Ofsted.

Ofsted (2008) *Geography in Schools: Changing practice*. London: Ofsted.

Ofsted (2011) *Geography – learning to make a world of difference*. London: Ofsted.

Rawling, E. (2001) *Changing the Subject: The impact of national policy on school geography 1980–2000*. Sheffield: Geographical Association.

SCAA (1995) *Planning the Curriculum at Key Stages 1 and 2*, London: SCAA.

Swift, D. (2010) *From False Dilemmas towards (re) Empowerment* Available from: http://www.tidec.org/ [Accessed 8 August 2012].

Woodhouse, S. (2006) 'But I didn't think that was geography!' *Primary Geographer*, 60, 28–9.

Chapter 2

What is Key Stage 3 for?

John Hopkin

> He would refer admiringly to the French Minister who could tell what
> was being taught at every minute in each school in France. He wanted
> up to 90% of the school day dictated nationally. If a ruler fell from any
> desk in the land, Mr Baker would metaphorically scoop it up. To this end
> he introduced the Great Education Reform Act.
>
> (Jenkins, 1995, quoted in Morrell, 1996)

Introduction

The story of geography at Key Stage 3 is of course the story of geography in
the National Curriculum: the very idea of the different phases of compulsory
education being formalised in Key Stages is an invention of the 1988 Education
Reform Act. Whether or not Kenneth Baker, the architect of the Act, really saw
himself in this way, the quotation is a reminder of the tensions inherent within
the National Curriculum; for example between different views about the purposes of the curriculum, between central control and professional autonomy
in selecting content, and between different concepts of 'entitlement' and
'standards'. In exploring the question 'What is Key Stage 3 geography for?' this
chapter focuses on the development of the National Curriculum for this age
group and asks how effective it has been in providing pupils with a high-quality
geography education.

GEOGRAPHY BEFORE THE NATIONAL CURRICULUM

The period between 1970 and 1988 is often portrayed as an era of extensive
school-based curriculum development in geography. One source of support on a
national scale came from the Schools Council, which funded three significant
geography projects focused on pupils aged 14 to 19 (see Chapter 3, in this
volume). These had an enduring influence which can still be detected in some current examination specifications, as well on the theory and practice of geographical

enquiry (Roberts, 2003). Rawling (1993) maintains their importance in engaging teachers in the process of rethinking school geography and argues that, because one of the National Curriculum's key political aims was to reassert central control over what was taught, one of its biggest casualties was a significant weakening of this kind of school-based curriculum development (Rawling, 2000, p. 13, 2001, p. 35).

However, these projects were not of course mandatory, and were inevitably taken up rather more by those teachers most open to change; so their reach was by no means universal. The projects were also focused on older secondary pupils; it was perhaps significant that the Schools Council project for the 8–13 age group focused on humanities rather than geography.

Another source of support and advice came from Her Majesty's Inspectorate (HMI), which produced a series of discussion documents designed to support schools in planning the curriculum, culminating in the Curriculum Matters series for the whole curriculum (DES, 1985) and for geography (DES, 1986). The last set out detailed aims for geography, with broad objectives and advice on teaching strategies for each phase of education, together with advice on planning and organisation, progression and continuity, and assessment.

This support for structuring the curriculum focused on the secondary phase as a whole, rather than identifying any distinctive aims or objectives for geography for ages 11–14, leaving the selection of content up to teachers themselves. Arguably school textbooks had more influence on shaping the lower secondary school curriculum (Walford, 1989). There was nothing new in this: the use of textbook series to help to define the curriculum was a tradition stretching back to the Victorian origins of school geography (Marsden, 1988, 1989, 1995); it was one which continued through the National Curriculum era.

So teachers' freedom to select aims, content and approaches (or textbooks) ensured that pupils' experience of geography in lower secondary schools varied considerably from one to another; indeed Bale suggests that it was quite possible to find three or more contrasting approaches existing alongside each other in the same school (Bale, 1993, p. 96). As HMI noted on the eve of the National Curriculum:

> There is also much variety between schools in the content of geographical work and the ways in which it is tackled. Although popular textbook series and ... inservice training help to provide some unifying influences, many kinds of programme can be identified.
>
> (DES, 1986, p. 21)

It is important to remember that this heterogeneity of approaches had weaknesses as well as strengths. It was a period that Lawton (1980, p. 22) called 'the golden age of teacher control (or non-control) of the curriculum', when many schools did little to ensure progression and continuity or a sufficiently broad and balanced set of experiences for their pupils (Simon and Chitty, 1993, p. 108).

In geography, Rawling reminds us that the period of curriculum development before the National Curriculum brought losses as well as gains, most notably leaving how to deal with place and locational knowledge unresolved (2001, pp. 40, 44). So although the Geography National Curriculum made much of the importance of knowledge, in reality school geography had already lost interest (Hopkin, 2011a), leaving the idea of knowledge resting on the shelf for another twenty years, waiting to be dusted off again in 2012–13 (see Chapter 4, in this volume).

On the eve of the first National Curriculum then, the lack of clear national guidelines and objectives or programme of curriculum development meant that there was little sense of either what pupils in this age group should be entitled to learn, or agreement about what standards they should achieve. Compared with the 14–16 and 16–19 age groups, supported by the structure of exam syllabuses and guidance from several curriculum development projects, geography for ages 11 to 14 was relatively neglected.

GEOGRAPHY IN THE NATIONAL CURRICULUM

The general aims for the National Curriculum were set out in a consultation document (DES, 1987), including the need 'to raise standards' and 'develop the potential of all pupils and equip them for the responsibilities of citizenship' (1987, pp. 2–3). These broad aims were to be achieved by securing:

> ... for all pupils in the maintained schools a curriculum which equips them with the knowledge, skills and understanding that they need for adult life and employment ... ensuring that all pupils study a broad and balanced range of subjects ... setting clear objectives for what children over the full range of ability should be able to achieve (and by) checking on progress towards these objectives and performance achieved at different stages

> (DES, 1987, pp. 3–4)

A National Curriculum would also facilitate the movement of pupils between schools, secure progression, continuity and coherence and enable schools to be more accountable for pupils' achievements.

A key concern of the GNC was to re-establish knowledge and understanding of places at the heart of school geography, including locational knowledge (Walford, 1992; Rawling, 1992, 2001), aims which are set out in the Geography Working Group's final report (DES, 1990). Although geographers were delighted that geography was included in the National Curriculum (Walford and Haggett, 1995), there was considerable concern from the start about weaknesses in the structure of the Geography Order. In particular, unlike history, each key stage was sampled from the whole of geography, leading to an overload of content and the lack of an effective model for progression. Liz Taylor's

chapter in this volume explores further the issue of how better to describe and understand progression in geography.

At the time of writing, the GNC for Key Stage 3 has gone through four different versions (DES, 1991 [for 1992]; DFE, 1995; DES/QCA, 1999 [for 2000]; and DCSF/QCDA, 2007 [for 2008]), with another planned for 2013. Table 2.1 summarises its development, using headings suggested by the structure of the earlier versions of the GNC (Programme of Study, Attainment Target/s, Skills (and enquiry), Places and Themes, together with those aspects whose origins lie in geography's earlier humanistic and welfare approaches. A summary of *Geography from 5–16* (DES, 1986) has been added for comparison.

A number of developments are evident over the first four versions of the GNC:

- An increased articulation of aims for geography and, in the 2000 version, an attempt at defining what is distinctive about learning in geography at Key Stage 3.
- Within the Programme of Study, an increasingly extended sequence of geographical enquiry and reduction in the prescription of geographical skills.
- In response to demands from schools and in common with other subjects, an overall reduction in content (especially between the 1991 and 1995 versions), together with reductions in the detail specified and more use of illustrative examples to frame teachers' increased choice.
- Considerable continuity in content, especially between 1991 and 1999; for example in locational knowledge, knowledge and understanding of places and geographical themes, albeit with reduced prescription.
- A development of themes based in geography's humanistic and welfare traditions.
- Significant changes to the Attainment Target/s between 1991 and 1995, a major focus for the Dearing Review (Dearing, 1994), then considerable continuity between 1995 and 2007.
- Some coherence between the 1999 and 2007 versions and the pre-GNC *Geography from 5–16*, including support for geographical enquiry; the influence of humanistic and welfare approaches to geography, including understanding diversity and controversial social, economic and environmental issues; and, latterly, the re-emergence of concepts in the development of geographical understanding.

Taking the long view, the GNC's twenty-year evolution has produced a curriculum which would be recognisable in a number of significant respects to geographers teaching in 1987. The move from the original highly detailed compulsory curriculum document to a more minimal framework, designed to secure a basic entitlement, helps explain this process, leading to increased responsibility for teachers to develop a balanced curriculum (Lawton, 1996).

Table 2.1 The evolution of the Geography National Curriculum

	Aims	POS	Enquiry and skills	Places	Themes	Humanistic and welfare	AT
Precursor: HMI 1987	Extensive aims for geography	No POS	A wide range of skills suggested – contributing to geographical enquiry	Locational knowledge 'essential' Places: Local area Global view (otherwise not specified)	Not specified: • people environment interactions, patterns and processes	• Understanding the nature of multicultural societies, sensitivity to prejudice & injustice • Controversial social, economic & environmental issues • Acting in the environment	None
First version: 1991	No geography aims in the Order; brief aims in non-statutory Guidance, and in Geography Working Group Final report.	Two sections: • Geographical skills • Places and themes (6 pages) Some content defined by level No distinctive key stage definition.	Brief statement on enquiry 'an enquiry approach should be adopted' Detailed list of specific skills	Locational knowledge: • Identify places on 6 maps Places: • Localities in local area, a developing country, an EC country • Home region • EC country and theme • USA, USSR, Japan		• To compare differences in economic geography and welfare in different parts of the world • Causes and effects of global environmental change	Five Attainment Targets: • Geographical skills • Knowledge and understanding of places • Physical geography • Human geography • Environmental geography 114 statements of attainment for KS3 (levels 3–7)

(Continued)

Table 2.1 (Continued)

	Aims	POS	Enquiry and skills	Places	Themes	Humanistic and welfare	AT
Revision: 1995	Overview of the Geography POS for KS3: 'pupils should be given opportunities to …'	Three sections: • Geographical skills • Places • Thematic studies (5 pages) Opportunities set out for each key stage.	Outline of investigation process Detailed list of skills	Locational knowledge: • Identify places on 3 maps Places: • Two countries in different 'states of development' (List A, List B)	Nine themes, at a range of scales, in context of the local area, UK, EU, different parts of the world (28 bullets)	• Issues that arise from people/environment interactions • Countries' global context and interdependence • Differences in development and their effect on quality of life, interdependence • Environmental issues: sustainable development, stewardship and conservation	One Attainment Target Eight level descriptions focused on attainment outcomes
Revision: 1999	Values, aims and purposes for the school curriculum (pp. 10–13) Importance statement for geography (p. 98) Statement of learning for Key Stage 3 (p. 100)	Knowledge skills and understanding • Geographical enquiry and skills • Knowledge and understanding of Places • Patterns & processes • Environmental change and sustainable development Breadth of Study sets out content to be studied in the Key Stage	Extended enquiry sequence; less detailed list of skills	Locational knowledge: • Detailed list of exemplar places (e.g. the 9 largest world cities, pp. 104–5) Places: • Two countries in 'different states of development'	Ten themes, in context of the local area, UK, EU, different parts of the world	• Values and attitudes in relation to contemporary issues • Interdependence and global citizenship • Sustainable development • Development, quality of life and interdependence • Places: changes and the issues arising • Topical issues	One Attainment Target Eight level descriptions (slightly revised)

2007		Key Processes	Range and content:	Range and content:	Key concepts	
Curriculum purposes, values and aims for the whole curriculum (pp. 5–7) Curriculum aims for geography are generic (p. 101) Importance statement for geography (p. 101)	POS reorganised around seven key concepts, then • Four key processes (skills and processes) • Range and content (breadth of study) • Curriculum Opportunities (for learning)	Extended enquiry sequence Reduced list of skills	Locational knowledge (unspecified) Places: Unspecified; studies at • Variety of scales • Key aspects of the UK, different parts of the world including the EU, regions, countries in different states of development	• Physical geography, human geography • Interaction between people and environments (minimal definition)	4. Interdependence 6. Environmental interaction and sustainable development (including climate change) 7. Cultural understanding and diversity *Range and content* Interactions between people and environment *Curriculum Opportunities* Participate in informed responsible actionGeographical issues in the news	One Attainment Target Eight level descriptions (slightly revised to strengthen progression)

In addition we can see a shift in the balance of influence on National Curriculum policy between the politicians (strong in the first GNC) towards professionals, represented by SCAA/QCA/QCDA and the subject associations. We may also detect a degree of rebalancing between geography's subject, educational and social dimensions (Marsden, 1995), as well as a caution about the risks of over-emphasising the latter, ever present in the history of geography education (Marsden, 1997; Lambert and Morgan, 2009).

As in the years before the GNC, textbooks became surrogates for curriculum planning and a significant force in interpreting the curriculum. In particular, a single textbook series, Key Geography (Waugh and Bushell, 1991), quickly achieved market dominance (Lambert, 2000). Its reach was extensive: Key Geography's choice of country studies influenced the selection of case studies by other publishers, leading in the longer term to a lack of curriculum innovation and so to a view of the world in danger of becoming distorted or out of date (Hopkin, 2011b). In addition, Roberts (1995, 1998), researching teaching before and after the implementation of the GNC, found considerable continuity in teachers' practice, based on strongly held values, or ideologies of geography education which predated and survived the National Curriculum.

THE OFSTED REPORTS: THE IMPACT OF THE NATIONAL CURRICULUM

The Office for Standards in Education (Ofsted) came into being in 1992 and, since the first year of the National Curriculum, has regularly reported its findings from inspections of schools, including reports on the National Curriculum subjects. The analysis below is based on these subject reports, supplemented by two annexes to HMCI annual reports (Ofsted, 1993a, 1993b, 1995, 2001, 2002a, 2002b, 2004, 2005, 2008, 2011). It uses three of the main section headings adopted in the most recent Ofsted frameworks (achievement, teaching and curriculum) and picks out comments specifically about Key Stage 3, rather than generic evaluations of secondary geography. Although Ofsted's frameworks have changed somewhat over the period, and there are some variations in style and detail, overall the reports for geography give us a good fix on the development of the subject at Key Stage 3 over two decades, and an opportunity to review the impact of the GNC on pupils' learning.

Achievement

Achievement was graded specifically for Key Stage 3 in the period between 1992–93 and 2004–5 when it showed a steady improvement: in this period lessons where achievement was good or better doubled from one third to two-thirds. However, alongside this long-term improvement, a consistent theme is the significant proportion of under-achievement at Key Stage 3, especially compared

with geography at Key Stage 4 and with other subjects (Ofsted, 2002a, 2002b, 2005, 2011). For example: 'In Key Stage 3 geography is weaker than most other subjects in terms of both teaching and pupils' achievement. Often, this is because teachers' expectations are insufficiently high' (Ofsted, 2002b, p. 4). One area of weakness leading to poor standards relates to geographical knowledge and skills:

> In some schools, pupils' development of knowledge, understanding and skills was not even. For example, skills in mapping were not always linked sufficiently to knowledge or understanding of contexts to apply them.
>
> (Ofsted, 1995, p. 8)

> Most of the students had poorly developed mapwork skills. Predominantly, this was because using maps was often limited to ... a unit on geographical skills, usually early in Key Stage 3 ... The students were expected to understand places and issues but they did not know where the places were, what they were like or the characteristics of their landscapes.
>
> (Ofsted, 2011, p. 22)

This theme is also taken up in other reports in relation to teaching (Ofsted, 1993a) and curriculum (Ofsted, 2005, 2008).

Teaching

Ofsted's evaluation of teaching shows a similar pattern to achievement; the two are of course closely related. Between 1993–94 and 2002–3 the proportion of teaching graded good or better improved from 42 per cent (of lessons) to 65 percent (of schools). Specific examples of good teaching include good questioning, well-planned and managed lessons with clear objectives, a variety of methods and effective use of resources. For example:

> The quality of teaching is now judged to be good or very good in the majority of schools. In some schools this can be linked to a recent emphasis on developing pedagogy using National Key Stage 3 training materials. These schools are frequently making good use of a good range of teaching and learning approaches including thinking skills, paired and group work.
>
> (Ofsted, 2005, p. 4)

These general examples are backed up by numerous case studies of good practice, especially in the later reports. Again, however, in spite of the generally improving picture, a consistent theme is that there is too much unsatisfactory teaching, more than in most other subjects, and that teaching at Key Stage 4 is better than at Key Stage 3 (Ofsted, 1993a, 2002a, 2002b, 2004, 2005, 2011).

Some weaknesses in teaching persist throughout the series, in particular, low expectations and limited challenge (especially for more able pupils) with limited differentiation overall and limitations in the use of ICT:

> A number of recurring limitations characterised the unsatisfactory lessons. Usually the teachers had low expectations of their pupils and their learning objectives were vague. The methods used, including the choice of learning aids, were unimaginative and ineffective. Often the pupils were required to listen to dull and over-long explanations by the teacher or to undertake low-level tasks such as copying or labelling maps and diagrams ....
> (Ofsted, 1993a, p. 11)

At Key Stage 3, in mixed-ability classes in more than half of the schools visited, more able students were often underachieving because many of the activities, intended primarily for middle- and lower-ability students, lacked challenge (Ofsted, 2011, p. 24).

Many of these features are linked; for example, common weaknesses are limitations in subject knowledge and teaching by non-specialists (Ofsted, 1993a, 1993b, 1995, 2001, 2002a, 2004, 2005, 2008, 2011) and overreliance on mundane exercises from limited textbooks:

> An increasing number of lessons in Years 7 to 9 are taught by non-specialists ... in general they do not have the technical subject knowledge to explain geographical concepts or an understanding of the quality of work required to reach higher levels. The lack of professional development opportunities available for geography teachers frequently compounds this problem.
> (Ofsted, 2004, p. 6)

> In far too many classes there was an over-reliance on text books, especially by non-specialist teachers ... a narrow range of textbooks and a focus on factual recall rather than on exploring ideas failed to capture students' interest. Higher-attaining students, in particular, were rarely challenged.
> (Ofsted, 2011, p. 26)

A particular and enduring difficulty for many geography teachers at Key Stage 3 has been their assessment of pupils' progress, in particular inconsistent use of marking and assessment data to promote improvement, and assessment for learning (formative assessment) (Ofsted, 1993a, 1993b, 2001, 2002a, 2011). In spite of significant training through the Key Stage 3 and Secondary National Strategies (DfES, 2002, 2004, 2005), this remained an issue up to 2011:

> Many departments have sound policy statements on assessment, but too often policies are not followed by all of the teachers, leading to inconsistencies and variations in, for example, the quality of marking. Also, in too many

departments teachers fail to recognise the potential of assessment information for monitoring progress in standards and quality of teaching, and
informing and improving lesson planning.

(Ofsted, 2001, pp. 3–4)

Curriculum

Alongside improvements in achievement and teaching, a consistent theme is
the improvement in planning and schemes of work over the last two decades,
sometimes linked to positive changes in the National Curriculum and support
materials such as the Key Stage 3 Scheme of Work, (QCA/DfEE, 2000).
Fieldwork is particularly singled out for praise, for example: 'a well-organised
programme of fieldwork for all pupils in Years 7-9, integrated into the scheme
of work' (Ofsted, 2002a, p. 2) and 'much of the field-study work ... was of
high quality' (Ofsted, 1993, p. 11). However. fieldwork is also identified as a
weakness in several reports (Ofsted, 2002a, 2004, 2005). For example:

> There is insufficient opportunity for fieldwork in many schools, particularly
> at Key Stage 3. This distracts from the overall quality of geography, and may
> be associated with a continuing decline in numbers of pupils opting for
> geography at examination level.
>
> (Ofsted, 2004, p. 11)

Weaknesses in the geography curriculum, also linked to poor teaching and low
standards, particularly focus on inadequate attention to real places and locational
knowledge, and planning for progression in geographical skills (Ofsted, 1993a,
1993b, 1995, 2005, 2008). For example:

> The majority of students, especially at Key Stage 3 in the weaker schools,
> had poorly developed core knowledge in geography. Their mental images
> of places and the world around them were often confused and lacked spatial
> coherence.
>
> (Ofsted, 2011, p. 6)

Other areas for development consistently singled out are weak or non-existent
continuity and progression from primary schools, out-of-date or irrelevant
schemes of work and other weaknesses in planning. Whole-school arrangements
causing concern in the early days of the National Curriculum were humanities
courses with little geography teaching and pressure on curriculum time, issues
which re-emerge in the 2008 and 2011 reports:

> In over half the schools visited there was increasing evidence that curricular
> changes were ... frequently reducing time for geography in Key Stage 3 ....
> In almost a third of the schools visited, initiatives such as a two-year Key

Stage 3 programme or teaching a broad humanities course in Year 7 were having an impact on the quality of what was provided as well as the time available.

(Ofsted, 2011, p. 31)

Summary

It is important to remember that this series of Ofsted reports shows steady improvements in achievement, teaching and curriculum over two decades. However, they also highlight some weaknesses persistent since the early years of the National Curriculum, many identified as key issues for improvement in successive reports. Some, for example limitations on curriculum time for geography, the use of non-specialist teachers and the impact of integrated humanities, can be seen as whole-school issues, perhaps related to geography's enduring relatively low status in the curriculum. However, other necessary improvements, such as teaching with appropriate expectations, challenge and differentiation; the planning and teaching of locational knowledge, places and geographical skills; and assessment that supports progress and improvement are arguably fundamental to geography teachers' professional repertoire, and so less easy to dismiss.

A number of reports (for example for 1993a, 1993b, 1995, 2008, 2011) point out the strong (usually generic) association between good leadership and management, good teaching and high standards, suggesting how this underperformance might be tackled – for example citing effective subject-specific support through the Action Plan for Geography[1] as important in the implementation of the revised 2007 National Curriculum (Ofsted, 2011, p. 32).

Conclusion

In answering the question, 'What is geography at Key Stage 3 for?' we are in a position to evaluate to what extent the National Curriculum's aims have been met for this age group. A key aim of the first GNC was to re-establish a balanced geography curriculum by reviving the knowledge and understanding of places, including locational knowledge; as the above analysis suggests, even by 2011 this aim was not met for many, perhaps the majority of pupils. A key general aim of the National Curriculum was to raise standards; here geography can claim some success, although at a slower rate compared with many other subjects and with persistent low expectations and lack of challenge for some groups of pupils. Continued weaknesses in primary liaison and inconsistent planning for progression within Key Stage 3 and into Key Stage 4 suggest that the aim of securing progression and continuity tends to be met only in strong departments. There has been some success in improving formative assessment, but it remains inconsistent in improving standards.

Finally, the recent re-emergence of integrated courses based on 'themes' (positively encouraged in the 2007 Key Stage 3 reforms) and restrictions on teaching time for geography have both limited pupils' experience of a high-quality geography curriculum, and put at risk the notion of a broad and balanced range of subjects. The key debate that emerges here concerns the form and function of Key Stage 3: as an extension of primary education (with its traditional emphasis on integration) or as the platform for secondary education with its emphasis on the development subject knowledge, conceptual depth and intellectual challenge.

So although the Geography National Curriculum established a framework for pupils' geographical education in the (previously neglected) first three years of secondary schools, it has been only modestly successful in some significant aspects. These are issues that predate the National Curriculum, suggesting that they are deep-seated within school geography. The Key Stage 3 geography curriculum in 2011 bears a number of similarities to its pre National Curriculum identity, suggesting a remarkable ability for school geography to recreate itself partly in the image of former times, and for teachers' (and authors') ability to interpret and adapt what geography is taught and learned, whilst perhaps not questioning too closely what should be distinctive about geographical learning for this age group. There are many advantages to professional control over the curriculum. However, these unresolved issues suggest there may also be disadvantages, particularly without the systematic professional development needed to foster a 'cultured profession' (HoC, 2009, para 47) able to take responsibility for keeping itself up to date in geographical knowledge, as well as in curriculum, pedagogy and assessment. In asking 'what is Key Stage geography 3 for?' it is worth considering whether we have made significant progress beyond HMI's rather bland definition of its purpose three decades ago:

> When geography is optional in years 4 and 5,[2] pupils' experience in earlier years should be designed to provide a satisfactory programme for those who do not continue with the subject as well as those who do.
>
> (DES, 1981)

Notes

1 www.geography.org.uk/projects/actionplanforgeography.
2 That is, Years 10 and 11.

Key readings

1. Oates, T. (2010) *Could do better: Using international comparisons to refine the National Curriculum in England*, Cambridge: Cambridge Assessment. Tim Oates's paper 'Could Do Better' made an important contribution to thinking before the 2011–12 review of the National Curriculum. It discusses the (controversial) concepts of 'curriculum control' and 'curriculum coherence'.

2. Marsden, W.E. (1995) *Geography 11–16: Rekindling good practice*, London: David Fulton. Bill Marsden takes a long-term, at times rather sceptical view of the development of geography and the tendency to conflate change with progress:

> We are the inheritors, not the inventors of good practice .... Hardly any of the dramatic developments in geographic education over the last 30 years have not been anticipated in previous periods. We have invented few, if any, wheels .... What might be a new wheel, however, would be the achievement of a better balance between the elements of good practice. (Marsden, 1995, pp. vii–viii)

References

Bale, J. (1993) 'Geography Teaching, Postmodernism and the National Curriculum', in R. Walford (ed.), *Viewpoints on Geography Teaching: The Charney Manor Conference Papers 1991*. London: Longman.

DCSF/QCA (2007) *The National Curriculum: Statutory requirements for Key Stages 3 and 4*. London: DCSF/QCA.

Dearing, R. (1994) *The National Curriculum and its Assessment*. London: SCAA.

DES (1981) *Geography in the School Curriculum*: a working paper by the geography committee of HM Inspectorate.

DES (1985) *The Curriculum from 5–16* (HMI Curriculum Matters Series, 2). London: HMSO.

DES (1986) *Geography from 5–16* (HMI Curriculum Matters Series, 7). London: HMSO.

DES (1987) *The National Curriculum 5–16: A Consultation Document*. London: DES.

DES (1990) *Geography for Ages 5 to 16* (The final report of the Geography Working Group). DES: London.

DES (1991) *Geography in the National Curriculum (England)*, London: HMSO.

DES/QCA (1999) *The National Curriculum Handbook for secondary teachers in England, Key Stages 3 and 4*. London: DES/QCA.

DFE (1995) *Geography in the National Curriculum*. England, London: HMSO.

DfES (2002) *Training Materials for the foundation subjects*. London: DfES Publications.

DfES (2004) *Pedagogy and Practice: Teaching and learning in secondary schools*. London: DfES Publications.

DfES (2005) *Assessment for Learning: Guidance for senior leaders*, London: DfES Publications.

DFES/QCDA (2007) *The National Curriculum: Statutory requirements for key stages 3 and 4*, London: DCSF/QCDA.

Hopkin, J. (2011a) 'Progress in geography', *Geography*, 96 (3), 116–23.

Hopkin, J. (2011b) 'Sampling the World', *Teaching Geography*, 36 (3), 96–7.

House of Commons (2009) House of Commons Children, Schools and Families Committee, *National Curriculum: Fourth Report of Session 2008–9*, London: The Stationery Office.

Jenkins, S. (1995) 'Rimbaud without a Cause', *The Times*, 25 January.

Lambert, D. (2000) 'Textbook Pedagogy: Issues on the use of textbooks in geography classrooms', in C. Fisher and T. Binns (eds.), *Issues in geography teaching*, London: Routledge Falmer.

Lambert, D. and Morgan, J. (2009) 'Corrupting the curriculum? The case for geography', *London Review of Education*, 7 (2), 147–57.

Lawton, D. (1980) *The Politics of the School Curriculum*, London: Routledge, Kegan & Paul.

Lawton, D. (1996) *Beyond the National Curriculum: Teacher professionalism and empowerment*, London: Hodder & Stoughton.

Marsden, W.E. (1988) 'Continuity and Change in Geography Textbooks: perspectives from the 1930s to the 1960s', *Geography*, 73 (4), 327–43.

Marsden, W.E. (1989) '"All in a good cause": Geography, history and the politicisation of the curriculum in nineteenth and twentieth century England', *Journal of Curriculum Studies*, 21, 509–26.

Marsden, W.E. (1995) *Geography 11–16: Rekindling good practice*, London: David Fulton.

Marsden, W.E. (1997) 'On Taking the Geography out of Geographical Education', *Geography*, 82 (3), 241–52.

Morrell, F. (1996) *Continent Isolated: A study of the European dimension in the National Curriculum in England*, London, Federal Trust.

Oates, T. (2010) 'Could do better: Using international comparisons to refine the National Curriculum in England', Cambridge, Cambridge Assessment, Available from: http://www.cambridgeassessment.org.uk/ca/digitalAssets/188853_Could_do_better_FINAL_inc_foreword.pdf [Accessed 20 January 2011].

Ofsted (1993a) *Geography: Key Stages 1, 2 and 3 – First Year, 1991–92*, London: HMSO.

Ofsted (1993b) *Geography: Key Stages 1, 2 and 3 – Second Year, 1992–93*, London: HMSO.

Ofsted (1995) *Geography: A Review of Inspection Findings 1993–94*, London: HMSO.

Ofsted (2001) *Ofsted Subject Reports, 1999/2000: Secondary Geography*, London: Ofsted.

Ofsted (2002a) *Secondary Subject Reports 2000/01: Geography*, London: Ofsted.

Ofsted (2002b) *Secondary Subject Reports 2001/02: Geography*, London: Ofsted, Available from: http://www.ofsted.gov.uk/resources/annual-report-200102-ofsted-subject-reports-secondary [Accessed 1August 2011].

Ofsted (2004) *Geography in Secondary Schools: Ofsted subject reports series 2002/03*, London: Ofsted, Available from: http://www.ofsted.gov.uk/resources/annual-report-200203-ofsted-subject-reports-secondary [Accessed 1August 2011].

Ofsted (2005) *The Annual Report of Her Majesty's Chief Inspector of Schools 2004/5: Geography in secondary schools*, Available from: http://live.ofsted.gov.uk//publications/annualreport0405/4.2.6.html [Accessed 1 August 2011].

Ofsted (2008) *Geography in Schools: changing practice*, London: Ofsted, Available from: http://www.ofsted.gov.uk/resources/geography-learning-make-world-of-difference. [Accessed 1 August 2011.]

Ofsted (2011) *Geography: Learning to make a world of difference*, London: Ofsted, Available from: http://www.ofsted.gov.uk/resources/geography-schools-changing-practice [Accessed 1 August 2011.]

QCA/DfEE (2000) *Geography: A Scheme of Work for Key Stage 3*, London, QCA/DfEE.

Rawling, E. (1992) 'The Making of a National Geography Curriculum', *Geography*, 77 (4), 292–309.

Rawling, E. (1993) 'Innovations in the geography curriculum 1970–1990: A personal view', in R. Walford (ed.), *Viewpoints on Geography Teaching: The Charney Manor Conference Papers 1991*, London: Longman.

Rawling, E. (2001) *Changing the Subject: The impact of national policy on school geography 1980–2000*, Sheffield: Geographical Association.

Roberts, M. (1995) 'Interpretations of the Geography National Curriculum: Aa common curriculum for all?' *Journal of Curriculum Studies*, 27 (2), 187–205.

Roberts, M. (1998) 'The Impact and the Legacy of the 1991 Geography National Curriculum at Key Stage 3', *Geography*, 83 (1), 15–27.

Roberts, M. (2003) *Learning through Enquiry: Making sense of geography in the Key Stage 3 classroom*, Sheffield: Geographical Association.

Simon, B. and Chitty, C. (1993) *Save Our Schools*, London: Lawrence and Wishart.

Walford, R. (1989) 'On the Frontier with the New Model Army: Geography publishing from the 1960s to the 1990s', *Geography*, 74 (4), 308–20.

Walford, R. (1992) 'Creating a National Curriculum: A view from the inside', in D. Hill (ed.), International Perspectives on Geographical Education, Boulder, CO: Centre for Geographical Education, University of Colorado.

Walford, R. and Haggett, P. (1995) 'Geography and Geographical Education: Some speculations for the twenty-first century', *Geography*, 80 (1), 3–14.

Waugh, D. and Bushell, A. (1991) *Key Geography*, Cheltenham: Stanley Thornes.

Chapter 3

What is geography's place in post-14 education?

David Gardner

> What counts as an educated 19 year old in this day and age?
>
> (Pring et al., 2009, p. 12)

Introduction

This quotation reminds us that debates about post-14 education are about far more than what frames, structures and calibrates the examination system. In outlining what I consider to be the key debates in this phase of education I shall also try to keep in mind a broad view. I do so as a former school teacher and author of classroom materials but also as the geography subject officer at the now defunct Qualifications and Curriculum Development Agency (QCDA). The chapter is therefore written from a practitioner-policy perspective rather than a purely academic analysis.

CONTEMPORARY PERSPECTIVES

Why study geography post 14? How we see this question depends on our perspective. From the students' point of view they need to make decisions about which subjects to opt for in year 9, and this has been the subject of considerable research interest in recent years (e.g. Biddulph and Adey, 2003). They consider advice, or influence, from many quarters and factors including:

- how well they performed in the last assessment;
- what their friends are going to do;
- whether they like the teachers of different subjects;
- which subjects they think are the 'easiest' and therefore their best chance of achieving a good grade in two years' time;
- whether they have enjoyed their Key Stage 3 experience of the subject; and
- which subjects they think are most 'useful' or 'important'.

In other words, it is a complicated mix of approaches to decision making.

The teacher's perspective is, of course, different: it is, presumably, in the teacher's interest to influence the students' choices, and maximise take up. Although there is plenty of support material available for teachers to act in this way, there has apparently been relatively little research on this – although the available data (from examination entries at 16 years) do suggest that the attitudes and actions taken by teachers (and this might include the content of year 9 programmes) are vital (Weeden, 2007; Weeden and Lambert, 2011). Another aspect that might benefit from research, in an era of transparent accountability through published league tables, is the operation of the 'specifications market'. It is important for teachers to select a GCSE specification, which seems to 'best suit the learning needs of the students', of course. But what is perhaps more important are the grades that the specification is likely to yield. These two things are not necessarily the same thing, although it is surely the case that teachers will look for specifications with fresh and exciting contents and modes of assessment, but possibly not if changing the specification risks the grade profile of the subject. At the time of writing (early 2012), this matter has become heated and the Secretary of State is said to be interested in radical reform in order to ensure the maintenance of academic standards at GCSE and A level.

Specifications and their examinations are handled by just three Awarding Bodies in England. Each of these markets their specifications as the best route to success for the most students. It is a highly competitive market place, which, it is possible to hypothesise, provides the circumstances that will encourage grade inflation. Where subject advisers are in place, offering online support and resources, teachers may justifiably feel well supported. But where awarding bodies have signed deals with (or own) publishers, who contract chief examiners to write the textbook for the specification, it is possible to at least imagine the possibility for corruption, driven by needs other than 'what constitutes an educated person in this day and age'. Mick Waters, former Director of Curriculum at QCA, went as far as saying: 'the exams system is "diseased" and "almost corrupt"' (Bangs et al., 2011, pp. 34–5). We discuss this in a little more detail later in the chapter.

What is clear from this brief overview of the contemporary context is that geography's place in the post-14 curriculum is not determined simply by our views on whether geography is a good thing or not. The Geographical Association's manifesto (GA, 2009) makes some powerful statements about geography as does the GA's submission in support of geography in the English Baccalaureate, introduced in 2010 (GA, 2011). But these attempts to argue a 'case for geography' cut little ice in comparison with the real *politik* laid down in policy, which is characterised by instability. New qualifications such as diplomas (developed and then abandoned), vocational qualifications, new GCSEs and A levels – the introduction of AS and A2, new higher grades A*, changing benchmarks for measuring school performance (with the English Baccalaureate the latest in a long line of measures): this is the day-to-day reality of schools,

teachers and learners trying to make decisions about how to occupy 14–19 educational space.

HISTORICAL PERSPECTIVES

A number of trends and landmarks in education as a whole have had a significant influence on geography and its place in a post-14 curriculum in the twentieth and early twenty-first centuries (see Walford, 2000 for a detailed account of most of this story). During the early part of the nineteenth century, the geography taught (mainly to younger children of primary age) was very 'fact' based, consisting largely of the rote learning of names of places and features, such as the rivers of Britain, and the location of these places and features: a 'capes and bays' approach. By the late nineteenth century, there was growing interest in geography in schools perhaps symbolised by the establishment of the GA in 1893 (Balchin, 1993), and a trend towards commercial geography and a greater focus on the links between physical and human phenomena. But the subject was not yet seen as an academic discipline for older students or university study.

In 1903 Brereton stated, in his analysis of the teaching of geography in secondary schools, that

> Geography has been till recently the Cinderella of secondary education …. However, powerful influences outside the school have been working in its favour – the Imperialist movement, the need for wider commercial knowledge, the growing recognition of the intimate connection between geography and many kindred sciences, such as astronomy, physics, geology, meteorology, ethnology, history, and the like.
>
> (Brereton, 1903, p. 107)

By the beginning of the twentieth century, in grammar and independent schools, geography was still a subject of minor importance. In 1922 the Board of Education Regulations for Secondary Schools recognised advanced courses in geography for the first time. This raised profile for the subject was a reaction to increasing pressure fuelled by growing public interest in international affairs as a result of the First World War. In terms of examinations, pupils entered for School Certificate examinations were awarded for performance across a number of subjects. Between 1918 and 1939 the number of examination entries for geography gradually increased, and it gained popularity and acceptance as a university subject too – partly, or even mainly, to supply graduates to become secondary school teachers. By the mid-twentieth century, with its main focus on regional geography, about two-thirds of school pupils were entered for the School Certificate examinations – the 'E.Bacc' of its time – which included geography as one of their five choices.

During the 1940s many universities and professions began to request a national examination system that would be more effective in filtering out the type

of pupils suited to their needs. As a result, in 1951 GCE Ordinary and Advanced levels were introduced. These examinations were initially adopted by selective grammar school pupils. Unfortunately, as King (1997) points out, these grammar schools were not evenly distributed across the country leading to inequalities of opportunities for pupils, for example Westmorland entered 42 per cent of pupils for O Levels, whilst Gateshead only managed 9 per cent. It is interesting to note that such an uneven geography of geography educational opportunity still persists today (Weeden and Lambert, 2011).

Marchant (1964), as staff inspector of geography at the then Department of Education and Science, characterised O and A level examinations as having to 'include papers on systematic physical and human geography and on the regional geography of certain selected areas' (1964, p. 178). More significant, in the context of contemporary perspectives, was Marchant's observation that examinations in 1964 strongly reflected the move from geography being a test of memory to developing a more analytical approach which stressed understanding.

Such approaches, which exhibit the growing influence of educational thought at the time (see Lambert, 2009), reposition geography not so much as an end in itself, but more as means to educational purpose and value. This was expressed well by Michael Naish, leader of the very influential Geography 16–19 Project in the early 1980s, who described geography as a '*medium* of education' (Naish, 1997; my emphasis) rather than an end in itself. Such approaches certainly influenced the new Certificate of Secondary Education (CSE) examinations introduced in 1963, and designed initially for 16-year-old pupils in Secondary Modern schools. The School Examinations Council recommended that field-work be a compulsory component of CSE examinations, and also suggested that questions be more resource based. Photographs, large-scale maps, statistics, pieces of first-hand description were data offered for observation and analysis, and the examination questions concerned with thinking rather than memorising. The development of CSEs led to a greater emphasis on coursework and other innovative practices. CSE quickly became popular, and within ten years entry numbers equalled GCE O level.

Continued pressure to merge O level and CSE over a period of ten years ultimately led to the creation of the General Certificate of Secondary Education in 1988. GCSEs, common to all pupils, are developed from common national criteria general to all subjects and also subject-specific criteria. The geography criteria for GCSE introduced in 1986 reflected changes in geographical curriculum thinking and assessment practice over the previous twenty years, and many syllabuses were brought much more up to date, with approaches based on concepts and key ideas, enquiry approaches, and recognition of the importance of values and attitudes in dealing with issues.

For many these were heady days for school geography. This period was marked by a confident and expanding teaching profession working with a vibrant discipline fired up by the conceptual revolution that brought with it

'new geography'. Teacher innovators were well supported not only by academic geographers anxious to spread the word (notably following the legendary Madingley Hall summer schools reported by Walford (2001)) but also by a highly regarded team of subject specialist HMIs, well-qualified subject specialist local authority 'advisers' and a highly productive university-based teacher education infrastructure providing the background intellectual 'heavy lifting' that guided curriculum development projects: for example, Hall (1976), Marsden (1976), Graves (1979), and Slater (1982).

THE NATIONAL CURRICULUM AND AFTER

The 1988 Education Reform Act legislated that geography was to be a foundation subject in the new national curriculum and would be taught to all children in England and Wales from 5 to 16. Compulsory geography post 14 was short-lived but led to the high watermark for geography in terms of entries in 1994–96. However, it soon became recognised that the curriculum was seriously overloaded and geography lost its post-14 compulsory status in the Dearing Review (1995). From 1995 to 1999 geography entries at GCSE declined by 12.85 per cent, whereas the total cohort of pupils increased by 15.34 per cent.

By 2005, although geography was still a significant option subject ranked eighth for GCSE and nineth at A level, GCSE entries had declined by 29.3 per cent since 1996 and A level by 26 per cent since 1998. Westaway and Rawling (2001) were keen to point out, however, that 'geography numbers tend to be more buoyant where geography is taught most successfully. A stimulating, challenging, enjoyable key stage 3 experience … is a powerful factor in maintaining numbers'. The QCA monitoring reports (2005) acknowledged that there were a range of factors influencing this decline, but stated in 2005: 'there is now sufficient evidence of the negative effect of tired and dated content in existing specifications on the one hand and of the positive effect of the GCSE pilot innovations on the other hand, to make curriculum renewal 14–19 a priority'. The report went on to state that 'geography is at a crucial point in its development … opportunities provided by the current curriculum reviews should be seized' (QCA, 2005, p. 6).

This sentiment was also evident in a succession of Ofsted reports for the same period. These pointed to

> … the small but steady fall in numbers of pupils choosing to study geography at GCSE, AS and A level. To some extent this may be attributed to an increase in the number and range of other courses, particularly more vocationally orientated courses such as leisure and tourism. Ultimately, however, pupils make choices based largely on their Key Stage 3 experience. Pupils who have chosen geography say that they have done so because of high quality teaching and their own enjoyment of it.
>
> (Ofsted, 2008, p. 23)

Nevertheless, one attempt to instil creativity and innovation into the 14–19 arena for geography was the so-called 'GCSE pilot'. The pilot aimed to provide a lively and innovative geography course for 14–16-year-olds that reflected pupils' needs and current thinking in the subject, particularly in higher education. The pilot GCSE was in effect part of the larger QCA 'Futures Project' launched in 2004. This had a remit to rethink the aims, purpose and future direction of the school curriculum, with seminars for each subject, including geography. The Geography Futures Seminar in February 2005 allowed the subject community to make progress in outlining geography's distinctive contribution to the school curriculum. The findings of this meeting were summarised in a publication (QCA, 2005b, pp. 18–19): what was needed in geography was a move to an aims-led, more flexible curriculum with a sound conceptual, skills-based framework, with improved links with other subjects and higher education.

Over the next five years the secondary curriculum review, with greatest fanfare reserved for the KS3 revised programme of study introduced in 2008, resulted in a government-funded implementation programme, the Action Plan for Geography (also government-funded), GCSE and A level reviews, and ultimately the GA's 2009 'manifesto' *A Different View*. Arguably, all these initiatives were influenced by and developed the findings from QCA's Futures seminar.

TAKING STOCK: GCSE AND A LEVEL REFORM

The government's 14–19 White Paper (DfES, 2005) had clear objectives for GCSEs and A levels – designed principally to preserve them as the golden standard of English education. At GCSE level a key issue was to review 'coursework', originally introduced in 1986 in order to broaden the assessment base and increase the 'validity' of the examination. Now the imperative was to reduce the assessment burden on teachers and at the same time neutralise the criticism in some quarters that coursework could no longer be trusted (and indeed was open to 'cheating' – through plagiarism and/or undue help from parents or even teachers). At A level a key concern was to address the widely reported perception that disciplinary 'rigour' was no longer what it was: thus the need to increase 'stretch' for the most able by introducing optional harder questions with separate sections at the end of A level papers. The review also reduced the numbers of assessment units in A levels from 6 to 4, again to lessen the assessment burden on students and teachers.

Although QCA was remitted to review both GCSE and A level with these objectives in mind, it also took the opportunity to address content issues, working with Awarding Bodies and key subject stakeholders effectively to modernise these qualifications (QCA, 2007b). At GCSE, attempts were made, in writing the subject criteria, to more clearly signpost continuity and progression from Key Stage 3. This was hampered, however, by a number of technical issues – not least the revision itself of the KS3 programme of study (introduced in 2008)!

At A level a certain level of content prescription was removed (QCA, 2006) enabling the Awarding Bodies (ABs) to draft new specifications with less constraint on content. The ABs were thus able to produce specifications that were significantly different in content, structure and approach.

These changes to the post-14 offer in geography need to be understood in context. As John Hopkin explores in detail in this volume, the KS3 programme of study was radically transformed. Although the official rationale was to sharpen the approach to subject study in the early secondary years by specifying the essential or 'key' concepts and skills rather than delivering a long shopping list of prescribed topics, the overall impact on geography (and history) was mixed. There is evidence that in many schools leadership teams interpreted the key messages of the new secondary curriculum in a manner which was damaging to a number of foundation subjects including geography (CfBT, 2009). In many schools senior leadership teams interpreted the review as an opportunity to introduce skills-based schemes under the banner of competency and 'learning to learn', at the expense of foundation subjects. Schools were encouraged to innovate – and innovation often began and ended with 'humanities': some schools reduced teaching geography to one year in Y8, with pupils expected to choose option subjects to GCSE after just two terms of being taught geography. Although it is difficult to quantify, there is little doubt that less geography was being taught, including in KS4, by the end of the New Labour period in 2010. The 2011 Ofsted report for geography provides some evidence of this:

> In almost a third of the schools visited, initiatives such as a two-year Key Stage 3 programme or teaching a broad humanities course in Year 7 were having an impact on the quality of what was provided as well as on the time available. Broad humanities courses tended to focus on teaching generic learning skills rather than knowledge and understanding that was specific to geography. Many students also had little or no specialist geography teaching at Key Stage 3, particularly in Year 7.
>
> (Ofsted, 2011a, pp. 31–2)

Indeed the evidence suggests that New Labour's 14–19 review actually accelerated the decline in geography entries post-14 which started in the mid 1990s. However, the fact that in 2011 history GCSE entries dropped by about 2700 (1.2 per cent), whilst geography saw a drop of 13,800 (7.1 per cent), suggests factors beyond merely the structural.[1] A very good debating point is to explore the possible reasons for this. In practice this is highly contentious for all manner of local issues intervene. Thus, for example, Weeden and Lambert (2010) have identified a regional pattern to geography's GCSE candidature. The data reveal that inner-city areas with a relatively large proportion of schools with students from deprived households are more likely to have lower geography entries than suburban or rural areas with more affluent households. In London, eight (62 per cent) of Inner London local authorities had low entries, while only two (15 per cent)

had high entries. In contrast, Outer London had only two local authorities (11 per cent) with low entries and seven (37 per cent) with high entries. The geographical pattern of candidature for geography GCSE shows in general a greater uptake in county comprehensive schools and independent schools and a lower uptake in city comprehensives and academies. Lambert and Weeden conclude that in some low-performing urban schools, leadership teams have taken strategic decisions to restrict student choice in an attempt to boost the school performance scores through the introduction of vocational qualifications that gave the equivalent of four GCSEs but required proportionately less timetable time. Some schools have boosted their five A*–C scores by introducing these qualifications and restricting the subjects that students can choose.[2] As the 2011 Ofsted report found:

> Most worrying was the trend in the number of schools not entering students for GCSE geography. In 2007, this figure was 86; in 2008, it stood at 99 and by 2009 it had risen to 123 maintained schools. The trend in academies was more marked. In 2007, six academies did not enter students for geography; in 2008, this had increased to 12 and, in 2009, the figure had risen to 19 academies, representing almost one in 10 academies overall.
>
> (Ofsted, 2011a, p. 23)

Weeden and Lambert (2010) concluded that it was of 'great concern that the pressure of school "league tables", and the current obsession with generic skills and competences, is depriving many students, especially in urban areas, of the opportunity to explore the geographical'.

THE QUALIFICATIONS MARKET

The previous section provides a glimpse of a period of relentless though well-meant reform in the post-14 secondary curriculum. The overarching themes are curriculum 'modernisation' and raising performance, achieved through the use of simple market mechanisms, for example to incentivise the take-up of vocational options – albeit hurriedly introduced and found to be fundamentally flawed (Wolf, 2011).

The Awarding Bodies (ABs) responsible for GCSE and GCE specifications and examinations also operate in a market (Hopkin, 2011). For Mick Waters, this has incentivised ABs to increase market share through some fairly questionable tactics as we have already observed in this chapter – even marketing their new specifications at GCSE and A level as relatively 'easy routes' to success for schools under pressure from league tables:

> Exam boards are competing in the market place by implying to schools that their qualifications are easier than their competitors …. In previous jobs,

> I had seen people from awarding bodies talk to headteachers implying that their examinations are easier.
>
> (Bangs et al., 2011, pp. 34–5)

Not only that, but many specifications have the textbook to help you through. Ofqual, Waters argued, should 'immediately' stop chief examiners from writing textbooks aligned to the specific specifications they examined, a practice which he said was akin to 'insider dealing'.

This is, of course, of great concern, for at the very least it suggests that some ABs and schools may have lost sight of the wider purposes of studying geography post 14 in the dash for market share and performance points. This issue became national headline news in December 2011 when the *Daily Telegraph* revealed that 'teachers are paying up to £230 a day to attend seminars with chief examiners during which they are advised on exam questions and the exact wording that pupils should use to obtain higher marks' (*Daily Telegraph*, 7 December 2011). The chief examiner for one GCSE geography specification was reported as boasting that 'there's so little [in the exam] we don't know how we got it through [the exam regulator]'.

There are clearly significant pressures in the system, and these have consequences. A recent Ofsted history report (2011b) commented that at A level, the mushrooming of course-endorsed and linked textbooks was having a negative impact as they stultified teachers' thinking and restricted students' progress. Students relied on the textbook and were less willing to read beyond the 'set textbook'. Their written and oral work revealed how their understanding of the topics they studied was narrow. It can be concluded that such students are not well prepared for higher education, where independent learning and extensive reading are required. This analysis could equally be applied to geography students.

THE 2010 COALITION GOVERNMENT AND A CHANGE OF DIRECTION

With the election of the Coalition government and the publication of a new schools White Paper, *The Importance of Teaching* (DfE, 2010), it would seem much of the change initiated under New Labour is to be unpicked. It announced another review of the national curriculum as well as qualifications 14–19.

The new government has championed a return to traditional knowledge and subject 'rigour' with the introduction of the English Baccalaureate (Ebacc) as a measure of school performance. Geography is one of only two humanities subjects included in the Ebacc, which potentially raises the subject's status in schools. The national curriculum review expert panel report recommend that geography be part of the national curriculum in all Key Stages 1–4 (DfE, 2011, p. 25) This could restore geography to the high watermark position it attained at the introduction of the national curriculum in 1987 – with a key difference: the report favoured reducing Key Stage 3 to two years (11–13 years)

to enable Key Stage 4 to expand to three years. The panel believes that this would allow pupils to follow a wider range of subjects, avoid premature subject choices and enable essential knowledge to be taught in greater depth. For teachers working in the 'humanities', the significance of this is a potential end to the insidious choice required of 14-year-olds to drop either history or geography: they could do both over three years (DfE, 2011, pp. 32–3). It remains to be seen whether this opportunity is grasped, although it is already the *de facto* case that in many schools Key Stage 3 is already reduced to two years.

It is, at the time of writing, difficult to see what will be the impact of these changes. Could the introduction of the English Baccalaureate reverse the slide in the number of geography entries at GCSE and A level, and encourage a resurgence of specialist geography at Key Stage 3? These early signs of new policy seem very encouraging for the future of geography 14–19; the question still to be debated, however, is what kind of geography this will be and how well it is taught across a wider spectrum of the age cohort.

Conclusion

This brief review of the place of geography in the post-14 curriculum identifies a number of recurring themes. The development of the subject is influenced by changes in society as a whole. This is as it should be because dynamic change is a vital element of living geography, but it also proves to be a challenge for governments, school leaders and parents coming to understand the nature of the subject.

But there are also examples of history repeating itself. It is not a story of unfolding progress. Thus, the regional disparities evident with the introduction of O level in 1951, with pupil entry dependent on the number of grammar schools in a Local Authority, were still visible in the 2000s with inner-city schools replacing subjects like geography with vocational courses. Even when these are displaced, will the establishment of high-achieving Academies and 'Free Schools' result in the introduction of a tiered education system as in the 1950s? No politician dare support the reintroduction of grammar schools, but maybe the market will achieve this through the back door. And so what of geography post 14: an academic subject for the few (as before) or a component of a general education for all? In the next few years, as the Coalition's curriculum review unfolds, there will no doubt be much continuing debate of the central question of the Nuffield Review of 14–19 Education and training: 'what counts as an *educated* 19 year old in this day and age?' (Pring et al., 2009, p. 12, my emphasis).

Note

1 According to 2012 figures this decline has been reversed - a direct result of the introduction of the Ebacc. It remains to be seen whether the trend will be reversed into a period of year-by-year growth in examination enteries.

2 In January 2012 the Coalition government announced its intention to tackle this issue by removing over 1,000 vocational options qualifying for the published school

league tables. This follows the Wolf Report of 2011 in which Alison Wolf showed that many of these options were of extremely limited currency on the job market.

Key readings

1. Pring, R., Hayward, G., Hodgson, A., Johnson, J., Keep, E., Oancea, A., Rees, G., Spours, K. and Wilde, S. (2009) *Education for All: The Future of Education and Training for 14–19 Year Olds*, Abingdon: Routledge. A six-year independent review of 14–19 education and training from October 2003 to September 2009. It was shaped throughout by the answers to the question: 'What counts as an educated 19 year old in this day and age?' An excellent overview of the findings is available from <http://www. nuffieldfoundation.org/14-19review>.
2. GA (2011) *Learning to be human and the English Baccalaureate: Geography and history: Evidence from the Geographical Association*. The GA's evidence paper in support of the inclusion of geography in post-14 education, this provides an excellent overview of their rationale.

References

Balchin, W.G. (1993) *The Geographical Association: The first hundred years*, Sheffield: The Geographical Association.

Bangs, J., MacBeath, J. and Galton, M. (2011) *Reinventing Schools, Reforming Teaching: From Political Visions to Classroom Reality*, London: Routledge.

Biddulph, M. and Adey, K. (2003) 'Perceptions v. reality: Pupils' experiences of learning in history and geography at key stage 4', *The Curriculum Journal*, 14 (3), pp. 291–303.

Brereton, C. (1903) 'The Teaching of Geography in Secondary Schools', *The Geographical Teacher*, 2 (3), 107–13.

CfBT (2009) *Moving from implementation to impact: A report on the subject specific support for the New Secondary Curriculum*, CfBT Education Trust July 2009.

Daily Telegraph (2011) Watt, H. Newell,C. Winnett, R. and Paton,G. 'Exam boards: How examiners tip off teachers to help students pass', Daily Telegraph 7 December 2011 Available from: http://www.telegraph.co.uk/education/secondaryeducation/8940781/Exam-boards-how-examiners-tip-off-teachers-to-help-students-pass.html [Accessed 12 April 2012].

Dearing, R. (1995) *Review of 16–19 Qualifications: Interim report*, London: SCAA.

DfES (2005) *14–19 Education and Skills White Paper*, Available from: https://www.education.gov. uk/publications/standard/publicationDetail/Page1/CM%206476 [Accessed 12 April 2012].

DfE (2010) *The Importance of Teaching: The Schools White Paper*, Available from: https://www. education.gov.uk/publications/standard/publicationDetail/Page1/CM%207980 [Accessed 12 April 2012].

DfE (2011) *The Framework for the National Curriculum A report by the Expert Panel for the National Curriculum Review*, London: Department for Education. See page 2 of report at https://www.education.gov.uk/publications/eOrderingDownload/NCR-Expert%20 Panel%20Report.pdf

Geographical Association (2009) *A Different View: A manifesto from the Geographical Association*, Sheffield: GA, also Available from: www.geography.org.uk/adifferentview [Accessed 12 April 2012].

GA (2011) *Learning to be human and the English Baccalaureate: Geography and history: evidence from the Geographical Association*, Available from: www.geography.org.uk/download/ GA_AUEBacSelectCommitteeEvidence.pdf [Accessed 12 April 2012].

Graves, N. (1979) *Curriculum Planning in Geography*, London: Heinemann.

Hall, D. (1976) *Geography and the Geography Teacher*, London: George Allen and Unwin.

Hopkin, J. (2011) *Progress in Geography*, GA Presidential Lecture given at Geographical Association Annual Conference University of Surry, Guildford, April 2011 Available from: http://www.geography.org.uk/download/GA_Conf11PresidentialLecture.pdf [Accessed 12 April 2012].

King, S. (1997) 'Geography and the GCSE', in D. Tilbury and M. Williams (eds.), *Teaching and learning geography*, London: Routledge.

Lambert, D. (2009) *Geography in Education: Lost in the Post?* Professorial Inaugural lecture, London Institute of Education.

Marchant, E.C. (1964) 'Geography in Education in England and Wales', *Geography*, 49 (3), 173–91.

Marsden, W. (1976) *Evaluating the Geography Curriculum*, Edinburgh: Oliver and Boyd.

Naish, M. (1997) 'The scope of school geography: A medium for education', in D. Tilbury and M. Williams (eds.), *Teaching and learning geography*, London: Routledge.

Ofsted (2008) *Geography in schools: Changing practice*, Available from: http://www.ofsted.gov.uk/resources/geography-schools-changing-practice [Accessed 12 April 2012].

Ofsted (2011a) *Geography Learning to make a world of difference*, Available from: http://www.ofsted.gov.uk/resources/geography-learning-make-world-of-difference [Accessed 12 April 2012].

Ofsted (2011b) *History for all History in English schools 2007–10*, March 2011, Available from: http://www.ofsted.gov.uk/resources/history-for-all [Accessed 12 February 2012].

Pring, R., Hayward, G., Hodgson, A., Johnson, J., Keep, E., Oancea, A., Rees, G., Spours, K. and Wilde, S. (2009) *Education for All: The Future of Education and Training for 14-19 Year Olds*, Abingdon: Routledge. Also see: www.nuffieldfoundation.org/14-19review.

QCA (2005) *Geography monitoring report 2004–2005*, Available from: http://www.geography.org.uk/download/GA_NKS3QCAreport.pdf [Accessed 12 February 2012].

QCA (2005) *Futures: A curriculum for the future subjects consider the challenge* QCA, pp. 18–19. London: QCA, Available from: http://www.bgfl.org/bgfl/custom/files_uploaded/uploaded_resources/19021/futures_report_rgb_qca_05_1615.pdf.

QCA (2006) *GCE AS and A Level subject criteria for geography*, QCA Available from: http://www.ofqual.gov.uk/files/qca-06-2852_geog_asandalevel_sc.pdf [Accessed 12 February 2012].

QCA (2007a) *The New Secondary Curriculum What has changed and why?*, Available from: http://dera.ioe.ac.uk/6564/1/qca-07-3172-new_sec_curric_changes.pdf [Accessed 12 February 2012].

QCA (2007b) *GCSE subject criteria for geography*, QCA, Available from: http://www.ofqual.gov.uk/files/qca-07-3452_GCSEcriteriageography.pdf [Accessed 12 January 2012].

QCA (2007c) The National Curriculum statutory requirements for key stages 3 and 4 from September 2008 (originally published on the National Curriculum website but now programmes of study available at DfE website, Available from: http://www.education.gov.uk/schools/teachingandlearning/curriculum/secondary [Accessed 12 February 2012]. Archived version of the National Curriculum website developed by QCA, Available from: http://teachfind.com/content/national-curriculum [Accessed 12 March 2012].

Slater, F. (1982) *Learning Through Geography*, Oxford: Heinemann Educational.

Walford, R. (2001) *Geography in British Schools 1850–2000: Making a world of difference*, London: Woburn Press.

Weeden, P. (2007) 'Students' Perceptions of Geography: Decision making at age 14', *Geography*, 92 (1), 62–73.

Weeden, P. and Lambert, D. (2010) 'Unequal Access: Why some young people don't do geography', *Teaching Geography*, 35 (2), 74–5.

Westaway, J. and Rawling, E. (2001) 'The rises and falls of geography', Teaching *Geography*, 26 (3), 108–11.

Wolf, A. (2011) *Review of Vocational Education, The Wolf Report* [online] Available from: https://www.education.gov.uk/publications/eOrderingDownload/The%20Wolf%20Report.pdf [Accessed 3 November 2011].

Part II

'Classroom' Debates

Chapter 4

What constitutes knowledge in geography?

Roger Firth

> The shift from an emphasis on disciplinary knowledge in the curriculum to the pedagogy of social constructivism and the blurring of the distinction between the curriculum and pedagogy has major implications for what knowledge is taught in schools and how it is taught.
>
> (Rata, 2012, p. 107)

Introduction

The focus of this chapter is knowledge and the geography curriculum, and specifically how we might conceptualise knowledge and its impacts on the curriculum. While such considerations may at first seem a world away from the geography curriculum and teaching geography in schools today, this is not the case. Different conceptions of knowledge (and truth) imply and encourage different ideals of thinking, learning, teaching and curriculum in geography. The background to the chapter is the review of the National Curriculum, which is now taking place in England which David Lambert (2011) has described as a 'knowledge turn' in schools, as well as recent debate within education about the question of knowledge. The National Curriculum review serves to exemplify the importance of attentiveness to how knowledge is conceptualised.

Three conceptions of knowledge are introduced: absolutism, relativism and realism. The main interest is with realism or, to be more exact, *social realism*. Absolutism and relativism are briefly presented through social realist argumentation. These conceptions have fundamental importance for educational policy, theory and practice. In recent times relativism has usually been considered the only alternative to absolutism. Social realism, however, understands itself as an alternative to both absolutism and relativism. The terms 'absolutism' and 'relativism' are used to depict a general understanding of and approach to knowledge whereas social realism is a school of thought which is becoming increasingly influential in education. It is for this reason that social realism is given attention in this chapter.

Social realism makes a defence of knowledge in opposition to absolutism (the usual referent is positivism) and relativism (social constructivism) as well as arguing against recent trends in curriculum policy. Social realist theorists such as Michael Young emphasise the way education has had difficulties with the very idea of knowledge in recent decades. 'The basis of this problem is a long-standing belief ... that the only choice is between positivist absolutism or constructivist relativism' (Maton and Moore, 2010, p. 1). This false dichotomy has deleterious implications for understanding education, for policy and practice, and for social justice (2010, p. 2).

Social realist theorists have been concerned about how recent curriculum policy and the school curriculum have neglected or marginalised the question of knowledge. Knowledge is either taken for granted or is 'something we can make fit our political goals' (Young, 2010, p. 21). Yet, as Young points out,

> If we are to give the importance to education in a knowledge society any serious meaning, we need to make the question of knowledge our central concern and this involves developing a knowledge-led and subject-led, and not, as much current orthodoxy assumes, a learner-led approach to the curriculum.

> (2010, p. 21)

For Young 'this is the 'radical' option – not, as some claim, the 'conservative' option – provided we are clear about what we mean by knowledge' (2010, p. 21). Here, 'radical' refers to the persistence of social inequalities in education.

The chapter is in four parts. First, I draw on the recent policy context. The second part introduces social realism and recent debate about the question of knowledge. Third, the three conceptions of knowledge are presented through a social realist perspective; and in addition three scenarios of 'possible educational futures'[1] identified by Young and Muller (2010), both with the aim of distinguishing their different assumptions about knowledge and the implications for the curriculum and pedagogy. The fourth part draws out the implications of social realism as a developing theory of knowledge and how it might support a knowledge-based or subject-based curriculum that is progressive and democratic. It is not possible in a chapter of this length for the arguments to be exhaustive or definitive. Instead, the aim is to draw attention to the assumptions that underlie different conceptions of knowledge and their implications for the curriculum.

POLICY CONTEXT

The recent publication of *The Framework for the National Curriculum* (DFE, 2011), a report by the Expert Panel for the National Curriculum review, makes clear the significance of subject knowledge for the National Curriculum within the overarching aim of providing a broad and balanced curriculum (1.5):

it is helpful from the start to be aware of some fundamental educational considerations. Perhaps the most significant concerns the nature of knowledge and of learners, and crucially, the interactions between them.

(DFE, 2011, 1.1)

The Coalition government's proposals for the National Curriculum have stirred up considerable controversy. Some of the recent utterances of Michael Gove, the Secretary of State for Education, suggest that the National Curriculum review could turn the curriculum clock back decades. Some commentators dismiss the government's emphasis on subject knowledge as backward-looking, elitist and likely to lead to new inequalities. Others welcome putting subjects strongly to the fore in the school curriculum. Yet others see the proposals as nominally supporting a return to subjects, but question the coherence and sense of direction of the Coalition's educational strategy.

The current government's wider approach to education isn't convincing because their arguments aren't theoretically grounded. Subject-centred teaching can't simply be asserted as something worthwhile. It must be argued for if teachers are to become engaged and convinced of its necessity.

(Institute of Ideas, 2010, p. 3)

As for geography, Morgan (2011) is concerned that

a return to a focus on subject-based teaching and within that a concern with the core knowledge that makes up the subjects, may for many geography teachers seem to be an alarming prospect, signalling a return to long lists of content to be covered, and threatening the pedagogical developments around enquiry and learning that are increasingly seen as 'best practice'.

(2011, p. 90)

The GA's recent Geography Curriculum Consultation,[2] which set out its response to the Schools White Paper *The Importance of Teaching* (DFE, 2010), has provided an evidence base of teacher comments, which confirm strong support for the creation of a rigorous geography curriculum. However, the Geography Curriculum Consultation Full Report makes it clear

that a line-by-line, detailed list of geography's contents is not the best way to draw a positive response from teachers ... though there is strong support for the national curriculum achieving greater clarity over the core and essential knowledge contents of geography.

(Geographical Association, 2011, p. 2)

Three significant issues emerged from the consultation: distinguishing curriculum from pedagogy, defining the school subject and getting the level of

detail right. The first directly maps onto the recent debate within education about the question of knowledge and is taken up below. The other two issues are not considered and it is, perhaps, important to explain why. The GA consultation was mainly concerned to identify the 'core' knowledge that ought to be included in the National Curriculum. While this is understandable and important in the context of the review, it is not enough when the matter in hand is the justification and establishment of a knowledge-based/subject-based curriculum. The GA Consultation absented any consideration of the epistemological nature of knowledge itself. Questions about knowledge as a *phenomenon* were left outside its frame of reference.

The concept 'core knowledge' is somewhat of a blunt instrument. No matter how defined,[3] the concern is always with the marking out of knowledge, with specifying or delineating *what* knowledge is to be taught. This points us towards specific kinds of cognitive material only ('what to teach'). 'That the issues in front of us can be reduced to such mundane dimensions is to be avoided' (Barnett, 2009, p. 429). 'Core' knowledge tells us nothing about knowledge as a phenomenon (its structure, modes of production and development, its values and conventions and uses). Whatever one's view about knowledge and its importance or otherwise at this time, the National Curriculum review requires that we ask: what kind of knowledge turn is this? The question that immediately follows is: what theoretical frameworks do we have to interpret a 'knowledge turn'?

SOCIAL REALISM

Social realism has emerged over the last decade in the sociology of education. It is a sociological rather than a philosophical approach to knowledge. It is concerned to define the social basis of objectivity in knowledge in relation to education in order to bring into view the epistemological principles that should underpin the use of disciplinary knowledge within the school curriculum which can support meaningful learning. The aim of social realist theorists is not just to 'bring knowledge back in' (Young, 2008a) to education but to redefine and reconfigure the central issues around knowledge and the curriculum. Outlining some of the arguments of social realism will also help to illustrate the way that theorising about knowledge has been a missing piece of the educational puzzle (policy, theory and practice) in recent times – and the need to ground educational policy and practice in a social theory of knowledge.

Social realist theorists argue for a strong conception of knowledge; one that 'recognises *contra* positivism, the inescapably social character of knowledge but, *contra* constructivism, does not take this to inevitably entail relativism' (Maton and Moore, 2010, p. 2). For social realism the rational objectivity of knowledge is acknowledged as itself a fact: that is, we do actually have knowledge, it is a social phenomenon (it is produced in socio-historical contexts) and it is fallible

rather than absolute or merely relative (2010, p. 2). 'This allows knowledge to be seen in itself, not merely as a reflection of some essential truth or social power but as something in its own right whose different forms have effects for intellectual and educational practices' (2010, p. 2).

Social realists are particularly concerned about the neglect of disciplinary knowledge in recent years, both in curriculum policy and in classroom practice that has followed from such policy. During the 13 years of New Labour, policy knowledge came in for a hard time as an educational aim. Two assumptions came to the fore about the knowledge basis of the school curriculum: that subjects and subject knowledge are less important than the emphasis on learners and making the curriculum relevant to their experience and future life and employability, and that reducing social inequalities requires a reduced role for school subjects (Yates and Young, 2010, p. 8). In consequence knowledge has lost ground in the school curriculum and in teachers' thinking and practice.

The core argument of social realism is that the acquisition of disciplinary knowledge is the key purpose that distinguishes education from all other activities (Moore, 2004; Young, 2008a); that disciplinary knowledge acquired in schools is fundamentally more powerful than the knowledge gained from everyday life (social knowledge) because of its explanatory power. This critical conceptual knowledge is the knowledge that enables a higher form of thought in which the learner is able to deduce abstract and generic ideas from a mass of factual data. It can move young people, intellectually at least, beyond their local and particular circumstances. Here, Young lays emphasis on what the knowledge can do[4]: enable the next generation to participate in a society's conversation about itself and its future (Wheelahan, 2010, p. 1). It follows, therefore, that schools need teachers with that specialist disciplinary knowledge who are subject specialist teachers.

CONCEPTIONS OF KNOWLEDGE AND THE CURRICULUM

Three conceptions of knowledge are presented as a useful device with which to consider the National Curriculum review, to distinguish the different assumptions about knowledge and their implications for the curriculum and pedagogy and to engage with current curriculum debates in geography (see Figure 4.1) The conceptions of knowledge are used to represent:

- Absolutism: Coalition government curriculum policy.
- Constructivism: the situation in schools today regarding the geography curriculum based on New Labour's neo-liberal approach to education.
- Realism: an alternative viewpoint of knowledge and the curriculum.

Figure 4.1 Three conceptions of knowledge.

View of knowledge (epistemology)	Absolutism (Positivism is the usual referent)	Constructivism (Social constructivism/postmodernism)	Realism (Social realism)
	Knowledge as external, fixed, universal and certain	Knowledge as situated, ideological and relativist	Knowledge as objective and fallible
	Knowledge is independent of the social and historical contexts in which it is developed	Socially produced	Socially produced
	Knowledge is discovered and verified through direct observations or measurements of phenomena	Knowledge is established through the meanings attached to the phenomena studied; researchers interact with the subjects of study to obtain data; research changes both researcher and subject; knowledge is context and time dependent	Knowledge is revisable by constant and systematically institutionalised critique
	Objective standards whereby truth is determined	No objective standards with which to compare different representations of reality and all opinion and beliefs are equally true	There are specific kinds of conditions under which knowledge is produced. These conditions are not given; they are historical and social but also objective and confirm truth
	Boundaries are given and fixed	The end of boundaries	Disciplinary boundaries are recognised and maintained but also crossed for the creation and acquisition of new Knowledge
Ontology	Reality exists independently of what anyone knows, thinks or believes about it – it 'is'	Reality is socially constructed. We are never able to transcend or suppress our own situatedness and interests. Thus even if there is some ultimate fixed reality we would not be able to know it as it 'really is'	Reality exists independently of what anyone knows, thinks or believes about it but human knowledge and perceptions are an integral part of reality
Curriculum	'Traditional' curriculum	Boundary weakening and de-differentiation of knowledge	Intimate link between knowledge structure, form and concepts and curriculum organisation
	Subject knowledge is abstracted from the particular contexts and human interests which render it meaningful	the stipulation of curricular content in generic, usually skill, 'learning to learn and outcome terms	Differentiation *both* between disciplines and between theoretical and everyday knowledge as fundamental, even though the form and content of the differentiation is not fixed and will change
	Content-driven Socially conservative	the *'integration' of school subjects*	
	A curriculum of compliance	A curriculum of generic skills and instrumental outcomes	A curriculum of engagement

Aims of education	Induction into the dominant knowledge traditions/'the canon'	Learning to learn and learning for life and work	Acquisition of powerful knowledge
Future scenario	Future 1	Future 2	Future 3:
	Boundaries are given and fixed. The 'Future' is associated with an 'a-social' or 'under-socialised' concept of knowledge	The end of boundaries. The 'Future' is associated with an 'over-socialised' concept of knowledge	Boundary maintenance as prior to boundary crossing. In this 'Future' it is the variable relation between the two that is the condition for the creation and acquisition of new knowledge in the emerging global context
	Education and the wider context will continue to exist as two parallel worlds	In 'progressive' opposition to future 1	
		The boundedness of absolutism is seen to be the main problem, and the condition for greater social justice and less inequality is the removal of these boundaries	The de-differentiation approach of Future 2 is most likely to achieve not the dissolving of boundaries, but to render them invisible - an invisibility that is exaggerated for the more disadvantaged
	Maintaining and legitimising existing power relations and restricting access to knowledge		
	An education system overtly stratified along social class lines, with schooling as its principal instrument of stratification	A steady weakening of boundaries, a de-differentiation of knowledge and institutions, a blurring of labour market sectors, and a greater emphasis on generic outcomes rather than inputs as instruments of equalisation and accountability	Future 2 as the deprofessionalisation of teaching
			F2 replaces unequal access to knowledge by increasing access to qualifications leading to credential inflation as qualifications are competed for but have less and less worth — either as use value or exchange value
	Recipe for social divisiveness, inequality and conflict	Learner-directed trends	
			Both F1 and F2 end up with an instrumental view of knowledge

The term absolutism is used to refer to the view that there is knowledge (and truth) that is external and universal. This position generally assumes that there is a given and fixed reality and a neutral observer who can observe the external world objectively. Knowledge is objective because of its direct correspondence with the objects of an external reality. It implies that we have some purely objective method of knowing, which allows us to know reality as it 'really' is, independently of our own interests, needs and situatedness. The natural sciences, particularly physics, provide the model for all the sciences, including the social sciences, and where the task of science is to enable the prediction and control of social and natural events.

A traditional subject-based curriculum assumes a given and fixed concept of knowledge. The curriculum is seen as a body of received wisdom inherited from the past, whereby students are inducted into the dominant knowledge traditions that keep them dominant. The educational rationale for this traditional model (Future 1) is found in its respect for knowledge as something to be valued 'for its own sake' (Young, 2011, p. 267). It is driven by the view of a relationship of deference to a given body of knowledge, whereby traditional disciplines promote proper respect for authority and protect traditional values. 'Such ideals of knowledge, truth and reality are seen as desirable because they are thought to provide us with absolute certainty' (Bleazby, 2011, p. 454). This is a view of the curriculum that is 'overwhelmingly static because [its] boundaries are fixed by social imperatives that override the conditions for knowledge and its innate dynamism, fecundity and openness to change' (Young and Muller, 2010, p. 17). It is socially conservative and underpins the Coalition government's[5] policy and rhetoric in terms of the National Curriculum.

One example of such an approach to the curriculum is Hirsch's (1987, 2007) notions of 'core' knowledge and 'cultural literacy'. They attempt to make explicit the core knowledge that every student should know and emphasise the need to create a public sphere of knowledge that enables all cultural groups to engage in common issues. This would ensure 'our cultural inheritance'. Hirsch's ideas are likely to have influenced the Coalition government's writing of the 2010 Schools White Paper. Coalition policy appears to look to the past to secure the future for young people. In geography this view is represented by Alex Standish, who argues for a return to a 'pure' form of geography. Unquestionably a knowledge-based/subject-based curriculum defined in traditional terms has historically been associated with acute inequalities in access and opportunity. But does a knowledge-based curriculum inevitably mean social inequality?

'Relativism is usually considered the only alternative to absolutism' (Bleazby, 2011, p. 455). It stands in 'progressive' opposition to absolutism. It envisages a steady weakening of boundaries, a de-differentiation of knowledge. Relativists deny that there is a knowable, static reality, and consequently deny the possibility of absolute truth. According to relativism, knowledge and truth are no longer 'out there'; they are constructed and relative to particular cultures, times, places and individuals. Any observer, implicitly or explicitly, influences what is observed.

An observer's prior beliefs, theories and expectations mould what they assume to be 'out there'. Each particular body of knowledge vies for attention but none has more validity than any other. Relativists argue that we are never able to transcend or suppress our own situatedness and interests. It follows that there are no objective standards with which to compare different representations of reality and all opinions and beliefs are equally true. Clearly this suggests a radically different approach to education.

Policy and practice in more recent times (Future 2) has certainly rejected the 'givenness' of knowledge and instead sees knowledge as a 'social construct' and therefore a product of and responsive to changing social and economic demands (Young, 2011, p. 267). It leads to an increasingly instrumental view of knowledge and of the curriculum. 'The emphasis is invariably on learners, their different styles of learning and their interests, on measurable learning outcomes and competences and making the curriculum relevant to their experience and their future employability' (Young, 2010, p. 21). As Young stresses:

> Often these reforms are well intentioned and have progressive aims. They stress open access, widening participation, and promoting social inclusion. This makes them difficult to question without being seen as elitist and conservative.
>
> (2010, p. 21)

This has seen a steady weakening of the boundaries between disciplinary knowledge and everyday knowledge (social knowledge).

This has usually been through a constructivist logic whereby the student has been increasingly constructed as an active being rather than a cognitive being. There is also 'a sense that disciplinary knowledge is obscure and strange and its possession difficult, and thereby, somewhat elitist' (Barnett, 2009, p. 431). This idea 'lurks in the view that knowledge is "socially constructed", a view that often carries the silent "only" or "merely" before the socially constructed' (2009, p. 431). The idea that the boundaries between subjects and between disciplinary knowledge and everyday knowledge might express epistemological realities is set aside (Young, 2011, p. 267). Arguments in favour of subjects have been increasingly seen as conservative and backward-looking; out of alignment with the world in which young people are growing up.

The emphasis on constructivist pedagogies has also placed stronger emphasis on students' own social experience (social knowledge). However, as Rata (2012) emphasises, when there is an over-dependence on social experience as the means and content of knowledge, such knowledge becomes not only a pedagogical resource but also the main resource for the curriculum' (p. 104). And at this point, curriculum and pedagogy are treated as the same process.

For Young (2011), curriculum and pedagogy should be seen as conceptually distinct. Curriculum and pedagogy 'refer to the distinct responsibilities of curriculum designers and teachers and each depends on the other' (p. 267).

The blurring of the distinction, Young, argues, arose out of two genuine problems that were 'not unique to England: an "over-crowded-curriculum" and too many disaffected students' (2010, p. 23). 'Attempts to include the experiences of students in a "more motivational" curriculum' (2010, p. 23), however, are for Young, inappropriate.

> As most teachers know well, they have to take account of the experiences and prior knowledge that students bring to school and what initially motivates them. These are part of the resources teachers have for mobilising students and are the basis for students to become active learners. That is quite different, however, from including these experiences in the curriculum.
>
> (p. 24)

It is to misunderstand what any curriculum can do and confuses two critically separate educational ideas. In consequence of all of this, there has been a significant weakening of the concept of knowledge within education and an associated loss of disciplinary knowledge within the school curriculum.

Distinguishing curriculum from pedagogy raises a critical question about the GA's idea of 'curriculum making' in teachers' work. As the Full Report of the Geography Curriculum Consultation (Geographical Association, 2011) states, 'there is very strong endorsement in the consultation of the GA's idea of curriculum making. It expresses where curriculum and pedagogy come together. But there may need to be additional clarity made between this and how it relates to a National Curriculum document' (p. 4). Such clarity will need to build on epistemological foundations.

The Coalition review of the National Curriculum raises important questions about the direction and consequences of recent curriculum policy. As argued above, however, it offers us two polarised alternatives for the curriculum based on their assumptions about knowledge:

> *Future 1* denies the social and historical basis of knowledge and its organisation into subjects and disciplines, *Future 2* treats the ways that knowledge is organised as historically arbitrary and in some forms little more than expressions of power.
>
> (Young, 2011, p. 268)

Absolutism emphasises the objectivity of knowledge but ignores the socio-historical basis of knowledge. Relativism (constructivism) denies the objectivity of knowledge, that knowledge may not only represent 'knowledge' of the powerful', but also the most reliable ways we have of understanding the natural and social world – and therefore for structuring and sequencing knowledge in the curriculum. In its most extreme form, relativism (constructivism) argues that 'because we have no objective way of making knowledge claims, the curriculum should be based on the learner's experience and interests and that

somehow these can be equated with the interests of society' (Young, 2011, p. 268). Absolutism and constructivism are not the only options. Social realism makes a defence of knowledge in opposition to both epistemological absolutism and epistemological relativism (constructivism), as will be explored below.

A SOCIAL REALIST MODEL OF THE CURRICULUM

From a social realist viewpoint, both absolutism and constructivism are wrong about the assumptions they make about knowledge. Absolutism and social realism 'do both start with knowledge and not the learner, nor the contexts faced by learners' (Young, 2010, p. 22). Social realism treats knowledge as external to learners, as absolutism does, but it recognises that this externality is not given, but has a social and historical basis (2010, p. 22). Knowledge is understood as emergentist and objectivist. Social realism is concerned with the social basis of knowledge production and the endorsement of a strong conception of knowledge that reconciles the objectivity of knowledge with its sociality.

The social realist view of the objectivity of knowledge is based on the assumption that there are specific kinds of conditions under which powerful knowledge is acquired and produced. These conditions are not given; they are social and historical but also objective. The objectivity is located in the specialist communities of researchers in different fields of knowledge (disciplines) who produce that knowledge. Here, it is emphasised that disciplinary knowledge has its own internal authority – the authority of procedures of review and criticism which are institutionalised, occur over time and allow for the separation of the ideas from their original socio-historical location (Rata, 2012, p. 106). In this way, Young (2008b, p. 14) differentiates between *context-independent* knowledge (disciplinary knowledge) and *context-dependent* (everyday, social knowledge) knowledge. Context-dependent knowledge allows the individual to cope within the particulars of their everyday life. Context-independent knowledge is the conceptual knowledge of disciplines that is not tied to particular cases and forms of life and therefore provides a basis for generalisation, moving beyond specific context and making claims towards universality (2008b, p. 15).

Social realism thus understands knowledge as emergent from the specialised collective practices of knowledge generation within specialist/epistemic communities. In this sense, it relies on a regulatory rather than an absolute notion of truth and an inescapable ontological realism, but recognises the fallibility of even the most reliable knowledge. Knowledge develops on the basis

> of its conceptual or explanatory power, which allows researchers/scientists to make choices between competing theories. Such knowledge develops into non-arbitrary forms that have their own necessary constraints – and it is argued curriculum designers and teachers have to take this into account
>
> (Yates and Young, 2010, p. 8).

What is particularly significant about social realism is its emphasis on the nature of knowledge itself (knowledge as a *phenomenon*) and its epistemological integrity. Social realist theorists are making more explicit the *internal* or *cognitive* nature of disciplinary knowledge; in particular the structures and 'grammars' of knowledge. These are concepts which offer a possible means of systematically describing the particular nature of disciplines in terms of the organising principles of their knowledge formation. What social realism tells us is that knowledge is not just an object that can be taken for granted and unproblematically included in the curriculum. Instead, 'the relationship of knowledge to its referents and the way it is structured and built has implications for the way in which it should be included in curriculum' (Wheelahan, 2010, p. 1) and taught. Social realism thus raises important questions about the centrality of epistemological constraints on curriculum and pedagogy. To secure social justice in terms of the school curriculum, social realist theorists argue, requires close attention to such issues. What is very apparent about the Coalition review of the National Curriculum and its recent discussion within the geography education community is a lack of attention to knowledge as a phenomenon.

What is evident here, social realist theorists emphasise, is that students will need access to the underlying principles/epistemic standards of knowledge production, to the generative mechanisms of knowledge itself. It is only through these generative mechanisms that the generic metaphors of 'deep understanding', 'higher order thinking' and 'personal constructions of knowledge' can be translated into specific, actionable ways of working with geographical knowledge.

For geography educators the social realist approach to knowledge opens up three key questions about the conditions for geographical learning:

(a) What is the epistemic/internal/cognitive structure of geography?
(b) What are the relations between geography's knowledge structures and curriculum and pedagogic structures?
(c) What kinds of limits does the disciplinary structure place on how the curriculum and its pedagogy are constituted?

Social realism raises important questions about the coherence of the curriculum and pedagogic practice in terms of the epistemic nature of geographical knowledge.

Conclusion

Attention has been called to the fact that in recent years knowledge has receded from view in curriculum policy and classroom practice using three conceptions of knowledge to do so, and presented from a social realist perspective. Social realism was presented as an alternative to the limitations of absolutism

(a traditional model of the curriculum) and to those of relativism/constructivism (a 'progressive' instrumentalist curriculum). Social realist theorists emphasise that social realism contains both the commitment of the 'progressivists' to education as a means of social justice and the commitment of 'traditionalists' to disciplinary knowledge (Rata, 2012, p. 120). They put knowledge as a phenomenon centre-stage in thinking about education (Maton and Moore, 2010, p. 2).

Without necessarily endorsing the social realist position in its entirety, the aim has been to emphasise the need to begin to grapple with the epistemological basis for an appropriate geography curriculum for the 21st-century. Whether social realism as an emergent theory of knowledge provides possible ways forward for the school curriculum was within this aim, not the main concern. What is clear, however, is that there is more to the curriculum than the concern with the delineation of core knowledge; in evolving a subject-based model of the curriculum, knowledge is not something that can be taken for granted and unproblematically included in such a curriculum. What can be said about social realism is that it is a timely and valuable articulation of the centrality of knowledge to education that goes beyond critique to offer useful concepts about the nature of knowledge and how a subject-based curriculum has the potential to be a form of radical intellectual development for all students, whatever their backgrounds.

Eight key ideas can be drawn from the chapter. First, there is a need for a strong conception of knowledge in education. Second, we need to better understand bodies of knowledge, the subject disciplines – and how they can be used within educational settings. Third, there is a need for a more theoretically informed articulation of knowledge and of the relation between knowledge and the curriculum and pedagogy. Fourth, whatever the approach to knowledge we might adopt as geography educators we do need to address the right to knowledge emphasised by social realism and the social justice issues it raises. 'This means that if schools are to play a major role in promoting social equality, they have to take the knowledge base of the curriculum very seriously – even when this appears to go against the immediate demands of pupils' (Young, 2009, p. 15). It does not guarantee that all schools will be successful in enabling students to acquire powerful knowledge, but 'is this curriculum a means by which students can acquire powerful knowledge' (2009, p. 15), is a question that needs to be asked. Fifth, an educational theory of knowledge can only be of worth if at the same time we consider where the student stands, epistemologically, in relation to knowledge and the geography curriculum (space has not allowed its consideration here). Sixth, in all of this we also need to recognise the distinction between the school subject and the academic discipline. Subjects as forms of conceptual and social organisation have been the most reliable ways we have developed of enabling students to acquire disciplinary knowledge. The issues highlighted in this chapter, however, do raise a vital question about the need for a stronger and more mutually supportive relationship between higher

education and school geography. Seventh, 'the subject expertise of teachers should be re-invigorated if they are to make the best of the opportunities offered in a revised National Curriculum' (CfSA, 2011, p. 1). Eight, the ideas presented are ultimately as much about learning as they are about the curriculum and knowledge. Reconceptualising learning is a necessary act within the reconceptualisation of the curriculum and knowledge. At the beginning of 2012 and as the National Curriculum review begins to unfold there is an urgent need for creative and critical thinking about the relationships between curriculum, knowledge, learners, learning and society.

I acknowledge that the direction of the arguments presented in the chapter may be met with resistance from teachers struggling to maintain their established professional identity and practice having been subjected to a protracted process of curriculum and pedagogic renewal in working conditions that involve inspection surveillance and accountability criteria. For this reason, however, I would suggest that the willingness to (re)engage with the power relations inherent in and reaffirmed by curriculum and knowledge is something that teachers need to continue to demonstrate in their work and to push for in others (Penney, 2007, p. 152) if the relative degradation of teacher professionalism which has occurred since the 1980s is to be reversed.

Notes

1 This has been done 'not as a futuristic or predictive exercise, but through an analysis of current trends in educational policy.
2 This took the form of a web-based consultation where teachers responded to a curriculum framework, key stage expectations and a set of principles guiding a statutory geography subject component in the National Curriculum for ages 5–16.
3 Core knowledge is commonly defined in terms of factual knowledge only. The GA Geography Curriculum Consultation Document, however, distinguishes between three forms of geographical knowledge: factual 'core' knowledge, conceptual content knowledge and applied practical knowledge.
4 Traditionally in education, emphasis has been placed on the 'knowledge of the powerful', which refers to what Young (1971) once termed 'high status' knowledge and Bourdieu (1986) would describe as the 'cultural capital' of the dominant or ruling classes. Many sociological critiques of school knowledge have focused on the dominant relations between knowledge and power and the inequalities that have been embodied historically in the disciplinary and subject basis of school curricula. It is not that these issues are not important, but the fact that some knowledge is 'knowledge of the powerful', Young argues, tells us nothing about the knowledge itself or what it can do for young people. Sociological critiques of school knowledge have neglected the extent to which the knowledge from which the disadvantaged are disproportionately excluded – disciplinary knowledge – is not just the knowledge of the powerful, which it has been for too long, but is also, in an important sense, 'knowledge itself', that is, 'powerful knowledge' that is valued in particular ways within society.
5 This is certainly the case based on the 2010 Schools White Paper The Importance of Teaching (DFE, 2010). The publication of a report by the Expert Panel for the National Curriculum The Framework for the National Curriculum (DFE, 2011), might suggest a shift in emphasis.

Key readings

1. Firth, R. (2011) 'Making geography visible as an object of study in the secondary school curriculum', *Curriculum Journal*, 22 (3), 289–316. This article focuses on the increasingly influential social realist school of thought and the endeavour to 'bring knowledge back' into education. It engages with some of the key theoretical ideas of social realism, in particular its 'structure of knowledge' approach. Consideration is also given to the nature of geographical knowledge and to how these ideas about the 'structuring of knowledge' might influence thinking about the geography curriculum and pedagogy. The article recognises both the significance of the social realist approach to knowledge as well as offering some thoughts about its possible limitations as an overarching theory of knowledge for educational purposes. It is more theoretical than the current chapter, where the main concern has been to flag up the importance of how we might think about knowledge.
2. Maton, K. and Moore, R. (eds.) (2010) *Social Realism, Knowledge and the Sociology of Education*, London: Continuum. The book provides key papers by leading authors about social realism. It provides an account of the difficulties education has had with the very idea of knowledge and a possible way out of an *impasse* that has debilitated thinking about knowledge and education for decades. It presents 'social realism' as a broad school of thought at first hand. It offers an alternative to current orthodoxies in education.

References

Barnett, R. (2009) 'Knowing and becoming in the higher education curriculum', *Studies in Higher Education*, 34 (4), 429–40.

Bleazby, J. (2011) 'Overcoming Relativism and Absolutism: Dewey's ideals of truth and meaning in philosophy for children', *Educational Philosophy and Theory*, 43 (5), 453–66.

Bourdieu, P. (1986) 'The forms of capital', in J. Richardson (ed.), *Handbook of Theory and Research for the Sociology of Education*. New York: Greenwood, pp. 241–58.

Council for Subject Associations (CfSA) (2011) *Putting Subjects at the Core of the Curriculum*. Available from: http://www.subjectassociation.org.uk/files/webdocs/Cfsa%20subjects %20thinkpiece%20Mar%202011.pdf [Accessed 24 August 2011].

Department for Education (DFE) (2011) *The Framework for the National Curriculum. A report by the Expert Panel for the National Curriculum review*, London: Department for Education.

Department for Education (DFE) (2010) *The Schools White Paper, The Importance of Teaching*, London: Department for Education.

Geographical Association (GA) (2011) *Geography Curriculum Consultation Full Report*, December 2011, Sheffield: Geographical Association.

Hirsch, E.D. (1987) *Cultural Literacy: What Every American Needs to Know*, Boston, MA: Houghton Mifflin.

Hirsch, E.D. (2007) *The Knowledge Deficit: Closing the Shocking Education gap for American Children*, New York: Houghton Mifflin Harcourt.

Institute of Ideas, (2010) 'A defence of subject-based education', *Institute of Ideas Education Forum*. London: IoI. Available from: http://www.instituteofideas.com/documents/subjects_ defense_ef.pdf [Accessed 24 August 2011].

Lambert, D. (2011) 'Reviewing the case for geography, and the "knowledge turn" in the English National Curriculum', *Curriculum Journal*, 22 (2), 243–64.

Maton, K. and Moore, R. (2010) 'Introduction: Coalitions of the Mind', in K. Maton and R. Moore (eds.), *Social Realism, Knowledge and the Sociology of Education*, London: Continuum.

Moore, R. (2004) *Education and Society*, Cambridge: Polity Press.

Morgan, J. (2011) 'Knowledge and the school geography curriculum: A rough guide for teachers', *Teaching Geography*, 36 (3), 90–2.

Penney, D. (2007) 'The curriculum of the future. Ahead of its time', *Critical Studies in Education*, 48 (1), 149–55.

Rata, E. (2012) 'The politics of knowledge in education', *British Educational Research Journal*, 38 (1), 103–24.

Wheelahan, L. (2010) *Why Knowledge Matters in Education: A Social Realist Argument*, Abingdon: Routledge.

Yates, L. and Young, M. (2010) 'Editorial: Globalisation, knowledge and the curriculum', *European Journal of Education*, 45 (1), 4–10.

Young, M. (1971) 'The return to subjects: A sociological perspective on the UK coalition government's approach to the 14–19 curriculum', *Curriculum Journal*, 22 (2), 265–78.

Young, M. (2008a) 'The future of education in a knowledge society: The radical case for a subject-based curriculum', *Journal of the Pacific Circle Consortium for Education*, 22 (1), 21–32.

Young, M. (2008b) 'What are schools for?', in H. Daniels, H. Lauder and J. Porter (eds.), *Knowledge, Values and Educational Policy*, London: Routledge.

Young, M. (2009) *Bringing Knowledge Back In. From social constructivism to social realism in the sociology of education*, Abingdon: Routledge.

Young, M. (2010) 'From Constructivism to Realism in the Sociology of Education', *Review of Research in Education*, 32 (1), 1–28.

Young, M. (2011) *Knowledge and Control*, London: Collier Macmillan.

Young, M. and Muller, J. (2010) 'Three Educational Scenarios for the Future: Lessons from the sociology of knowledge', *European Journal of Education*, 45 (1), 11–27.

Chapter 5

How do we understand conceptual development in school geography?

Clare Brooks

> Place, space and scale are arguably the three really big ideas that underpin school geography. Opening up these ideas a little ... shows their scope and potential. We can see the relevance of being able to 'think geographically' to anyone living in the world and wanting to understand and respond to the challenges facing them during the 21st century.
>
> (Lambert, 2009, p. 4)

Introduction

At the time of writing, a review of the English National Curriculum is underway. The Coalition government's preference for 'core' or 'essential' knowledge (as indicated in their White Paper, *The Importance of Teaching*, DfE, 2010) would suggest that the new national curriculum will articulate school geography in a different way to the 2007 version. The 2007 Geography National Curriculum (GNC) expressed the Programme of Study through Key Concepts and Key Processes. However, this approach has been critiqued due to its lack of specific reference to geographical knowledge, and the seemingly knowledge-weak school curriculum it produced. It is likely that the revised Geography National Curriculum will define the curriculum through identifying 'core' knowledge. The curriculum consultation exercise (conducted through the Geographical Association's (GA) website) highlighted that many geography teachers value the concept-based approach to the curriculum. This is a key time then to question what key concepts are, how they have contributed to geography education, and what will be lost if key concepts are removed from the formal curriculum documents. As the opening quotation to this chapter suggests, how we understand concepts determines how we use them and affects our understanding of geographical phenomena. In order to answer these questions, this chapter will explore how concepts have been used and understood in geography education, and how they relate to concepts as they are discussed and understood in academic geography.

WHAT IS A CONCEPT?

Before exploring the meaning of the term 'concept', and how it has been used in geography education, it is useful to consider why concepts have become part of the curriculum vocabulary. The Original Orders of the Geography National Curriculum represented a seminal moment in English geography education, as the content of school geography was described for the first time in a statutory document, even though much concern was expressed at the nature of how geography was defined within that document (see Rawling, 2001). The original National Curriculum lacked curriculum aims, and the Programme of Study defined content as a list of statements of attainment which reflected de-contextualised statements of knowledge (see Lambert, 2004). Rawling's account of the construction of Original Orders of the Geography National Curriculum shows how different ideological traditions of both geography and curriculum influenced the curriculum. The resulting document was not clear on how the geography statements of attainment developed geographical thinking or understanding. Their expression offered no guidance as to how they were linked or how they should be combined to facilitate geographical learning. Subsequent versions of the Geography National Curriculum reduced the content description (Lambert, 2011a) but it was not until the 2007 version that the curriculum included specific reference to key geographical concepts, even though their inclusion in the Geography National Curriculum did not necessarily reflect a consensus as to whether these concepts were indeed key to geography education, or whether they were solely geographical concepts. At the same time, debates were happening in other subject areas about the best ways to define and describe concepts within other disciplines.

'Concept' is a fairly general term that is used in a variety of contexts to mean different things. Concepts can be concrete and fairly unambiguous (like 'rain') or more abstract and difficult to define (like 'culture'). Within geography education, concepts have been used to describe and categorise geographical knowledge and understanding. However, there has not been a consensus as to which concepts are 'key' or how they should be used by teachers. To help us to understand these differences, I suggest that concepts are used from three different perspectives each relating to a different approach to teaching and learning. Key to this categorisation is an understanding that there are three dimensions to education: the curriculum, pedagogy and the learner (as represented in Lambert and Morgan's (2010) curriculum making diagram). Each of the categorisations below foreground one of these dimensions:

- *hierarchical* – concepts as a content container, with the focus on the subject;
- *organisational* – concepts helping the linking of ideas, experiences and processes, with the focus on pedagogy;
- *developmental* – concepts reflecting the process of deepening understanding, with the focus on the learner.

I suggest that these categorisations are useful to distinguish which particular perspective is being emphasised. However, these categorisations are not inherent to the concepts themselves but illustrate how they intended to be used in curriculum making. In this respect they are a useful tool for examining curriculum documents critically. In the section that follows, I take each dimension in turn.

HIERARCHICAL CONCEPTS

One of the most common uses of 'concepts' is to use them as a way of grouping the contents of the subject: as a container for geographical ideas or content. In this respect, the word is used to represent ideas, generalisations or theories. When concepts are used in this way, they are represented as hierarchical: so some concepts are described as 'key', or 'foundational' or 'main'. Taylor (2008) refers to concepts of this type as 'classifiers', as they classify the geographical knowledge to be taught.

In his review of concepts in geography (at the time of the introduction of the 'concept-free' Original Orders of the Geography National Curriculum), Marsden (1995) suggested that concepts have two dimensions: abstract–concrete, and technical–vernacular (everyday). In my adaption of Marsden's classification (see Figure 5.1), we can see how these dimensions result in different types of concepts.

It is worth noting that some readers may disagree with my categorisation in Figure 5.1. Indeed, it is debatable whether 'beach' is indeed a concrete concept. Geomorphologists and surfers may have some debate about what constitutes a 'beach'. The precise meanings of concepts are often debated, for example a concept such as 'place' will mean different things to different specialists: one person's concrete abstract, can be highly abstract for another. In addition, there will be some discussion as to whether some concepts are geographical: time is a key part of geographical analysis, but is not always considered a geographical concept.

The examples used in Figure 5.1 were chosen from a list of 'Main Concepts' taken from the Physical Geography section of a Singaporean Geography 'O' level (equivalent to GCSE) examination syllabus. My reason for doing this is twofold: first, to demonstrate how concepts can be used in different contexts (i.e. a 'main

		Dimension 2	
		Technical	Vernacular
Dimension 1	Abstract	Abstract-technical e.g. Adaption	Abstract-vernacular e.g: Erosion
	Concrete	Concrete-technical e.g. Abrasion	Concrete-vernacular e.g. Beach

Figure 5.1 Dimensions of hierarchical concepts (adapted from Marsden, 1995).

concept' in Singapore is not necessarily the same as a 'key concept' in the English Geography National Curriculum). Second, concepts can demonstrate both these dimensions of being abstract–concrete and technical–vernacular. The two dimensions are useful because they show that some concepts are more commonplace (vernacular) and more concrete than others. Concepts that are abstract–technical are more 'difficult' to understand than those that are concrete–vernacular. For curriculum makers this differentiates substantive geographical content, and enables them to structure content from the concrete–vernacular towards abstract–technical concepts: in this sense these concepts are hierarchical. This kind of classification is often used in examination specifications and other curriculum documents.

The key concepts in the 2007 Geography National Curriculum (e.g., Place and Space) can be viewed as hierarchical concepts. They are used to represent geographical ideas that are both technical and abstract. In Rawling's book *Planning your Key Stage 3 Geography Curriculum*, she refers to these concepts as 'fundamental ideas in geography' (2007, p. 17). Written specifically to support geography teachers implementing the 2007 Geography National Curriculum, Rawling's book breaks down each of the GNC key concepts, illustrating how the concept is understood within geography, and how students can experience them. This breakdown illustrates the hierarchical nature of these concepts, and Rawling shows how the curriculum can be designed to scaffold students' learning towards understanding the abstract–technical concepts. In particular, Rawling draws attention to the hierarchical nature of the key concepts, describing Space and Place as the most generalised and abstract of these ideas which are 'standing at the top of a hierarchy of ideas in geography' (pp. 23–4). Rawling's approach to the handling of these concepts is very clear. As content containers and abstract ideas, she argues that they should not be used as a starting point for curriculum planning, but more of a skeleton 'on which to hang the more detailed curriculum flesh' (p. 17). When concepts are used as content containers, it is possible to distinguish between the abstract–concrete, and technical–vernacular nature of content knowledge (and hence are often referred to in the academic literature as substantive concepts). In this respect they are helpful in determining the 'ends' or outcomes of the curriculum, but not necessarily the process or 'means' of how to achieve that end.

ORGANISATIONAL CONCEPTS

Another approach to the use of concepts in geography education is to view them as organisational. Whilst the hierarchical nature of concepts described above has a degree of organisation embedded within it, the focus is not on how the concept is used, but in how it relates to geographical knowledge. Both Leat's (1998) 'big concepts' and Taylor's (2008) 'organisational concepts' use concepts as a way of linking everyday experience with higher-level geographical ideas. The distinction here is that the concepts are seen as a tool in developing geographical learning.

Leat used the term 'big concepts' in his *Thinking Through Geography* publication (1998). This, and subsequent publications, became very influential in geography education, as the geographical interpretation of the Thinking Skills movement (and in line with other cognitive acceleration strategies). Thinking Skills were adopted as part of the New Labour Key Stage 3 Strategies and influenced geography education pedagogy in the first decade of the twenty-first century. *Thinking Through Geography* featured a series of thinking skills activities relevant to geography education. The focus of the publication (and the strategies contained within) was in promoting children's thinking, and so the concepts emphasised were those that would promote 'thinking'. Rather than seeing these concepts as goals of learning in geography education, Leat suggests they function as a way of developing understanding in geography:

> We believe that it is helpful to conceive of geography in terms of a number of central underpinning concepts, through which much subject matter is understood.
>
> (1998, p. 161)

He acknowledges that the list of Big Concepts is not a definitive one and is likely to change, but includes:

- cause and effect;
- classification;
- decision-making;
- development;
- inequality;
- location; and
- planning and systems.

Taylor (2008) describes these concepts as generic cognitive processes, and whilst they each have a role in geography education, they are not uniquely or distinctly geographical in nature. Indeed, a similar list would not look out of place in history or science education. Leat acknowledges this by arguing that 'the main concern of this book is students' learning, not the sanctity of the subject' (1998, p. 167), and that these concepts are useful to help students to make sense of the thinking scenarios that they are faced with, in the sense that they are used organisationally to develop the learning.

Taylor (2008) differentiates Leat's list of concepts from her own 'organisational' concepts. Taylor argues that her four organisational concepts were developed from engagement with the work of Massey (see 2005) and so they have a distinctively (but not exclusively) geographical function:

- diversity;
- change;

- interaction; and
- perception and representation.

The organisational nature of these concepts stems from how Taylor suggests they are used, particularly in how they create a bridge between the hierarchical substantive concepts of place, space and time and the geographical enquiry questions which relate to the topic being studied. This is illustrated in Figure 5.2 below, adapted from Taylor's original article (2008).

These concepts are organisational because they provide a link between the abstract concepts of place, time and space, and the enquiry questions that relate to the topic being studied. Taylor does not suggest that these concepts should necessarily be shared with students, but that these organisational concepts are useful in curriculum planning.

Taylor acknowledges that her work on organisational concepts has been influenced by 'second order concepts' as they appear within school history. (Indeed, it is also interesting to note that Taylor includes time as a geographical concept, when other categorisations explored in this chapter prefer to emphasise Place and Space as stronger geographical concepts.) In history education, second order concepts (cause, consequence, significance, change) are used to shape enquiry that will lead to deeper understanding of substantive concepts (such as democracy, revolution and empire). Within history education there is a clear demarcation between these second order concepts, which are organisational and enquiry–based, from the more substantive (content-based) historical concepts (see Counsell, 2011).

Organisational concepts are different in distinction and approach to hierarchical concepts, as they are not the goal of learning geography but a facilitating tool to get to those goals, and hence they emphasise linking processes and ideas rather than outcomes.

DEVELOPMENTAL CONCEPTS

The third approach to discussing concepts is the least common in geography education. The definition of key concepts in the 2007 Geography National Curriculum helped to define hierarchical concepts as the dominant approach in geography education. Prior to that, concepts were often referred to in relation to the child and their own learning, rather than on concepts as a way of structuring or organising knowledge. For example, Roberts (2003) describes the 'conceptual frameworks' used in learning and how an enquiry approach can help develop those frameworks. In this respect, concepts can be seen as starting with the learner rather than with the subject.

In Hopwood's research he explored students' own conceptualisation of school geography, which he argues is an important influence on their learning (2004, 2011). Hopwood demonstrates how students use their conceptualisation of the subject as a way of filtering and processing their geography lessons: as a way of making meaning. In this respect, concepts are ideas, internally held, that are adapted or modified in the light of new information.

PLACE		SPACE	TIME
DIVERSITY	INTERACTION	CHANGE	PERCEPTION AND REPRESENTATION
- How and why does it vary over space? (Differences in from, function, patterns of distribution etc.) - How does this affect different groups and how is it managed?	- How are different elements linked? (Inc. physical-human; human-human; physical-physical) - How does change in one element knock on to others? How might this affect different groups? - What are the 'power-geometries' of the links? -What can we learn about it by 'zooming in and out' of scales?	- How and why has it been different in the past? - What has the nature, rate and extent of the change been like? - How might it be different in the future? (Prediction) - Which of the different future paths are more/less desirable? - How can the more desirable outcomes be achieved?	- How do different people experience it? (Directly or indirectly) - How do they communicate this experience? How does this affect their own and other people's views and actions?

Figure 5.2 Questions afforded by each organising concept (adapted from Taylor, 2008, p. 52).

I have included this distinction because I think it is a particularly useful one for teachers. Research into concepts in education generally illustrates that views of knowledge in the curriculum can be divided into two schools of thought: exogenic and endogenic (Gergen, 2001). In the exogenic approach, knowledge is seen as external to the student, and the process of teaching is one in which 'outside' concepts are brought to the student. In this sense concepts are determined by the teacher (as the subject's conduit) and could be hierarchical and/or organisational. In the endogenic approach, knowledge is developed from within. In this respect, concepts are developmental, and are used internally by the student to make sense of a lesson's content. In this sense concepts are seen as internal, and taken from the students' perspective.

With this alternative way of understanding concepts, Hopwood's research is particularly important because he illustrates that students' conceptual understanding of geography is often different to the hierarchical or organisational way of presenting concepts, and also that students' concepts are unique to the individuals. The implication of this finding is that whilst teachers may organise their curriculums around hierarchical or organisational concepts, the way that students make sense of their lessons may be determined by their own conceptual frameworks.

USING CONCEPTS TO BUILD UNDERSTANDING

The 2007 Geography National Curriculum introduced concepts into geography curriculum documents, and has prompted a more nuanced and informed discussion about what concepts are and how they are useful to geography teachers. Whether concepts are seen as hierarchical, organisational or developmental, the debate around them is how they can support learners in developing geographical understanding, and how they can support teachers in planning geographical learning experiences.

Bennetts represents the process of developing understanding in geography education with the diagram in Figure 5.3.

In this diagram, concepts are grouped together with generalisations, models and theories as the ideas and mental constructs that enable learners to make sense of their experiences. To use the language analogy made popular by the Geographical Association's manifesto *A Different View* (2009), concepts can then be viewed as the 'grammar' of geography that we use to make sense of the world (or the vocabulary) and how we experience it. Bennett's diagram places concepts with both personal and public meanings, illustrating that they can come from the subject as well as from the student.

GEOGRAPHICAL CONCEPTS

The definition of concepts within geography education can be seen as a link between the school subject and the academic discipline. It has been argued that the link between school and academic geography has been increasingly weakened

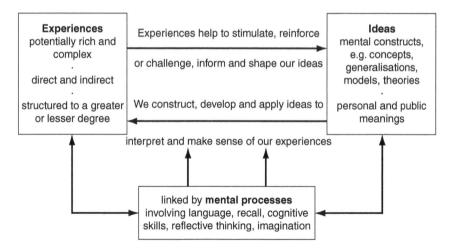

Figure 5.3 The roots of understanding (Bennetts, 2005).

over time. The key concepts as defined in the 2007 Geography National Curriculum were a bridge between the school subject and how the subject is understood in the academy. Lambert (2011a) argues that academic concepts matter because they are more independent than other definitions of concepts, and are less influenced by curriculum-politics. However, it is important to note that academic geography is subject to its own political influences that will affect how it categorises and defines geographical concepts, and there is much debate about what geographical concepts are and how they relate to each other in the conceptual hierarchy.

Concepts are important as their definition can affect the future development of the discipline. For instance, Matthews and Herbert (2004) have emphasised how shared concepts and methodologies can unify different positions within physical and human geography. They conclude that the core concepts of geography are space, place, environment and maps, and that these concepts (and in the case of maps, methodologies) can be used to link the subdivisions within geography. However, their position has been criticised by Johnston (2006) as he reasons that creating and sustaining an academic subject is a political process and the politics of silence can omit important areas. He explores how the geographical concept of spatial science is neglected in many undergraduate textbooks and in Matthews and Herbert's summary of the discipline. Johnston therefore argues that the omission of particular concepts can have a divisive effect within the discipline (Johnston, 2006).

The identification of key concepts can be seen as a defining force as well as a descriptive one. For example, Stoddart (1987) argues that the common purpose of geography is to answer the big questions in society, which can be achieved

through using location, position, distance and area as the 'building blocks' of the discipline. Clifford et al. (2003) also emphasise that there is a common set of geographical concepts but that these are used differently in human and physical geography (space, time, place and space, social formations, physical systems, and landscape and environment). Both note that the discipline is shaped by how we define and understand these concepts.

Acknowledging Johnston's important criticism, there does seem to be a gathering consensus on the defining concepts of geography. Areas of geography such as moral geographies (Smith, 2000) and hybrid geographies (Whatmore, 2002) bridge the physical and human divide. Analysis of first-year undergraduate human geography textbooks (Cloke et al., 1999; Holloway and Hubbard, 2001; Hubbard et al., 2002; Doring, 2005; Daniels et al., 2005) shows some agreement on key geographical concepts. Thrift and Walling's (2000) work on physical geography notes that the underlying concepts of place, scale and landscape are also prevalent in research.

Consensus on geography's concepts has also been used to justify an optimistic view on the future of geography as an academic discipline and as an important influence on policy and society (see Thrift, 2002, and responses from Johnston, 2002 and Turner, 2002). Indeed, Jackson (2006) has gone so far as to suggest that the geographical concepts of space and place, scale and connection, proximity and distance emphasise relational thinking, which he argues is a distinctive geographical contribution to knowledge.

Despite this sense of consensus on geography's concepts, views on the significance of certain concepts change. For instance, Castree (2005) presents a strong case for Nature as a powerful concept within geography. His book on nature is part of a series entitled Key Ideas in Geography that includes titles on *The City*, *Migration, Landscape, Citizenship, Rural, Mobility, Home, Scale*. Each of these titles can be seen as geographical concepts, and their focus as titles within this popular series illustrates a shifting dynamic in academic geography. This is symptomatic of the dynamic nature of disciplines, and is representative of our growing understanding of the world, and the ideas that shape it.

It is to be expected then that important concepts within the academic discipline will change over time. This will in turn influence school geography. Lambert and Morgan (2010) focus on the concepts of Place, Space, Scale and Interdependence, which they take care not to define in a hierarchical way (i.e., they don't refer to them as core or key), but as 'significant ideas' within geography. They argue that geography uses these 'ideas' to make sense of the world, whilst acknowledging the historical development of the concepts themselves. In the detail of their analysis they explore the development and interpretation of these concepts, and illustrate that the concepts are sites of contestation with the academic discipline, with multiple meanings. With each of the concepts they consider the implications this has for school geography.

Lambert and Morgan (2010) hold a position that a conceptual approach shows the promise of geography education. They see concepts as a powerful mechanism to support and develop geographical understanding.

THRESHOLD CONCEPTS

The categorisation I have used in this chapter has demonstrated that much of the discussion about concepts in geography has been with a focus on the substantive (hierarchical) and organisational nature of geographical knowledge. Although some work exists on learners' own concepts of geography (see Hopwood, 2011), this work is limited. Threshold concepts may be a way of bringing all viewpoints on concepts together, and whilst also underdeveloped in geography, the idea presents an exciting opportunity for rethinking the role of concepts in the curriculum.

The idea of threshold concepts was developed by Meyer and Land (2005) in relation to economics in higher education. They define a threshold concept as:

> A threshold concept can be considered as akin to a portal, opening up a new and previously inaccessible way of thinking about something. It represents a transformed way of understanding, or interpreting, or viewing something without which the learner cannot progress. As a consequence of comprehending a threshold concept there may thus be a transformed internal view of subject matter, subject landscape, or even world view.
>
> (p. 174)

They identify that threshold concepts have particular characteristics that distinguish them from other (lesser) concepts. For a concept to be 'threshold' it is likely to be:

- transformative;
- probably irreversible;
- integrative;
- possibly bounded; and
- potentially troublesome (in that they may be counter-intuitive).

Whilst some subjects have developed an understanding of threshold concepts in their discipline, little work in this area has been achieved in geography, and this is a fruitful area for new research. Jonathan Slinger, in his research for his MA in Geography Education, sought to identify a framework for looking at threshold concepts in school geography (2010). Slinger describes threshold concepts as 'existing in relational web-like patterns' which includes

- using the discipline as a resource
- viewing students as active, enquiring learners who bring their own experience to the learning processes; and
- teachers as working with the subject and the student to construct knowledge collaboratively.

Whilst Slinger doesn't go so far as to list what these concepts might be, he does acknowledge that they can operate at different levels (which he describes as basic,

disciplinary and procedural) and that they can adopt a relational and situated view of knowledge, acknowledging the contested and plural nature of approaches within the discipline. In this respect threshold concepts can be viewed from a variety of perspectives: the subject, the pedagogy and the learner, and so can be seen to cross the categorisations offered in this chapter.

Slinger's analysis highlights the geographical potential of threshold concepts, but he also concludes that defining threshold concepts in geography is not straightforward. I would contend that indeed, because of the transformative nature of threshold concepts, they may not be same for everyone.

Conclusion

In this chapter I have suggested a categorisation of concepts in geography education. Concepts can be seen as hierarchical, organisational and developmental. In each of these categorisations, concepts are used by geography educators to support the learning process, by emphasising the subject, pedagogy or the students' experiences (respectively). In this respect, and supported by the work of both Bennetts and Slinger, concepts can be understood as powerful tools for the geography curriculum maker. However, at the time of writing, the future of 'key concepts' as a curriculum tool looks bleak. The shift from a conceptual approach to one that defines content as core knowledge is a significant danger for geography education. Previous versions of the Geography National Curriculum that defined geography without a view to its conceptual structure limited both the content of the curriculum and how it was taught. I would contend then that how teachers see the relationship between geographical concepts and geographical content will determine how they change their practice and implement the new curriculum. The GA (Lambert, 2011b) has suggested that it is useful to distinguish between:

- core knowledge (the extensive world knowledge or vocabulary of geography);
- content knowledge (the key concepts and ideas, or grammar of geography); and
- procedural knowledge (thinking geographically, and the distinctly geographical approaches to learning such as enquiry).

Should geography teachers seek to adopt or develop this approach as a way of thinking about geographical content in the curriculum, then they will need to clarify which geography concepts they wish to focus on (hierarchical), and how they will support students to develop their understanding of those concepts (organisational) and the extent to which they will support students to develop their own conceptual frameworks (developmental). Further work on threshold concepts in geography could help to achieve this.

Key readings

1. Lambert, D. and Morgan, J. (2010) *Teaching Geography 11–18: A conceptual approach*, Maidenhead: Open University Press. Anyone interested in exploring geography's key

concepts more should start with this book. In the opening chapters David Lambert and John Morgan outline their approach to teaching with concepts, and subsequent chapters take key concepts in turn and explore how they have changed over time and their relevance for school geography.

2. Taylor, L. (2008) 'Key concepts and medium term planning' in *Teaching Geography*, 33 (2), 50–54. This article is a good introduction to organisational concepts. In this article, Liz Taylor outlines her interpretation of them, how they relate to more substantive concepts and how they can be used to identify enquiry questions.

References

Bennetts, T. (2005) 'Progression in Geographical Understanding', *International Research in Geographical and Environmental Education*, 14 (2), 112–32.

Castree, N. (2005) *Nature*, London: Routledge.

Clifford, N.J., Holloway, S.L., Rice, S.P. and Valentine, G. (eds.) (2003) *Key Concepts in Geography*, London: Sage.

Cloke, P., Crang, P. and Goodwin, M. (eds.) (1999) *Introducing Human Geographies*, London: Arnold.

Counsell, C. (2011) 'What do we want students to do with historical change and continuity?', in I.Davies (ed.), *Debates in History Education*, Abingdon: Routledge.

Daniels, P., Bradshaw, M., Shaw, G. and Sidaway, J. (eds.) (2005) *An introduction to Human Geography: Issues for the 21st Century* (2nd edn), Harlow: Pearson Prentice Hall.

Department for Education (DfE) (2010) *The Importance of Teaching: the Schools White Paper*, London: HMSO.

Doring, D. (2005) *Human Geography of the UK*, London: Sage.

Geographical Association (2009) *A Different View: A manifesto from the Geographical Association*, Sheffield: Geographical Association.

Gergen, K. (2001) 'Social construction and Pedagogical Practice', in K.Gergen (ed.), *Social Construction in Context*, London: Sage.

Holloway, L. and Hubbard, P. (2001) *People and Place: The extraordinary geographies of everyday life*, Harlow: Prentice Hall.

Hopwood, N. (2004) 'Pupils' Conceptions of Geography: Towards an Improved Understanding International Research', in *Geographical and Environmental Education*, 13 (4), 348–61.

Hopwood, N. (2011) 'Young People's Conceptions of Geography and Education', in G.Butt (ed.), *Geography, Education and the Future*, London, Continuum.

Hubbard, P., Kitchin, R., Bartley, B. and Fuller, D. (2002) *Thinking Geographically: Space, theory and contemporary human geography*, London: Continuum.

Jackson, P. (2006) 'Thinking Geographically', *Geography*, 91 (3), 199–204.

Johnston, R.J. (2002) 'Reflections on Nigel Thrift's optimism: Political strategies to implement his vision', *Geoforum*, 33 (4), 421–5.

Johnston, R.J. (2006). 'The politics of changing human geography's agenda: Textbooks and the representation of increasing diversity', *Transactions of the Institute of British Geographers*, 31 (3), 286–303.

Lambert, D. (2004) 'Geography', in J.White (ed.), *Rethinking the School Curriculum; Values, Aims and Purposes*, Abingdon: RoutledgeFalmer: 75–86.

Lambert, D. (2009) 'Introduction – part 1: What is living geography?', in D.Mitchell (ed.), *Living Geography*. Cambridge: Chris Kington Publishing.

Lambert, D. (2011a) 'Reviewing the case for geography, and the "knowledge turn" in the English National Curriculum', *Curriculum Journal*, 22 (2), 243–64.

Lambert, D. (2011b) *The Geography National Curriculum: GA Curriculum Proposals and Rational*, Sheffield, Geographical Association.

Lambert, D. and Morgan, J. (2010) *Teaching Geography 11–18: A conceptual approach*, Maidenhead: Open University Press.

Leat, D. (1998) *Thinking Through Geography*, Cambridge: Chris Kington Publishing.

Marsden, W. (1995) *Geography 11–16: Rekindling good practice*, London: David Fulton Publishers.

Massey, D. (2005) *For Space*, London: Sage Publications.

Matthews, J.A. and Herbert, D.T. (eds.) (2004) *Unifying Geography: Common Heritage, Shared Future*, Abingdon: Routledge.

Meyer, J.H.F. and Land, R. (2005) 'Threshold Concepts and troublesome knowledge (2), Epistemological considerations and a conceptual framework for teaching and learning', *Higher Education*, 49, 373–88.

Rawling, E. (2001) *Changing the Subject: The impact of national policy on school geography 1980–2000*, Sheffield: Geographical Association.

Rawling, E. (2007) *Planning your Key Stage 3 Geography Curriculum*, Sheffield: Geographical Association.

Roberts, M. (2003) *Learning through Enquiry*, Sheffield: Geographical Association.

Slinger, J. (2010) 'Threshold Concepts in Secondary Geography Education', Unpublished dissertation, Institute of Education: University of London.

Smith, D.M. (2000) *Moral Geographies: Ethics in a World of Difference*, Edinburgh: Edinburgh University Press.

Stoddart, D.R. (1987) 'To claim the high ground: Geography for the end of the century', *Transactions of the Institute of British Geographers*, 12, 327–36.

Taylor, L. (2008) 'Key concepts and medium term planning', *Teaching Geography*, 33 (2), 50–54.

Thrift, N. (2002) 'The future of geography', *Geoforum*, 33 (3), 291–8.

Thrift, N. and Walling, D. (2000) 'Geography in the United Kingdom 1996–2000', *The Geographical Journal*, 166 (2), 1–29.

Turner, II, B.L. (2002) 'Response to Thrift's "The future of geography"', *Geoforum*, 33 (4), 427–9.

Whatmore, S. (2002) *Hybrid Geographies: Natures cultures spaces*, London: Sage.

Chapter 6

What is the rightful place of physical geography?

Duncan Hawley

> Recently physical geographers have tended to overemphasize the importance of process and hence function and explanation at the expense of pattern and the spatial approach.
>
> (Kent, 2009, p. 99)

Introduction

When the revisions to the curriculum and GCSE and GCE AS/A2 examination specifications were about to be published (in 2008) a topic thread on the popular SLN internet forum for geography teachers asked 'Will students know less about physical processes?' (SLN Geography Forum, 2008). The discussion by the teachers in the forum raised on-going and not uncommon concerns, issues and mixed views about the nature, purpose, and approaches to teaching physical geography in schools. In essence, the discussion was centred on the place of physical geography in a 21st-century geography education.

The title question of this chapter asks about 'rightful place'. Place is a familiar term to geographers and has two key ideas embedded in the concept: (1) location, and (2) meaning and/or significance attached to, or associated with, locations (Cresswell, 2004). 'Rightful' is taken as implying a reasoned position that gives a just claim to distinction whilst acknowledging a relationship with surrounding 'places'.

This chapter attempts to open up some important discussions to help grapple with both of these ideas. In terms of location, the debate attempts to tackle the position and relationship of physical geography to the broader collective of ideas within the geography as a discipline and with cognate disciplines with which it shares content and contexts of study. In terms of meaning, the discussion will explore what types of knowledges (ways of seeing, doing and understanding) exist within physical geography as a discipline, how these have influenced, and perhaps continue to dominate, thinking and approaches to physical geography in the curriculum and its teaching in schools.

WHAT IS PHYSICAL GEOGRAPHY AND CAN IT BE DEFINED BY THE SUBJECT MATTER?

The answer to the question may seem self-evident and in need of no further discussion, but to what extent are our notions of physical geography in agreement? How do we conceive physical geography? Frequently, geographers and geography teachers claim their sub-identities as 'physical' or 'human' geographers (Barratt-Hacking, 1996).

Roger Trend (1995) noted the perception of a simplistic model of school geography, which comprises discrete physical and human elements, is common and often pervasive. The issue is not new. Ron Johnston (1986) asserted that physical and human geography diverged (in the 1960s) because they deal with fundamentally different subject matter and find their inspirations from different bodies of knowledge. I mention this dichotomy not to pass any value judgement on self-identified 'types' of geographers; everyone has personal preferences and enthusiasms, but to raise questions about the implications this might have for what geography is taught in schools.

Physical geography is a complex blend of various sub-disciplines, shifting emphases and methodologies that in recent years, at university level, has been increasingly positioned within larger units of environmental or Earth sciences (Matthews and Herbert, 2004; Pitman, 2005), making a comprehensive definition difficult (Tadaki et al., 2012). However, Gregory (2000) attempts this by exploring what and how physical geographers study, think and do and offering a synopsis of future trends in his book *The Changing Nature of Physical Geography*, to arrive at a working definition (p. 288). Trend (2008), in a GA think piece, provides a simple and brief definition of physical geography, regarding it 'as dealing with all the non-human processes and features which occur on or near the Earth's surface'. This is a wide remit and offers a 'traditional' view of physical geography with which most geography teachers would probably agree.

However, these definitions are not unproblematic, as they overlap with other cognate disciplines and subjects taught in schools and universities. The study of ecosystems is (naturally) part of the biological sciences; studies of earthquakes, volcanoes and tectonics form fundamental aspects of study in geology, which draws on strong connecting roots in physics and chemistry; climatology and weather are allied with physics. These rooted links prompts Gregory to ask: 'Is the position of physical geography within geography as a whole appropriate?' (Gregory, 2000, p. 22). Collectively, these are the Earth sciences and this content overlap provokes debate about the school subject in which Earth science content should be situated.

SHOULD ASPECTS OF PHYSICAL GEOGRAPHY BE PART OF THE SCIENCE CURRICULUM?

The debate about what and where content relating to the physical aspects of the Earth should be taught is not new. During the development and revisions of the

National Curriculum in the 1980s, 'territorial' claims and counter-claims were made for what should be taught in science and what aspects are taught in geography (King, 1986; Wilson, 1990; Trend, 1995; Hawley, 1997). Despite a gradual 'slimming' process, key aspects relating to physical geography remained in the geography curriculum but the study of rock types, the rock cycle and plate tectonics was also in the Science Programmes of Study (DfES/QCA, 2004).

The National Curriculum Review (2011–14), with a remit for children to acquire a core of 'essential knowledge' in the key subject disciplines and an aim for the curriculum to 'create coherence in what is taught in schools' (DfE, 2012), implies any duplication in subject content is not acceptable. The 'dilemma' over the place of Earth science in the curriculum is evident in the generic label given to this aspect of understanding the planet. Earth is 'naturally' seen as the study domain of geography but a claim is also made by some in the science education community for science being the rightful place to teach this aspect. Chris King has summarised this in an article 'Where should Earth science be situated in the science curriculum? (King, 2011). Using international test data for comparative purposes, King argues that in countries where Earth science is a significant and distinct part of the science curriculum and is taught by teachers who are Earth science specialists, the students outperform students from the UK and elsewhere where Earth science is not so strongly demarcated. One principal aim of the National Curriculum Review (2011–14) is focused on developing a curriculum that compares favourably with other successful international curricula in the highest performing jurisdictions, so King's argument for Earth science being a distinct 'strand' of the science curriculum could be said to have some legitimacy.

Concerned about possible duplication in teaching about the Earth, in the autumn of 2011 the Department for Education asked The Royal Society to collate views about the place of Earth science in a revised curriculum. A meeting was arranged and invitations issued to all 'stakeholders' with an interest in Earth science education so that positions on the matter could be debated. The Geographical Association's position argued for a complementary approach to understanding the physical aspects of the Earth, claiming physical geography 'naturally' sets the study of earth processes in real-world contexts that aid the capacity for interpretation and meaning, for understanding the moral and ethical implications and their application and usefulness. They distinguished this from a concept of 'deep' Earth science, which they suggested focuses on the investigation and explanation of the chemical and physical properties of the earth, such as the composition and viscosity of magmas or the mechanics of seismic waves, and argued these are best developed in the context of science lessons. However, they suggested a full understanding of the geographical perspectives of Earth science would need to draw on the concepts and principles developed in 'deep' earth science. They concluded by arguing that, if harnessed in an appropriate way, the commonalities of earth science in physical geography and 'deep' earth science do not duplicate learning but are complementary, and both perspectives are advantageous

and essential for effective learning about the Earth, its systems and how people respond to its environments.

The idea of 'deep earth science' playing a part in understanding physical geography has become widely practised in higher education in recent years through inter-disciplinary collaborative work that seeks to find new ways of understanding environmental issues. As Urban and Rhoades (2003, pp. 212–13) state: '... physical geography draws on knowledge of a wide range of ancillary disciplines including physics, chemistry and biology', so in this sense it is a composite science with a 'strong dependency on theoretical knowledge drawn from other natural sciences, many of which are viewed as foundational with respect to physical geography'. Earth System science is similarly aimed at creating a (holistic) synthesis of disciplines, which accepts and emphasises a scientific process-oriented approach. Pitman (2005) argues that Earth System science is geography but Kent (2009) maintains that in recent years physical geography has tended to overemphasise the importance of process and hence function and explanation at the expense of pattern, the spatial approach and characterisation of place. This shift in the starting point and the focus of study in physical geography promote a more distinctive perspective on the physical world that, whilst overlapping, is different from that offered by other more conventional sciences and which is less diluted in global modelling approaches such as Earth System science (Gregory, 2009; Inkpen, 2009).

The outcome of the meeting fostered a further collaborative venture creating a curriculum 'map' outlining how Earth science concepts can be rationally divided between geography and science, and identifying a progression suitable for key stages (Table 6.1).

So the debate for physical geography (teachers) has become less about 'territory' without, but more about its place within, geography.

SHOULD PHYSICAL GEOGRAPHY ALWAYS BE TAUGHT WITHIN A SOCIAL/ENVIRONMENTAL ISSUES CONTEXT?

Curriculum-making has become a prominent professional development focus for geography teachers in recent years as it is realised that potentially different geographies and the learning students derive in lessons stem from how their teachers select geographical content. The debate revolves around how (critically) active teachers can be in formulating lesson content (Morgan, 2006). Questions about the curriculum-making of (school) physical geography have existed for some time. David Pepper was, perhaps, the first to resonate with his article 'Why teach physical geography?' (Pepper, 1985), in which he railed against what he saw as the predominant mode of school physical geography at that time (driven by exam syllabus content), arguing it didn't allow students (and teachers) to set knowledge within the context of human society and problems. He thus claimed the physical environment was seen as a system entirely separated from society.

Twenty years on, Clare Brooks (2006) questioned the types of geographical knowledge represented in the classroom, illustrated by reference to three lessons. One of these related to 'solving acid rain', in which the main aim was 'to identify the causes and effects of acid rain' by looking at the environmental impacts (in Europe and Canada) and identifying some of the ways they can be managed. From this, it might be assumed this lesson goes some way to satisfying Pepper's need for 'relevance' in placing the acid rain problem in a social context. However, Brooks comments that whilst the lesson tasks and activities allowed students to gain knowledge about the physical processes and impacts of acid rain, the teacher didn't draw attention to the borderless nature of acid rain and how this could result in different 'solutions' depending on which side of a geopolitical border you happen to live. Her question is whether the knowledge presented by the teacher as a simple understanding of cause, effect and symptoms based on the physical process would likely leave students thinking the solution to acid rain is a simple issue rather than one that cannot be easily resolved. The argument Brooks advances is that knowledge and understanding of physical processes are not sufficient without these being referenced in the wider geographical (social) context, even if they appear to be set within the frame of an 'environmental issue'.

What lies at issue here is the prevailing divide between human and physical geography in schools, even though the intention is for the context to create integration. Over the last two decades there has been a substantial debate amongst academic geographers about the nature of this gap and how there are productive ways to narrow it and unify geography (Matthews and Herbert, 2004) but at school level this issue has been dealt with simplistically, often by creating 'applied problem-solving' tasks rather than teasing out the complexities of a holistic approach that involves people's perspectives on the physical environment (Newson, 1992; Tadaki et al., 2012). David Pepper would probably still be dissatisfied.

SO IS THERE LESS PHYSICAL GEOGRAPHY NOW TAUGHT IN SCHOOLS, OR DOES IT TAKE A DIFFERENT FORM COMPARED WITH FORMER TIMES?

Rachel Atherton (2009) suggests that new ideas in physical geography only trickle through to schools and into the curriculum when it appears that they pass through a test for 'how does this apply to humans?' which aims to ensure relevancy of the content to young people. Atherton gives the example of tackling sea level rise from the point of view of its impacts rather than studying the underlying scientific processes. In this approach, the processes are supplementary and only introduced to further the understanding of the component of human impact. However, Gregory (2000) contests this approach, stating

Table 6.1 A curriculum map of earth science and physical geography in the National Curriculum[2]

Fieldwork Observation and description of what is around you	Fieldwork Observe and record local fossils and rock types	Lab/Fieldwork Observe, record and experiment to test hypotheses about past processes and environments	Science programme of study Observation of the present and evidence about past processes and environments can be used to model future change
	Fossils are a record of past life forms and the extinction of life forms that no longer exist	Life has evolved over billions of years – observing fossils and properties of rocks in the geological record informs our understanding of past environments and the development of life and the planet	Life has evolved over billions of years and continuously modifies Earth systems
Rocks: Sorting and grouping rocks based on physical properties	Identification and classification of sedimentary, igneous and metamorphic rock types based on key lithological characteristics	The Rock Cycle-formation and cycling of igneous, metamorphic and sedimentary rock by Earth processes Earth structure – core, mantle and crust The age of rocks at the Earth's surface can be estimated by their pattern of distribution and radiometric dating	Earth and its atmosphere consist of dynamic and complex interacting systems of rock, water, ice, air and life; feedbacks operate, and energy and mass are cycled Greenhouse effect – composition of the atmosphere controls the balance of incoming and outgoing energy, and hence the temperature and climatic conditions for life The carbon cycle – fossil fuels, limestone, etc., as sinks which lock away atmospheric carbon, which is rapidly released when fuels are burnt
	Formation of soils and their resultant properties.		Global distribution of mineral resources depends on past geological processes
	Solar system – Sun, Moon and Earth and their effects – light, heat and seasons, night and day.	Formation of the solar system and of the Earth; evolution of atmosphere, oceans and solid Earth Climate has varied through Earth history and continues to do so	Plate tectonics as a unifying theory caused by mantle convection Plate tectonics has shaped the continents, ocean circulation and climate, and the development of landforms and active geological processes at plate margins
KS1 -The world is made up of what you see around you	**KS2** - Natural processes shape the Earth and its surface	**KS3** - The Earth, its environments and landscapes change and evolve over time	**KS4** - Earth and its environments as dynamic and complex systems

(Continued)

	The world's major physical features– locations, patterns, characteristics and scale: continents, oceans and currents, mountain chains, river basins and hot and cold deserts	The processes shaping the Earth's surface including the role of water, weathering and erosion and the formation of soils. Landscapes as distinctive collections of landforms, soils and Earth surface processes;	Ecosystems as the balance and interconnections between climate, soil, water, plants and animals	**Geography programme of study**
	World climate zones and distribution and characteristics of major ecosystems	Weather systems, climate zones and ocean currents; their properties, processes and patterns	Fragile landscapes and environments e.g. deserts, polar regions, mountains and reefs, are vulnerable to change, especially through human interventions and choices.	
Landscapes and Environments: Identifying key landforms, soil, vegetation, water bodies and weather	The water cycle: major phases and flows; atmosphere to surface and sub-surface, surface to lakes/oceans, oceans/lakes to atmosphere.	People-Environment interactions Humans depend on resources provided by the Earth and its atmosphere. Human activity affects climate, oceans and landscapes. Parts of the planet are more prone to natural hazards than others. Humans are affected by natural hazards.	Human life has rapidly modified Earth's systems and surface resulting in climate change; ocean pollution, land degradation and flood risk.	
	The UK: Climate and weather patterns; types of landscapes		Use and sustainability of renewable and non-renewable resources.	
			Geohazards are managed by assessing risk perception, monitoring events and evaluating mitigation strategies.	
Fieldwork Observation of what is around you	Fieldwork Observe and record local landscapes and weather	Fieldwork Observe, map, measure, analyse and interpret UK landscapes/ surface processes	Fieldwork Observe, map, measure,analyse, interpret and evaluate landscapes/surface processes.	

the greater tendency at pre-university level to focus on the impact of human activity and upon management of the environment, with much less, if any, emphasis on the mechanics and principles of landscape development, is rather like putting the cart before the horse. It is very difficult later to take up the study of the horse when all the emphasis has been placed upon the cart!
(p. 109).

Gray (2009) agrees, stating that despite our dominantly egocentric view of the world, physical form is largely untouched and remains essentially natural over large parts of the world. The physical layer (landforms, materials and processes) provides the foundation for superposed biological and cultural layers that make up the landscape, so landforms and their character first need to be studied in their own right before being able to make sense of and develop a full appreciation of the other layers in understanding the character of landscapes, their management and restoration.

Atherton further suggests that the teaching and delivery of many physical geography topics in school tends to rely on extreme simplification of complex topics, especially at Key Stage 3, due to students' level of intellectual capacity and lack of time to explore the concepts in any depth (Atherton, 2009). This raises a question about the extent to which placing the teaching of physical geography in a 'social context' leads to superficial approaches in understanding the way the natural world works and/or develops misconceptions, which somehow diminishes a key aim of the social context approach of enabling and empowering individuals to participate in decisions and actions affecting the physical world in an informed way.

An underlying assumption of Atherton's 'applicability test' is that relevance is recognised by students as being something worthwhile and so becomes of interest. Decisions about the context of teaching are usually made by teachers, with little regard for students' views, which begs the question of whether students prefer physical geography being taught within a social (issues-based/integrated) context or as a branch of geography in its own place. Referring to Earth science in mass popular culture, Iain Stewart asserts that social contexts are interesting but it is the awe and wonder that captivates and inspires, stating 'that modern Earth science is ripe for public consumption but ironically, this ripeness stems less from "pressing social relevance" than from an inherent sense of narrative' (Stewart, 2012).

There are few studies that have looked into physical geography as a focus of students' interest (Trend, 2009) but, in researching interest in geosciences, Trend (2005) found 'Girls have a preference for phenomena perceived as aesthetically pleasing and boys have a preference for the extreme and catastrophic' (p. 271). Hopwood (2006) researched the responses of students to their experiences of physical geography and their conceptions of the people–environment theme. He discovered different understandings and not all were persuaded by the 'social context' despite being acknowledged as part of geography. He reports 'evidence suggests equally if not more strongly that physical phenomena *per se* interest Matt, and his desire to study them reflects a fascination with the physical

world and how it works rather than an ultimately social concern' (p. 5). Perhaps physical geography being always passed through the 'applicability test' risks negating the spiritual and intellectual stimulation (the awe and wonder) to find out about the natural world. As Hopwood asks, 'Are we in danger of losing sight of education about the environment?' (p. 5).

Concerns about the 'weakening' of physical geography in the school curriculum have surfaced periodically. These began to appear in the 1980s following the rise of humanistic geography and as the environment emerged as an important focus of political concern leading to a drift towards 'concentrating attention on human geography in the school curriculum', which was perceived as a potentially damaging neglect of the physical environment (Mottershead, 1987, p. 80). For a number of geographers the people–environment framework did not provide the rigour required to give proper attention to physical process (Adamczyk et al., 1994), giving some academic physical geographers some concerns over whether appropriate and up-to-date knowledge and ideas are being taught in schools (Keylock, 2006; Knight, 2007).

Inman (2006) suggests that physical geography in higher education has enjoyed significant development and attention in recent years. However, these have not been matched by innovations in physical geography pedagogies in schools, which Inman considers have been neglected in the development of the 'thinking skills' curriculum. He suggests that, despite physical geography continuing to feature in GCSE and A level specifications, there is evidence of poor understanding and lack of confidence and motivation with regard to physical geography, resulting in students not having the foundation needed to move to higher education. This concern is also voiced by academics in physical geography, as Keylock (2006) comments: 'The lack of sufficient scientific grounding at A-level means that we may serve the interests of our students better by telling them that if they wish to succeed in a physical geography degree, they should pursue maths, physics, chemistry or biology instead of geography, at least in their A2 year' (p. 272).

The key debate revolves around the extent to which physical geography within a social context or a people–environment, issues-based approach weakens or strengthens engagement with and understanding of the natural world, together with its attendant effect on potential participation in appropriate environmental decision-making. This diverts us back to the opening question raised by the forum contributors mentioned in the introduction: 'Will students know less about physical processes?', and we are forced into considering the pedagogical implications.

WHAT COUNTS AS 'KNOWLEDGE' IN PHYSICAL GEOGRAPHY?

So far this discussion on the rightful place of physical geography has focused on how it is situated in terms of knowledge, content and context. I now want to turn attention to the process and production of (new) knowledge in physical geography.

John Morgan recounts his experience of physical geography at school in the 1980s, describing how there was a lot of teaching about hydrology, drainage basins and catchments which involved quantification, measuring correlations between stream order and other variables, and this was symptomatic of physical geography thereby studying glaciers as a 'system' and coasts as 'process studies'. He suggests this approach was aimed at students learning to experience how geographers practised the subject, but critiques it as an inculcation into one particular type of knowledge that breaks the world down into discrete parts studied in their own right. The processes were small-scale, and the focus was on the data and number crunching rather than seeing how the river formed part of the wider landscape. What was portrayed as a neutral and objective scientific approach is only one way of constructing meaning about the river, which is built on assumptions (J. Morgan, 2006). Newson (1997) illustrates this construction of different meanings with an anecdote based on a conversation with a Lake District farmer: 'I wish the bloody boffins would come here in a spate and watch how this beck eats my land; they'd not waste money making it deeper then – it's deep water what drowns sheep' (p. 22).

Morgan suggests that if teachers are aware of types of knowledge (and how these are produced) they are more likely to be able to give a considered answer to what it is they want students to learn. It raises questions about the process of how we teach physical geography and what meaning students are likely to derive from what they are being taught. Morgan is not alone; debate about the meaning of 'scientific' knowledge and method in physical geography is alive in academic physical geography (Trudgill and Roy, 2003). How is physical geography portrayed through teaching, is it taught as the 'truth' or explored as different forms of 'truth'? (Inkpen, 2005).

A useful framework for this discussion can be drawn from a set of stories to be told about landscapes (Huggett and Perkins, 2004; Bloomer and Atherton, 2006), adapted to physical geography and how it can be 'read' in ways that produce different knowledges, each occupying a different place in constructs of meaning. These knowledges create physical worlds that are (i) machine and system driven by processes; (ii) text – constructed through heuristic and swayed by paradigm (see Kennedy, 2006); (iii) palimpsest – where understanding the current 'layer' is contingent, for example river landforms in the British landscape can only be fully understood by reference to the last glacial period; (iv) providers for taste and value – aesthetic value and/or spiritual/recreational nourishment, for example the picturesque or special designation as a conservation area; (v) drivers of social and political process, for example hazard geography.

The dominant type of knowledge experienced in school physical geography tends to be that of machine and system driven by process (Lambert and Morgan, 2010, p. 138), portraying physical geography as determining the way nature works in geography through a set of stable, 'fixed' processes where facts fit together in a given way according to 'laws', that is a positivist perspective. It is manifested through predetermined models presented in the classroom by descriptions,

diagrams and definitions and/or in the classic hypothesis-testing approach. At one level, this knowledge as a system can convince of rational explanation and is intellectually seductive (Harrison, 2009). However, it can also lead to belief in an outdated machine that doesn't match with a dynamic understanding of nature, leading teachers passively to depict a machine that doesn't exist. It can encourage students to learn the model and slot the components in, even if they don't fit: the so-called 'tyranny of models' (Trudgill, 2003, p. 34).

Academic understanding has shifted from this empirical and 'rigid' world to acknowledge 'simplicity' doesn't exist and the real world is more 'naughty', complex, approximate and our perceptions of it are socially constructed (Kennedy, 1979; Tadaki et al., 2012). There is no objective 'truth' but there are better approximations to the truth (Inkpen, 2005). This philosophy has more in common with the pluralities of knowledges outlined above. In 'knowledge as text', the information isn't just 'out there' but is constructed or created in specific contexts for particular purposes. In this sense, physical geography should be exploratory as well as explanatory as it can be created in different ways through prior experience or constructs (interpretative frameworks) offered by teachers that help to stimulate seeing the world in new ways (Trudgill, 2003).

So are paradigms useful in teaching physical geography or can learning be swayed by paradigms? When a construct is oversimplified, outdated, offered as the sole explanatory model, as though no understanding about the physical world existed previously and without critical evaluation, it can obfuscate rather than clarify. For example, swayed by the paradigm of climate change being a process of rapid change and negative impact, every natural event of magnitude (e.g. Queensland floods 2010–11 or increased frequency of earthquakes) is interpreted as a symptom of climate change. If the paradigms taught in school are not explored, it can make it difficult for students to distinguish 'trend' (nearer the truth) from the 'noise' (exceptions that don't fit) in the real world. Atherton (2009) suggests students develop skills of acceptance rather than enquiry, whereas in reality the world is riddled with uncertainty so that students should be taught to deal with ambiguities, and therefore a constructivist approach is more appropriate to physical geography teaching. Trend (2009) and A. Morgan (2006) advocate the use of argumentation as a pedagogic approach to empower students with a more critical understanding of the world's natural systems.

Thus, the key debate revolves around how best to help students make sense of a complex and dynamic physical world: whether, when and how to use paradigms as constructs and simple and singular explanatory tools, or whether it is more appropriate and effective to introduce a range of different (sometimes historical) interpretive models to explore the validity of ways of explaining and understanding.

Conclusion

This exploration of the 'rightful place' has clearly identified that school geography could not exist without physical geography; the interdependence between

the physical world and cultural and social worlds, in a range of direct and indirect ways, is too strong to be dismissed. However, the physical world is wide-ranging, complex and dynamic. The content matter of physical geography lies within a collective of scientific disciplines called Earth sciences, but our current understanding shows that there is value in a geographical dimension brought to a 'hard science'-driven systems approach (Pitman, 2005). The debate for teachers is a curriculum debate over what to emphasise in choosing to teach in physical geography and how to develop students' thinking to enable a fresh, distinctive perspective to be gained in understanding the physical world. The idea of physical geography as emphasising the surface, spatial and social, as opposed to 'deep' Earth science, is attractively simple, but this throws up debates about the balance of studying processes, for it is in understanding processes and principles that the power of prediction and applicability lie. Applicability seems to be a current filter for much physical geography taught in school that gives a social justification to the place of physical geography. The dilemma of 'cart before horse' (Gregory, 2000) can lead to insufficient knowledge and understanding in how the physical world works, and so the application becomes detached from reality. Applicability could also limit the development of a 'richer', more spiritual, appreciation of the physical world. The challenge for teachers is in deciding appropriate starting points and routes for study. Recent shifts in constructing our understanding have shifted from a fixed positivist view of the physical world as a stable place to exploring multiple knowledges which interpret and aim to reveal evermore 'approximate truths'. The challenge for geography teachers is to critically examine their own biographical knowledge of physical geography so as to evaluate decisions over how best to portray to students, and develop their understanding of, the 'naughty world'.

The rightful place of physical geography is dependent on the context in which we find ourselves making sense of the world, so cannot be thought of as a fixed location in the minds of geography teachers or their students.

Notes

1   SLN is the Staffordshire Learning Net, its Geography pages are available at http://www.sln.org.uk/geography/
2   Table 6.1 is a curriculum map of earth science and physical geography in the National Curriculum based on a document produced jointly by The Geographical Association, The Geological Society, The Earth Science Teachers' Association, The Royal Geographical Society and The Royal Meteorological Society and submitted to assist with the review of the National Curriculum for England (December 2011).

Key readings

1. Gregory, K.J. (2000) *The Changing Nature of Physical Geography*, London: Arnold. The focus of Ken Gregory's book is self-explanatory and whilst there have been some further changes in the last decade it provides an enduring overview of ideas that have influenced our conceptions of physical geography as taught in schools.

2. Trudgill, S. and Roy, A. (eds.) (2003) *Contemporary Meanings in Physical Geography: From what to why?*, London: Arnold. Stephen Trudgill and André Roy's book offers refreshing, stimulating, reflective, cultural interpretations of physical geography which challenge how meanings derived from physical geography are framed.

References

Adamczyk, P., Binns, T., Brown, A., Cross, S. and Magson, Y. (1994) 'The geography-science interface: A focus for collaboration', *Teaching Geography*, 19 (1), 11–14.

Atherton, R. (2009) 'Living with natural processes – physical geography and the human impact on the environment', in D. Mitchell (ed.), *Living Geography*, Cambridge: Chris Kington Publishing.

Barratt-Hacking, E. (1996) 'Novice teachers and their geographical persuasions', *International Research in Geographical and Environmental Education*, 5 (1), 77–86.

Bloomer, D. and Atherton, R. (2006) 'Understanding Landscape', in D. Balderstone (ed.), *Secondary Geography Handbook*, Sheffield: Geographical Association.

Brooks, C. (2006) 'Geography Teachers and Making the School Geography Curriculum', *Geography*, 91 (1), 75–83.

Cresswell, T. (2004) *Place: A short introduction*, London: Wiley-Blackwell.

Department for Education and Skills/Qualification and Curriculum Authority (DfES/QCA) (2004) *The National Curriculum for England: Science Key Stages 1–4 (Revised 2004)*, London: HMSO.

Department for Education (DfE) (2012) *Remit for Review of the National Curriculum in England*, Available from: http://www.education.gov.uk/schools/teachingandlearning/curriculum/nationalcurriculum/b0073043/remit-for-review-of-the-national-curriculum-in-england [Accessed 2 March 2012].

Gray, M. (2009) 'Landscape: The Physical Layer', in N.J. Clifford, S.L. Holloway, S.P. Rice and G. Valentine (eds.), *Key Concepts in Geography*, 2nd edn, London: Sage Publications.

Gregory, K.J. (2000) *The Changing Nature of Physical Geography*, London: Arnold.

Gregory, K. (2009) 'Place: The Management of Sustainable Environments', in Clifford, Holloway, Rice and Valentine (eds.), *Key Concepts in Geography*, 2nd edn, London: Sage Publications.

Harrison, S. (2009) 'Environmental Systems: Philosophy and Applications in Physical Geography', in Clifford, Holloway, Rice and Valentine (eds.), *Key Concepts in Geography*, 2nd edn, London: Sage Publications.

Hawley, D. (1997) 'Cross-curricular concerns in geography Earth science and physical geography', in D. Tilbury and M. Williams (eds.), *Teaching and learning geography*, London: Routledge.

Hopwood (2006) *Pupils' perspectives on environmental education in geography: 'I'm not looking at it from a tree's point of view'*, Paper presented at the University of Bath Centre for Research in Education and the Environment, 16 February 2006. Available from: http://www.bath.ac.uk/cree/resources/hopwood.pdf [Accessed 30 March 2012].

Huggett, R. and Perkins, C. (2004) in J.A. Matthews and D.T. Herbert (eds.), *Unifying geography: Common heritage, shared future*, Abingdon: Routledge.

Inkpen, R. (2005) *Science, Philosophy and Physical Geography*, Abingdon: Routledge.

Inkpen, R. (2009) 'Development: Sustainability and Physical Geography', in J. Clifford, S. Holloway, S. Rice and G. Valentine (eds.), *Key Concepts in Geography*, 2nd edn, London: Sage Publications.

Inman, T. (2006) 'Let's get physical', in D. Balderstone (ed.), *Secondary Geography Handbook*, Sheffield: Geographical Association.

Johnston, R. (1986) 'Four fixations and the quest for unity in geography', *Transactions of the Institute of British Geographers*, 11, 449–53.

Kennedy, B.A. (1979) 'A Naughty World', *Transactions of the Institute of British Geographers*, 4 (4), 550–8.

Kennedy, B.A. (2006) *Inventing the earth: Ideas on landscape development since 1740*, Malden, MA: Blackwell Publishing.

Kent, M. (2009) 'Space: Making room for space in physical geography', in J. Clifford, S. Holloway, S. Rice and G. Valentine (eds.), *Key Concepts in Geography*, 2nd edn, London: Sage Publications.

Keylock, C.J. (2006) 'Reforming AS/A2Physical Geography to Enhance Geographic Scholarship', *Geography*, 91 (3), 272–9.

King, C. (1986) 'Will Physical Geography join the sciences?', *Teaching Geography*, 12 (1), 32.

King, C. (2011) 'Where should Earth science be situated in the curriculum?', *Teaching Earth Sciences*, 36 (2), 56–60.

Knight, P. (2007) 'Physical geography: Learning and teaching in a discipline so dynamic that textbooks can't keep up', *Geography*, 92 (1), 57–61.

Lambert, D. and Morgan, J. (2010) *Teaching geography 11–18 A Conceptual Approach*, Maidenhead: Open University Press.

Matthews, J.A. and Herbert, D.T. (2004) 'Unity in geography: Prospects for the discipline', in J.A. Matthews and D.T. Herbert (eds.), *Unifying geography: Common heritage, shared future*, Abingdon: Routledge.

Morgan, A. (2006) 'Argumentation, Geography Education and ICT', *Geography*, 91 (2), 126–40.

Morgan, J. (2006) 'Geography – a dynamic subject', in D. Balderstone (ed.), *Secondary Geography Handbook*, Sheffield: Geographical Association.

Mottershead, D. (1987) 'Physical Geography', *Teaching Geography*, 12 (2), 80–81.

Newson, M. (1992) '20 years of systematic physical geography: issues for a new environmental age', *Progress in Physical Geography*, 16 (2), 209–21.

Newson, M. (1997) *Land, water and development: Sustainable management of river basin systems*, 2nd edn, London: Routledge.

Pepper, D. (1985) 'Why teach physical geography?' *Contemporary Issues in geography and Education*, 2 (1), 62–71.

Pitman, A.J. (2005) 'On the role Geography in Earth System Science', *Geoforum*, 36, 137–48.

SLN Geography Forum (2008) 'Will pupils know less about physical processes? Available from: http://www.learning net.co.uk/ubb/Forum5/HTML/o16909.html [Accessed 2 August 2011].

Stewart, I. (2012) *Tell me a story*. Available from: http://www.geolsoc.org.uk/page11347.html [Accessed 10 March 2012].

Tadaki, M., Salmond, J., Le Heron, R. and Brierley, G. (2012) 'Nature, culture, and the work of physical geography', *Transactions of the Institute of British Geographers*, 37 (12), 1–16.

Trend, R. (1995) *Geography and Science: Forging Links at Key Stage 3*, Sheffield: Geographical Association.

Trend, R. (2005) 'Individual, situational and topic interest in geoscience among 11 and 12 year old children', *Research Papers in Education*, 20 (3), 271–302.

Trend, R. (2008) *Think Piece, Physical Geography (secondary)* [online] Available from: http://www.geography.org.uk/gtip/thinkpieces/physicalgeography(secondary)/ [Accessed 31 March 2012].

Trend, R. (2009) 'Commentary: Fostering Students' Argumentation Skills in Geoscience Education', *Journal of Geoscience Education*, 57 (4), 224–32.

Trudgill, S. (2003) 'Meaning, knowledge, constructs and fieldwork in physical geography', in S. Trudgill and A. Roy (eds.), *Contemporary Meanings in Physical Geography: From what to why?* London: Arnold.

Trudgill, S. and Roy, A. (eds.) (2003.) *Contemporary Meanings in Physical Geography: From what to why?* London: Arnold.

Urban, M. and Rhoads, B. (2003) 'Conceptions of Nature', in S. Trudgill, and A. Roy (eds.), *Contemporary Meanings in Physical Geography*.

Wilson, R.C.L. (1990) 'National Curriculum Geography Working Group: Comments on the Interim Report of the National Curriculum Geography Working Group, Submission from the Association for Science Education', *Teaching Earth Sciences*, 15 (1), 18–22.

Chapter 7

Whatever happened to the enquiry approach in geography?

Jane Ferretti

> The GA believes that teachers should be accountable, but also that they are autonomous professionals driven by educational goals and purposes.
> (Geographical Association, 2009, p. 27)

Introduction

In geography 'enquiry learning' has long been advocated as an important approach for teachers; however, evidence (Ofsted, 2008, 2011) suggests that, although excellent in some schools, its use in both Key Stage 3 (KS3) and Key Stage 4 (KS4) is limited. This chapter starts by discussing different interpretations of the term pedagogy and goes on to consider ideas surrounding geographical enquiry starting by linking enquiry to established learning theories, particularly constructivism, and the importance of students being actively involved in their own learning and the key role that teachers play in facilitating this. Although there may be a lack of consensus about what teachers understand by the term 'geographical enquiry', the key debate must be about why only limited use of an enquiry approach is used in schools, whether or not this is an inevitable result of the current demands being made on teachers and schools, and whether the educational goals and purposes advocated by the Geographical Association (GA) in this quote are being lost as a result of the pressures of the performativity agenda.

WHAT IS PEDAGOGY?

The term pedagogy is used frequently by academics, PGCE tutors and even Office for Standards in Education (Ofsted) inspectors but perhaps less so by teachers themselves, who may prefer just to talk about 'teaching'.[1] I would argue that pedagogy is more complex than the rather simplistic definition 'the process of teaching' (Wikipedia) or 'the study of teaching methods' (Oxford Advanced online dictionary). Pedagogy was defined by the DfES in its 2007 National Strategy publication as

the act of teaching, and the rationale that supports the actions that teachers take. It is what a teacher needs to know and the range of skills that a teacher needs to use in order to make effective teaching decisions.

(p. 1)

This echoes, and is probably derived from, Alexander's (2004) definition of pedagogy as 'the act of teaching together with its attendant discourse' (p. 11), which he amplifies by saying 'it is what one needs to know, and the skills one needs to command, in order to make and justify the many different kinds of decisions of which teaching is constituted' (p. 11). Alexander further argues that teachers are professionals who should make their own decisions about teaching based on their skills, knowledge and understanding; they are not technicians who implement the ideas and procedures of others.

Teachers have for many years been swamped by changing policies and frequently repeated dogma, so it is understandable that for some there is a tendency to comply with rather than question the demands made of them. It is perhaps unsurprising that many rarely challenge what they are asked to do, although, as Adams (2008) points out, many feel 'frustrated and constrained' (p. 379) by the expectation that they should teach in a particular way. The danger is that teachers will increasingly focus on their daily routine, rarely drawing on their wider professional knowledge and beliefs unless specifically encouraged to consider evidence, look at research and discuss and reflect on their practice. There is even a concern that teachers may be susceptible to government rhetoric that adopting particular methods and approaches will lead directly to better teaching and increased pupil progress as measured by test scores (Adams, 2008).

The National Strategy publication *Pedagogy and Personalisation* (DfES, 2007) suggests it is helpful to consider pedagogy in four domains: namely subject and curriculum knowledge; teaching repertoire of skills and techniques; teaching and learning models; and conditions for learning. Lists of bullet points explain to teachers how they can improve their understanding of each of these domains, all of which, it suggests, will transform teaching and learning in schools. The document introduces pedagogy as 'what teachers need to know and the range of skills that a teacher needs in order to make effective teaching decisions' (p. 1). It is clearly based on Alexander's (2004) definition; however, it does not reflect Alexander's view that 'pedagogy is a somewhat more complex enterprise than may be recognised by those who reduce effective teaching to "what works" or "best practice" lessons downloaded from government websites' (p. 13).

In July 2011 the General Teaching Council for England (GTCE) published a series of Policy Papers (GTCE, 2011) designed in part as a legacy to remain when the GTCE is abolished as recommended in the 2010 Schools White Paper (DfE, 2010). These Policy Papers are evidenced-based and consider ways in which teaching quality in schools can be enhanced, and how this could be achieved through government policy, the actions of school leaders and teachers themselves. Paper 7, entitled 'Pedagogy', advocates that there should be greater focus

on how teachers acquire and develop their 'expert professional knowledge' starting with initial teacher education and continuing with more meaningful Continuing Professional Development (CPD) for experienced teachers. The paper argues that teaching quality is the strongest influence on learning and that in order for pupil outcomes to improve, more emphasis should be put on improving pedagogy; it considers that 'a crucial part of pedagogic expertise comes from engaging in, and with, research ideas and evidence, which can stimulate reflective analysis of issues and deepen the professional judgements a teacher makes' (GTCE, 2011, p. 93). It is clear that the GTCE views pedagogy as being complex and important and that teachers need time, opportunities and support in order to develop their pedagogical expertise in the interests of the students they teach.

THEORY INTO PRACTICE

One way in which teachers might build up their pedagogical expertise is through developing a better theoretical understanding of what goes on in the classroom. Freeman (2010) suggests that '[F]for many teachers the notion of engaging with theory may seem like an additional burden on their time; a distraction from the real world of teaching and learning' (p. 139); however, key questions such as 'how do young people learn?' and 'how can teachers encourage and support their learning?' require us to engage with and develop an understanding of learning theories. Moore (2000) provides a useful summary of the ideas developed by Skinner, Piaget, Vygotsky and Bruner, discussing both the value and some of the limitations of each of these well-established learning theories, and also points out that many classroom teachers have little explicit knowledge of these theories despite the fact that most would have studied them at some time during their training. Constructivists including Piaget, Vygotsky and Bruner believe that learners need to build on ideas they already have in order to understand and internalise new information. This is summarised by Barnes (2008), who writes that 'The central contention of this view of learning which is nowdays called "constructivism", is that each of us can only learn by making sense of what happens to us in the course of actively constructing a world for ourselves' (p. 3). The role of teachers is vital in providing the structure in which young people can progress by setting up situations which will challenge and enable them to improve their understanding; providing information which has no connection with a learner's current view will soon be forgotten. It is important to emphasise that the constructivist view of learning stresses that learners need to be *actively* involved in their own learning, which Barnes (2008) suggests 'does not imply moving about the room or manipulating objects (though either of these might be involved), but rather attempting to interrelate, to reinterpret, to understand new experiences and ideas' (p. 2). The link between this and enquiry learning is clear and indeed is developed by Roberts (2003) who relates geographical enquiry to constructivism and especially the work of Vygotsky. The essence of enquiry learning is that students are 'enquiring actively into questions, issues or problems'

(Naish et al., 1987, p. 45), and in order to do this they are using some form of data or evidence to find out more and to develop their knowledge and understanding. It involves students being stimulated by something which has inspired curiosity, and asking and answering questions to generate knowledge and increase understanding.

WHAT IS GEOGRAPHICAL ENQUIRY?

An enquiry approach is by no means unique to geography and indeed is identified as a key process in the 2007 programmes of study for Key Stage 3 for other subjects including history, citizenship and science. Within geography this approach has long been advocated as important and indeed enquiry has been included within the programme of study for Key Stages 1, 2 and 3 in the Geography National Curriculum (GNC) since its inception in 1991. Even before this, the term geographical enquiry was used within the Schools' Council geography projects developed in the 1970s and 80s; the Geography 16–19 project particularly encouraged geographical enquiry, which it defined as

> a range of teaching methods and approaches by which the teacher encourages students to enquire actively into questions issues and problems rather than merely to accept passively the conclusions, research and opinions of others.
>
> (Naish et al., 1987, p. 45, cited in Rawling, 2001)

During the early 1990s, Margaret Roberts (1998, 2003) undertook research to discover what secondary geography teachers understood by the term geographical enquiry and how they incorporated it into schemes of work for Key Stage 3. She found an impressive variety of enquiry work going on in schools, both inside and outside the classroom, with students working individually and in groups. However, perhaps her most striking finding was the considerable range of different understandings of geographical enquiry held by the teachers she interviewed, and the differences in the extent to which enquiry-based work was incorporated into lessons, not only between schools but also within departments. She found some schools making extensive use of enquiry-based learning but others only incorporating enquiry into fieldwork investigations and rarely using it in the classroom.

Roberts developed her ideas about geographical enquiry in her book *Learning through Enquiry* (2003). She emphasises the need for students to be actively involved in their own learning and identifies four essential characteristics of enquiry, starting by creating a need to know, then using data, making sense of the data and finally reflecting on learning. She recognises that geographical enquiry may take different forms and that it is not always appropriate for classes to have an open-ended project, based on independent research lasting several weeks and suggests that 'by narrowing the scope of enquiry work, it is possible to carry out

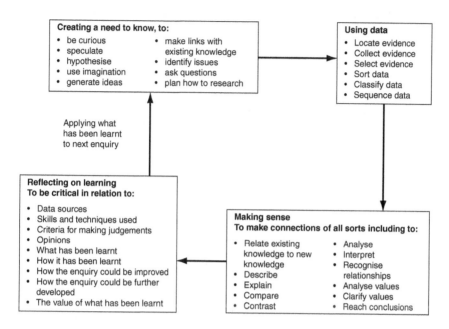

Figure 7.1 A framework for learning through enquiry (Roberts, 2003, p. 44).

a complete enquiry from initial stimulus to the reaching of conclusions and debriefing within one or two lessons' (p. 46).

The framework which Roberts suggested is not intended to show a prescribed route that all geographical enquiries should follow, although that is what some teachers may think. An investigation which is structured by the teacher but worked on independently by students is at one end of a spectrum of enquiry approaches which also includes much more tightly structured activities where teachers provide a stimulus that generates students' questions and help them to find answers. Any activity which opens up problems and issues, encourages questions and begins to find solutions can be described as enquiry and the key to this is the teacher who provides the structure to allow this to occur (Rawling, 2001). Most important of all, in my view, is the way in which teachers inspire curiosity and 'a need to know'; failing to do this will inevitably lead to lessons that simply cover prescribed content which may not interest or have any relevance to students and is thus likely to limit their learning.

The 2007 programme of study (POS) for KS3 geography (QCA, 2007) puts considerable emphasis on geographical enquiry which is highlighted as one of four key processes, itself a change from the previous three POS where it was listed as a skill. The 2007 POS states that 'pupils should carry out a range of enquiries, from structured to more open ended and active' (p. 4). It provides a list of seven

aspects of geographical enquiry which pupils should be able to do, the first of which is to 'ask geographical questions, thinking critically, constructively and creatively' (p. 4). Beyond the list little guidance is provided, meaning teachers must make their own decisions about how, and how often to include geographical enquiry in schemes of work, nor does it clarify that it is not necessary for all these steps to be followed at the same time. Sadly, evidence from Ofsted's 2011 report into geography teaching *Learning to make a world of difference* suggests that in many schools very little enquiry learning takes place at all, reporting that '[I]in too many of the lessons seen, there were not enough opportunities for enquiry through research, discussion, collaboration and allowing pupils to use their initiative' (p. 26); they also observed that starter activities often had little relevance to the main part of the lesson and plenaries were weak and unlikely to stimulate reflection (Ofsted, 2011). This highlights the reluctance of some teachers to engage with geographical enquiry, which may reflect a lack of understanding of generally accepted ideas about how people learn.

Perhaps there is another related issue here too in terms of how teachers see their role: is it simply the transmission of information or should teachers be enabling students to investigate something geographical? Some of the most familiar Key Stage 3 textbooks such as Waugh and Bushell's Key Geography series tend to present information without encouraging students to question or challenge and indeed the increasing use of PowerPoint® presentations can tempt teachers simply to provide information as fact rather than inspire their students to ask questions and investigate for themselves. As Margaret Roberts has pointed out, enquiry as a teaching method implies a state of mind which is not about the transmission of information but about engaging students with data and in making meaning (Roberts, 2011).

The lack of consensus about the meaning of geographical enquiry which Roberts identified in her research during the 1990s is almost certainly the same for today's teachers, who will also have different understandings of the term geographical enquiry. Rawling (2007) suggests that '[S]some people think of enquiry as meaning open ended activities in which students are independently discovering things for themselves; others see it, certainly at key stage 3, as a tightly controlled set of training activities' (p. 42) but she points out that neither of these views is entirely correct because geographical enquiry can include both, and a range of other 'more-or-less structured approaches in between' (p. 42). Differences in interpretation and the issue of whether geographers need consensus are worth considering and discussing but are probably not a 'key debate'. What matters is that teachers are able to stimulate curiosity, help their students learn by investigating issues and considering evidence, and can encourage them to adopt a critical and questioning approach, which in turn helps them to widen their geographical knowledge and understanding. Of course there are schools with strong geography departments where students are involved in geographical enquiry and where geography is seen as relevant and important but perhaps too few of them. The debate must therefore be about what is threatening the place of

geographical enquiry and why it is not used more frequently in geography class-rooms. Young people need to be engaged in challenging enquiries to help them to develop their ability to 'think geographically' perhaps best defined as 'a unique way of seeing the world, of understanding complex problems and thinking about inter-connections at a variety of scales' (Jackson, 2006, p. 199).

WHY IS THERE A LACK OF GEOGRAPHICAL ENQUIRY IN SCHOOLS?

In this section I consider three concerns which may be responsible for a lack of geographical enquiry in schools. These are lesson structure, assessment and issues related to skills, competencies and core knowledge.

Lesson structure

Over the last decade or more, teachers have been given extensive advice, particularly through the National Strategy, about teaching and learning strategies, learning styles, assessment, behaviour management and lesson structure. The publications produced by the National Strategy were advisory rather than statutory, however, schools often felt pressured to adopt advice given by Local Authorities through their Strategy consultants and also by Ofsted, whose inspectors expected to see evidence of these preferred practices. One of the results has been that teachers feel, and sometimes are, obliged to structure learning by planning three-part lessons including a starter, development activities and a plenary, and to share lesson objectives and learning outcomes with the class at the start of each lesson. There is much which could be debated about the three-part lesson but one particular aspect to consider is the impact it can have on enquiry learning. Roberts' (2003) four essential characteristics of the enquiry process can certainly be incorporated into the three-part model, for example by creating 'a need to know' as a starter and using the plenary as an opportunity to 'reflect on learning', but it seems this rarely happens. One reason for this, as Davidson (2006) points out, is the impact which sharing learning objectives at the start of lessons can have on the way students engage with lessons. Davidson stresses the importance of starting lessons in ways which stimulate and engage students, providing them with a purpose for learning and encouraging them to ask questions and make sense of information for themselves, and points out that sharing lesson objectives at the start of lessons can have a demotivating effect and curtail the process of enquiry. Furthermore, opportunities for linking with students' own lives and experiences are lost and there is a tendency for information to be presented as fact rather than debatable issues worth investigating (Davidson, 2006). This is supported by more recent comments from Ofsted (2011), which reports seeing geography lessons where lesson objectives were simply copied off the board, starters had little relevance to the rest of the lesson and plenaries were no more than a summary, often foreshortened by lack of time.

Unfortunately, some teachers have focused on lesson structure at the expense of adopting teaching strategies, such as geographical enquiry, which might not fit easily into the three-part formula. Starters may be chosen to grab the class's attention rather than to encourage curiosity or speculation about a geographical issue, and plenaries may simply summarise rather than encourage reflection. School leaders often implement changes hoping to impress Ofsted and certainly the three-part lesson is now almost ubiquitous, thus it is somewhat ironic that Ofsted's 2011 report into geography found that

> [L]lessons which consistently used a rigid three-part structure did not allow sufficiently for spontaneity and creativity in students' learning. Such lessons also did not always allow them opportunities, the most academically able pupils in particular, to develop the skills of planning and organisation, take responsibility for their own learning or work independently.
>
> (p. 26)

In other words the three-part lesson, especially when rigidly adhered to, can stifle geographical enquiry.

Assessment

Another concern is to do with assessment. Since 1997 the UK government has increasingly 'sought to inform teachers not only what to teach ... but also how to teach' (Adams, 2008, p. 377). Adams points out that government guidance, such as that issued through the National Strategies, clearly suggests that adopting particular teaching methods 'will directly lead to high quality teaching that will result in increases in pupil attainment' (p. 377). Going hand in hand with this is an assumption that test results are the only way to demonstrate student attainment, with little acknowledgement that learning can take place in different ways and with different outcomes. A consequence of this results-driven approach is the unrelenting pressure on teachers to show that pupils are making progress week by week, term by term, and year by year, resulting in frequent 'levelled' assessments with increasing use of sublevels to show the all-important 'progression'. Teachers are accused of 'teaching to the test' especially at GCSE and A Level but who can blame them? This quote from Barker (2010) will resonate with many:

> the dominance of the performance regime has masked ... the extent to which official curriculum requirements, and the selected measures of success (e.g. the five A* to C GCSE grades threshold), have distorted and changed the nature of education. Schools teach to the test ... reduce the time devoted to non-examinable activities and concentrate attention on borderline candidates.
>
> (pp. 113–14)

It may also explain why some teachers are rarely using geographical enquiry, as evidenced by Ofsted (2011), which refers to narrow prescriptive approaches

and a focus on covering the content suggesting that 'teaching programmes met the examination requirements but lacked imagination and stimulus for the students' (p. 33). Teachers naturally worry about examination results but this concern can lead them to focus on 'delivering' content and they perhaps feel that using an enquiry approach will impact on their results. On the other hand some examination specifications explicitly advocate enquiry learning; for example, both the Edexcel GCSE Geography specifications (A and B) 'give[s] students opportunities to actively engage in the process of geography to develop as effective and independent learners' and to 'use geographical skills, appropriate technologies, enquiry and analysis' (Edexcel, 2008a, 2008b, p. 1) and the AQA GCSE Geography A specification states that it 'allows enquiry-based learning to be at the forefront of the teaching of the subject' (AQA, 2008, p. 3).

Teachers often remain unconvinced by this rhetoric, anxious to focus on the content and examination skills they feel are needed for success. Even the opportunities for geographical enquiry through fieldwork have been curtailed by the introduction of controlled assessment, which tends to encourage teachers to set up a tightly structured activity based on a question set by the examination board.

Skills, competencies and core knowledge

A further concern relates to the different emphasis placed on skills, competencies and 'core' knowledge in the curriculum. The 2007 KS3 Curriculum review resulted in the publication of a curriculum overview called the Big Picture (QCDA); this emphasised the importance of skills, particularly personal, learning and thinking skills (PLTS), and led some schools to redesign their KS3 curriculum with a focus on competencies and skills-based curricula often through the integration of geography with other humanities subjects. Lambert (2008) points out the dangers of this asking: 'Don't we care *what* young people are taught? Aren't we interested in *what* they are learning?' (p. 209). Reorganising the curriculum to focus on skills instead of subjects threatens geography in a number of ways, including threatening investigative geography and geographical enquiry. It usually leads to less time being allocated to the subject and a reduced focus on subject knowledge; if cross-curriculum courses or projects, such as the Royal Society for the encouragement of Arts, Manufactures and Commerce (RSA)'s Opening Minds, are introduced in Year 7 then KS3 geography must be squeezed into Year 8 and 9, indeed in schools introducing GCSE courses into Year 9, geography can be squeezed in this way too. In addition, these changes may also involve non-specialists teaching geography and geographers themselves teaching other subjects. Although we should be pleased that geography is a subject which can contribute to developing skills, there is a risk that this approach devalues it as a subject in its own right; it should be emphasised that genuine geographical enquiry is not a means of learning transferrable skills but an approach to learning *geography* and developing a better understanding of geographical issues.

On the face of it, the White Paper *The Importance of Teaching* (DfE, 2010) might be seen to address this issue. It indicates that teachers should be given more responsibility for what they teach, claiming that 'at present, the National Curriculum includes too much that is not essential knowledge, and there is too much prescription about how to teach' (p. 10) and that this is 'weighing teachers down and squeezing out room for innovation, creativity, deep learning and intellectual exploration' (p. 40). It also promises a revised National Curriculum with a greater focus on subject content which will 'outline a core knowledge in the traditional subject disciplines' (p. 42). It further announces the introduction of the English Baccalaureate (E.Bacc) awarded to students who secure A* to C passes at GCSE in English, mathematics, a science, a language and a humanity which must be either history or geography. Clearly this provides opportunities for geography; the status of the subject may improve and uptake at GCSE may increase as schools strive to improve the percentage of students achieving the E.Bacc. At the time of writing, specifics of the new Geography National Curriculum and in particular the required 'core knowledge' are not known. We must hope that the recognition that 'Teachers, not bureaucrats or Ministers, know best how to teach' (p. 41) and the promise that they will be given 'space to create lessons which engage their pupils' (p. 42) will be prominent, encouraging teachers to develop a range of teaching and learning strategies including geographical enquiry. Indeed we must hope that geographical enquiry continues to be a required element within the GNC and that the term 'core knowledge' is interpreted widely to include key concepts, skills and geographical procedures, the very heart of which is geographical enquiry (GA, 2011). Encouraging young people to ask questions about real issues, to search for answers using a wide range of skills and information, and to think critically about issues is an essential ingredient in helping them to 'think geographically' and I see it as important that this is not thrown out in a rush to rationalise and create space in the curriculum.

Conclusions

Teachers need to have time to read and reflect on their pedagogy, not only independently but with other teachers and teacher educators. Their reflection should go beyond simply deciding what particular teaching strategy or approach to use and most teachers certainly realise that improving their practice depends on more than adopting particular approaches advocated by government agencies, and that these alone are not the key to transforming their own performance or that of the young people they teach. Indeed it could be argued that some of these approaches, including the three-part lesson, have had a negative impact on geography lessons and may be partly responsible for the fact that geographical enquiry is not a strong feature of practice in many schools. Both Davidson (2006) and Roberts (2010) have raised concerns about the way in which starters and plenaries are used as part of a routine and that lessons can lack any focus on geography's big

ideas or how students' *geographical* understanding can be developed. Ofsted continues to see schools where geography teachers are reluctant to change teaching approaches in order to make geography more relevant and challenging and rely on textbooks and work that occupies rather than engages students (see Ofsted, 2011, p. 26).

An enquiry approach to geography starts with an engaging and worthwhile question about a real issue, something which intrigues learners and inspires them to find out more. It leads them to use different kinds of information and skills to find answers and construct their own knowledge. It helps them to evaluate information and to empathise and respect the views of others. It is a very powerful way in which young people can understand contentious issues and develop their geographical knowledge and understanding. So is this incompatible with the demands of teaching today? In my view the very opposite is true. Young people learn when they are interested and engaged and when they have questions for which they want answers; they are less likely to learn if they are told the answers or if information is simply provided for them by the teacher, from a PowerPoint® slide or a textbook. Many geography teachers responded to the changes brought by the new KS3 POS in 2007, which had less prescription and more opportunities to innovate, by redesigning their schemes of work and incorporating current and relevant topics which appeal to young people. The efforts of the GA and RGS-IBG to encourage teachers to make changes through the Action Plan for Geography, has helped many to have the confidence to become curriculum makers. As the GA points out, teachers should be accountable but they are also professionals with educational goals and perhaps all they need is the confidence to be autonomous in their classrooms and focus on inspiring young people and encouraging them to ask questions and engage with the geography around them, something which is at the heart of the enquiry approach.

Note

1 The phrase 'teaching and learning' was prevalent between 1997 and 2010 during the period of the Labour government; however, since the change to the Coalition government there has been a marked return to the use of the term 'teaching' evidenced in the 2010 Schools White Paper, *The Importance of Teaching* (DfE, 2010) and the new 'Teachers Standards' (DfE, 2011).

Key readings

1. Roberts, M. (2003) *Learning through Enquiry*, Sheffield: Geographical Association. This book draws on the author's own research and her experiences as a PGCE Tutor. It outlines the key characteristics of geographical enquiry and provides suggestions for how teachers might incorporate enquiry into their teaching.
2. Barker, B. (2010) *The Pendulum Swings. Transforming School Reform*, Stoke on Trent: Trentham Books. This book is a fascinating discussion of education reform since 1988 and particularly of New Labour's education policies. The author argues that teaching and learning will not improve through regulation, inspection and measurement,

and that the time is right for completely new thinking from policy makers. Published in 2010, it is particularly interesting to read as the Coalition government's education policies become clearer.

References

Adams, P. (2008) 'Considering "best practice"; the social construction of teacher activity and pupil learning as performance', *Cambridge Journal of Education*, 38 (3), 375–92.

Alexander, R.J. (2004) 'Still no pedagogy? Principle, pragmatism and compliance in primary education', *Cambridge Journal of Education*, 34 (1), 7–33.

AQA (2008) *GCSE Specification Geography A*, Available from: http://web.aqa.org.uk/subjects/geography-specifications.php [Accessed 20 February 2012].

Barker, B. (2010) *The Pendulum Swings. Transforming School Reform*, Stoke on Trent: Trentham Books.

Barnes, D. (2008) 'Exploratory Talk for Learning', in N. Mercer and S. Hodgkinson (eds.), *Exploring Talk in School*, London: Sage.

Davidson, G. (2006) 'Start at the beginning', *Teaching Geography*, 31 (3), 105–108.

Davidson, G. (2009) GTIP *Think Piece – Geographical Enquiry*, Available from: http://geography.org.uk/gtip/thinkpieces/geographicalenquiry [Accessed 8 September 2011].

Department for Education (DfE) (2010) *The Importance of Teaching: Schools White Paper*, Available from: https://www.education.gov.uk/publications/standard/publicationdetail/page1/CM%207980 [Accessed 22 August 2011].

Department for Education (DfE) (2012) *2011 Performance Tables*, [online] Available from: http://www.education.gov.uk/performancetables/index.shtml [Accessed 22 February 2012].

Department for Education and Skills (DfES) (2007) *Pedagogy and Personalisation*, Available from: http://www.teachfind.com/national-strategies/pedagogy-and-personalisation [Accessed 20 August 2011].

Edexcel (2008a) *Specification. Edexcel GCSE in Geography A (2GAO1) Issue 2*, Available from: http://www.edexcel.com/migrationdocuments/GCSE%20New%20GCSE/GCSE%20in%20Geography%20A%20spec%20issue%202%2020160112.pdf [Accessed 20 February 2012].

Edexcel (2008b) *Specification. Edexcel GCSE in Geography B (2GBO1) Issue 2*, Available from: http://www.edexcel.com/migrationdocuments/GCSE%20New%20GCSE/GCSE%20in%20Geography%20B%20spec%20issue%202%2020160112.pdf [Accessed 20 February 2012].

Freeman, D. (2010) 'Engaging with Theory', in C. Brooks (ed.), *Studying PGCE Geography at M Level*, London: Routledge.

General Teaching Council for England (GTCE) (2011) *Teaching quality: Policy Papers, Paper 7*, 88-97. reference: P-TQLP-0711 Available from: http://gtce.org.uk/documents/publicationpdfs/teach_quality7_ped0711.pdf [Accessed 20 August 2011].

Geographical Association (2009) *A Different View: A manifesto from the Geographical Association*, Sheffield: Geographical Association.

Geographical Association (2011) *Curriculum Proposals and Rationale*, Available from: http://www.geography.org.uk/download/GA_GIGCCCurriculumProposals.pdf [Accessed 20 August 2011].

Jackson, P. (2006) 'Thinking Geographically', *Geography*, 91 (3), 199–204.

Lambert, D. (2008) 'Why are School Subjects important?', *Forum*, 50 (2), 207–13.

Moore, A. (2000) Teaching and Learning: Pedagogy, Curriculum and Culture, London: RoutledgeFalmer.

Naish, M., Rawling, E. and Hart, C. (1987) *Geography 16–19: The contribution of a curriculum project to 16–19 education*, London: Longman.

Ofsted (2008) *Geography in Schools: Changing Practice*, London: Ofsted, Available from: http://www.ofsted.gov.uk/resources/geography-schools-changing-practice [Accessed 12 August 2011].

Ofsted (2011) *Geography: Learning to make a world of difference*, London: Ofsted, Available from: http://www.ofsted.gov.uk/resources/geography-learning-make-world-of-difference [Accessed 12 August 2011].

QCA (2007) Geography National Curriculum [online] Available from http://curriculum.qcda.gov.uk/key-stages-3-and-4/subjects/key-stage-3/geography/index.aspx [Accessed 12 September 2011].

Rawling, E. (2001) *Changing the Subject: The impact of national policy on school geography 1980–2000*, Sheffield: Geographical Association.

Rawling, E. (2007) *Planning your Key Stage 3 geography curriculum*, Sheffield: Geographical Association.

Roberts, M. (1998) 'The nature of geographical enquiry at key stage 3', *Teaching Geography*, 23 (4), 164–7.

Roberts, M. (2003) *Learning through Enquiry*, Sheffield: Geographical Association.

Roberts, M. (2010) 'Where's the Geography? Reflections on being an external examiner', *Teaching Geography*, 35 (3), 112–13.

Roberts, M. (2011) *What makes a geography lesson good?* Available from: http://www.geography.org.uk/download/GA_PRMGHWhatMakesAGeographyLessonGood.pdf [Accessed 12 March 2012].

Chapter 8

What is personalised learning in geography?

Mark Jones

Personalised learning would provide children with a greater repertoire of scripts for how their education could unfold. At the core would still be a common script – the basic curriculum – but that script could branch out in many different ways, to have many different styles and endings.

(Leadbeater, 2004a, p. 68)

Introduction

This chapter begins by tracing the emergence and conceptualisation of personalised learning in UK educational discourse. For Charles Leadbeater (2008) personalised learning, with its emphasis on student choice and voice, offers an alternative to the rigidity of schools where restrictive organisation, curriculum and pedagogy is representative of an outdated 'one size fits all' education system. While personalised learning may appeal as more befitting of 21st-century education, it is, however, a contested concept and, as will be seen, has varying interpretation in practice including association with differentiation, Assessment for Learning and an expansive range of teaching and learning considerations.

In the opening quotation, Leadbeater (2004a) emphasises personalised learning's potential for increased choice in what students learn, how they approach learning and where and when learning occurs. However, it is *voice* that potentially provides students with more say in their experience of school and schooling. Where students are provided with opportunities to operate as 'co-author[s] of the script' (Leadbeater, 2004b, p. 16), then this more 'radical collegiality' (Fielding, 2004) challenges the traditional roles of students and teachers. In the second part of this chapter we explore the transformative potential of personalising learning in geography through teachers and students co-constructing learning and 'curriculum making'. However, opportunities for these deep forms of personalising learning are not without their dilemmas and are further challenged by the Coalition's renewed emphasis on 'core knowledge' and 'teaching' as described in the White Paper *The Importance of Teaching* (DfE, 2010).

CAN WE DEFINE PERSONALISATION AND PERSONALISED LEARNING?

An important role of the geography teacher is to make the curriculum exciting, engaging and translate it into 'meaningful educational encounters' (Lambert and Morgan, 2010, p. 52). This process, however, does not occur in a vacuum, since teachers work within the policies, procedures and *politics* of schools as well as responding to what seems to be constantly changing national priorities. One priority, that of personalisation, was originally conceptualised as part of a philosophical reform and policy agenda which lay at the heart of New Labour's plans for transformation of public services, e.g. health, adult social care and children's services. Personalisation promised to give choice and voice to people by placing them at the heart of public services (DfES, 2004a). Whilst already acknowledging the concept's ambiguity, Leadbeater (2004b) characterised personalisation as having a number of levels moving from 'shallow personalisation' (giving people more say in public service interfaces, pathways and spending) to 'deep personalisation' (public involvement in the design and delivery of the services themselves). Education quickly became subsumed within this reform agenda, with the term 'personalised learning' becoming common in UK educational discourse in the early 2000s.

The concept of personalised learning appeared in New Labour ministerial speeches and policy from 2003 (see Miliband, 2003). Tony Blair, at the 2003 Labour Party Conference, declared education as the party's number one priority, announcing at secondary level the provision of 'personalised learning for every child in new specialist schools and City Academies'. David Miliband (2004a), the then School Standards Minister, explained that personalised learning was to be the defining feature of New Labour's education system and was to cover every aspect of teaching. However, ministerial speeches, at the time, clarified what it was not, rather than what it was. 'It is not individualised learning where pupils sit alone at a computer. Nor is it pupils left to their own devices' (p. 3). Against a backdrop of centralised initiatives, Miliband asserted that personalised learning should not be imposed from above but developed school by school, taking account of individual context and 'building the organisation of schooling around the needs, interest and aptitudes of individual pupils' (p. 3). Declared as '*the* debate in education' (Miliband, 2004b, p. 24 original emphasis), personalised learning was to become one of the most debated and contested concepts in education during the early 2000s. Arguably, the 2010 White Paper signals a conscious change at the policy level as we shall see later, but ideas of choice, voice and the individual are of course deeply rooted in western capitalist thought and are unlikely to go away.

Personalised learning had multiple meanings and was open to interpretation. For the Labour Government, it was an educational aspiration reflecting moral purpose in pursuit of reducing educational inequality. The DfES wanted to make best practice in schools universal across the state education system in order to

reduce the achievement gap between different groups of young people; it was 'a big idea for education' (Pollard and James, 2004). However, Johnson (2004) suggests it was simply 'a development of the standards agenda' (p. 4), supporting the government's pursuit of maximising students' attainment by paying attention to individuals. Meanwhile, Leadbeater promoted it as a 'powerful solution' (2004b), one which would fix the current education system. For Stephen Ball, such a policy provided evidence of the 'further decomposition of a common and universal system of education' (2008, p. 132). While debate continued at policy level and in academic arenas, one aspect was clear; New Labour's grand ambition would require further conceptual and practical clarification if there was to be a smooth transition from policy to practice.

PERSONALISED LEARNING: AMBITION AND AMBIGUITIES

A number of ambiguities surround both the theory and practice of personalised learning (Campbell et al., 2007). First, it is not a new idea, a point that is acknowledged in the publication, *A National Conversation on Personalised Learning* (DfES, 2004a), as it clearly supports previous governmental emphasis on the need to educate in ways that suit young people (DfES, 2001). According to the DfES (2004a), personalised learning translates into five key components: assessment for learning; effective teaching and learning strategies; curriculum entitlement and choice; a student-centred approach to school organisation; and strong partnership beyond the school. Pollard and James (2004) noted that these components projected an extensive 'but loosely defined range of policies and practice' (p. 4). The principle of personalisation was strongly supported through *Every Child Matters* (DfES, 2004b) and the White Paper (DfES, 2005), which devoted a whole chapter to it, although narrowing the focus to a commitment to providing extra support and tuition for children with particular needs, e.g. Special Educational Needs; Gifted and Talented; and those falling behind in English or mathematics. Thus, despite considerable policy support, the concept remained poorly defined and underdeveloped, accounting for what Pykett (2010) has called its 'amorphous and vague reputation' (p. 3).

One reason for this was that despite its beguiling commonsense appeal, personalised learning lacked underpinning from academic research (Johnson, 2004; Campbell et al., 2007). In terms of policy consistency or authenticity, while the official language increasingly emphasised 'learners', this contrasted with initiatives focusing on centralised teaching approaches endorsed by the National Strategies. Pollard and James (2004) warned of the potential to lose sight of the focus on learners and learning by more restricted interpretations based on 'teaching provision and associated systems' (p. 5). In his paper, *Personalised learning – an emperor's outfit?* Johnson (2004) critiqued DfES rhetoric, noting the lack of clarity concerning definition and purpose, suggesting that it really provided little more than a 'box' for all the good practice already in existence in many schools.

For Hartley (2006) it represented a form of 'personalised standardisation: a personalised pick and mix of pedagogy and curriculum' (p. 13) merely to offer some surface variety to the approved standard menu. The origins lay less in educational theory and more in contemporary marketing theory (Hartley, 2009). If personalised learning were merely a packaging of particular pedagogical approaches (Burton, 2007), this would account for the varying interpretation seen in schools (Sebba et al., 2007).

Whilst many agreed on personalised learning's lack of clarity (Hopkins, 2006; Hartley, 2008), this vagueness provided an opportunity to develop the concept further. David Hargreaves adopted a distributed approach working with head teachers to produce six pamphlets (Hargreaves, 2004a; 2004b; 2005a–2005c; 2006a), claiming to give the concept substance through nine themes or 'gateways' (see Table 8.1). Assessment for Learning (AfL) was identified by many as the most developed aspect in their schools (Hargreaves, 2006a) and it quickly became a key feature of personalised learning (NCSL, 2008). For Hargreaves (2004a) the gateways represent routeways away from a 19th-century 'educational imaginary' towards a more transformative 21st-century vision of education summaried into four 'Deeps': deep learning; deep support; deep experience; and deep leadership (Hargreaves, 2006b). Hargreaves' focus on the 'Deeps' went far beyond early government conceptions of personalised learning with his work ultimately advocating complete system redesign with its reconfigurations of institution, leadership and role (see Hargreaves, 2008).

An independent review of teaching and learning, chaired by former Chief HMI for England, Christine Gilbert, presented a summary of the existing situation in schools and a vision of how personalised learning could become a reality in every classroom by 2020 (Gilbert et al., 2006). This interpretation concluded that personalised learning was strongly connected with developing a shared understanding of pedagogy, although the recommended model was so wide-ranging it could be 'interpreted as almost anything and everything in the school system' (Campbell et al., 2007, pp. 144–5). Further publications included *Pedagogy and Personalisation* (DfES, 2007) and *Personalised Learning: A Practical Guide* (DCSF, 2008). In the latter, nine features of the pedagogy of personalisation were identified and accompanied by practical guidance. The promise of personalised learning as a deep culture shift had been reduced to a standardised checklist for schools to audit themselves against, stripping away any 'radical democratic potential' (Williamson and Morgan, 2009, p. 290). Sebba et al. (2007) reported that a lack of clarity among school leaders and teachers was still widespread. Further discontinuity in practice was found amongst managers, teachers and learners (Courcier, 2007; Underwood and Banyard, 2008). Furthermore, in government policy and exemplification documents there was little emphasis on Leadbeater's (2004a) deep personalisation in which user voice was central; the learner as a 'co-author of the script' was silent. This is not uncommon since Stephen Ball (2008) in his discussion of education policy models and public service reform reminds us that student voice often resides 'at the very margins of policy' (p. 132).

Table 8.1 Conceptions of personalised learning

Five Key Components (DfES, 2004a)	Nine gateways (Hargreaves, 2004a) Four Deeps (Hargreaves, 2006)	Nine features of Pedagogy of personalisation (DCSF, 2008)
1. Assessment for learning	1. Assessment for learning (DL)	1. High-quality teaching and learning
2. Effective teaching and learning strategies	2. Student voice (DL)	2. Target setting and tracking
	3. Learning to learn (DL)	
	4. Curriculum (DE)	3. Focused assessment
3. Curriculum entitlement and choice	5. New Technologies (DE)	4. Intervention
	6. Mentoring and coaching (DS)	5. Pupil grouping
	7. Advice and guidance (DS)	6. The learning environment.
4. A student centred approach to school organisation	8. Design and organisation (DLe)	
	9. Workforce reform (DLe)	7. Curriculum organisation.
5. Strong Partnership Beyond the School	DL Deep Learning	8. The extended curriculum.
	DE Deep Experience	
	DS Deep Support	9. Supporting children's wider needs.
	DLe Deep Leadership	

During the period 2003–9, geography teachers may have had variable engagement with the debates surrounding personalised learning since it may have been subsumed within the numerous centrally driven initiatives that beset schools during the 2000s.[1] Before exploring personalised learning in a geography-specific context, it is worth pausing to consider the emphasis placed on different aspects of teaching and learning in particular representations of personalised learning and some of the issues raised in this section. This has been summarised in Table 8.1.

PERSONALISED LEARNING IN GEOGRAPHY

This section moves us from a system level (a policy and whole school focus) towards the level of classroom practice. Teachers, naturally, try to make sense of ideological or policy shifts in the context of often habitual practices. Thus, for some geography teachers, personalised learning is synonymous with or at least associated with differentiation, a term that took hold in schools following the introduction of GCSE in the mid 1980s. Indeed, Burton (2007) has argued that personalised learning's 'pedagogical and political roots' are located in the concept of differentiation (p. 14). This close association reflects New Labour's educational philosophy of making the basic curriculum accessible to all through meeting individual needs and, as we have seen, the 2010 Coalition Government appears to have taken exception to this. Even though differentiation and personalised learning have not been presented as the same in practice (Burton, 2007, p. 14), later publications reinforce differentiation as fundamental to the success of personalised learning (see DCSF, 2008). A helpful summary of practical advice

and considerations influencing successful differentiation is provided by Lambert and Balderstone (2010, pp. 205–6). However, with the exact relationship somewhat complicated and potentially blurred, Courcier (2007) has reported confusion among teachers concerning the differences between 'differentiation' and 'personalised learning'.

A persistent question that arises concerning differentiation, specifically because of its concern for the individual is: *who to differentiate for?* Is it all students or just those with *identified* learning needs? The orthodoxy seems to be that any interventions should 'make a difference for all pupils' (Lambert and Balderstone, 2010, p. 205) and, as Battersby (2002) reminds us, differentiation should occur at the planning stage in all classrooms and for all pupils. This is a fine aspiration but difficult to achieve with integrity. Ofsted has reported that differentiation in geography lessons still needs to improve as 'too often, teaching is directed at pupils of average ability' (2008, para 42), teaching to the majority of students with little deviation from a single script. However, where teachers meet the needs of particular groups of students, Sebba et al. (2007) have equally identified concerns over teachers' lack of engagement with *invisible* middle-ability students.

In broad terms, there are two approaches to differentiation: by task[2] or by outcome. Whichever approach is utilised, if differentiation simply means engaging students and then monitoring their progress, it inevitably results in accepting different levels of attainment. This fuels the current vogue for 'differentiated learning objectives', where objectives with tripartite stems such as *All, Most, Some* or *Must, Should, Could* can place artificial ceilings on students' attainment. While well intentioned as tools to support students making *measurable* learning gains in lessons (and signalling progression to Ofsted), such differentiated objectives (often imbued with levels and sublevels) may be misdirected, bound up with what Lambert (2010) has called the 'AfL paraphernalia' – that is, bureaucratic systems to demonstrate compliance with AfL policies but which, literally, get in the way of planning and teaching motivating worthwhile geography. Burton (2007) reminds us that whilst theory and ideas concerning learning develop, educators should 'resist reductionist attempts to produce neat, digestible, commercialised chunks of pedagogy' (p. 16). Therefore, whichever approaches to differentiation are utilised in the geography classroom, teachers need to have sound pedagogic reasoning for their inclusion and constantly review their effectiveness through conversations with colleagues and with students.

If differentiation dominated educational discourse in the 1990s then personalised learning, particularly through the visible form of AfL, has dominated the 2000s. But if AfL is, as recently announced in the educational press, 'here to stay' (Lucey, 2011, p. 4) then it may need to adjust to new policy and mood music. While original work on formative assessment produced evidence of subsequent improvement by two GCSE grades (Black and Wiliam, 1998) and improved attainment in the core subjects at KS3 (Black et al., 2003), this effectiveness can be lost in superficial representation of AfL in many classrooms. Recently, Lambert (2010) has warned how the principles of formative assessment may have been 'lost in translation' (p. 1). In geography, Ofsted (2011) has reported that

AfL has had a limited impact on improving teaching and learning ... what schools needed to focus on was how best to ensure that the students actually made progress ....

(para. 58)

In moving beyond superficial understanding of AfL, Pollard and James (2004) have argued that teachers use of AfL requires 'deeper changes in practices and relationships' (p. 6). For deep changes to occur this presents considerable challenges for teachers operating within mandated national agendas and restrictive school policies, often-reinforcing formulaic lesson beginnings and endings (see Roberts, 2010). Familiarity with differentiation and AfL is therefore only the beginning of understanding personalised learning in geography, since sharing differentiated objectives at the start of a lesson or AfL through modelling, questioning or peer-assessment may merely represent what Hartley (2006) calls 'personalised standardisation'.

PERSONALISING GEOGRAPHY IN SCHOOLS

Differentiation can equally be about students' interests as well as needs (DCSF, 2008). Connecting with students' everyday lives and interests or 'living geography' (Mitchell, 2007) presents opportunities for personalising learning through increased student choice and voice. Hargreaves' (2005b) preference for 'personalising learning' over 'personalised learning' reinforces its dynamism as an ongoing process rather than an end product. What this opens up, as the Geographical Association has tried to show in its consultation report (GA, 2011), is the need to distinguish pedagogy from curriculum. In this section, I shall briefly explore some approaches to personalising geography in secondary schools, mindful of the Young People's Geographies Project (Biddulph, 2011a) finding that although pedagogically more voice and choice are productive, students do not see themselves as curriculum makers: this is primarily teachers' work.

Personalising learning in geography is a collective act in which group dynamics and the social construction of meaning between teachers and students are central to unlocking young people's interests. Leadbeater's (2004a) aspiration of teachers and young people collaborating as co-constructors of learning is consistent with more radical forms of student voice (see Fielding, 2004) and the upper rungs of Roger Hart's (1992) ladder of participation. Where student voice activities involve *students as co-researchers* and have a pedagogic or curriculum focus, these occur often as projects between universities and schools (e.g. Kellett, 2005; Ruddock et al., 2006; Morgan, 2011). *Genuine* student voice was key to successful examples of personalised learning in the case study schools researched by Sebba et al. (2007). Whilst, in some areas, the voice of students in curriculum making has been mostly silent and generally marginalised (Brooker and Macdonald, 1999), research in geography has problematised aspects of 'student voice' and 'curriculum making'. Two projects funded by the Action Plan for Geography are particularly valuable here: 'Young People's Geographies' (YPG)[3]

and 'Making Geography Happen' (MGH).[4] YPG brought together young people, geography teachers and academics for a geography 'curriculum-making' project (see Firth and Biddulph, 2009; Biddulph, 2011a). Through respectful 'conversations' and inclusive pedagogies students co-constructed a range of geographical experiences for their school curriculum, from exploring feelings about different local places to scenarios such as 'What if gas was cut off tomorrow?' Through using dialogic pedagogies, outcomes included increased student enthusiasm and motivation. However, the YPG also showed up dilemmas relating to curriculum, and in particular the teachers' and students' roles in its formation (see Biddulph, 2011b, pp. 395–6).

For many geography teachers not involved in funded projects or research, opportunities for co-construction in curriculum making in any case may appear somewhat limited, due to the high stakes accountability context of their work. Underwood and Banyard (2008) found secondary pupils perceived that personalisation declines over time in school. The accountability agenda and preparing students for high stakes examinations can render student choice as somewhat artificial, confined to choice of data-collection techniques within controlled assessment or case study selection for examinations. With emphasis on content coverage and 'teaching to the test', any *real* choice for students can disappear altogether after Key Stage 3 (KS3). A lack of real choice can exist where teachers utilise the approaches and case studies as presented by Awarding Body core texts, training and examinations. This narrowing of opportunity provides some evidence for Lambert's (2010) question as to whether a gap has opened up between geography as experienced at KS3 and as expressed in Awarding Body specifications. However, despite the pressure to perform, opportunities can exist for negotiated decision-making when selecting new specifications and within specifications on what optional modules to study (see Morgan, 2010; Jones, 2011), particularly as Ferretti (2007) reminds us that teachers' perceptions of what makes for engaging geography may differ from students' views. Where teachers are adventurous and able to deviate from annual recycling or tweaking of 'old favourites', this can create the potential for co-construction of new schemes of work.

KS3 provides most opportunity for increased student choice and voice in geography. In Figure 8.1, I offer a number of aspects that geography teachers may consider when making decisions concerning possibilities for co-construction in the curriculum-making process at KS3.

Flexibility within the KS3 geography curriculum (QCA, 2007) means that teachers working in more dialogic classrooms, where conversations are valued, may offer students choices in topic (curriculum), approach (pedagogy) and outcome (assessment) although there may be significant variation in what represents choice. Opportunities exist for student choice within project-based learning and through enquiry, although the latter may vary from tightly controlled teacher-led to more flexible and dynamic student-led enquiry (Roberts, 2003). *Restricted* choice is where a teacher decides the overall theme and students have options within, for example, giving students' choice over which country to study in a project on 'development'. Within an established 'geography of sport' unit, Berry

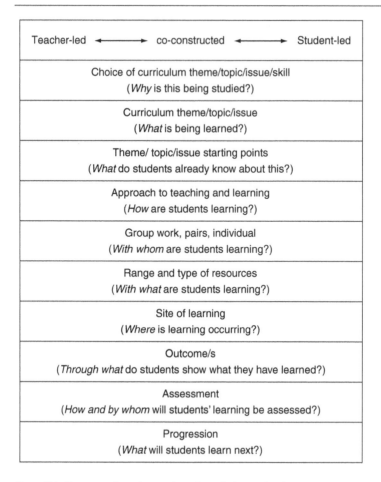

Figure 8.1 Degrees of teacher and student choice and voice.

(2011) acknowledges that while allowing students choice over groups and out-comes, all students carried out the same enquiry on 'child labour', thus restrict-ing choice and allowing the teacher to maintain control. In the MGH project, one school provided Year 7 students with a choice of four different assessment approaches including making an artefact to show their understanding of a unit on Australia. With more *open* choice, Morgan (2010) permitted Year 8 students freedom of choice for planning lessons to be taught by teachers. The Year 8 stu-dents confidently created lessons covering super-volcanoes, endangered species and environmental impacts of music festivals. Students clearly valued the experi-ence and wanted more *negotiated* choice of topic and activities (Morgan, 2010) but respected the teacher's vital role in the curriculum-making process (Hopwood, 2007; Morgan, 2011). This is further supported by Campbell et al. (2007), who have identified important features of effective personalised pedagogy including

teachers' high level of subject expertise; and their control of the overall structure of the lesson; its 'pace, direction and transition' (p. 150).

Conclusion

The aspect of personalised learning emphasised in this chapter is that of increased student choice and voice through co-construction of the curriculum-making process. However, under the Coalition Government the somewhat prophetic headline 'Whatever happened to personalised learning?' (see Wilby, 2009) has renewed emphasis, with 'essential knowledge' and 'teaching', not learning, in the ascendancy. Whilst affording teachers 'renewed freedom and autonomy' (DfE, 2010, p. 10), the White Paper refers to too much non-essential knowledge and more emphasis on 'essential knowledge'.

New Labour's appetite for 'personalised learning' and the Coalition's thirst for 'essential knowledge' raise important questions for geography teachers. One concerns the origins and practicalities of government policy. What informs policy and how policy translates into practice should demand teachers' attention since policies may be underpinned, partly by theory and research but more significantly by government ideology. At the time of writing, this is represented by the Coalition's focus on 'core' knowledge, an emphasis on teaching over learning and the importance of particular 'academic' subjects in the English Baccalaureate. Geography teachers therefore will need to be attentive to how, once the geography curriculum is rewritten and presented, they can continue to enact their pivotal role as 'curriculum makers'.

Within this curriculum-making process, a second question concerns the extent to which teachers will feel able to provide opportunities for student choice and voice. Sebba et al. (2007) reported that schools where personalised learning is a perceived strength see 'learners as co-investors in education' (p. 72); however, opportunities for co-construction may be further challenged by the Coalition's focus on 'core' and 'essential' knowledge – knowledge that is 'adult prescribed'. This potentially restricts space for more creative conversations between geography teachers and their students on what essential knowledge in geography might look like.

Whether the vogue is for 'personalised learning' or 'teaching essential knowledge', it is only where geography teachers take account of their students' motivations, preferences and interests that policy can translate into educational encounters which have shared meaning, significance and relevance.

Notes

1 Ofsted's review of the National Strategies reported as many as 111 separate programmes in secondary schools (Ofsted, 2010).
2 'Task' here is used as an umbrella term to include the activities, resources, grouping and support.
3 YPG (2006–11) has been promoted to the wider geography community through the YPG website (launched 2008); the Summer 2010 edition of *Teaching Geography*,

which focused entirely on young people's geographies and the projects page of the GA website.

4   MGH (2009–11), see the projects page of the GA website and Paul Weeden's chapter in this volume.

Key readings

1. Biddulph, M. (2011) 'Young People's Geographies: Implications for Secondary School Geography', in G. Butt (ed.), *Geography, Education and the Future*. Using the metaphor of *conversations*, Mary Biddulph's chapter provides a valuable insight for teachers wanting to collaborate with students in the curriculum-making process.
2. Firth, R. and Biddulph, M. (2009) 'Whose life is it anyway? Young people's geographies', in D. Mitchell (ed.), *Living Geography*, London: Chris Kington Publishing, a useful highlighting of academic geography's engagement with young people's lives and explanation of the YPG approach.

References

Ball, S. (2008) *The Education Debate*, Bristol: The Policy Press.

Battersby, J. (2002) 'Differentiation in teaching and learning Geography', in M. Smith (ed.), *Teaching Geography in Secondary School*, London: RoutledgeFalmer.

Berry, S. (2011) 'What are the barriers to achievement for Year 9 boys within geography and how can the classroom teacher begin to narrow the gap?' Unpublished dissertation, University of the West of England, Bristol.

Biddulph, M. (2011a) 'Young People's Geographies: Implications for Secondary School Geography', in G. Butt (ed.), *Geography. Education and the Future*, London: Continuum.

Biddulph, M. (2011b) 'Articulating student voice and facilitating curriculum agency', *The Curriculum Journal*, 22 (3), 381–99.

Black, P. and Wiliam, D. (1998) *Inside the Black Box: Raising Standards through Classroom Assessment*, London: King's College.

Black, P., Harrison, C., Lee, C., Marshall, B. and Wiliam, D. (2003) *Assessment for Learning: Putting it into practice*, Maidenhead: Open University Press.

Brooker, R. and Macdonald, D. (1999) 'Did we hear you: Issues of student voice in a curriculum innovation', *Journal of Curriculum Studies*, 31 (1), 83–97.

Burton, D. (2007) 'Psycho-pedagogy and Personalised Learning', *Journal of Education for Teaching*, 33 (1), 5–17.

Campbell, R., Robinson, W., Neelands, J., Hewston, R. and Mazzoli, L. (2007) 'Personalised Learning: Ambiguities in theory and practice', *British Journal of Educational Studies*, 55 (2), 135–54.

Courcier, I. (2007) 'Teachers' Perceptions of Personalised Learning'. *Evaluation and Research in Teacher Education*, 20 (2), 59–80.

Department for Children, Schools and Families (DCSF) (2008) *Personalised Learning: A Practical Guide*, Nottingham: DCSF publications.

Department for Education (DfE) (2010) *The Importance of Teaching: the Schools White Paper*, London: The Stationery Office.

Department for Education and Skills (DfES) (2001) *Schools Achieving Success*, Norwich: The Stationery Office.

Department for Education and Skills (DfES) (2004a) *A National Conversation about Personalised Learning*, Nottingham: DfES publications.

Department for Education and Skills (DfES) (2004b) *Every Child Matters: Change for Children in Schools*, Nottingham: DfES publications.

Department for Education and Skills (DfES) (2005) *Higher Standards, Better Schools for All*, London: DfES publications.

Department for Education and Skills (DfES) (2007) *Pedagogy and Personalisation*, Nottingham: DfES publications.

Ferretti, J. (2007) 'Education Matters: What Influnces Students to Choose Geography at A' level', *Geography*, 92 (2), 137–47.

Fielding, M. (2004) 'Transformative Approaches to Student Voice: Theoretical Underpinnings, Recalcitrant Realities', *British Educational Research Journal*, 30, 295–311.

Firth, R. and Biddulph, M. (2009) 'Whose life is it anyway? Young People's Geographies', in D. Mitchell (ed.), *Living Geography: Exciting futures for teachers and students*, Cambridge: Chris Kington Publishing,

Geographical Association (2011) *Curriculum Consultation Full Report* [online] Available from: http://www.geography.org.uk/getinvolved/geographycurriculumconsultation/ [Accessed 11 December 2011].

Gilbert, C., August, K., Brooks, R., Hancock, D., Hargreaves, D. and Pearce, N. (2006) *2020 vision: Report of the Teaching and Learning by 2020 Review Group*, Nottingham: DfES publications.

Hargreaves, D. (2004a) *Personalising Learning 1: next steps in working laterally*, London: Specialist Schools Trust.

Hargreaves, D. (2004b) *Personalising Learning 2: student voice and assessment for learning*, London: Specialist Schools Trust.

Hargreaves, D. (2005a) *Personalising Learning 3: learning to learn and the new technologies*, London: Specialist Schools Trust.

Hargreaves, D. (2005b) *Personalising Learning 4. curriculum and advice & guidance*, London: Specialist Schools Trust.

Hargreaves, D. (2005c) *Personalising Learning 5: mentoring and coaching workforce development*, London: Specialist Schools Trust.

Hargreaves, D. (2006a) *Personalising Learning 6: the final gateway school design and organisation*, London: Specialist Schools Trust.

Hargreaves, D. (2006b) *A new shape for schooling*, London: Specialist Schools and Academies Trust.

Hargreaves, D. (2008) *Leading System Redesign-1*, London: Specialist Schools and Academies Trust.

Hart, R. (1992) *Children's participation: From tokenism to citizenship*, Innocenti, Essays 4, Florence: UNICEF. Available from: http://www.unicefirc.org/publications/pdf/childrens_participation.pdf [Accessed 25 August 2011].

Hartley, D. (2006) 'Excellence and Enjoyment: The logic of a 'contradiction', *British Journal of Educational Studies*, 54 (1), 3–14.

Hartley, D. (2008) 'Education markets and the pedagogy of personalisation' *British Journal of Educational Studies*, 56 (4), 365–81.

Hartley, D. (2009) 'Personalisation: The nostalgic revival of child-centred education? *Journal of Educational Policy*, 24 (4), 423–34.

Hopkins, D. (2006) 'Introduction', in OECD/CERI (2006) *Schooling for Tomorrow. Personalising Education*, Paris: OECD Publishing.

Hopwood, N. (2007) *Young People's Geography Evaluation Report*. Available from: http://www.youngpeoplesgeographies.co.uk/about-ypg/evaluation-reports/ [Accessed 12 July 2011].

Johnson, M. (2004) *Personalised learning: an Emperor's Outfit?* London: Institute for Public Policy Research.

Jones, M. (2011) *Making geography personal*, Geographical Association Annual Conference, University of Surrey. 14–17 April 2011.

Kellett, M. (2005) *Children as active researchers; a new research paradigm for the 21st Century*, UK: ESRC.

Lambert, D. (2010) *Issues in Geography Education No.8 Progression*. [online] Available from http://www.geography.org.uk/download/GA_PRMGHProgressionThinkPiece.pdf [Accessed 12 September 2011].

Lambert, D. and Balderstone, D. (2010) *Learning to Teach Geography in the Secondary School*, 2nd edn, Abingdon: Routledge.

Lambert, D. and Morgan, J. (2010) *Teaching Geography 11–18: A Conceptual Approach*, Maidenhead: Open University Press.

Leadbeater, C. (2004a) *Personalisation through participation: A new script for public services*, London: DEMOS.

Leadbeater, C. (2004b) *Learning about Personalisation: How can we put the learner at the heart of the education system*, London: DfES/ NCSL.

Leadbeater, C. (2008) *We-think; Mass Innovation not Mass Production*, London: Profile.

Lucey, C. (2011) 'Why AfL is not a passing fad', *Tespro*, 16 September, 4–7.

Miliband, D. (2003) 'Opportunity for all: Targeting disadvantage through personalised learning', in *New Economy*, 10 (4), 224–9.

Miliband, D. (2004a) *Personalised Learning: Building a New Relationship with Schools*, North of England Education Conference, Belfast, 8 January, 2004.

Miliband, D. (2004b) *Choice and voice in personalised learning*. DfES Innovation Unit/ DEMOS/OECD conference: *Personalising Education: the future of public sector reform*, London, 18 May 2004.

Mitchell, D. (ed.) (2007) *Living Geography: Exciting futures for teachers and students*, Cambridge: Chris Kington Publishing.

Morgan, L. (2010) 'Young People's voice in Geography today: to what extent can they be heard in curriculum development?' Unpublished dissertation. University of the West of England, Bristol.

Morgan, L. (2011) Research Paper: How far can young people's voices be heard in geography today? Geographical Association Annual Conference University of Surrey, 14–17 April, 2011.

National College for School Leadership (NCSL) (2008) *Leading personalising learning national survey*, Available from: www.nationalcollege.org.uk/index/leadershiplibrary/leadingschools/personalisedlearning/leading-personalised-learning-survey. [Accessed 10 August 2011].

Ofsted (2008) *Geography in Schools: Changing Practice*, London: Ofsted, Available from: http://www.ofsted.gov.uk/resources/geography-schools-changing-practice [Accessed 12 August 2011].

Ofsted (2010) *The National Strategies: a review of impact*, London: Ofsted, Available from: http://www.ofsted.gov.uk/node/2416 [Accessed 18 August 2011].

Ofsted (2011) *Geography: Learning to make a world of difference*, London: Ofsted. Available from: http://www.ofsted.gov.uk/resources/geography-learning-make-world-of-difference [Accessed 15 August 2011].

Pollard, A. and James, M. (eds.) (2004) *Personalised Learning: A commentary by the Teaching and Learning Research Programme*, London: Economic and Social Research Council/TLRP.

Pykett, J. (2010) 'Personalised governing through behaviour and re-education', 60th Political Studies Association Conference, Edinburgh, 29 March to 1 April 2010.

QCA (2007) Geography National Curriculum [online] Available from: http://curriculum. qcda.gov.uk/key-stages-3-and-4/subjects/key-stage-3/geography/index.aspx [Accessed 12 September 2011].

Roberts, M. (2003) *Learning Through Enquiry*, Sheffield: Geographical Association.

Roberts, M. (2010) 'Where's the geography? Reflections on being an external examiner', *Teaching Geography*, 35 (3), 112–13.

Ruddock, J., Brown, B. and Hendy, L. (2006) *Personalised Learning and Pupil Voice: The East Sussex Project*, Nottingham: DfES publications.

Sebba, J., Brown, N., Steward, S., Galton, M. and James, M. (2007) *An Investigation of Personalised Learning Approaches used by Schools*, Nottingham: DfES Publications.

Underwood, J. and Banyard, T.S. (2008) 'Managers', teachers' and learners' perceptions of personalised learning: Evidence from Impact 2007', *Technology, Pedagogy and Education*, 17 (3), 233–46.

Wilby, P. (2009) 'Intellectual guru seeks "system redesign" of secondary education', *The Guardian: Education Guardian section*, Tuesday 22 September 2009, p.1.

Williamson, B. and Morgan, J. (2009) 'Educational reform, enquiry based learning and the re-professionalisation of teachers', *Curriculum Journal*, 20 (3), 287–304.

Chapter 9

Where is the curriculum created?

Mary Biddulph

> What counts as an educated 19 year old in this day and age?
>
> (Pring et al., 2009, p. 3)

Introduction

The title of this chapter could be misleading. It is not about the technicalities of prescribing a geography curriculum nor to advocate particular planning frameworks: planning grids and structures or curriculum maps, etc. It is more to explore where the geography curriculum comes from and how it comes into being – what shapes and informs it. Exploring this question is important because whilst the ideas of a 'curriculum' may seem, on first encounter, relatively straightforward (a curriculum is what we teach in school isn't it?), when we try to define curriculum a little more precisely we soon find that this straightforward idea is less clear-cut than we think;. Closer inspection reveals that curriculum is in fact a highly contested concept, *because* what we think we should be teaching connects directly with what we think is the purpose of education in the first place:

> Is education primarily to serve the needs of society and economy (providing skilful and employable people for the world of work in the global market place), or is it mainly to provide worthwhile experiences and knowledge to help individuals 'live sanely in the world' ... Or has education to serve both these purposes and more besides?
>
> (Lambert, 2003, p. 159)

This chapter attempts to raise some important questions about the nature of the school curriculum, with a particular focus on school geography. It takes curriculum as a highly significant idea and discusses some of the key influences on how this idea has emerged and developed. It concludes with an exploration of some of the consequences of curriculum thinking for teachers and students studying geography.

THE MAKING OF THE GEOGRAPHY CURRICULUM:
AN HISTORICAL CONTEXT

John Kerr defined the curriculum as 'All the learning which is planned and guided by the school, whether it is carried on in groups or individually, inside or outside the school' (quoted in Kelly, 1983, p. 10). This is supported by Oates (2011), who distinguishes between 'the national curriculum' and 'the curriculum' arguing that

> The curriculum – taught and untaught – represents the totality of the experience of the child within schooling (aims, content, pedagogy, assessment). It includes unassessed and uncertificated elements – including opportunities to acquire vital 'personal' and 'social' capitals. A national curriculum cannot specify and control all elements of the 'real' curriculum – and will run into terrible difficulty if it attempts so to do.
>
> (p. 133)

Both constructions are explicit about the responsibility of schools and teachers in making the curriculum, drawing on formal and informal contexts in order to meet the needs of young people. The implication here is that that the curriculum is not a neutral entity; it is 'a human creation' serving a range of needs and purposes, reflecting and responding to changes in wider society (Morgan and Lambert, 2005, p. 25). This lack of neutrality in the curriculum is illustrated in the history of curriculum theory. At a societal level the late nineteenth – early twentieth century saw marked changes in working practices driven by rationalistic management ideals. The impact of these ideals on education was marked by the development of an objectives-led approach to curriculum planning advocated by North American curriculum theorists such as Franklin Bobbit, and later Ralph Tyler. The objectives-led model, described by Graves (1979) as a linear model of curriculum planning, presented education as the means by which to change behaviours. For Bobbit and others:

> The first task of the scientific curriculum maker is the discovery of those social deficiencies that result from a lack of historical, literary and geographical experiences. Each deficiency found is a call for direct training; it points to an objective that is to be set up for the conscious training.
>
> (Bobbit, quoted in Flinders and Thornton, 2004, p. 16)

The generation of lists of behavioural objectives, the achievement of which could then be measured by simple testing techniques (Smith, 2000, p. 5), became a means by which this perceived 'lack of historical, literary and geographical experiences' was to be rectified. Defined by Smith (2000) as 'curriculum as product', this objectives-led approach to curriculum design, that took form in North America, interpreted the curriculum-making process as an entirely technical-rational exercise.

The development of this rationalistic approach to curriculum planning is well documented in historical accounts of curriculum change in UK schools. In the context of school geography the ground-breaking work of Norman Graves in *Curriculum Planning in Geography* (1979) plus the work of others (Marsden, 1997, 2003; Naish, 1997; Rawling, 2001) all provide comprehensive accounts of geography curriculum changes in the twentieth century.

Whilst the rationalistic approach *per se* provides us with a sense of the hierarchical nature of the curriculum decision-making process at this time, with teachers being close to the bottom of this hierarchy, it is important to also consider the *content* of the school geography curriculum. Whereas curriculum design was influenced by changes taking place beyond the academy, the geography curriculum tended to be heavily influenced by university-level geography which in turn determined the content of examination syllabuses. Whilst this geography may have been mediated by teachers, in essence it passed into schools relatively uncontested, tending to represent authoritative knowledge for teachers to 'deliver'. The prevailing geographical paradigm of the day was regionalism, emphasising the differences between places and reinforcing notions of imperialism and colonialism. As Heffernan (2003) argues, for university geography 'the otherwise vague and underdeveloped idea of the region emerged as the single most important intellectual contribution of interwar geography' (p. 17). School geography drew on this paradigm and so comprised 'relatively unchanging features of physical geography, on a mainly static, deterministic view of human societies and racing through a regionally based coverage of world geography' (Rawling, 2001, p. 22). Characterised by a 'capes and bays' curriculum, school geography tended to be learned 'by rote' (Naish, 1997, p. 49). It is worth noting here that despite there being no national curriculum at this time pupils across the country were learning more or less the same geographical content (Rawling, 2001).

A turning point for education generally and school geography specifically was the establishment of the Schools Council in 1964. Universal education, the raising of the school-leaving age plus concurrent technological and social shifts in wider society necessitated a shift in the purpose of education, and in response to these shifts the curriculum also changed (see Lambert and Morgan's 2010 account of this – chapters 1 and 2). The Schools Council was responsible for curriculum and assessment developments, including supporting teachers in their newly emerging role as curriculum makers.

Curriculum planning and development in the 1970s and 1980s was characterised by notions of collaboration and cooperation – between teachers, schools, educational infrastructures (examination boards, professional development initiatives, etc.) and the academy. Eleanor Rawling (2008) provides clear and helpful distinctions between planning and development. Curriculum planning, she argues, comprises the 'organising and sorting of material' and curriculum development has more of a creative dimension to it, 'taking things beyond what is stated or provided'. Whilst such terms are often used interchangeably, it can be said that curriculum development involves planning but not all planning

involves wider curriculum development. Margaret Roberts (1997) develops these ideas when she states that both curriculum planning and development 'encompass the thinking and documentation that occurs before, during and after teaching and learning takes place' (p. 35).What she implies here is that the making of the curriculum is both an intellectual process and a practical product, and that the curriculum is in a constant state of review and change because of this. She argues, despite the curricula shifts and turns at a political and policy level, what goes into the curriculum is 'ultimately a matter of professional judgement' (1997, p. 35). Perhaps this is so but, to balance concerns about the possibilities of a somewhat permissive approach to curriculum development, it was the varying levels of cooperation and collaboration between interested parties that ensured that school geography was not underpinned by an 'anything goes' philosophy; the Schools Council provided frameworks that supported teachers' selection of both content to be taught and processes for learning. Before the 1988 Education Reform Act and the advent of the national curriculum in England and Wales, it was professional judgement in the absence of any statutory guidelines which produced a very localised process of planning and development; a state of affairs seen as problematic by the central government of the day.

The publication in 1991 of the first national curriculum for geography provided a radical shift in where the geography curriculum was made. The curricula freedoms, enjoyed under the guidance of the Schools Council projects, were lost and according to Rawling's authoritative account this marked the end of a golden age of curriculum *development* (Rawling, 2008). The curriculum became statutory and its implementation was shored up via a new school inspection regime (Education (Schools) Act 1992). A requirement of the inspection framework, criticised for being shaped around absolutist criteria (Richards, 1999), included reporting on schools' implementation of the national curriculum, thus suggesting a new 'regulated autonomy' for teachers:

> ... a view that teachers (and other professions) need to be subjected to the rigours of the market and/or greater control and surveillance on the part of the re-formed state.
>
> (Whitty, 2000, p. 283)

This 'regulated autonomy' has had significant implications for the geography curriculum ever since.

Whilst the initial premise of the new curriculum was to prescribe content to be taught, freeing teachers to decide on learning processes, in actuality the geography curriculum was so content heavy that teachers' roles changed considerably. For many the pressure was to 'deliver' the content knowledge and the '*curriculum as product model*', discussed by Smith (2000) and conceptualised by Bobbit and others, resurfaced (Rawling, 1996). For others, more confident in their capacities to reinterpret and make sense of the GNC, the new rules represented an opportunity to structure the requirements of the national curriculum in educationally more

valuable ways (see Roberts, 1997). Generally, however, teachers' professional judgement was no longer trusted and curriculum development, the intellectual process advocated by Roberts above, was, at least in relation to the curriculum, much more difficult to exercise. One consequence, arguably, was that the curriculum links between school and university geography were severed: at a time when university geography was taking a new turn to the left with developments in cultural geography (Jackson, 1989), school geography was being forced to turn to the right, driven by the ideologies of the New Right and a 'capes and bays' perception of the subject; the school geography curriculum became 'fossilised' in an outdated view of the discipline (Lambert, 2004).

Since 1991 the national curriculum has undergone several further revisions (DfE, 1995; DfEE/QCA, 1999; QCA, 2007). However, these revisions have been accused of 'keeping interest groups happy rather than developing well-theorised content' (Oates, 2010, p. 2). For school geography this meant that the national curriculum saw merely a *reduction* in what was to be taught rather than comprising any new interpretations of what actually constituted geography as a discipline. The 2007 revision was more radical, significantly loosening up the factual knowledge content to be taught, and framing the curriculum around seven 'key concepts'. Teachers were once again in a position to 'make' the curriculum for themselves, taking into account their students' views and their own geographical enthusiasms. In addition, the curriculum also comprised a series of cross-cutting themes such as 'cultural understanding and diversity', the claim being that these themes would enable greater curriculum flexibility and ensure students experienced some degree of curriculum coherence (Nightingale, 2007). This was a complex policy setting, in which teachers had to operate after many years during which 'curriculum thinking' had been severely eroded in the professional preparation of teachers. The Action Plan for Geography (GA and RGS-IBG, 2011) explicitly emphasised curriculum making, precisely because of the need to rediscover and encourage curriculum thinking in schools.

CURRICULUM MAKING: THE CURRENT CONTEXT

As we saw earlier, the term curriculum making has a historical context which is important to understand – we are where we are because of where we have been. However, at the end of the first decade of the twenty-first century, the idea of making the curriculum in school geography has acquired new significance. This is partly through the activities of the Action Plan for Geography (2006–11) and its attempts to encourage principled, localised curriculum thinking. Thus Brooks (2006) writes that

> 'curriculum-making' therefore reflects 'the curriculum which is experienced by students and made by teachers in school' (ibid). Although the localised curriculum is influenced by the macro-level curriculum design, the responsibility for ensuring that it is responsive to the local needs of the school and the

individual classes remains in the hands of the individual teacher. The concept of curriculum-making firmly places the ownership of the 'local' curriculum in the hands of each geography teacher.

(p. 77)

The Geographical Association (GA)'s 2009 *Manifesto* for school geography also presents curriculum making as an important professional activity. Here it is said metaphorically to draw from three separate sources of 'energy':

- The teachers' own practical skills and expertise: the craft teaching and pedagogic choice
- The interests and needs of students: getting to know students, what motivates them and how they learn
- The dynamic, changing subject discipline has to offer: drawing from the concepts and ideas in the discipline that help us understand aspects of the world (p. 27).

Lambert and Morgan (2010) present this idea in the form of a diagram (see below) where the three 'sources of energy' are presented as interacting with and mutually dependent on each other. The following discussion explores the role of each as a means of unravelling the complexity of relationships between teachers, students and the discipline in the curriculum-making process.

a. Teachers

The interaction between the teacher and the learner is dependent not only on subject knowledge and skills but it is also an expression of personal values and beliefs about teaching.

(Burgess, 2000, p. 416)

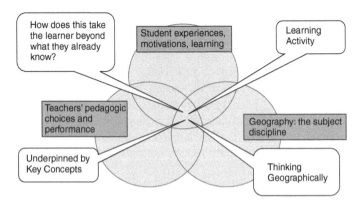

Figure 9.1 Curriculum making (see Lambert and Morgan 2010, p. 50; see also www.geography.org.uk/cpdevents/curriculummaking

In order to plan, develop and make a curriculum that meets the educational aims of a democratic society, the selection, ordering and interpretation of what young people learn is a tall order and carries with it enormous responsibility. Nonetheless, once a national curriculum has been constructed (with or without consultation with education professionals including teachers), it is still the case that any prescription still has to be interpreted and implemented by teachers and subsequently taught to students. Kelly (2009) describes the 'make or break role that teachers have in all curricular activities, even in relation to those which originate outside the school' (p. 13), a view supported by Pring (2011), who calls into question the much used 'delivery' metaphor when talking about teachers' work; teachers do not 'deliver' anything, and such an idea is, he argues, a significant distraction from what it really means to be a teacher.

In the context of school geography Lambert and Morgan (2010) develop this further when they suggest that 'the curriculum *as experienced* by children and young people is, at least in part, one that has been made by teachers. Teachers are the curriculum makers' (p. 49). Their argument runs that, in spite of prevailing political ideologies resulting in curriculum prescription, and in spite of the influences of accountability systems such as Ofsted, ultimately the curriculum comes *into being* in the day-to-day interactions between teachers, their students and the subject discipline, and it is impossible to have a living geography curriculum without this dynamic interaction. To a certain extent it is *because* of the centralisation and institutionalisation of curriculum decisions that teachers have a moral responsibility to re-present the *curriculum as given* in ways that bring meaning and critical insight to *their* students in *their* context; without this re-presentation young people will be learning inert, irrelevant content:

> Designing a curriculum is not just a technical matter, specifying objectives and a course of study to meet them. It is a moral concern and should reflect what we think we should be teaching.
>
> (Geographical Association, 2009, p. 27)

Such a notion of curriculum making is a radical and somewhat liberating departure from the objective-led planning approaches espoused by Bobbit, Tyler and others all those years ago, which still prevails today. Whilst Lambert and Morgan do not deny the significance of systematic curriculum planning and curriculum development (after all, decisions and choices about what and how to teach still have to be made), what this alternative take on curriculum making does is force us to see the curriculum as a *process* rather than a product (Smith, 2000) and for this process to succeed it requires creative contributions from teachers, students and geography. What this means for geography teachers is that they themselves have to 'think geographically' (Jackson and Massey, 2005; Jackson, 2006), as opposed to generically, in order to make intelligent decisions about *what* as well as how to teach. In many respects teaches are the drivers here and, as Smith (2000) points out, 'The approach is dependent upon the cultivation

of wisdom and meaning making in the classroom. If the teacher is not up to this, then there will be severe limitations on what can be achieved educationally' (p. 10). Teachers are not the only limitation to the process model, there are others; the pursuit of curriculum uniformity and accountability mechanisms such as examination results do little to encourage the professional individualism that characterises the process model.

b. Geography

In 2010 Margaret Roberts raised concerns that judgements about teaching quality of new teachers were too frequently based on proficient instrumental generic aspect of lessons rather than on the geographical understanding being developed:

> I am not arguing that teachers don't need generic skills: it is clearly necessary for classes to be well managed if students are going to learn anything. In my opinion, however, the over-riding purpose of geography lessons is to develop geographical understanding, to give students access to geographical ways of thinking, to help them make sense of their worlds. The use of starters or plenaries is not intrinsically good; it depends on whether they enhance learning or are mere routines.
>
> (p. 113)

A great deal of attention and a significant amount of public money has been spent in recent years on attending to issues of pedagogy. National Strategies in literacy and numeracy, initiatives such as SEAL (social and emotional aspect of learning), the proliferation of learning styles inventories and the notion of generic thinking skills have dominated education policy and school-based curriculum development for some years now. When mired in all of this 'professional paraphernalia' (see Lambert, 2011) – the three-part lesson, target setting, explicit learning objectives, etc. – we could be forgiven for thinking that 'what' we teach is almost irrelevant; the subject seems to have been forgotten.

However, the curriculum-making diagram above makes a clear case for refocusing on the subject because without this the dynamic equilibrium necessary for successful curriculum making is lost. Curriculum making at any level – national, school or classroom cannot proceed without an intellectual engagement with the kind of geographies we believe appropriate for young people growing up in the twenty-first century.

The 2011 Ofsted report for geography entitled *Learning to Make a World of Difference* is bold not just in its attention to how students learn, but also it articulates the significance of what they learn if geography is to contribute to pupils' broader education. The report more than suggests that school geography needs to reconnect with its disciplinary roots. This is not to say that university geography has an automatic right to shape the school curriculum, but it does suggest that while school geography has in many respects been 'prevented from

a sustained engagement with developments in the discipline' (Morgan and Lambert, 2005, p. 3), the process of making a *geography* curriculum actually requires engagement with geography at a disciplinary rather than popular culture level. This engagement with disciplinary thinking is crucial because it provides ways of 'understanding the world and interpreting facts about the world' (Gardner, cited in Brooks, 2011, p. 173).

This returns us to the question: 'What kind of geography is appropriate "*in this day and age*"? The government's 2010 White Paper (DfE, 2010) advocates a 'core knowledge' curriculum (see Roger Firth's chapter in this volume). The tone of the White Paper suggests a return to an 'essentials' curriculum that is modelled around 'core' factual knowledge which is disconnected from both the needs and interests of young people. This 'essentials' curriculum risks failing to make a contribution to young people's understanding of the issues of the day: climate change, mass movement of people across space, global consumerism, the global economic crisis, water security, power security, contested borders and more. I am not suggesting the need for a 'here today/gone tomorrow' curriculum built around media events and popular 'everyday' culture, but a curriculum that enables a sustained and thoughtful engagement with the space/place dimension of significant matters of our time – or, to use John Morgan's phrase, to teach geography 'as if the planet matters' (Morgan, 2011). Morgan (2008, 2011) contends that insights from social and cultural geography could make a significant contribution here, and others (Stannard, 2002; Brown, 2002; Huckle, 2002) make a clear case for a school/university interface in order to sustain the relevance of the subject in schools.

c. Students

John Dewey, a contemporary of Franklin Bobbit, argued that an effective education needed a curriculum that started with the capabilities and interests of children, and that learning was essentially a social and interactive process. He was an advocate of a curriculum that enabled children to relate new learning to prior experiences and that comprised significant and relevant content: '*It is not a question of how to teach the child geography, but first of all the question what geography is for the child* (Dewey, 1972 [1897], cited in Brooks, 2009, p. 203).

Starting with the interests and capabilities of students is a challenge in the face of curriculum prescription. However, Paechter (2009), Hall and Thompson (2008), Biddulph (2011) and others suggest that failure to do so has significant consequences for many young people. They argue that many who struggle to engage with school do so because they do not acquire from *outside* school (in their homes and in their communities), the kind of elitist knowledges validated *inside* the school system.

An exclusive and excluding curriculum that only values certain kinds of knowledges and experiences signals to many young people how we, as a society, value them now – as individuals, as members of diverse communities

and as contributors to wider society. It could be deemed educationally care-less to ignore the social and cultural capital of young people whose spatial lives are shaped by powerful global forces: ignoring these geographies runs the risk of alienating significant proportions of young people and runs the risk of leaving school geography out of kilter with their needs and interests.

(Biddulph, 2011, p. 56)

Students do bring into their geography lessons pre-existing 'geographical behaviours perceptions and skills '(Lambert and Morgan, 2010, p. 50; Brooks, 2011); the lives that they lead, the places and spaces that they occupy, the real and virtual connections they make and the concerns that they have are part and parcel of young peoples' individual and collective identities all of which contribute, either consciously or subconsciously, to their geographical imagina-tions. But how can, or even should school geography utilise these pre-existing geographies and in doing so '... include and validate within school more non-school student centered knowledge ...?' (Paechter, 2009, p. 165).

In answering 'should' school geography utilise these pre-existing geographies, Yi-Fu Tuan (2008), the Chinese-American geographer, suggests that:

Blindness to experience is in fact a common human condition. We rarely attend to what we know. We attend to what we know about ... we know far more than we can tell [yet] .... Experiences are slighted or ignored because the means to articulate them or point them out are lacking.

(p. 201)

If there is any validity in Dewey's notion of learning, then it may just be the case that in 'attending' to what young people already know, that is, their pre-existing geographies, rather than just what we want them to know about, school geography may be the means by which teachers can unlock and value this knowledge and in doing so create a more inclusive curriculum experience for all students.

What we are exploring here is something akin to a 'curriculum as praxis' model (Smith, 2000, p. 11), namely an approach to the curriculum that is both committed to sense-making but in addition has at its core an explicit com-mitment to emancipation. The implications of such a model are not insignificant for school geography? How can we ensure that the everyday experiences of young people are visible, valued *and* valuable to geographical understanding, and in doing so take young people beyond what they already know? Curriculum devel-opment projects such as 'Living Geography' and the 'Young People's Geographies Project'[1] have sought to better centralise the knowledge that young people bring to school with them. The outcomes of these curriculum-making opportunities demonstrate the means by which the discipline, teachers and students can col-laborate in order to construct the school geography curriculum.

Conclusions

To bring this curriculum 'story' to some sort of conclusion it seems appropriate to return to our question at the beginning of this chapter:

> *What counts as an educated 19 year old in this day and age?*
> (Pring et al., 2009, p. 3, emphasis added)

I argue that it would be difficult to claim that the education system has done its job well if our '19-year-old' left school without a critically informed understanding of the social, environmental and cultural challenges confronting us in the twenty-first century. The question is what kind of school geography would be required in order to achieve this critically informed understanding? Without a doubt geography as a discipline has a distinct contribution to make here. However, the success of this endeavour is dependent on a number of variables, not least of which is how we construct the geography *within* the curriculum.

As this chapter has argued, and as the curriculum-making diagram suggests, the curriculum will be what teachers and their students choose to make of it. It is in a constant state of becoming and so risks being pulled in all manner of directions – and possibly badly distorted if any one interest or influence becomes too dominant. Teachers have to accept quite a lot of responsibility for holding things in balance.

And so decisions have to be made regarding what to teach (subject discipline), when to teach it (progression) and how to teach (pedagogy), and to enact all three (what, when and how) we must return to the distinction between curriculum planning, curriculum development and curriculum making and the interlocking levels at which these activities are played out. At the time of writing another review of the national curriculum is underway, but regardless of the national geography curriculum we end up with what we can be sure of is that it will need interpreting and developing (the creative process referred to by Eleanor Rawling) and at the classroom level it will need bringing to life through the curriculum-making process. As Tim Oates (2011) states:

> A national curriculum should include that which is essential for participation in a modern, democratic society .... It is for teachers and schools to construct programmes of learning which will be motivating for their learners – it is teachers who understand the specific keys to unlocking the motivation of their learners
> (Black et al., 2003) in respect of essential bodies of knowledge.
> (p. 129)

What Oates is reminding us of here is of both the relationship between the curriculum and the broader purposes of education for a democratic society

(for more see Kelly, 2009) and that a national curriculum document is, in itself, neither boring nor exciting, neither inspirational nor dull. But teachers can be all of these things. It is almost certainly the case that excitement and motivation can be encouraged best when the students are involved, but also when the teacher is oriented by a clear sense of purpose and convinced about the significance of what she or he is doing. External political and social influences play their role but ultimately it is up to teachers and students to take what the discipline has to offer, work it into something tangible and realise the opportunities it offers.

I want to give the final word in this 'story' to students who, when given the opportunity, can provide us with some wise words to reflect upon. The following quote is from a student participant in the YPG project, and it captures for me the essence of what a geography curriculum is all about. For this 15-year–old, school geography clearly isn't just about locational knowledge (but he concedes that it is partly about this). What he expresses here is a more sophisticated take on the discipline, capturing his own position within it and a sense that geography connects him to others and elsewhere. School geography is not just inert content but is both present and influential in our everyday; it is up to the curriculum and those who enact it to bring this into being.

> Geography is all around us, Geography effects [*sic*] us all. *Me, I'm geography.* This building is part of geography; everything is geography. Geography isn't just about Jamaica's there, Africa's there, Britain's there, it's about us as a community.
>
> (Anton, age 15 years)

The skilful curriculum maker not only recognises and values this, but also finds way to induct Anton to ways of understanding the world using ideas that may be new, challenging and sometimes requiring painstaking effort.

Note

1 Living Geography and The Young People's Geographies Project, both funded by The Action Plan for Geography (DfES), are curriculum development projects where expertise across a range of institutions (universities, schools, the GA, and other non-education specific organisations such as town planning departments) collaborate to develop school geography. For more go to: http://www.geography.org.uk/projects/livinggeography and http://www.youngpeoplesgeographies.co.uk/

Key readings

1. Firth, R. and Biddulph, M. (2009) 'Whose life is it anyway? Young People's Geographies', in D. Mitchell (ed.), *Living Geography: Exciting futures for teachers and students*, Cambridge: Chris Kington Publishing, pp. 13–27. This chapter discusses how the academic discipline has engaged with young people's lives and the opportunities this presents for the geography curriculum in schools.

2. Smith, M.K. (1996, 2000) 'Curriculum theory and practice', *The encyclopaedia of informal education* [online] Available from: www.infed.org/biblio/b-curric.htm. This article is generic and provides interesting models of curriculum with sensible criticism.

References

Biddulph, M. (2011) 'Young People's geographies: Implications for school geography', in G. Butt (ed.), *Geography, Education and the Future*, London: Continuum.

Brooks, C. (2006) 'Geography teachers and Making the School Geography Curriculum', *Geography*, 91 (1), 79–83.

Brooks, C. (2009) 'Teaching living Geography – making a geography curriculum', in D. Mitchell (ed.), *Living Geography: Exciting futures for teachers and students*, Cambridge: Chris Kington Publishing.

Brooks, C. (2011) 'Geographical knowledge and professional development', in G. Butt (ed.), *Geography Education and the Future*, London: Continuum.

Brown, P. (2002) 'The erosion of geography', *Geography*, 87 (1), 84–5.

Burgess, H. (2000) 'ITT: New curriculum, new directions', *Curriculum Journal*, 11 (3), 405–17.

Department for Education, (2010) *The Importance of teaching: The Schools White Paper*, London: DfE.

Flinders, D.J. and Thornton, S.J. (2004) *The Curriculum Studies Reader*, New York and Abingdon: RoutledgeFalmer.

Geographical Association (2009) *A Different View; A Manifesto from the Geographical Association*, Sheffield: Geographical Association.

Geographical Association/Royal Geographical Society (2011) *The Action Plan for Geography 2006–11*, online, Available from: http://www.geography.org.uk/projects/actionplanforgeography/.

Graves, N.J. (1979) *Curriculum Planning in Geography*, London: Heineman Educational Books.

Hall, C. and Thompson, P. (2008) 'Opportunities missed and/or thwarted? "Funds of knowledge" meet the English national curriculum', *Curriculum Journal*, 19 (2), 87–103.

Heffernan, M. (2003) Histories of Geography, in N.J. Clifford, S. Holloway, S. Rice and G. Valentine (eds.), *Key Concepts in Geography*, London: Sage.

Huckle, J. (2002) 'Reconstructing nature', *Geography*, 87 (1), 64–72.

Jackson, P. (1989) *Maps of Meaning: An introduction to cultural geography*, London: Unwin Hyman.

Jackson, P. and Massey, D. (2005) *Thinking Geographically*, Geographical Association. Available from: www.geography.org.uk/download/NPOGThinking.doc [Accessed 6 October 2011].

Jackson, P. (2006) 'Thinking Geographically', *Geography*, 91 (3), 199–204.

Kelly, A.V. (1983) *The Curriculum. Theory and practice*, 1st edn, London: Paul Chapman.

Kelly, A.V. (2009) *The Curriculum: Theory and practice*, 6th edn, London: Sage.

Lambert, D. (2003) 'Effective approaches to curriculum development', in R. Gerber (ed.), *International Handbook on geographical education*, Netherlands: Kluwer Academic Publishers.

Lambert, D. (2004) 'Geography', in J. White (ed.), *Rethinking the school curriculum: Values, aims and purposes*, London: Routledge.

Lambert, D. (2011) 'Reviewing the case for geography and the "knowledge turn" in the English National Curriculum', *Curriculum Journal*, 22 (2), 243–64.

Lambert, D. and Morgan, J. (2010) *Teaching Geography 11–18: A conceptual approach*, Maidenhead: McGraw-Hill.

Marsden, W. (1997) 'The place of geography in the curriculum: An historical overview 1886–1976', in D. Tillbury and M. Williams (eds.), *Teaching and Learning Geography*, London: Routledge.

Marsden, W. (2003) 'Geography curriculum planning in evolution: Some historical and international perspectives', in R. Gerber (ed.), *International Handbook on geographical education*, Netherlands: Kluwer Academic Publishers.

Morgan, J. (2008) 'Curriculum development in new times', *Geography*, 3 (1), 17–24.

Morgan, J. (2011) *Teaching secondary geography as if the planet matters*, London: Routledge.

Morgan, J. and Lambert, D. (2005) *Geography: Teaching school subjects*, Abingdon: Routledge.

Naish, M. (1997) 'The scope of school geography: A medium for education', in D. Tillbury and M. Williams (eds.), *Teaching and Learning Geography*, London: Routledge.

Nightingale, P. (2007) 'A Level English Literature: Learning and Assessment', *Changing English: Studies in Culture and Education*, 14 (2), 135–44.

Oates, T. (2010) *Missing the point: Identifying a well-grounded common core: Comment on trends in the development of the National Curriculum. Cambridge Assessment.* Available from: http://www.cambridgeassessment.org.uk/ca/digitalAssets/185415_Missing_the_point. pdf [Accessed 30 September 2011].

Oates, T. (2011) 'Could do better: Using international comparisons to refine the National Curriculum in England', *Curriculum Journal*, 22 (2), 121–50.

Ofsted (2011) *Learning to make a world of Difference.* Available from: http://ofsted.gov.uk/ publication/090224 [Accessed 6 October 2011].

Paechter, P. (2009) 'Schooling and the ownership of knowledge', *Pedagogy, Culture and Society*, 6 (2), 161–76.

Pring, R. (2011) Talk given to the post-graduate students' summer conference. University of Nottingham, School of Education.

Pring, R., Hayward, G., Hodgson, A., Johnson, J., Keep, E., Oancea, A., Rees, G., Spours, K. and Wilde, S. (2009) *Education for all: The future of education and training for 14–19 year olds*, London: Routledge.

Rawling, E. (1996) 'The Impact of the National Curriculum on school-based curriculum development', in A. Kent, D. Lambert, M. Naish, and F Slater (eds.), *Geography in Education: Viewpoints on teaching*, Cambridge: Cambridge University Press.

Rawling, E. (2001) *Changing the subject: The impact of national policy on school geography 1980– 2000*, Sheffield, Geographical Association.

Rawling, E. (2008) *Planning your Key Stage 3 Curriculum*, Sheffield: Geographical Association.

Richards, C. (1999) Memorandum sent to the Select Committee on Education and Employment: Appendix 69. Appendices to the Minutes of Evidence. Available from: http://www.publications.parliament.uk/ [Accessed 6 October 2011].

Roberts, M. (1997) 'Curriculum planning and course development: A matter of professional judgement', in D Tillbury and M. Williams (eds.), *Teaching and Learning Geography*, Routledge: London.

Roberts, M. (2010) 'Where's the geography? Reflections on being an external examiner', *Teaching Geography*, 35 (3), 112–13.

Smith, M. K. (2000) 'Curriculum theory and practice' *The encyclopaedia of informal education*, Available from: www.infed.org/biblio/b-curric.htm [Accessed 6 October 2011].

Stannard, K. (2002) 'Waving not drowning', *Geography*, 87 (1), 73–83.

Tuan, Yi-Fu (2008) *Space and Place: The Perspective of Experience* 6th edn, Mineapolis, MN: University of Minnesota Press.

Whitty, G. (2000) 'Teacher professionalism in new times', *Journal of In-service Education*, 26 (2), 281–95.

Chapter 10

How do we link assessment to making progress in geography?

Paul Weeden

> Progression is a complicated matter, especially when linked to the technical processes of assessment. Assessing progress is particularly challenging in a subject like geography which is not learned in a cumulative or linear sequence.
>
> (Lambert, 2011, p. 5)

Introduction

To assess students' progress teachers need to have a vision both of what makes 'better' geography and how students learn the subject. English assessment models are based on a hierarchical linear sequence of performance which implies that learning is a series of steps. Some other countries view progression differently (DfE, 2011). Some problems associated with the English model have been identified in the 2011 review of the English National Curriculum:

> We are concerned by the ways in which England's current assessment system encourages a process of differentiating learners through the award of 'levels', to the extent that pupils come to label themselves in these terms. Although this system is predicated on a commitment to evaluating individual pupil performance, we believe it actually has a significant effect of exacerbating social differentiation, rather than promoting a more inclusive approach that strives for secure learning of key curricular elements by all. It also distorts pupil learning, for instance creating the tragedy that some pupils become more concerned for 'what level they are' than for the substance of what they know, can do and understand. This is an unintended consequence of an over-prescriptive framework for curriculum and assessment.
>
> (DfE, 2011, p. 44, para. 8.4)

Implicit or explicit beliefs about learning and the model of progression adopted can therefore have important implications for assessment. If the assumption is

that learners 'capacity to learn, and achieve, is determined by innate endowment of fixed intelligence (ability)' (DfE, 2011, p. 45, para. 8.6) then this can limit expectations of children and have a negative impact on performance. Expectations of 'intelligence' can be further complicated by socio-economic factors such as class, gender, race and ethnicity. Overall performance in England, as measured by test and examination outcomes, has improved significantly over the last thirty years but the gap in the performance of different sub-groups has widened. For example, about 75% of candidates of Chinese origin get at least five A*–C grades at GCSE compared with about 35% of Black African or Caribbean candidates (Torrance, 2009, p. 223). White working-class boys have the lowest performance at GCSE (Cassen and Kingdon, 2007). Data from the 2011 school performance tables have been used to highlight these issues with blame and solutions focused on schools and teachers.

> Children only have one chance at education. These tables show which schools are letting children down. We will not hesitate to tackle underperformance in any school, including academies. Heads should be striving to make improvements year on year, and we will not let schools coast with mediocre performance. ... We have introduced a tough new inspection regime targeted at the weakest performing schools and Ministers now have clear new powers to intervene when schools are failing.
>
> (DfE, 2012)

The issue here is the role of 'assessment' outcomes in quantifying complex social issues and influencing practice in schools through the threat of punitive measures (Ball, 2008, pp. 153–92). Does accountability raise 'standards' overall or merely focus teaching and learning too much on 'passing the test', which can limit the curriculum (Torrance, 2009)? How can 'an approach to pupil progression that emphasises "high expectations for all"' (DfE, 2011, p. 47, para. 8.17) operate effectively alongside a meritocratic system that condemns some students to failure? Teachers have a role to play in improving performance although it is debatable whether education can be the panacea for all society's social and economic problems. A useful starting point is the recognition that learning is related to interest and motivation (Trend, 2005) and some topics engage and motivate some students more than others (Hopwood, 2004; Biddulph and Adey, 2004). Learning can be shallow or deep, forgotten or retained and the type of assessment used can influence the student's approach (Harlen and Deakin-Crick, 2002).

Approaches to handling these issues in the classroom are illustrated by the Making Geography Happen Project (Geographical Association, 2010). At the start of a module on uneven development Year 9 students completed the phrase 'Uneven Development is ...'. The teacher used student responses to identify their understanding at the start of the unit:

Pupils are aware that it is about difference and there are multiple reasons for it. Some are aware that it is about change though very few refer to scale or place except to refer to the familiar terms 'rich and poor countries'. Many related the term to their own lives in a rich country. Many referred to the selfishness of rich countries.

(Cooper, 2010)

The teacher in designing the module made decisions about three assessment issues which will be considered here: assessing progress; integrating assessment with teaching and learning; and fitness for purpose. The 'golden thread' of progression was the concept of uneven development (QCA, 2008). This was explored in different places and scales so students considered the complexity of their place in the world as well as developing their criticality and precision in handling geographical ideas. Assessment purposes were mostly formative and choices were made about content, teaching and assessment methods. The assessment was varied and practical arising out of day-to-day work. It was not 'polished and neat' and 'oral evidence was particularly valued and recorded' (Cooper, 2010). Assessment purposes were mostly formative (Gardner, 2006; Gardner et al., 2010).

Lesson planning became very interesting as I tried to plan the appropriate 'next step' for students rather than simply teach the next thing on a scheme of work. I found that we were not labouring points but rather moving on with our thinking and the ongoing dialogue with students provided evidence of progression in understanding and also helped me tailor lessons to their needs.

(Cooper, 2010)

By the end of the unit the teacher was able to identify the progress made by both individuals and the group. By incorporating the assessment into day-to-day work she used her knowledge of the strengths and weaknesses of different assessment instruments and the evidence they provided. This allowed her to both evaluate whether the assessment was 'fit for purpose' and to build up a profile of evidence that was not just based on one assessment. She was focused on the evidence of progress in geographical understanding, not merely on collecting the grades or marks that so often are the outcome of end-of-unit assessments. Her purpose here was to help ALL the students develop their understanding of ideas associated with uneven development, not to grade them for management and tracking purposes.

One point to make here is that giving grades can get in the way of the dialogue with students. If a grade is attached to a piece of work the student will tend to focus on the grade rather than the comments the teacher has made (Black and Wiliam, 1998a, 1998b; Weeden and Lambert, 2006, p. 13). It can be difficult to get students, parents and school managers to accept that if the purpose is to

improve dialogue and engage students with analysing their own work, grades can get in the way but the outcomes have been shown to be beneficial (Black et al., 2003, pp. 43–9).

ASSESSING PROGRESS IN GEOGRAPHY

One of the challenges therefore is conceptualising progress in geography in a way that is helpful for learning. How has progression in geography been defined and established over time? Is there a theoretical underpinning for progression in geography and how are standards maintained over time? The commonest method has been to draw on the practice and understanding of teachers but a second approach has been to analyse students' responses and to link them to theoretical models (Davies, 2002, p. 185).

The original National Curriculum in England attempted to define progression largely by content and skills through 'huge numbers of atomistic and trivial statements of attainment' (DfE, 2011, p. 43) which was highly problematic (Rawling, 2001, pp. 52–64; Davies, 2002). For example, if the content is 'rivers' what knowledge, understanding and skills might be expected of a 7-year-old (Y2) or a 16-year-old (Y11) and how might they be expressed? Meanders could be taught to students of any age but decisions have to be made about the level of detail to be included and assessed. In terms of teaching what happens to progression when the next topic is climate change or urbanisation? How can these topics be taught and assessed at an appropriate level of performance?

This led to the introduction of National Curriculum levels written by a group of 'expert' geographers (primary and secondary teachers, examiners, advisers and QCA subject specialists) who tried to encapsulate and communicate their understanding of progression in a way that could be used consistently by teachers. The levels provide broad brush criteria statements of progress that attempted to remove specific 'content' from assessment and identified progression in terms of:

- Increasing breadth of study
- Wider range of scales studied
- Greater complexity of phenomena studied
- Increasing use made of generalised knowledge about abstract ideas
- Greater precision required in undertaking intellectual and practical tasks
- More mature awareness and understanding of issues and of the context of differing attitudes and values in which they arise.

(Rawling, 2008; Weeden, 2010; Lambert, 2011, p. 5)

Levels therefore require interpretation within the context in which the assessment will take place. For the National Curriculum the original intention was that level descriptions would be used as end of key stage judgements. They were not intended for use on a daily basis for individual pieces of work because they do not provide focused statements of performance. The trend to subdivide levels for

tracking purposes is therefore inappropriate and is the result of the assessment and reporting regime (Hopkin, 2006; DfE, 2011, p. 50, para. 8.24).

At GCSE and A-level performance is defined by senior examiners who use both their own experience and statistical data to make judgements about grade boundaries (Lloyd, 1999). These examinations have past papers, mark schemes, textbooks and awarding body meetings to provide guidance about examiner expectations of performance. There is a risk of 'teaching to the test', focusing on parts of the syllabus that are likely to be examined and drilling students rather than developing understanding (Black and Wiliam, 1998a, 1998b; Harlen et al., 2002).

The second method of defining progression arose from an analysis of students' responses to questions that was then linked to the Structure of Observed Learning Outcomes (SOLO) taxonomy (Davies, 2002; Biggs, 2011). Categories such as specificity, completeness and judgement were used to develop hierarchies of response that show how descriptions, explanations and judgements become more complex and interrelated as students become more expert geographers (George et al., 2002; Davies and Durbin, 2005). While this analysis uses different 'levels', these are not directly linked to GNC levels. Another more recent example of this approach uses models of increasing complexity in student responses (Budke et al., 2011).

Thus a day-to-day issue facing teachers is how to identify progression within a topic. As the experience of the first version of the National Curriculum shows, it is difficult to do this in terms of specific content because understanding and engagement with geography is more than merely recalling facts, but also involves making connections and comprehending relationships (Bennetts, 2005). How then has progression been defined so that assessment is possible?

One method used has been to identify 'strands' (such as enquiry or pattern and process) within the level descriptions where progression in more focused aspects of geography can be identified. This was done after the first revision of the National Curriculum when exemplar assessment materials (Kobe Earthquake, Swanage) were produced for both England and Wales (SCAA, 1996; Tidmarsh and Weeden, 1997). Other possible organising frameworks for progression include using the concepts (Place, Space, Scale, Interdependence, Physical and human processes, Cultural understanding and diversity, Environmental interaction and sustainable development) of the most recent version of the National Curriculum (Rawling, 2008), the development of knowledge and understanding (Bennetts, 2005), enquiry (Roberts, 2003) and geographical literacy (Lambert and Morgan, 2010; Jenkinson, 2011). These headings by themselves do not identify progression of knowledge, understanding and skills, and require further development as illustrated earlier (Cooper, 2010).

Each provides a potential framework for progression but does not provide an off-the-peg model that can be used on a day-to-day basis. This has been one of the major challenges for geography teachers over the last twenty years where there has been an increasing emphasis on having clearly defined criteria that exemplify performance. Are there some aspects of progress that can be more easily identified? It has been suggested that there are some skills such as map reading that can be

defined relatively easily (Lambert, 2010). Other examples include factual recall of place names and explanations of landforms although it is difficult to see how progress can be made other than knowing more places or more obscure places. It has also been argued that 'knowing how' rather than 'knowing what' is more important today because of the growth of the internet. This leads to another current debate in education – what is the core and essential knowledge that is required for the subject (Lambert and Morgan, 2010; Hopkin, 2011; Kinder and Lambert, 2011) and how will it be assessed? How will this knowledge be updated over time?

To summarise, there are a number of frameworks available that exemplify progression in geography. The criteria available for progression are generalised and not content-specific so need contextualising for individual topics. There have been attempts to formalise these and break them down into more bite-sized chunks but there is a danger that making criteria too specific and competence-based can impose a rigid strait-jacket where the assessment becomes the priority not the geography (Rawling, 2008; Weeden, 2010; Lambert, 2010).

Finally, the system of assessing progression within the English National Curriculum is contested. In early 2012 there are proposals that the revised National Curriculum should abandon level descriptions and replace them with an alternative that has yet to be agreed or rationalised.

> 7.6 Instead, and consistent with separating 'what is to be taught' from 'statements of standards', we suggest an approach in which the Programme of Study is stated as a discursive statement of purposes, anticipated progression and interconnection within the knowledge to be acquired. Attainment Targets should then be statements of specific learning outcomes related to essential knowledge. This approach has the benefit of greater precision – both in orienting teaching and giving a clear rationale for teaching content – and in respect of assessment, since the Attainment Targets would be both detailed and precise.
>
> (DfE, 2011, pp. 42–3)

The question here is how teachers can develop their knowledge and understanding of progression in geography so that they feel confident in making judgements or helping students make next steps without being constrained by formal assessment structures. This leads to the next section where the influence of assessment on teaching and learning is considered.

INTEGRATING ASSESSMENT WITH TEACHING AND LEARNING

Teachers use assessment on a daily basis to collect data about students but the important issue is purpose. Is the assessment going to be for formative, used synonymously here with Assessment FOR Learning (AFL) or summative (end of key stage, examination results) purposes (Assessment OF Learning). In most day-to-day teaching situations the purposes will be formative but in reality the assessment is often summative.

An assessment activity can help learning if it provides information to be used as feedback by teachers, and by their students in assessing themselves and each other, to modify the teaching and learning activities in which they are engaged. Such assessment becomes *formative assessment* when the evidence is used to adapt the teaching work to meet learning outcomes.

(Black et al., 2003, p. 2)

There are two implications of this statement, first that formative assessment involves dialogue between student and teacher and secondly that it is more important to be able to identify next steps (progression) than to be able to give a specific grade or level (Weeden and Lambert, 2006; Weeden and Butt, 2009; Weeden, 2010). This means that teachers need to use assessment as a means of developing a dialogue with students through strategies such as more effective questioning (Hodgen and Webb, 2008; Wood, 2009) or feedback (Weeden, 2005; Weeden and Lambert, 2006; Rooney, 2006, 2007; Swaffield, 2008).

Teaching and learning tend to be driven by summative outcomes because teachers and schools in England are increasingly judged by performance through the league tables (James, 1998; Black et al., 2003; Harlen, 2006, 2007; Stobart, 2008). This results in 'teaching to the test' to maximise performance rather than learning. In the most effective situations the teacher will be using formative processes because they have assessed current performance, know what needs to be learnt and will give guidance on next steps (progression). The question here is whether the learning is deep (resulting in understanding) or surface (knowledge sufficient to pass the assessment).

The research evidence suggesting that a focus on deep learning can boost performance because learning is more effective (Black and Wiliam, 1998a, 1998b; Black et al., 2003) has resulted in a growth in the use of AFL within schools during the last decade. In the process of dissemination has it been watered down to a series of strategies that are used without full understanding of the underpinning principles (Marshall and Drummond, 2006)? The issue here is whether the assessment is used to provide effective feedback about current attainment and feed-forward about next steps or whether it is merely a bureaucratic data-collecting exercise for accountability purposes. There may be a conflict between teacher values which support AFL and the requirements of a school system that is judged by performance outcomes (James and Pedder, 2006; Lambert, 2010).

There can therefore be a tension between the increasing collection of data on a regular basis to track performance over time and its impact on learning. Increasingly schools in England are using sophisticated data analysis (Midyis, Yellis, Allis; FFT; Raiseonline: Value Added[1]) to 'predict' student progress or to evaluate the performance of departments compared with other departments or schools (Howes, 2009; FFT, 2011; CEM, 2011). How does the conception of formative assessment relate to the use of 'AFL' data collection procedures such as detailed mark schemes, self-assessment charts, peer-assessment criteria that are used on a regular basis to collect detailed numerical or grade information about performance? These ostensibly AFL tools are used to set on-going targets and to

track progress but do they help learning? Current performance has only a partial relationship to future performance (FFT, 2007) and while a useful tool for highlighting expectations it can become a self-fulfilling prophecy that may limit some students' opportunities.

This leads to another debate in the literature about whether different purposes of assessment can easily sit together (Black et al., 2003; Taras, 2005). Can one assessment serve a number of different purposes? This has implications for classroom practice because if summative and formative purposes can be more closely linked then assessment for learning will not be an additional burden on teachers (Harlen, 2007; Weeden, 2008).

FITNESS FOR PURPOSE

Having identified the purpose of the assessment it is then necessary to consider whether the assessment is 'fit for purpose'. Areas that might be considered are the types of assessment instrument available (Lambert and Lines, 2000; Weeden, 2003), more technical assessment issues such as whether the comparisons of progress would be ipsative, normative or criterion referenced (Harlen, 2007, p. 19) and questions about reliability (Black and Wiliam, 2006) and validity (Stobart, 2006).

In the example at the beginning of this chapter the teacher had to make decisions about the best method of assessment (Cooper, 2010). In this case the purpose was a 'baseline' assessment of the students' prior knowledge, understanding and attitudes at the start of the unit to give a clearer focus about what to include and what to leave out (Black et al., 2003). In choosing to ask the students to write definitions she felt that a relatively open task was likely to provide a richer picture of their current knowledge and understanding. However, there are other ways of collecting baseline assessment data such as tests or whole class questioning.

Having collected assessment data teachers have to decide how they will judge performance. There are three main ways: by comparison with everyone else in the group or cohort (normative); by comparison with previous performance of the individual (ipsative) or against descriptions of expected performance (criteria). Teachers have to make judgements about which to use in different situations. The National Curriculum levels are criteria based and rely on the premise that reliable, valid and consistent judgements can be made about quality of performance so that students can be assigned a level or a grade that summarises their performance. This hierarchical grading can enable both comparisons with other students (normative) and allow individual progress over time to be tracked (ipsative).

For the grade to be useful there needs to be confidence that the judgement is sound and some common understanding of what that grade means. For example, the 'C' grade at GCSE has obtained the status of the benchmark of a 'good' pass grade with the implication that anything lower than this is less worthwhile. In reality the students on either side of the boundary between C and D will have very similar performance and where the boundary is drawn is the result of examiner judgements and not any very significant differences. Grades therefore have

limitations in helping define progression, especially if attempts are made to have a fine-grained scale that subdivides grades or levels.

This is compounded if the reliability of assessment is considered. No assessment is perfectly reliable because it will only sample learning, student performance may vary from day to day and markers can vary in their judgements. Assessment outcomes may be contradictory and high stakes judgements should not be made on the basis of one assessment (Lambert and Lines, 2000, pp. 89–95; Black and Wiliam, 2006, pp. 120–21). Assessments also need to be valid. Does it give 'an accurate measurement of whatever it is supposed to measure' in an appropriate manner? Does it sample the content covered and is it 'fit for purpose'? If students are supposed to be able to demonstrate skills do they have the practical opportunity to do so (CIEA, 2012)? Assessments therefore should be valid and assessing learning appropriately. Writing tests or asking questions in the classroom are complex skills. Questions can either allow students to demonstrate what they know or be so specific that they are limiting. Even experienced examiners may write questions that are restrictive in terms of learning (QCA, 2008).

Finally, testing can have significant effects on student motivation and self-esteem. 'A strong emphasis on testing produces students with a strong extrinsic orientation towards grades and social status, that is a motivation towards performance rather than learning goals' (Harlen and Deakin-Crick, 2002, Introduction). There are a number of different views about the impact of testing on motivation with some believing that it raises level of achievement; another view is that it is only motivating for those who anticipate success which has the effect of widening the gap between high- and low-achieving students (ARG, 2002, p. 1). The implication is that a focus on measurement and grades can limit the scope and range of the geography taught increasing the gap between low and high attainers.

Conclusion

Attempts to define progression in geography have led to the development of a hierarchy of criteria which suggests that progression in geography is encapsulated by students' ability to demonstrate learning through their increasingly complex use of scale, breadth, depth, context, interaction, diversity, generalisation, precision and communication. The tension continues to be about whether assessment is dominated by the need to collect data that are used for target setting and school performance measures or is a tool for teachers and students that helps them enter into a dialogue about learning which develops geographical knowledge and understanding.

Finally, has the requirement to label and track progress for accountability purposes led to a loss in teachers' confidence in their own ability to judge progress and a concentration on summative assessment rather than assessment for learning? Second, are students 'labelled' by their 'level', lowering expectations for some and widening the gap between high and low achievers or do teachers expect 'high standards for all' believing that all students have the potential to make progress in geography? These issues have been brought more into focus with the

publication of the White Paper on a revised National Curriculum for England, where progression and the current system of attainment targets is being questioned (DfE, 2011).

Note

1 Raiseonline [online] available from: https://www.raiseonline.org/login.aspx?ReturnUrl=%2f [Accessed 12 November 2011].

Key readings

1. Black, P., Harrison, C., Lee, C., Marshall, B. and Wiliam, D. (2003) *Assessment for Learning: Putting it into Practice*, Maidenhead: Open University Press.
   The report of a two-year research project into Assessment for Learning that describes how teachers put AFL into practice in their schools.
2. Weeden, P. and Lambert, D. (2006) *Geography inside the black box*, London: nfer Nelson/GA.
   One of a series of booklets about AFL offering advice to teachers on how to interact more effectively with students, on a day-to-day basis, promoting their learning.

References

Assessment Reform Group (ARG) (2002) *Testing, Learning and Motivation*, Cambridge: University of Cambridge, Faculty of Education.

Ball, S. (2008) *The Education Debate*, Bristol: The Policy Press.

Bennetts, T. (2005) 'The links between understanding, progression and assessment in the secondary geography curriculum', *Geography*, 90 (2), 152–70.

Biddulph, M. and Adey, K. (2004) 'Pupil Perceptions of effective teaching and subject relevance in history and geography at Key Stage 3', *Research in Education*, 71, 1–8.

Biggs, J. (2011) *The SOLO Taxonomy* [online] Available from: http://www.johnbiggs.com.au/solo_taxonomy.html [Accessed 12 November 2011].

Black, P. and Wiliam D. (1998a) 'Assessment and classroom learning', *Assessment in Education*, 5, 7–74.

Black, P. and Wiliam, D. (1998b) *Inside the Black Box*, Slough: NFER/Nelson.

Black, P. and Wiliam, D. (2006) 'The Reliability of Assessments', in J. Gardner (ed.), *Assessment and Learning*, London: Sage.

Black, P., Harrison, C., Lee, C., Marshall, B. and Wiliam, D. (2003) *Assessment for Learning: Putting it into Practice*, Maidenhead: Open University Press.

Budke, A. Schiefele, U. and Uhlenwinkel, A. (2011) 'I think it's stupid' is no argument: Investigating how students argue in writing', *Teaching Geography*, 35 (2), 66–9.

Cassen, R. and Kingdon, G. (2007) *Tackling low educational achievement*, York: Joseph Rowntree Foundation.

Centre for Educational Measurement (CEM), (2011) [online] Available from: http://www.cemcentre.org/ [Accessed 12 November 2011].

Chartered Institute of Educational Assessors (CIEA), (2012) *Assessment Validity* [online] Available from: http://www.ciea.org.uk/knowledge_centre/articles_speeches/general_articles/assessment_validity.aspx [Accessed 29 January 2012].

Cooper, P. (2010) *Making Geography Happen: Uneven Development* [online] Available from: http://www.geography.org.uk/projects/makinggeographyhappen/unevendevelopment/ [Accessed 12 November 2011].

Davies, P. (2002) 'Levels of attainment in Geography, *Assessment in Education: Principles, Policy and Practice*, 9 (2), 185–204.

Davies, P. and Durbin, C. (2005) *It's long, it's neat and it's coloured in nicely: Approaches to assessment for learning to improve geographical writing*, Stafford: Staffordshire County Council.

Department for Education (DfE), (2011). *The Framework for the National Curriculum. A report by the Expert Panel for the National Curriculum review*, London: Department for Education.

Department for Education (DfE), (2012) *New data reveals the truth about school performance*: Press release [online] Available from: http://www.education.gov.uk/a00202531/secperftables12 [Accessed 28 January 2012).

Fischer Family Trust (FFT), (2011) *Data Analysis Project for Schools and LAs* [online] Available from: http://www.fischertrust.org/dap_overview.aspx [Accessed 12 November 2011].

Fischer Family Trust (FFT), (2007) *Making Best use of FFT Estimates* [online] Available from: http://www.fischertrust.org/downloads/dap/Training/Making_best_use_of_FFT_estimates.pdf [Accessed 12 November 2011].

Gardner, J. (ed.) (2006) *Assessment and Learning*, London: Sage.

Gardner, J., Harlen, W., Hayward, L. and Stobart, G. with Montgomery, M. (2010) *Developing Teacher Assessment*, Maidenhead: Open University Press.

Geographical Association (2010) *Making Geography Happen* [online] Available from: http://www.geography.org.uk/projects/makinggeographyhappen/ [Accessed 25 January 2012].

George, J., Clarke, J., Davies, P. and Durbin, C. (2002) 'Helping students to get better at geographical writing', *Teaching Geography*, 27 (4), 156–9.

Harlen, W. (2006) 'The Role of Assessment in Developing Motivation for Learning', in J. Gardner (ed.), *Assessment and Learning,* London: Sage.

Harlen, W. (2007) *Assessment of Learning*, London: Sage.

Harlen, W. and Deakin-Crick, R. (2002) 'A systematic review of the impact of summative assessment and tests on students' motivation for learning', *Research Evidence in Education Library*, London: EPPI-Centre, Social Science Research Unit, Institute of Education, University of London [online] Available from: http://eppi.ioe.ac.uk/cms/Default.aspx?tabid=108 [Accessed 12 November 2011].

Hodgen, J. and Webb, M. (2008) 'Questioning and dialogue', in S. Swaffield (ed.), *Unlocking Assessment: Understanding for reflection and application*, Abingdon: Routledge.

Hopkin, J. (2006) *Level descriptions and assessment in geography: a GA discussion paper* [online] Available from: http://www.geography.org.uk/download/GA_AULevelAssessments InGeography.pdf [Accessed 12 November 2011].

Hopkin, J. (2011) 'Progress in geography', *Geography*, 96, (3), 116–23.

Hopwood, N. (2004) 'Pupils' Conceptions of Geography: Towards an Improved Understanding', *International Research in Geographical and Environmental Education*, 13 (4), 348–61.

Howes, N. (2009) 'How can working assessment data help students make progress in geography?' in P. Weeden and G. Butt (eds.), *Assessing progress in your key stage 3 geography curriculum*, Sheffield: Geographical Association.

James, M. (1998) *Using Assessment for School Improvement*, Oxford: Heinemann.

James, M. and Pedder, D. (2006) 'Beyond method: assessment and learning practices and values', *Curriculum Journal*, 17 (2), 109–38.

Jenkinson, C. (2011) 'Using empathy to encourage extended writing at key stages 3 and 4', *Teaching Geography*, 35 (2), 62–5.

Kinder, A. and Lambert, D. (2011) 'The National Curriculum Review: What geography should we teach? *Teaching Geography*, 36 (3), 93–5.

Lambert, D. (2010) *Think Piece: Progression* [online] Available from: http://www.geography.org.uk/download/GA_PRMGHProgressionThinkPiece.pdf [Accessed 12 November 2011].

Lambert, D. (2011) *The Geography National Curriculum: GA Curriculum Proposals and Rationale*, Sheffield: Geographical Association [online] Available from: http://www.geography.org.uk/download/GA_GIGCCCurriculumProposals.pdf [Accessed 25 January 2012).

Lambert, D. and Lines, D. (2000) *Understanding Assessment: Purposes, Perceptions, Practice*, London: RoutledgeFalmer.

Lambert, D. and Morgan, J. (2010) *Teaching Geography 11–18: A Conceptual Approach*, Maidenhead: Open University Press.

Lloyd, J.G. (1999) *How Exams Really Work*, London: Cassell.

Marshall, B. and Drummond, M. (2006) 'How teachers engage with Assessment for Learning: Lessons from the classroom', *Research Papers in Education*, 21 (2), 133–49.

QCA (2008) *Inter-subject comparability studies Study 1a: GCSE, AS and A level geography and history London* [online] Available from: http://www.ofqual.gov.uk/downloads/category/105-comparability [Accessed 12 November 2011]

Rawling, E. (2001) *Changing the Subject: The impact of national policy on school geography 1980-2000*, Sheffield: Geographical Association.

Rawling, E. (2008) *Planning your KS3 Geography Curriculum*, Sheffield: Geographical Association.

Roberts, M. (2003) *Learning Through Enquiry: Making sense of geography in the key stage 3 classroom*, Sheffield: Geographical Association.

Rooney, R. (2006) 'Effective feedback as a focus for CPD with a developing Geography Department, *Teaching Geography*, 31 (2), 84–6.

Rooney, R. (2007) 'Using Success Criteria', *Teaching Geography*, 32 (1), 51–5.

SCAA (1996) *Non-statutory Test Material in Geography, Key Stage 3*, London: SCAA.

Stobart, G. (2006) 'The Validity of Formative Assessment', in J. Gardner, (ed.), *Assessment and Learning*, London: Sage.

Stobart, G. (2008) *Testing Times: The uses and abuses of assessment*, London: Routledge.

Swaffield, S. (ed.) (2008) *Unlocking Assessment: Understanding for reflection and application*, Abingdon: Routledge.

Taras, M. (2005) 'Assessment – Summative and Formative – Some Theoretical Reflections', *British Journal of Educational Studies*, 53 (4), 466–78.

Tidmarsh, C. and Weeden, P. (1997) 'Using Optional Tasks and Tests', *Teaching Geography*, 22 (2), 71–6.

Torrance, H. (2009) 'Using assessment in education reform', in H. Daniels, H. Lauder and J. Porter (eds.), *Knowledge, Values and Educational Policy: A critical perspective*, London: Routledge.

Trend, R. (2005) 'Individual, situational and topic interest in geoscience among 11- and 12-year-old children, *Research Papers in Education*, 20 (3), 271–302.

Weeden, P. (2003) 'Fit for purpose: choosing the right assessment task', *Curriculum Briefing*, 2 (1), 31–5.

Weeden, P. (2005) 'Feedback in the Geography Classroom', *Teaching Geography*, 30 (3), 161–3.

Weeden, P. (2008) *Think Piece – Assessment for Learning* [online] Available from: http://www.geography.org.uk/gtip/thinkpieces/assessmentforlearning/#6878 [Accessed 12 November 2011].

Weeden, P. (2010) *Making Geography Happen: Thinking about progression in geography* [online] Available from: http://www.geography.org.uk/projects/makinggeographyhappen/progression/ [Accessed 12 November 2011].

Weeden, P. and Butt, G. (2009) *Assessing progress in your key stage 3 geography curriculum*, Sheffield: Geographical Association.

Weeden, P. and Lambert, D. (2006) *Geography inside the Black Box*, London: nferNelson.

Wood, P. (2009) 'What helps to improve Assessment for Learning in the geography classroom?', in P. Weeden, and G. Butt (eds.), *Assessing progress in your key stage 3 geography curriculum*, Sheffield: Geographical Association.

Chapter 11

Examining geography

What geography is examined in schools and colleges?

Bob Digby

> *Man [sic]* is not divided into subjects. He lives his life as a whole, and it is
> in preparation for this life that children come to school.
>
> (Fairgrieve, 1926, p. 282)

Introduction

Does it matter how geography is examined? Let us assume that, like James Fairgrieve almost a century ago, we do care where we want to get to with our students studying geography. And in that case, it does matter how the subject is examined – how the specifications, the assessment framework, the questions and the mark schemes are structured. This chapter aims to set out a context for anyone interested in exploring some of the key debates in this particular aspect of geography education.

In the late 1980s, the Thatcher government undertook the most comprehensive review of what is taught in schools in modern times. Rawling (2001) has written an authoritative account of the nature and impact of government policy changes between the late 1970s and 2000, particularly analysing how the curriculum has become a vehicle for almost constant cyclical review and for introducing political initiatives. Thus, political influence upon the curriculum is by no means recent, though it varies in nature. In recent years, some initiatives have focused upon qualifications, such as the introduction of the AS qualification in 2000; others have been curriculum-focused, such as the introduction of national Subject Criteria for A level (from 1994) and GCSE. Each can result in substantial changes to examination specifications, to examination requirements, and therefore to what is taught in geography classrooms.

Teachers across two decades have faced cyclical changes to examination specifications. Revisions occurred in 1995, 2000 and 2008 for the Key Stage 3 of the National Curriculum and for post-16 specifications, and in 1994, 2001 and 2009 for GCSE. Each change was preceded by a review by government resulting in the development of Subject Criteria, to which different examination specifications must adhere. As each new set of Subject Criteria was revised and published,

Awarding Bodies (formerly referred to as Examination Boards) revised their different specifications. Teachers in schools would then select a specification for their post-14 and post-16 classes, each selection requiring some adaptation of existing schemes of work to match new specification and examination requirements, and potentially investment in new resources.

Teachers face a wide choice of specifications. As of 2012, each of the four Awarding Bodies in England and Wales offered a single specification at AS/A2, and two at GCSE. Teachers could therefore select from eight GCSE and four AS/A2 specifications. In addition to these choices, there were international specifications for GCSE, known as iGCSE, which, since 2011, had been made available to all state schools in the UK, as well as the International Baccalaureate.

Faced with such choices, how do teachers make sense of what is on offer? What makes them select a particular specification? Is it simply a matter, as BBC News (2011) reported, of 'price, service and support', a driving factor cited by a representative of Edexcel? Or are there other factors in play? Do teachers have a clear sense of 'where (they) want to get to'? Perhaps they are influenced by their personal preferences for what a geography curriculum should look like, attaching importance to particular subject paradigms. Perhaps their degrees, their professional training and experience have developed preferences for a particular pedagogy. Amid these decisions, what kind of school geography emerges that their students will experience? And how far should teachers care?

WHOSE GEOGRAPHY?

Before the introduction of a national qualification began with the School Certificate in 1918, examination syllabuses were determined largely by universities, who initially set examinations to suit their own entry requirements. Even after its creation, the School Certificate (later redeveloped as Ordinary ('O') and Advanced ('A') levels), universities retained a large measure of independence over what each examination syllabus should contain, and examination style. From 1953, there were nine GCE examination boards, including the Associated Examining Board (AEB) initially formed by City and Guilds to offer technical and vocational subjects (Sheldon, 2011).

However, a decision by Wilson's Labour government in 1964 to create the Schools Council led to a political drive to influence the curriculum, as opposed to its assessment. Together with the Nuffield Foundation, the Schools Council made funds available to pilot new curricula up to 'O' level, and later to 'A' level. The main purpose of these funds was to meet the curriculum needs of a wider-ability school population with the spread of comprehensive schools in the 1960s, and later, from 1973, the raising of the school-leaving age to 16.

In geography, all funding derived from the Schools Council for curriculum development was placed within Higher Education Institutions (HEI), whose influence in school geography in the 1970s and early 1980s continued to be considerable. The Schools Council funded a number of curriculum projects across

a range of school subjects, and established three landmark projects in the geography curriculum. In the 14–16 age range, two projects were especially influential:

- the 'Bristol Project' was developed around Bristol University; its focus was what Butt (2000) has described as 'a project noted for its teacher-centred strategy for curriculum development in school Geography and its role in developing new approaches to assessment' (p. 188). It sought to develop teacher creativity and professionalism in creating a curriculum for more able students, which had as its framework a range of ten themes in geography across a spectrum from physical to human, and scales ranging from local to global. Content within this framework was defined and decided by the individual teacher. Its assessment was a mix of coursework (created by the teacher) and examination, the latter assessing generic concepts in order to draw out the knowledge, application and understanding of geographical ideas.
- the 'Avery Hill' Project, otherwise known as the 'Geography for the Young School Leaver' (GYSL), was based at Avery Hill, a teacher training college in south London. The Project's focus was to develop ways in which geography could make a significant contribution to a new generation of school leavers whose educational attainment was below the range of normal 'O' level examinations. It sought to develop a more limited curriculum in terms of range, but one which focused on issues considered relevant to the generation of young people in the 1970s and 1980s. Initially created as a course for less able students, it widened its remit and, like the 'Bristol Project', became a popular 16-plus and, later, GCSE course.

By the mid-1990s, each of these projects had created a curriculum legacy, insofar as they had embedded themselves in two separate GCSE specifications, lasting well into the 2000s.

For the post-16 age group, a new '16–19 Project' was based around the University of London's Institute of Education. Beginning as a curriculum project in the late 1970s, it had rapidly gained support in schools by the late 1980s, and, by the early 1990s had the largest A level candidature in England and Wales. It sought to establish first, not subject content, but ways in which geography could be relevant to the lives of 16–19-year-olds. Like the Bristol Project, teacher professional development lay at its heart, in that teachers could build their own content from a conceptual framework with limited compulsory content, and select option topics that suited their interests, those of their students, and their own expertise.

Outside these projects, the curriculum for students aged between 14 and 18 was largely influenced by syllabuses controlled by examination boards. Until 1995, these were university-based; for example:

- the University of London gave its name to an exam board which until the late 1990s was based on the site of its main campus;

- the Joint Matriculation Board (JMB) brought together a consortium of the Universities of Manchester, Liverpool, Leeds, Sheffield and Birmingham;
- Oxford and Cambridge had their respective examination boards; the Associated Examining Board (AEB) was an amalgamation of what had been Oxford Examinations.

These boards were often quite adventurous in bringing change in the curriculum and assessment to schools. In the 1970s, for example, AEB offered an 'A' level syllabus for which 20% was assessed by a fieldwork log, supported by an oral examination. At the same time, JMB introduced a new 'A' level syllabus, known at the time as syllabus B, which was the first to bring the positivist revolution into schools. It was focused on thematic teaching of physical and human geography, supported by data response and fieldwork in which data collection and analysis were essential.

As well as the curriculum and assessment, HEI geographers also played a large role in influencing school geography through the publication of textbooks. Between the 1960s and 1980s, leading academics in their fields – for example, Monkhouse (1962), Bradford and Kent (1977) – gained a younger audience for their work through a range of physical and human geography textbooks. As experts, they wrote textbooks which were unaligned with any particular syllabus, aiming instead for a general market in the age group. Even with the introduction of the GCSE qualification in 1986, academic geographers and geography educators, such as Keith Orrell and Harry Tolley, were among popular textbook authors. Even where written by academics involved in the different Schools Council projects, textbooks had no formal allegiances to any particular syllabus or exam board. A few teachers wrote textbooks, too, some of which were widely adopted, such as Young and Lowry (1984), together with a few written by Local Authority Advisers for Geography.

Increasingly, specifications are revised to comply with the requirements of central government. The post-14 and post-16 curriculum and assessment are broadly defined by subject requirements known as Subject Criteria, which until 2010 (when the Qualifications and Curriculum Development Agency, a government quango, was abolished) set a framework against which new submissions by the Awarding Bodies, known as specifications (instead of syllabuses), could be approved. This should, in theory, have led to greater consistency between different Awarding Bodies, and therefore to what is taught from ages 14 and 16 in geography. In fact, as this chapter will show, English and Welsh specifications in geography remain very varied.

In addition, the requirement since the early 1990s that schools publish their examination results in order to assist in the production of national school league tables, is widely believed to have led to a 'results culture', whereby schools strive for the highest possible examination results. The push for results can lead to an innate conservatism, whereby inertia exists in both content and assessment style, mitigating against the introduction of progressive styles of content or assessment.

Compared with the 1970s and 1980s, during which time Schools Council syllabuses were widely adopted and accepted for their fresh approaches to teaching and assessment, the most recent GCSE Geography Project in the subject, known as the Pilot GCSE (2002), received only minority adoption between 2002 and 2009.

A further factor influencing both content and assessment of specifications is the control structure of different Awarding Bodies. To meet the needs of the new GCSE (a common examination for all 16-year-old students) in 1986, HEI-based Examination Boards merged with 14 Regional Boards which since 1963 had administered the Certificate in Secondary Education (CSE). For example, JMB merged with four northern CSE Boards to form the Northern Examinations and Assessment Board (NEAB). The new Boards were larger, because almost all students took GCSEs. Unlike the previous boards, which operated with few, largely administrative staff, a large professional structure took over the administration of subjects, all Boards having a professional Subject Officer to oversee syllabus development and assessment in a particular subject. Universities retained an influence only because they appointed representatives to sit as members of subject teams writing new syllabuses and reviewing examinations. Sheldon (2011) has shown how HEI effectively lost control of the new Boards after the introduction of the GCSE in 1986. For example, JMB links to its founders weakened when it became part of NEAB, and were lost completely in 2000 in the merger with AEB that created AQA. The University of London too became a minority player when its examinations merged with BTEC[1] to create Edexcel in the mid-1990s, and then altogether when Pearson purchased it in 2002 (Tattersall, 2007, pp. 73–8, quoted in Sheldon, 2011).

Thus, in the 2010s, project managers (who may not be geographers) now coordinate the writing of new specifications, with teams which normally consist of a Chief Examiner and other Principal Examiners responsible for particular papers. In this respect, examiners form a majority over professional full-time staff, even though they are part-time and employed on a needs basis. For example, the Development Team for one of the GCSE Awarding Bodies for the 2009 series consisted of four senior examiners (a Chief plus three Principals), a Project Manager from the Awarding Body, and a Chair of Examiners. The four examiners were mostly teachers past and present; only one had worked in HEI.

Ownership of the Awarding Bodies has also altered, from a majority working as university trusts. In 2011, of the four main bodies responsible for examinations and assessment in England and Wales:

- AQA is an education charity, run on a not-for-profit basis;
- Edexcel is part of a multinational publishing company, Pearson;
- Oxford, Cambridge and RSA (OCR) remains owned and run by Cambridge University;
- Welsh Joint Education Committee (WJEC) is run by a consortium of Welsh local authorities, though as an independent organisation.

In spite of this variety, there exists a common adherence to market values. All four Awarding Bodies are concerned about market share, even though in public some deny it (BBC, 2011). In the most recent revision to post-16 AS/A2 specifications in 2008, each Awarding Body was required to merge its previous two specifications into one; in all cases, the 'majority' specification with the greater number of candidates emerged as the model for the new specification, and the 'minority' one was dropped.

In effect, all four Awarding Bodies are run largely as though they were private companies, where market values dominate. Chief and Principal Examiners are valued for their insight into the examinations process by publishers and companies providing Continuing Professional Development (CPD). Many textbooks pass through a formal process of endorsement by relevant Awarding Bodies, who in turn may take a royalty. CPD is carried out largely by examiners and private consultants with experience of examining. CPD provision for teachers is largely based around three themes:

- teaching a specification, offering assistance in planning and teaching;
- preparing for examinations, offering tips on preparing students for examinations and marking strategies;
- reflection and evaluation, looking back on previous examinations, and considering where students (and therefore teachers) showed strengths and weaknesses.

Both textbooks and CPD provision are each linked closely to specification requirements, and their authors and providers are mainly teachers and examiners, rather than HEI subject specialists who play a limited role.

A consequence of the diminished role of HEI in school geography is the significant gap between the subject as taught in schools and in HEI. This was recognised as significant by Heeley and Roberts (1996), and many others such as Rawling (2001) continue to identify this as an issue. While HEI largely focus on their own research assessments, bids for research funding, and inspections of teaching quality, many academics give little attention to curriculum and assessment in schools. Similarly, as many senior examiners are approaching or are post retirement, the influence of contemporary subject content, philosophies and approaches is reduced. There have been attempts to improve the relationship between HEI and the school curriculum, for instance via the Geographical Association's 'Top Spec' series of student textbooks from 2009, which have been jointly authored by university specialists and practising teachers in schools, but to date these have had limited impact in terms of numerical sales.

WHAT CONTENT?

At the time of writing, the QCA Subject Criteria for Geography (2006) are generic; none requires particular content that students must study, only that both

physical and human geography should be incorporated. It is left to individual Awarding Bodies to decide what content should be included in specifications. The result is a varied patchwork of themes and content (Figure 11.1). In the example of human geography, there is no common theme taught to all AS or A2 students, across two years. Population comes closest; three specifications include it as a compulsory topic. Some optional themes are found in most or all specifications, such as Development, but, as options, there is no guarantee that significant numbers of students will study these. Specifications vary in terms of compulsory and optional topics; Edexcel's specification has more compulsory topics than the remaining Bodies combined, whilst neither OCR (2009) nor Pre-U (University of Cambridge, 2008) specifications has any compulsory content.

Awarding Bodies also differ in their requirements of 'core' and compulsory themes, and at what level of difficulty these should be studied. Energy, for example, is compulsory within the Edexcel specification at A2, whilst for AQA (the largest provider) Energy Issues, an AS option, is considerably outstripped in terms of candidate numbers by Health Issues. Other topics are ascribed different levels of importance or difficulty; for example, Water is a compulsory topic at A2 with Edexcel, is optional for WJEC, but is not even included among the rest. Almost all topics are thematic; only 'Emerging Asia' (WJEC/CBAC, 2009) is place-focused.

At A2, courses are even more varied in terms of coverage, where option topics abound. There is a clear focus on research rather than content, together with opportunities for both teachers and students to develop particular interests and specialisms. Some specifications, notably Edexcel and WJEC, offer varied option topics at A2 whereby students are encouraged to select and research a theme of their choosing, so that even within a single cohort of students in a school or college several different themes may be studied.

SHIFTING PARADIGMS AND APPROACHES

Even simple analysis of post-16 specifications portrays evidence of particular geographical approaches. Traditionally, those specifications produced by examining teams at AQA and OCR have their roots in traditional thematic geography, in which physical and human geography are largely portrayed as separate themes within the subject, whereas the backgrounds of senior examiners for Edexcel and WJEC, mainly in the '16-19 Project', tend to follow people–environment perspectives. There is, it appears, a strong adherence to particular approaches in particular specifications. How this has occurred is an interesting story in its own right and is partly a result of geography's dynamic development after the overturning of the long-established regional 'paradigm', which in school lasted well into the 1970s. Influenced by Thomas Kuhn's influential book, *The Structure of Scientific Revolutions* (1962), many writing about the development of geography as a discipline, both in HE and in the school curriculum, used the idea of 'paradigm shift' to capture the significance of different approaches to the subject. It is

Theme	AQA	Edexcel	OCR	WJEC	Pre-U
Population / migration	AS	AS		AS	
Global economy		AS			
Food					
Energy		A2			
Health					
Climate change and risk		AS		AS	
Hazards and risk		AS		AS	
Unequal spaces/deprivation					
Urban change/rebranding				AS	
Rural change/rebranding				AS	
Tourism					
Crime					
Housing					
Development/trade		A2			
World of work					
Superpowers		A2			
Technological fix		A2			
Water		A2			
Contemporary conflict					
Emerging Asia					
Retailing					
Pollution					
Cultural diversity					

Key

Compulsory topics

Option topics

Not offered

Figure 11.1 Thematic coverage of human geography among the five Awarding Bodies in England and Wales[2].

a useful analytical device, as we shall see below, but it remains controversial. Indeed, the 16–19 project's people–environment approach was explicitly adopted to avoid having to select one or other of the 'paradigms' of geography that were on offer: it was a form of compromise.

Until the 1970s, school geography was mostly 'regional' in nature – what Butt (2000) has referred to as 'an approach to geography concerned with the study of regions and their areal differentiation' (p. 157). School textbooks, in lower secondary school years at least, were based on international regions (e.g. 'The Southern Continents') and emphasised description and explanation. Their coverage was broad, particularly in lower secondary school, so that Walford (2001) described the approach as 'inevitably superficial'. Continents and regions were routinely described with maps and photographs accompanying text. For many, the Ministry of Education (1960) included, felt this approach offered 'an understanding of the interaction of all those complex factors which go to make up the personality of a region' (p. 38). JMB's own 'A' level 'Syllabus C' retained this approach until the 1990s when reduced candidate numbers led to its withdrawal.

The 'quantitative revolution' of the late 1960s radically altered 'A' level geography, filtering from universities so that it was commonplace by the late 1970s. Unwin (1992) has described the change from regional to 'an explanatory process-oriented science, based on the testing of theories and the construction of laws' (p. 106). The use of quantitative techniques was introduced to school students, and emphasised a scientific approach which Digby (2008) has described as 'based on the collection of data, hypothesis testing and a search for generalisations about spatial patterns and processes'. Textbooks and examination syllabuses included a range of theoretical models, and scientific enquiry as part of 'A' level syllabuses, such as JMB's 'Syllabus B' (1975), which attracted the largest number of candidates until the late 1980s.

By contrast, the emergence of 'humanistic geography' in school geography during the 1980s brought a sharp contrast to positivist approaches and the focus upon objective evidence. A new generation of GCSE syllabuses in 1986, particularly those derived from Schools Council curriculum projects, brought the values enquiry into school geography. Humanistic approaches had their shortcomings; different viewpoints in values-focused issues were often presented in textbooks as 'objective' evidence which students should accept, rather than consider as ways in which different people perceived the world. The Schools Council's '16–19 Project', offered by University of London Examinations in the 1980s and 1990s, was strongly influenced by this approach, together with aspects of radical geography.

Parallel with this, aspects of 'radical geography' also influenced the subject in schools in the 1980s. Johnston et al. (2000) has described this as a response of those who were 'critical of spatial science and positivism'. Typically, school geography adopted topics such as poverty, hunger and health and investigated contrasts in quality of life, inequality, and poverty. Physical geography shifted its focus from physical process to that of the environment and ways in which people could impact on physical processes, such as along coasts.

However, the diminishing role of HEI in school geography is reflected in the way that the dominant influence on geographical philosophy since the 1990s – that is, 'post-modernism' – has had little influence in school geography. Its rejection of what Valentine (2001) has called 'the claims of grand theories and metanarratives' (p. 345) has failed to make substantial impact, so that many students in the 2010s were still studying modernist geographical models such as the Demographic Transition Model. The acknowledgement by post-modernists that, in the words of Valentine, 'all knowledge is partial, fluid and ... emphasises a sensitivity to difference and an openness to a range of voices' (2001, p. 345) is hard to recognise in most GCSE and AS/A2 specifications from 2008 to 2009, as is the recognition by Morgan and Lambert (2005) of post-modernism as a 'plurality of explanations' (p. 54).

Digby (2008) has shown how, since the 1990s, academic geography in HEI has focused increasingly on 'the web of interconnections of places within a complex and changing world'. Difference and culture affect places and ways in which these are portrayed in text, or art and film, as well as environmental issues. A few influences have made their way into some post-16 specifications, such as Cultural Landscapes (Edexcel) or Environmental Psychology (WJEC). But Digby questions whether these have affected the *way* in which students learn.

THE INFLUENCE OF PEDAGOGY?

Having examined the relative influences of Awarding Bodies and HEI in the approach and content of examination specifications, this last section focuses on teaching and learning geography post 14. In considering this question, it is useful to draw on research carried out in KS3. In the early–mid 1990s, Roberts (1995, 2003) conducted research into how schools interpreted and planned the Geography National Curriculum. In spite of placing the National Curriculum at KS3 as her research focus, she found, significantly, that other curriculum choices that teachers had made had strongly influenced the ways in which they thought about KS3. She found that teacher choices about examination syllabuses were reflected in their planning and their views of teaching and learning, that is, their individual pedagogies. They approached planning and teaching units of work in very similar ways for all ages and key stages. Her ideas were informed and shaped by Barnes (1976), who contrasted transmission and interpretation views of teaching.

Roberts found that the ways in which teachers thought about and approached curriculum planning tended to occur in one of three, usually distinctive, ways which rarely overlapped. These were by content, using a framework, and enquiry-based.

1. Content

Roberts found that teachers who planned by content tended to value a more traditional curriculum, taught in traditional 'transmissive' ways. They presented

units of work as lists of items to be taught, usually within a thematic framework that tended, for example, to separate human and physical geography. Teaching was usually process-driven, with cause and effect; for example, river processes of erosion might be linked to the landforms that such processes produce. These processes and landforms would then be shown in units of work as content to be taught. Units were discrete, often unlinked to other areas of the subject; physical processes, for example, were often studied with little consideration of management issues or of human interference. A current example is shown from AQA's AS specification, for a unit on population (Figure 11.2).

- Population indicators – vital rates (birth rate, death rate, fertility rate, infant mortality rate, changes over time, life expectancy, migration rate and population density) for countries at different stages of development.

- Population change: the demographic transition model (5 stages), its validity and applicability in countries at different stages of development.

- Population structures at different stages of the demographic transition. The impact of migration in population structure. The implications of different structures for the balance between population and resources.

- Social, economic and political implications of population change. Attempts to manage population change to achieve sustainable development with reference to case studies of countries at different stages of development.

- The way population change and migration affects the character of rural and urban areas.

- Settlement case studies – comparing two (or more) of the following areas – an inner city area, a suburban area, an area of rural/urban fringe and an area of rural settlement. To include reference to characteristics such as: housing, ethnicity, age structure, wealth and employment and the provision of services. The implications of the above for social welfare.

Figure 11.2   A content approach to the subject – AQA's AS unit on Population (AQA, 2009).

2. Frameworks based upon key ideas

A second group of teachers tended to use what Roberts referred to as 'frameworks', consisting of key questions or key ideas by which to plan their teaching. They would often use issues and examples by which to generate interest and thematic content. Their units of work were usually designed such that content was focused upon key ideas, like those shown in the left-hand column in Figure 11.3. Focused concepts would therefore help students to learn about hazards, not in their entirety, but by using examples to illustrate fundamental concepts. This kind of planning was used in the early stages of the Schools Council '16–19 Project', where it was widely adopted by schools, and it now provides a commonly used format for presenting some GCSE and 'A' level specifications, such as that shown in Figure 11.3, from Edexcel's AS/A2 specification (2010).

What students need to learn	Suggested teaching and learning
Some types of hazards are increasing in magnitude and frequency, and having greater impacts upon people and their lives.	Researching databases (e.g. CRED) for evidence of the size and frequency of the top six global natural hazards (cyclones, droughts, floods, earthquakes, volcanoes and landslides/ avalanches) upon lives, property, infrastructure and GDP.
Natural disasters are increasing because of a combination of physical and human factors: • the unpredictability of global warming and El Niño events leading to increasing natural hazards. • the increasing exploitation of resources (eg deforestation), world poverty, rapid population growth and urbanisation.	Exploring examples of how natural and human activities are combining to cause increasing disaster scenarios, e.g. storms, floods and population change.
Trends show that the number of people killed is falling, whereas numbers affected and economic losses are escalating.	Developing an awareness of how and why disasters are affecting more people and causing more damage yet lives are being saved, using examples of hazard events.

Figure 11.3 A 'framework' approach: extract from Edexcel AS specification 'World at Risk' 2 Global hazard trends. Enquiry question: How and why are natural hazards now becoming seen as an increasing global threat?

3. The enquiry-based curriculum

Before the introduction of the National Curriculum for Geography in 1991, teachers could plan their own curriculum in ways that reflected their priorities and values. Roberts found that some teachers considered *how* students learned as fundamental, rather than *what* they learnt. Opportunities would be offered for students to decide for themselves some of what was learned by open-ended enquiry. Roberts (1995) found that such teachers explored ways to shape student learning even after the introduction of the National Curriculum, for example where students might investigate local villages near the school as part of a unit on settlement. This freedom of enquiry was embodied as a part of the '16–19 Project' (1982) for which, until 2000, students carried out individual enquiries which they devised themselves. The disappearance of coursework from AS and A2 Geography after 2008 removed any such freedom from students.

Pedagogic choices are important. Ofsted (2008) noted that 'limitations to the quality of teaching include a focus on content rather than learning' (para. 33). While teachers are held accountable through the examination results achieved by their students, many (particularly with PowerPoint® to help them) adopt more conservative learning strategies in their approaches to teaching older age groups. The need for pace in keeping to a specification, the time pressures of modular examinations, together with the readiness of their students to explain their grades as a consequence of their teaching, may condition the strategies for learning that teachers adopt.

Lessons, especially post-16, may be dominated by handouts or even dictated or closely guided notes, supported with exposition-style teaching strategies.

Conclusions and some speculations

At the time of writing, the curriculum and examination system is again under intense scrutiny by the government. An important issue is about preserving the 'gold standard' of GCSE and of A levels in particular, which has meant that the relationship between university academics and Awarding Bodies has come to the fore. In addition, the role of examiners in defining the specifications, in some cases writing textbooks *and* leading the professional development of teachers has been called into question (see David Gardner's chapter in this volume). The Minister for Education has on more than one occasion expressed an interest in the possibility of a single Awarding Body, or at least a single specification for each subject in England and Wales. A single definition of the subject might suit politicians, but its creation and development might result in more discontented than happy 'customers' – whether we think these are teachers or students.

Notes

1   Business and Technician Education Council. BTec now remains as a brand used by Edexcel for some of its vocational subjects; see http://www.edexcel.com/quals/introd/Documents/BTEC_Parents_Guide.pdf
2   NB: 'Climate change and risk', and 'Hazards and risk' are included in the table shown in Figure 11.1. Though the physical geography of climate change and of hazards is taught, the emphasis is on vulnerability and risk.

Key readings

1. Naish, M.C., Rawling, E. and Hart, R.C. (1987) *Geography 16–19: The contribution of a curriculum project to 16–19 education*, Harlow: Longman. This book details one of the most significant influences in post-16 geography teaching since the 1970s. The 16–19 Project questioned many of the content-heavy and positivist syllabuses available to teachers at the time. Its approach exemplifies what Roberts called both 'Framework' and 'Enquiry' teaching and learning.
2. Rawling, E. (2001) *Changing the subject: The impact of national policy on school geography 1980–2000*, Sheffield: Geographical Association. Rawling details more thoroughly than anyone the political influences which have affected geographical education in schools since the Thatcher government of the 1980s. This is essential reading in that it describes the process by which politicians take an active interest in education, and the means by which the curriculum is written in such a climate.

References

AQA (2009) 'GCE AS and A Level Specification: Geography' [online], Available from: http://web.aqa.org.uk/qual/gce/humanities/geography_noticeboard.php [Accessed 25 February 2012].

Barnes, D. (1976) *From Communication to Curriculum*, Harmondsworth: Penguin.

Bradford, M.G. and Kent, W.A. (1977) *Human geography: Theories and their applications,* Oxford: Oxford University Press.

BBC News (2011) 'Examiners reject cheat claims to MPs' 15 December 2011 [online], Available from: http://www.bbc.co.uk/news/education-16197500 [Accessed 24 February 2012].

Butt, G. (2000) *The Continuum Guide to Geography Education,* London: Continuum.

Digby, B. (2008) *Think Piece: Teaching 'A' level geography,* [online] Available from: http://www.geography.org.uk/gtip/thinkpieces/alevelgeography/ [Accessed 20 February 2012].

Edexcel (2010) 'Edexcel Advanced Subsidiary/Advanced GCE in Geography' Issue 3. Available from: http://www.edexcel.com/migrationdocuments/GCE%20New%20GCE/UA024843%20GCE%20Geography%20Issue%203%20210510.pdf [Accessed 20 February 2012].

Fairgrieve, J. (1926) *Geography in School,* London: University of London Press.

Heeley, M. and Roberts, M. (1996) 'Human and regional geography in schools and higher education', in E. Rawling and R. Daugherty (eds.), *Geography into the Twenty-First century,* Chichester: Wiley.

Johnston, R., Gregory, D., Pratt, G., and Watts, M. (eds.) (2000) *The Dictionary of Human Geography,* 4th Edn, Oxford: Blackwell.

Kuhn, T. (1962) *The Structure of Scientific Revolutions,* Chicargo IL: University of Chicargo Press.

Ministry of Education (1960) *Ministry of Education pamphlet, Issue 39,* London: HMSO.

Monkhouse, F. J. (1962) *Principles of Physical Geography,* London: University of London Press.

Morgan, J. and Lambert, D. (2005) *Geography: Teaching School Subjects 11–19,* London: Routledge.

OCR (2009) 'AS/A Level GCE Geography' Version 3. Available from: http://www.ocr.org.uk/download/kd/ocr_9630_kd_gce_spec.pdf [Accessed 24 February 2012].

Ofsted (2008) *Geography in Schools: Changing Practice,* Available from: www.ofsted.gov.uk/publications [Accessed 12 December 2011].

QCA (2006) 'GCE AS and A level subject criteria for geography' Available from: http://www.ofqual.gov.uk/files/qca-06-2852_geog_asandalevel_sc.pdf [Accessed 24 February 2012].

Rawling, E. (2001) *Changing the subject: The impact of national policy on school geography 1980–2000,* Sheffield: Geographical Association.

Roberts, M. (1995) 'Interpretations of the Geography National Curriculum: a common curriculum for all?', *Journal of Curriculum Studies,* 27 (2), 187–205.

Roberts, M. (2003) *Learning through Enquiry,* Sheffield: The Geographical Association.

Sheldon, N. (2011) 'History Examinations from the 1960s to the present day', [online] Available from: http://www.history.ac.uk/history-in-education/project-papers/topics [Accessed 20 February 2012].

Tattersall, K. (2007) 'A Brief History of Policies, Practices and Issues relating to Comparability', in P. Newton, J. Baird, H. Goldstein, H. Patrick, and P. Tymms (eds.), *Techniques for Monitoring the Comparability of Examination Standards,* London: Qualifications and Curriculum Authority.

University of Cambridge International Examinations (2008) 'Cambridge Pre-U Geography', Available from: http://www.cie.org.uk/qualifications/academic/uppersec/preu/subjects/subject/preusubject?assdef_id=973 [Accessed 20 February 2012].

Unwin, T. (1992) *The Place of Geography,* Harlow: Longman.

Valentine, G. (2001) *Social Geographies: Space and society,* Harlow: Prentice Hall.

Walford, R. (2001) *Geography in British Schools 1850–2000,* London: Woburn Press.

WJEC/CBAC (2009) 'GCE Examinations from 2009: Geography Available from: http://www.wjec.co.uk/uploads/publications/6312.pdf [Accessed 20 February 2012].

Young, E.W. and Lowry, J.H. (1984) *A Course in World Geography,* London: Hodder Education.

Chapter 12

How is the learning of skills articulated in the geography curriculum?

Phil Wood

> It would be desirable, in my view, to avoid simplistic, polarised debates which needlessly encourage the adoption of oppositional positions, particularly that old chestnut of knowledge v. skills.
>
> (Lambert, 2011, p. 245)

Introduction

Over the past 20 years there has been a growing interest in the development of skills in education (for example, Green, 2003), in large part a consequence of the growth of international economic markets with associated increases in labour mobility and flexibility. Education in this climate is increasingly seen as a driver for economic competitiveness and investment. Lyotard (1984) argues that the educational endeavour which has traditionally been driven by knowledge production and transmission is now being reconstructed as a process of developing and using generic skills which are thought of as important for efficient technological and economic use in the global economy (Usher and Edwards, 2008). The New Labour governments of 1997–2010 increasingly accepted this discourse and developed an emergent skills framework throughout all aspects of the curriculum, including geography. A similar process has occurred in Canada, where corporations have succeeded in embedding a 'skills agenda' as an accepted element of education policy (Taylor, 1998).

There is now, however, developing dialogue which identifies knowledge as the primary concern within the curriculum, leading to a need for a renegotiation of the roles and emphasis of skills within the geography curriculum. This debate focuses on the nature and roles of geographical skills, their place within the geography curriculum, and their relationship with knowledge, understanding and concepts.

WHAT ARE SKILLS?

The term 'skill' is used for many different activities and practices, for example, literacy/numeracy skills, map skills, thinking skills, enquiry-based skills, basic

skills, higher-order skills and learning skills. But what, within this wide spectrum of concepts, is a consistent basis for identifying the activity involved as a skill? Barrow (1999) argues that the skills agenda has led to what he calls the 'higher nonsense', terms which have become used in modern education which have little or no coherent meaning. He argues that 'skills' are often used synonymously to mean 'abilities', and as a result that all skills are seen as '... a specific, discrete, physical, trainable behaviour' (p. 133). Barrow sees this as problematic as he believes that it has become popular to believe that, through simplified development programmes, skills can be both developed and generalised beyond a particular context. Whether Barrow's critique is one with which we can agree or not, it does raise two issues: what are skills, and how should they be embedded within the curriculum; should they be developed as discrete entities, or within knowledge contexts?

Morlaix (2010) describes the move of the French government in 2005 to include skills as an explicit part of the country's national curriculum. Again, the definition of 'skills' is problematised. Morlaix states that 'Because the concept has many different facets, the task of rendering it operative is a particularly challenging one' (p. 396). Perhaps a simple way of beginning to do this is to use a basic dictionary definition, such as,

> The ability to utilize one's knowledge effectively and readily; 2. A developed aptitude or ability in a particular field.
>
> (Penguin Group, 1986)

Whilst this is a very general definition it does offer a clear process, a developing ability to apply knowledge within a particular field. Within an educational setting this suggests that the development of skills is actually the development of processes which allow for the use of emergent knowledge and understanding. Applying this description to the geography curriculum, a number of subject-led skills exist, including specific techniques such as fieldwork processes, and the use of maps and diagrams, as well as more generic cognitive activity such as describing, explaining and interpreting, thinking and enquiry skills. Bennetts (2002), suggests that,

> in geographical studies, they [skills] have to be applied in contexts which have geographical content, and which therefore require knowledge and understanding on the part of pupils.
>
> (p. 90)

Skills are intimately linked to geographical knowledge and understanding of content in Bennett's view, which opens up another facet of how we might understand skills. Are skills cross-disciplinary in nature, or specific to certain subjects; in other words, can we truly talk about *geographical* skills? One skills set which is

often associated with geography is map skills (for example Naish, 1997). Map skills are based around a number of competences, such as the use of coordinates and the reading of symbols. In the case of coordinates, the basic skill is also developed within the maths curriculum; in the case of reading symbols it could be argued that it is the learning of a new language. Other skills sets often associated with geography, such as fieldwork skills, are likewise multidisciplinary in nature.

In the case above, the skills developed within a geographical context can also be identified as having utility in other subjects. So are skills really identifiable as geographical? Perhaps both perspectives, of subject-specific versus generic, have an element of validity. Skills at a very general level might be seen as generic, for example, the development of the skill of using coordinates. However, the contexts in which coordinates are used are very different, and it is the knowledge and understanding of the subject which gives the skill meaning. The student needs to understand the subject context to make sense of, and develop their use of, the skill.

The above discussion demonstrates that skills are not easy to define, in part because of the wide spectrum of activities they might encompass, and also because their relationship to classifications of subjects is complex. However, it is at least possible to say that skills are competences which allow for the practical use and application of knowledge and understanding, and whilst there might be generic elements in their nature, they are also contextually located in relation to that specialist knowledge and understanding.

THE PLACE OF SKILLS IN THE GEOGRAPHY CURRICULUM

There are a large range of skills which geographers use and develop to aid understanding of the subject. The Geography National Curriculum at Key Stage 3 includes explicit skills foci: geographical enquiry, fieldwork, graphicacy and visual literacy and geographical communication, which are different to those in the Primary National Curriculum, which identifies a host of skills under a single heading 'Geographical enquiry and skills' encompassing enquiry and questioning skills, fieldwork, vocabulary and map skills. Other, perhaps generic, skills are not included in the programmes of study, but have been appropriated and developed within many geography classrooms, particularly the development of thinking skills. David Leat's *Thinking Through Geography* (2001) became very popular as a framework for developing thinking skills, heavily based on the CASE (Cognitive Acceleration in Science Education project) (Leat, 1997).

The statutory skills set described above, together with those which have developed from within the geography community itself, such as thinking skills approaches, are not immutable and never-changing, but have developed within the context of wider changes within the subject. The original National Curriculum (DES, 1991) had five Attainment Targets (AT), AT1 focusing on skills. The skills

mainly involved the development of map, fieldwork and communication skills, and were set out in fine detail. As the National Curriculum has developed, so the level of detail has diminished, and enquiry-based learning has become explicit. As skills have changed in nature, how have they related to other elements of the curriculum framework?

Traditionally, some skills have been taught as a discrete element of the curriculum. The stereotypical, but still common, example is the teaching of map and atlas skills, often as an introductory unit at the start of secondary level study. Students are taught the elements of map reading, such as how to use grid references, read contour information and measure distance. Further discrete, skills-based elements of the subject include fieldwork units, particularly at GCSE and A-level, where practical data collection skills and enquiry skills are developed. Having begun to understand and use map and field skills, to what extent are they then explicitly used and embedded in other areas of the curriculum? Ofsted (2011) emphasise that at primary level, most progression in map skills occurs where their use is woven into wider learning throughout the careers of children as they move through the primary curriculum. This indicates the importance of embedding skills progression within knowledge contexts.

Decisions about the incorporation of skills into the curriculum may relate to how the curriculum more generally is viewed by those who are creating it. Ross (2000) reviews three different visions of the curriculum:

- *Content-driven curricula*: formally delimited subjects each of which is tied to a recognised body of knowledge which needs to be conveyed to and understood by students;
- *Objectives-driven curricula*: objectives for the curriculum are set, such as employability objective, moral objectives and/or social objectives, and the curriculum is formed around these to ensure that those objectives are met;
- *Process-driven curricula*: the curriculum here is thought of as a framework for allowing students to explore and construct their learning, with the act of participating and growing within a curriculum being seen as more important than a focus on knowledge and understanding *per se*.

Even though the National Curriculum has existed since 1991 (DES, 1991) giving an 'official' view of the subject, the underlying curriculum philosophy of particular teachers varies greatly. As a consequence, the way in which knowledge, understanding and skills are brought together will be developed in a multitude of different ways. Departments, and even individual teachers, will develop different emphases in their curriculum, some focusing primarily on content, whilst others will foreground enquiry and other associated skills. Whatever the approach to the curriculum, consideration needs to be given as to how the elements will relate one to another if coherence and progression in geographical understanding is to be fostered.

The Geographical Association Manifesto (2009) highlights the notion of 'thinking geographically' and uses the analogy of a language:

> The grammar of geography is its 'big ideas', which help us organise and attach significance to the vocabulary (geographical information).
>
> (p. 10)

In this view of the curriculum, the geographical language is developed through a development of geographical knowledge (the vocabulary of the subject), which is organised and understood through geographical concepts. However, the role of skills is absent here, but might skills be seen as a form of 'syntax', that is, the rules or processes for ordering phrases? Skills are central in helping us construct geographical knowledge in a coherent way as they give us the capacity to structure, collect, manipulate, critique and discuss geographical knowledge and understanding.

The place of skills within the geography curriculum is mandated through lists in the National Curriculum and GCSE and A-level specifications, the way in which these skills are embedded in the curriculum and encountered by students will vary greatly from school to school. However, in developing the curriculum, careful thought needs to be given to the emphasis, role and relationships skills have with other elements of students' learning.

KNOWLEDGE VS SKILLS – IS THIS A NECESSARY DEBATE?

The nature of much of the geography curriculum has changed in emphasis since the birth of the National Curriculum (DES, 1991), alongside wider changes in educational thinking. As a result, thinking about both the nature and place of skills has also evolved. Geography up to the 1960s was predominantly characterised by regional geography, and the memorisation of large volumes of facts. However, Rawling (2001) describes the shift as,

> a more conceptual approach ... mak[ing] greater use of quantitative techniques and models, aiming to provide geography with greater rigour and a stronger claim to be part of the scientific community.
>
> (p. 22)

This created the need to develop numeracy and analytical skills as a requirement for learning, apparent as a consequence of the development of the Quantitative Revolution in geography. Subsequently, the introduction of the Schools Council (for Curriculum and Examinations) further developed an impetus for curriculum change and associated developments in new approaches to learning and skills development. An example of this was the introduction of the Geography 16–19 project which grew out of the Geography 14–18 project. This project emphasised

the development of enquiry and research skills, with areas of physical and human geography being treated together to demonstrate their interdependent nature. However, the development of the skills agenda led some to complain that knowledge was being diluted (Marsden, 1997; Walford, 2001) as the focus moved away from more traditional structures of knowledge and understanding within the subject, to more synthesised curricula which also introduced decision-making and problem-solving foci. Such debates mirrored a wider concern amongst what Ball (1990) called the 'New Right educationalists of the 1980s' (p. 47), who argued that education was being politicised and as such was no longer neutral and unbiased. This argument is clearly illustrated by Scruton et al. (1985, quoted in Rawling, 2001, p. 26),

> first difficult and disciplined parts of the subject are removed and downgraded, so that educational achievement can no longer be represented as mastery of a body of knowledge. Second, texts and subjects are chosen not for their intellectual and literary merit, or for their ability to further pupils' intellectual grasp, but for the political attitudes which are conveyed in them ....
>
> (Scruton et al., 1985, pp. 8–9)

From 2000 onwards the debate developed beyond subject boundaries with a surge in a focus on 'generic skills' which were promoted as embedded elements across the curriculum. The RSA 'Opening Minds' approach became popular, with some secondary schools replacing part of the subject-based curriculum with a competence focus in Year 7, leading to less focus on knowledge and understanding. However, Ofsted (2011) has reported that where such competency-based programmes have been developed, the learning of students within geography has suffered,

> poorly planned and taught integrated units of work in the humanities in Year 7, often linked to general skills-based initiatives, had resulted in less geography being covered.
>
> (Ofsted, 2011, p. 6)

Since 2010, the pendulum appears to be swinging back in the opposite direction. Lambert (2011) offers a view and critique of the emerging Coalition government's plans for the curriculum. Knowledge is once again central to curriculum planning, and the notion of 'core knowledge' is explored through a synthesis of the work of Hirsch (1987, 2007). Hirsch (2007) criticises process-oriented curricula, that is, those based around the development of skills sets which avoid a focus on knowledge, a 'how-to' rather than a 'know-what' approach. He advocates 'core knowledge', a collection of central, important knowledge which can act as a basis for further development. This thesis is critiqued by Lambert (2011), and is then used as part of a basis for an approach of 'deep learning'. Different forms

of knowledge are brought together to offer a multilayered notion of core knowledge (shallower facts and understanding), powerful knowledge (deeper, conceptual understanding) and the ability to think about geographical processes through various pedagogic experiences, decision making being used as one example by Lambert. However, what is of interest is the absence of skills as an explicit element in the weaving of such a framework. Why might this be the case? Has the recent history of skills as 'generic abilities' to be trained (Barrow, 1999) across the curriculum led to a negative view, even though the use of *geographical* skills has a long and central history in making the concepts and knowledge of geography concrete? It could also be argued that such swings between skills and knowledge are a 'bipolar illusion'. There seems to be a sub-text in arguments about curriculum that there must be a core focus on either skills (process-based), or knowledge (content-based), but can a position be put forward that rather than one or the other, a focus on both is fostered, the real questions becoming:

> What are the skills and knowledge that we feel are necessary for a clear and critical understanding of geography?
> At which point along a spectrum from skills-only focus to content-only focus do we want to position ourselves, and how might that position change with respect to age groups and time?

In this view there is an inherent belief that knowledge, concepts and skills all have a critical part to play in the developing geographical understanding and imagination of children. To see curricula as being solely beholden to content, objectives or processes (skills) is simplistic and unhelpful. A dynamic position which considers how each interweaves with the other is another potential position which perhaps needs to be made more explicit. Hence, in the debate of knowledge versus skills are we not able to be greedy and ask for both?

SUPPORTING PROGRESSION IN GEOGRAPHICAL SKILLS

Geographical skills cover a wide range of foci, including maps skills, decision-making skills, fieldwork skills, and enquiry skills to name but some. They are complex and multifaceted in nature, and are composed of a number of sub-skills (for example a spectrum of skills needed to complete successful fieldwork). It is also the case that some of the new, emerging skills in geography, such as Geographic Information Systems (GIS), involve aggregates of a number of families of skills. Such complexity brings with it the issue of progression. If skills are embedded with content and concepts to aid geographical thinking, in what order should they be developed? Also, how can we assess the developing skills to ensure that subsequent learning is securely built upon?

Many of the main areas of skills development in geography include the need to develop a number of different capacities. One example is the use of GIS.

A number of skills are important in developing capacities here, and it might even be argued that the term spatial literacy would be a better way of describing this area of skills development. There are different levels of GIS skills. Perhaps the most simple is being able to read the outputs of GIS packages, such as choropleth maps, or maps with proportional pie charts. In reading these outputs, there is an assumption that the student can read and understand base maps, with any associated symbols. There is then an assumption that they can understand what choropleth maps show and their potential shortcomings. Finally, there is an assumption that students can use spatial vocabulary (see Golledge, 2002; Golledge et al., 2008) to accurately describe the spatial patterns and relationships evident in the displayed data. To then move students forward to the production of GIS-generated maps, these skills are required plus others which might relate to datasets, the use of ICT packages and the underlying principles of GIS packages and their spatial constructions. Therefore, the use of GIS is not only a technical 'know-how' process involving an ICT package, but about a wider ability in spatial literacy.

In considering the integration of GIS into the curriculum, any planning of skills development needs to move forward in a number of ways to accommodate the outline as given above, including the order in which elements are presented and practised. Are some of the skills more 'foundational' than others? How can a framework be built that builds the skills for deep understanding in GIS rather than simplistic following of preconceived instructions? The same can be said of other geographical skills sets such as fieldwork and enquiry-based learning. Such 'networks of development' highlight the importance of building curricula over a number of years from Early Years, through primary and into secondary geography. Bennetts (2005) argues that understanding comes from an iterative process of experience and theory forming. Experiences are rationalised into mental constructs which are then interrogated and refined through subsequent experience. Skills development can be seen in this way, and serves to demonstrate the importance of repeated exposure to skills if they are to be internalised and understood in their support of emerging knowledge and understanding of geographical content. This has led to the popular use of the notion of 'spiral curricula' (Bruner, 1960) where a skill or area of content is encountered on a number of occasions, each time making its use more complex and difficult. However, this is perhaps too simplistic for the development of skills competence given the complex and interactive nature of skills sets, as outlined in the example of GIS. In the case of enquiry-based learning, Roberts (2003) suggests that an enquiry-based project cycle does not need to be completed in its entirety to develop enquiry skills. For example, it is possible to complete an activity which focuses on data analysis without collecting the data themselves, and still complete a meaningful learning experience. However, Roberts does highlight the need for meta-learning, where having completed the data analysis, students consider what they have learned, and how it might fit into a larger enquiry project where they themselves were collecting their own data.

Geographical skills are often extensive and complex in nature. An example is in the development of decision-making skills, which include the need to use generic skills such as critical and creative thinking, as well as numeracy and literacy. However, all of these skills rely on the use of geographical knowledge and understanding to give them meaning and context. Therefore, is the use of simple notions such as spiral curricula sufficient to capture the processes required for successful skills development? If, in Roberts' (2003) opinion, specific skills can be used and practised, and periodically brought together in larger, amalgamated projects, we need to be explicit about the spectrum of skills of interest, the content which they can be usefully applied to, and how they can be understood at a meta-level over a period of time. In practice, this can lead to a huge number of different formations, as to make sense the skills need to be linked positively to geographical content and concepts.

If the development of clear lines of progression in skills is not a simple issue, neither is the assessment of them. James and Gipps (1998) suggest that if high-order skills such as synthesis and interpretation, related to the geographical skills of enquiry-based learning or fieldwork, are to be developed it is important to use different modes of assessment. If skills are part of a holistic approach to curriculum, allied to knowledge and understanding, assessment needs to be able to offer advice on closing 'learning gaps' (Sadler, 1989) not only for knowledge but skills as well. This then suggests the need for carefully developed assessment opportunities which give clear feedback to both teacher and student concerning the degree to which skills have been mastered, knowledge understood, and the two brought together. Therefore, as well as integrating the use and development of skills into the curriculum, assessment frameworks must be carefully developed which give regular, critical and useful feedback and feed forward to aid further development in the use of skills, and their ability to enhance geographical knowledge and understanding.

Conclusion

The debates surrounding the place of skills in geography education are intimately linked with associated debates about the geography curriculum, and central to both is the question concerning the basis for the geography curriculum. Mills (1959) introduced the concept of 'sociological imagination', an ability to imagine and predict sociological processes and systems. In his view, to develop such capacities was at the centre of what it meant to be a good sociologist. A distinction can be drawn between someone who learns about sociology and someone who develops their understanding as a sociologist. The former can develop a knowledge and understanding of the main concepts and principles of the subject, but may have little understanding of how to think as a sociologist or to carry out their own work as a sociologist; for that they need to weave the skills of a sociologist into the fabric of their knowledge and understanding.

In a similar fashion, the degree to which skills are thought to be important in the development of geographical understanding in students depends upon the

aims of the curriculum which is created. At present, the nature and extent of the return to knowledge within the geography curriculum is still unclear. Knowledge is at the centre of any curriculum as it creates the framework for learning, but it is in its link to skills that the true nature of learning is revealed. If we only want students to know and understand some geographical content, then skills are not central to their development, but if the main intention is to aid students in beginning to act as geographers, to think geographically, then skills are an inherent element in learning the 'language' of geography. In thinking holistically about the interplay of concepts, content and skills, we may make the process of curriculum development more difficult as a number of interests and factors need to be held in positive association. However, can we say that to hold any of these elements of geographical thinking in less explicit regard is to help students develop their critical capacity to think independently and to think geographically? The 'knowledge turn' in geography education is still young; in emphasising this element of the curriculum, we must not forget the importance of the supporting role of a developed and mature approach to skills.

Key readings

1. Roberts, M. (2003) *Learning Through Enquiry*, Sheffield: Geographical Association. Margaret Roberts' book provides an excellent framework for the embedding and development of core skills within the geography curriculum.
2. Barrow, R. (1999) 'The higher nonsense: Some persistent errors in educational thinking', *Journal of Curriculum Studies*, 31 (2), 131–42. Barrow's paper focuses on a broader audience than the purely geographical, but offers an interesting critique concerning the way in which 'skills' have been conceptualised and embedded within wider educational debates.

References

Ball, S.J. (1990) *Politics and policy making in education: Explorations in policy sociology*, Vol. 1, London: Taylor & Francis.
Barrow, R. (1999) 'The higher nonsense: Some persistent errors in educational thinking', *Journal of Curriculum Studies*, 31 (2), 131–42.
Bennetts, T. (2002) 'Continuity and Progression', in M. Smith (ed.), *Teaching geography in secondary schools: A reader*, London: RoutledgeFalmer.
Bennetts, T. (2005) 'Progression in Geographical Understanding', *International Research in Geographical and Environmental Education*, 14 (2), 112–32.
Bruner, J. (1960) *The Process of Education*, Cambridge, MA: Harvard University Press.
DES (1991) *Geography in the National Curriculum*, London: HMSO.
Geographical Association (2009) *A Different View: A manifesto from the Geographical Association*, Sheffield: Geographical Association.
Golledge, R.G. (2002) 'The nature of geographic knowledge', *Annals of the Association of American Geographers*, 92 (1), 1–14.
Golledge, R.G., March, M. and Battersby S. (2008) 'Matching geospatial concepts with geographic educational needs', *Geographical Research*, 46, 85–98.
Green, A. (2003) 'Education, Globalisation and the Role of Comparative Research', *London Review of Education*, 1 (2), 84–97.

Hirsch, E.D. (1987) *Cultural Literacy*, Boston, MA: Houghton Mifflin.

Hirsch, E.D. (2007) *The knowledge deficit*, Boston, MA: Houghton Mifflin.

James, M. and Gipps, C. (1998) 'Broadening the basis of assessment to prevent the narrowing of learning', *The Curriculum Journal*, 9, 285–97.

Lambert, D. (2011) 'Reviewing the case for geography, and the 'knowledge turn' in the English National Curriculum', *Curriculum Journal*, 22 (2), 243–64.

Leat, D. (1997) 'Cognitive acceleration in geographical education', in D. Tilbury and M. Williams (eds.), *Teaching and Learning in Geography*, London: Routledge.

Lyotard, J.F. (1984) *The Postmodern Condition*, Minneapolis, MN: University of Minnesota Press.

Marsden, W. (1997) 'Taking the Geography out of Geographical Education: some historical pointers', *Geography*, 82 (3), 241–52.

Mills, C.W. (1959) *The Sociological Imagination*, London: Oxford University Press.

Morlaix, S. (2010) 'Assessing pupils' skills: Implications for research in education', *Journal of Curriculum Studies*, 42 (3), 395–409.

Naish, M. (1997) 'The scope of school geography', in D. Tilbury and M. Williams (eds.), *Teaching and Learning in Geography*, London: Routledge.

Ofsted (2011) *Geography: Learning to make a world of difference* [online] Available from: http://www.ofsted.gov.uk/resources/geography-learning-make-world-of-difference [Accessed 26 January 21].

Penguin Group (1986) *The New Penguin English Dictionary*, London: Penguin Group.

Rawling, E. (2001) *Changing the Subject: The Impact of National Policy on School Geography 1980–2000*, Sheffield: Geographical Association.

Roberts, M. (2003) *Learning Through Enquiry*, Sheffield: Geographical Association.

Ross, A. (2000) *Curriculum: Construction and critique*, London: Routledge.

Sadler, D.R. (1989) 'Formative assessment and the design of instructional systems', *Instructional Science*, 18 (2), 119–44.

Scruton, R., Ellis-Jones, A. and O'Keefe, D. (1985) *Education and Indoctrination*, Harrow: Educational Research Centre.

Taylor, A. (1998) 'Employability skills: From corporate 'wish list' to government policy', *Journal of Curriculum Studies*, 30 (2), 143–64.

Usher, R. and Edwards, R. (2008) *Globalisation and Pedagogy: Space, Place and Identity*, 2nd edn, New York: Routledge.

Walford, R. (2001) *Geography in British Schools 1850–2000*, London: Woburn Press.

Chapter 13

What is the contribution of fieldwork to school geography?

Alan Kinder

Geography wants to take children outside the school and into the streets and fields; it wants to take keyboard tappers out of their gloomy offices and into the rain or the sunshine.

(Bonnett, 2008, p. 80)

Introduction

Alistair Bonnett's assertion captures at least one essential element of geographical fieldwork: its sense of freedom, of breaking out from the constraints of the regular classroom environment, exposing both teachers and learners to the possibility of discovery and, perhaps, the opportunity to recover something of the spirit of exploration that helped to create the discipline we call 'geography'.

But Bonnett's claim also raises some rather challenging questions for teachers of geography. *Why* do geographers want to 'take children outside the school and into the streets and fields'? What do we want children to *do* when they get there and what do we want them to bring *back*? Does fieldwork have a positive effect on learning in geography? In seeking answers to these questions, this chapter explores the choices geography teachers might make in shaping 'fieldwork and outdoor learning' experiences for children and young people. The focus, therefore, is on the nature of fieldwork and the way in which this can help to enrich geographical learning, rather than the safe *management* of fieldwork (sources for which include May and Richardson, 2005; Holmes and Walker, 2006; CLotC, 2012). We also take it as read that there are many and various pressures which can lead to reduction in fieldwork provision as part of the curriculum experience (see Herrick, 2010).

THE PURPOSE OF FIELDWORK AND OUTDOOR LEARNING

Fieldwork can be defined as any component of the curriculum that involves leaving the classroom and learning through first-hand experience (Boyle et al., 2007). The need to define in more detail the purpose (or *range* of purposes) of fieldwork

might, at first glance, appear to be an unnecessary task for the busy teacher. It is, after all, a statutory requirement in Key Stages 1–3 and a component of the GCSE and A level criteria for geography which informs specification design. However, careful reading of such documentation suggests that it is in general stronger on exhortation *to* teachers than explanation *for* them. In KS1, learners 'should be taught to … use fieldwork skills' and 'carry out fieldwork investigations outside the classroom' (DfEE/QCA, 1999, pp. 110–11). By KS3, learners 'should be able to … select and use fieldwork tools and techniques appropriately, safely and efficiently' (QCA, 2007, p. 104) and 'undertake fieldwork investigations in different locations outside the classroom, individually and as part of a team' (2007, p. 107). The national curriculum therefore presents geography teachers with some rather circular thinking – that the purpose of undertaking fieldwork is to develop fieldwork skills. The lack of a rationale for fieldwork in such a statutory document is perhaps understandable: the failure to link it to other aspects of geographical learning less so.

As Table 13.1 makes clear, teachers designing a fieldwork programme or field excursion have a range of aims to draw upon, which take them well beyond the meeting of statutory requirements.

Table 13.1 The potential purposes of geographical fieldwork

Broad educational purpose	Geographical fieldwork aim	Outcomes for learners (from the Learning Outside the Classroom Manifesto)
Conceptual	Developing knowledge and understanding of geographical processes, landforms, issues	• Improved academic achievement • A bridge to higher-order learning • Opportunities for informal learning
Skills related	Developing skills in data collection, presentation and analysis with real data	• Skills and independence in a widening range of environments • The ability to deal with uncertainty
Aesthetic	Developing sensitivity to and appreciation of built and natural environments	• Stimulation, inspiration and improved motivation • Nurture of creativity
Values related	Developing empathy with views of others and care about/for the environment	• Development of active citizens and stewards of the environment
Social and personal development	Personal, learning and thinking skills such as independent enquiry, critical thinking, decision-making, team working	• Engaging and relevant learning for young people • Challenge and the opportunity to take acceptable levels of risk • Improved attitudes to learning • Reduced behaviour problems and improved attendance

(Source: adapted from Caton, 2006; Job, 1996 and DfES, 2006)

APPROACHES TO FIELDWORK

An effective fieldwork practitioner, like an effective classroom practitioner, is not only clear about purposes, aims and intended outcomes; they also possess a repertoire of approaches that can be adapted to a variety of contexts. There are countless ideas and strategies for geographical fieldwork and a rich library of texts from which to draw inspiration (e.g. Job et al., 1999; Holmes and Farbrother, 2000; Caton, 2006a; 2006b). However, the challenge for the geography teacher wishing to develop their practice is to:

- make sense of the choices available to them, by identifying a range of approaches and understanding how these can be of value in creating and shaping fieldwork experiences;
- learn to adapt and combine strategies to create worthwhile fieldwork experiences for learners – thereby extending their repertoire;
- select the strategies/activities most likely to meet the needs and interests of a particular group of learners.

As is often the case in geography, a system of classification can help to bring a sense of order to a highly complex landscape. A widely adopted way of thinking about fieldwork is as a continuum of types of activity, characterised by different forms and levels of learner and teacher involvement (Kent et al., 1997). Thus, from the learner's perspective, fieldwork can be placed along two continua – from passive observation to participation; and from dependency (on the teacher) to autonomy. An alternative approach is illustrated in Figure 13.1, which uses the degree of teacher 'control' and the degree of emphasis on quantification as continua for the classification of fieldwork activities.

These criteria can be re-phrased as questions:

- What degree of freedom for discovery and self-education is afforded by the strategy?
- What is the nature of the learning outcome (from highly specific and quantitative to broad sets of ideas and emotions)?

Five 'families' of strategies emerge from this analysis. As can be seen from the diagram, each of these can in themselves contain variety – the classification creates 'zones' rather than points on the diagram. Nor are these strategies mutually exclusive: some draw on elements from more than one approach (Balderstone, 2000).

1. Field excursions

Once seen as the 'traditional' approach to fieldwork, field excursions have been described by Lenon and Cleves (1994) as 'the guided tour' (p. 6). They are led

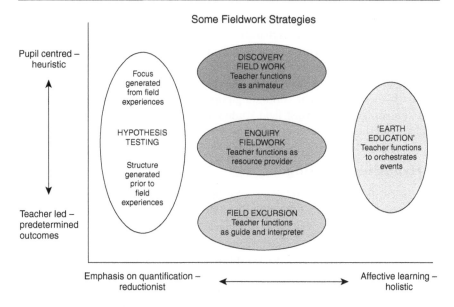

Figure 13.1 Aa classification of fieldwork activities (after Job, 1996).

by an expert (perhaps the teacher) whose role is to impart knowledge and under-standing to the group. The rationale for this approach might be summed up by the phrase, 'the more you know, the more you see'. It can be characterised as 'observational fieldwork', with a high degree of dependency on the teacher (Kent et al., 1997). Consequently, strategies based on this approach tend to be domi-nated by teacher exposition, note-taking, question and answer sessions (to check understanding) and field sketching.

Field excursions are therefore ordinarily regarded as most effective or appropri-ate in circumstances where the teacher chooses to 'transmit' information quickly and directly rather than design strategies for learners to uncover knowledge and understanding independently. For example, in order to develop learners' under-standing of the geomorphological processes at work in a landscape, learners are asked to notice subtle evidence they might otherwise miss. Other circumstances favouring this approach include: where the group is under pressure of time; where the environment is considered too hazardous for independent work; or where outside, perhaps non-teaching, expertise is available and a 'walk and talk' approach allows access to the specialised knowledge and perspective of the speaker.

However, teacher-led observation is also regarded as carrying with it a number of potential educational risks. No matter how enthusiastic and engaging the speaker, the reliance on listening and relatively passive role of the learner can lead to low degrees of engagement. The assumption that an explanation provided by the teacher promotes understanding in the mind of the student – that complex knowledge and understanding can be 'transmitted' relatively easily through

teacher exposition – is also one that is regarded critically. As Kent et al. (1997) put it, the principal problem 'is that students are only required to "be there" with the result that their attention may actually be elsewhere' (p. 315). In addition, the approach places a heavy reliance on teacher expertise – either site-specific knowledge or sufficiently developed subject knowledge to interpret the landscape accurately for students. The continuing popularity, despite the additional cost, of field courses led by specialist field studies staff suggests that not all geography teachers feel they have the required expertise in these respects.

2. Hypothesis testing

This 'scientific' approach to geography fieldwork gained currency during the 'quantitative revolution' of the 1960s and 1970s, and has remained a mainstay of geography fieldwork ever since. It is frequently, but not always, characterised by the collection and analysis of quantitative data, something that is supported by almost all current GCSE and A level specifications, since the data collected lend themselves readily to the types of data processing and representation credited by examiners. Hypothesis testing also promotes a 'rigorous' image of the subject as a scientific discipline. Typically, the hypothesis is generated from geographical models or theories and is 'applied' to specific locations. Lenon and Cleves (1994) distinguish between truly experimental work which attempts to 'find answers to previously unresearched problems' and *pseudo-experimental* fieldwork where 'measurements are taken but the outcome is probably already known' (p. 6). A good deal of hypothesis-testing conducted at school level is of this latter type. For example, the June 2012 'controlled assessment task' for one awarding body asks students to investigate how velocity changes downstream – something they could find a succinct answer to in the pages of the approved course textbook.

The hypothesis-testing approach is still seen as having a number of beneficial characteristics. The process promotes a logical and sequential approach to investigation, allowing students to make sense of highly complex situations through the careful examination of evidence. Students can 'test' general models and theories in specific locations, while gaining valuable experience in data-gathering methods and the use of a range of fieldwork equipment. However, assumptions about the active participation of students have been questioned (see Rynne, 1998). Caton (2006b) identifies a number of shortcomings including students' poor engagement with repetitive activities, the narrow focus of work which can limit an holistic appreciation of a place and the limited use made of the student's prior understanding or experience. Taylor (2004) asks pointedly, 'How often do we take students to interesting places, perhaps areas far removed from their normal range of experience, and then get them to spend most of their time looking at a clip board or measuring instrument?' (p. 53).

A more general criticism of the hypothesis-testing habits of school geographers is that this approach may be seen as relatively narrow and over-simplistic, ignoring as it does the 'cultural turn' of geography at university level and the

move towards more participatory approaches which attempt to take account of the complexity of real-world situations (Powell, 2002). To develop this point a little further and to provide something of a defence against this criticism, it is clear from Job's model that hypothesis testing may be organised deductively (teacher-led – with the introduction of geographical theory leading to the formulation of an hypothesis) or inductively (encouraging students to develop hypotheses based on initial observations in the field). In the deductive approach, where students are given an hypothesis and asked to undertake a phase of data gathering without recourse to discussion or reasoning, we should regard the degree of student autonomy in the field as being low. Interpretation and, it is assumed, gains in understanding appear separately from the 'fieldwork' element under this approach – sometimes much later and following a phase of data processing.

Whereas the deductive approach may be seen as having parallels with the 'traditional' descriptive-explanatory mode of teaching geography, an alternative model of 'analytical-predictive' teaching has gained ground (and support) in the teaching of physical geography within universities. In this mode of teaching, processes, principles and problems are analysed and their outcome or solution predicted. Fuller et al. (2000) suggest that fieldwork in this mode 'should make students aware of the nature of the subject and develop their understanding of key concepts by requiring the application of knowledge' (p. 201). For instance, an investigation of 'how velocity changes downstream' might, in the analytical-descriptive mode, require learners to identify the factors impacting upon river velocity, explain the effect that these seem to be having at each fieldwork site and predict the velocity of the stream before taking their measurements – providing them with an immediate purpose for 'looking at a clip board or measuring instrument'. This notion of providing what Roberts (2003) calls a 'need to know' is developed more fully below.

3. Enquiry

> The value of an academic subject lies in the extent to which it answers questions we are interested in.
>
> (Roberts, 2009)

Enquiry fieldwork is concerned with posing and investigating questions. The challenge for geography teachers is to ensure that these are indeed 'pertinent' questions – ones that are likely to engage learners and lead to worthwhile outcomes. Job (1999) proposes some 'well-conceived questions' that might underpin the design of good-quality enquiry fieldwork:

- What is this place like?
- What distinguishes it from other places that I know?
- What does it mean to me? What does it mean to other people who live here?
- How is it related to other places?

- How did it used to be? How might it change?
- Are there different views about change in the locality? How would we prefer it to change?
- Can it go on like this?

Whilst these questions are generic and may not translate directly into fieldwork activities in specific locations, they do draw on powerful geographical thinking and are therefore intended to unlock the curiosity of students in the field. Note also that, like any set of approaches, these questions are far from being 'value-free'. Many of them have a strong humanist or ecological slant. The issue of values is discussed later in this chapter.

Given the ease with which an hypothesis can be turned into a question ('The depth of a river increases downstream' becomes 'What happens to the depth of a river as it approaches its mouth?') some practitioners (and, it seems, some awarding bodies) make the mistaken belief that the two approaches are interchangeable. This is to misunderstand the nature of an *enquiry* question. Riley (2000) suggests that good enquiry questions:

- capture the interest and imagination of pupils;
- place an aspect of subject-specific, for example geographical thinking or investigating, at the forefront of the mind;
- result in tangible, lively, substantial, enjoyable 'outcome activities' (p. 8).

Riley's criteria suggest that the quality of the questions posed is crucial to the success of the enquiry approach. Questions that students can relate to, that they are beginning to pose themselves, that they want to know the answer to or that allow them to consider 'what might' and to develop their geographical thinking are all more likely to be successful enquiry questions. Other common enquiry pitfalls include not involving students (the teacher posing questions without reference to students' needs and interests) or posing questions that limit possibilities ('where should the factory go?' rather than 'should it be built?'). The relationship between a genuine enquiry approach and the 'analytical-predictive' mode of teaching described above is worthy of further consideration by teachers, awarding bodies and other stakeholders in school geography.

The final two types of fieldwork strategies are 'experiential', encourage learner participation and generally demand a higher degree of learner autonomy. This distinguishes them from the 'positivist' approaches discussed above. Their ethos is probably best captured by Van Matre (1979):

> Many of life's most rewarding, enriching and heartfelt experiences can barely be put into words, let alone placed on a scale. If we relied too much on the usual processes of collecting and testing, what would happen to our goals of instilling a sense of wonder, a sense of place and a reverence for life?
>
> (Van Matre, 1979, cited by Job, 2002, p. 134)

4. Discovery

Discovery fieldwork involves the teacher taking a calculated risk. In order to function as an *animateur*, the teacher provides opportunity and encouragement for learners to explore environments for themselves. New observations and personal discoveries are likely. Outcomes and even locations can be determined by the participants, not the teacher.

The emphasis of discovery fieldwork is on exploration and the development of independent learning skills. Typically, students are given the opportunity to use generic tools and techniques (e.g. taking photographs, making observations or collecting objects) driven by their own curiosity. As they discover features in an environment, the intention is for them to develop a sense of where they are and to begin to generate ideas and questions for further discovery. The results are inherently unpredictable – hence the sense of 'risk' in teaching terms.

A number of significant barriers to the use of discovery approaches have tended to limit their use in school geography. The perception that the location is not tightly prescribed or that supervision is compromised raises obvious concerns over the safety of learners. The limited sense of activity structure and relatively open-ended nature of the approach can leave teachers feeling a loss of control. Furthermore, the greater degree of freedom afforded to participants places a high degree of trust on children and young people, demands positive attitudes and assumes that learners will stay 'on task' without direct and close supervision.

Of course, the potential barriers identified above might also be seen as opportunities for promoting quality learning outcomes. This alternative view regards discovery approaches as *promoting* good behaviour, by placing increased responsibility on young people. Following this reasoning, learners are seen as more likely to develop skills for identifying and managing risks if they are required to explore environments independently – albeit in ways appropriate for their age and experience. Discovery also permits learners to focus on aspects of an area which are of interest and relevance to them. In this sense, it builds on their prior experience and understanding and promotes a constructivist approach to learning.

A range of strategies are available for providing structure in order to develop discovery skills (for both teachers and learners). For example, appropriate limits of exploration can be defined; maps, time frames and worksheets provided. Techniques such as 'scavenger hunts' or the use of 'journey sticks' allow even the youngest primary phase students to discover aspects of an environment by searching for objects and features that are of interest to them (Whittle, 2006). A variation on discovery fieldwork is to ask students to discover a place from a particular perspective. This can involve giving students roles and asking them to explore an area with particular needs in mind (e.g. imagining an area from an older person's point of view). Alternatively, students can engage in an ethnographic approach by closely observing or talking to members of a community. An innovative and even daring range of such approaches has been compiled as the *Mission: Explore* handbook (The Geography Collective, 2010).

5. Earth education

Whilst some educators prefer the term 'sensory fieldwork' to the more value-laden 'earth-education', the two terms are closely linked in the sense that they 'are most often aimed at re-establishing the somewhat fractured connections between people and nature' (Job et al., 1999, p. 16). By asking students to take 'time out' from the tasks we ordinarily ask them to undertake and instead to connect with their sense of smell, touch, sight, hearing and even taste, sensory approaches are designed to effect a deep emotional response to environments. Although these approaches were originally developed in natural and often remote environments as a way of reconnecting people and nature, they are increasingly being seen as a valid means of investigation in urban environments.

Like any approach to teaching, earth education is not value-free. Its origins are in environmental education, its objective to create concern and prompt action on environmental (and, more recently, social) issues. The 'model for outdoor education' (after Hawkins, 1987) provides a structured route through the earth education approach and is explicit about its aims and values. According to Hawkins, the first stage of this fieldwork approach is to raise awareness or provide 'acclimatisation' to the environment. Fieldwork activities aim to heighten the learner's awareness and develop their personal response to a place. This sharpening of perceptions and development of critical analysis can be prompted by depriving the leaner of one of their senses (e.g. removing their sense of sight with a blindfold) in order that they focus more keenly on other aspects of the environment, such as smell or sound. This initial 'stimulus' is followed by an investigation stage, wherein participants identify a focus for further investigation and carry out their own individual or group enquiry to further their knowledge and understanding. According to Hawkins, the aim of the final stage is to develop 'concern or action'. This involves the development of feelings of personal responsibility for a location or environment and a desire to participate in decisions which affect it. In other words, an element of participation which may result in direct action underpins the approach. Adopting this model in its entirety therefore presents teachers with practical and ethical challenges. As a result, earth education approaches which go beyond the first stage as a means of connecting learners to a place are relatively rare in schools, although there are notable exceptions (Doyle, 2006).

BENEFITS OF FIELDWORK

Having analysed the range of available strategies, we now critically examine the assumption that fieldwork is beneficial to the learning of students. Gold et al. (1991) have suggested that 'there is no clear evidence on the general value of fieldwork' (p. 27), a view echoed by Kent and Foskett (2002) who note that 'we often struggle to provide evidence to support our beliefs about the benefits of fieldwork' (p. 177). Whilst relatively little research has been conducted to investigate the cognitive gains of selecting first-hand investigation over classroom-based strategies, those who have ventured into this field tend to emphasise the affective benefits (Fuller et al., 2000; Herrick, 2010).

From a higher education perspective, Herrick (2010) defended fieldwork as 'an appropriate tool and setting' for observation-based knowledge acquisition, citing benefits such as the development of research, decision-making and team-work skills, as well as opportunities to bring learners into real-world settings and use active and experiential approaches, which contextualise and 'render visible' theoretical geographical ideas. Boyle et al. (2007) concluded that 'fieldwork is good if it triggers positive emotional responses', since these responses engender motivation, reduce anxiety about learning, develop constructive relationships, promote confidence and therefore foster deep rather than surface approaches to learning (p. 302). Dunphy and Spellman's (2009) empirical research found students rated the social aspects of fieldwork very highly. According to MacKenzie and White (1982), 'memorable episodes' such as reaching the top of a hill or paddling in water can aid long-term memory retention. Despite such 'undeniably comprehensive and holistic benefits' (Herrick, 2010, p. 109), the role of geography fieldwork in higher education is not uncontested. In sketching out a critique of fieldwork, Powell (2002) referred to earlier writers' views of fieldtrips as an 'initiation ritual of the discipline', one where 'students are taught to confront nature in the name of science', to engage in a masculine, intimidating and sometimes socially segregating experience (p. 263). The renewed interest in researching fieldwork in higher education may be due to the threat to its viability, but further research on the 'deep learning' impacts is also required.

For school geography, the available evidence suggests that prescription at policy level is no guarantee of quality outcomes for learners: nor does it ensure the position of fieldwork within the crowded school curriculum. Indeed, when seen only or predominantly as a statutory or examination requirement, significant numbers of teachers pay no more than 'lip-service' to fieldwork requirements, tend not to consider the fundamental educational need for it and therefore provide minimal programmes of limited impact (Ofsted, 2011). For some teachers, it seems that fieldwork has become peripheral to the subject (Cook et al., 2006). More encouragingly, inspectors found examples where 'good and regular fieldwork motivated pupils and enhanced their learning in geography' (Ofsted, 2011, p. 41). In the secondary phase fieldwork adds 'detail and depth to students' learning' and enables them to 'understand the relevance' of their studies (2011, p. 45). Overall, however, Ofsted concluded that fieldwork is 'underdeveloped' in the majority of secondary schools, with only around one fifth having an integrated programme to develop fieldwork skills progressively, and that almost half of schools have no significant fieldwork in Key Stage 3 and provide only the minimum needed to meet the demands of GCSE and A level examinations (Ofsted, 2011).

Nor do recent changes to examination specifications seem to have helped to shift practice in schools towards more productive modes of fieldwork. Pointon and Wood (2007) reinforce the impression of an educational culture in which geography teachers comply with requirements and have limited incentive to explore educational purpose. The replacement of A level coursework (which often incorporated the use of fieldwork evidence collected and analysed by the

candidate) with a limited range of ultimately predictable examination questions as a means to assess fieldwork skills risks encouraging rote learning rather than innovation in the field (p. 2). Perhaps the question to be asked of school geography fieldwork, then, is not *whether* it meets its stated objectives, but *how* we may encourage it to do so.

Conclusion

The purpose of this chapter has been to examine the choices made by teachers of geography when designing fieldwork experiences and the context within which these choices are made. Research and inspection evidence suggests that fieldwork is a vital and enriching element of the geography curriculum. The review by Rickinson et al. (2004), which drew on 150 examples of research published between 1993 and 2003, concluded that effective fieldwork has a range of positive benefits on participants. However, for fieldwork to be 'effective' it needs to be properly conceived; carefully planned; taught to a high standard and effectively followed up. It seems therefore that the potential of fieldwork and outdoor learning can only be fully realised if teachers are successful in clarifying their own educational purposes and selecting suitable strategies from a wider repertoire.

This conclusion is set within an interesting current policy context: successive iterations of the National Curriculum for geography have tended to reduce the degree of detailed content prescription, placing increased responsibility on the school, department and individual teacher to shape the curriculum locally. At the same time, the weakening of the direct link between 'the fieldtrip' and 'the coursework' post-14 presents challenges (e.g. to justify the field visit to senior leaders and parents) as well as opportunities (e.g. to widen the scope of fieldwork and use it to underpin geographical learning more generally). A decade ago, Kent and Foskett (2002) argued for the need to remake the case of fieldwork 'with each curriculum review' (p. 178). The contemporary case for fieldwork almost certainly includes the way in which it provides a challenge to the sedentary, indoor and increasingly online existence of young people – the so-called 'Nature Deficit Disorder' (Moss, 2012). Teachers of geography will need to continue to reflect on such debates as the discipline continues to evolve (Kent and Foskett, 2002; Pawson and Teather, 2002).

Engaging with the purpose(s) and associated methods of fieldwork – rather than setting out to meet statutory or examination requirements – is a challenge that numbers of geography teachers have risen to over the years. The geography community has a strong commitment to students' entitlement to fieldwork (Parkinson, 2009) through organisations such as the Geographical Association (which has a Fieldwork and Outdoor Education Special Interest Group) and recent initiatives such as the Action Plan for Geography. As is set out elsewhere in this volume (see chapters by Wood, Mitchell and Morgan), the challenge for geography teachers today is to find the time, energy and support required to pay more than 'lip-service' to this fundamental question of purpose.

Key readings

1. Caton, D. (2006) 'Real world learning through geographical fieldwork', in D. Balderstone (ed.), *Secondary Geography Handbook*, Sheffield: Geographical Association. In his chapter, Caton outlines the purposes of different fieldwork strategies. Recognising that many teachers continue to favour quantitative approaches, the benefits of alternative, more qualitative approaches are discussed. Two case studies, 'London Docklands' and 'Investigating rural settlements' are used to illustrate these alternative approaches.
2. Holmes, D. and Walker, M. (2006) 'Planning geographical fieldwork', in D. Balderstone (ed.), *Secondary Geography Handbook*, Sheffield: Geographical Association. In this chapter the authors provide practical advice for auditing and planning fieldwork as well as providing creative and innovative ideas, including the use of ICT in fieldwork.

References

Balderstone, D. (2000) 'Teaching styles and strategies', in A. Kent (ed.), *Reflective practice in geography*, London: Paul Chapman.

Bonnett, A. (2008) *What is geography?* London: Sage.

Boyle, A., Maguire, S., Martin, A., Milsom, C., Nash, R., Rawlinson, S., Turner, A., Wurthmann, S. and Conchie, S. (2007) 'Fieldwork is good: The student perception and the affective domain', *Journal of Geography in Higher Education*, 31 (2), 299–317.

Caton, D. (2006a) *Theory into Practice: New approaches to Fieldwork*, Sheffield: Geographical Association.

Caton, D. (2006b) 'Real world learning through geographical fieldwork', in D. Balderstone (ed.), *Secondary Geography Handbook*, Sheffield: Geographical Association.

Cook, V. A., Phillips, D. and Holden, J. (2006) 'Geography fieldwork in a "risk society"', *Area*, 38 (4), 413–20.

Council for Learning Outside the Classroom (CLOtC (2012) *Get Ready – managing risk* [online] Available from: http://www.lotc.org.uk/plan-deliver-lotc/planning-lotc-experiences/get-ready-managing-risk/ [Accessed 2 February 2012].

Department for Education and Employment/ Qualifications and Curriculum Authority (DfEE/ QCA) (1999) *The National Curriculum: Handbook for primary teachers in England*, Available from https://www.education.gov.uk/publications/eOrderingDownload/QCA-99-457.pdf [Accessed 2 October 2011].

Department for Education and Skills (DfES) (2006) *Learning outside the Classroom Manifesto*, Available from http://www.lotc.org.uk/getmedia/42c7c3e7-7455-43cc-a513-d6aef9654846/1.0-Learning-Outside-the-Classroom-manifesto.aspx [Accessed 2 October 2011].

Doyle, J. (2006) 'If you go down to the woods today', *Primary Geographer*, 59, 17–19.

Dunphy, A. and Spellman, G. (2009) 'Geography fieldwork, fieldwork value and learning styles', *International Research in Geographical and Environmental Education*, 18 (1), 19–28.

Fuller, I., Rawlinson, S. and Bevan, R. (2000) 'Evaluation of student learning experiences in physical geography fieldwork: Paddling or pedagogy?', *Journal of geography in Higher Education*, 24 (2), 199–215.

Gold, J., Jenkins, A., Lee, R., Monk, J., Riley, J., Shepherd, I. and Unwin, D. (1991) *Teaching geography in higher education: A manual of good practice*, Oxford: Blackwell.

Hawkins, G. (1987) 'From awareness to participation: New directions in the outdoor experience', *Geography*, 72 (3), 217–22.

Herrick, C. (2010) 'Lost in the field: Ensuring student learning in the "threatened" geography fieldtrip', *Area*, 42 (1), 108–16.

Holmes, D. and Farbrother, D. (2000) *A–Z: Advancing Geography Fieldwork*, Sheffield: Geographical Association.

Holmes, D. and Walker, M. (2006) 'Planning Geographical Fieldwork', in D.Balderstone (ed.), *Secondary Geography Handbook*, Sheffield: Geographical Association.

Job, D. (1996) 'Geography and environmental education: An exploration of perspectives and strategies', in A. Kent, D. Lambert, M. Naish and F. Slater (eds.), *Geography in education: Viewpoints on teaching and learning*, Cambridge: Cambridge University Press.

Job, D. (1999) *New directions in geographical fieldwork*, Cambridge: Cambridge University Press/Queen Mary Westfield College.

Job, D. (2002) 'Towards Deeper Fieldwork', in M. Smith (ed.), *Aspects of Teaching Secondary Geography: Perspectives on Practice*, London and New York: RoutledgeFalmer/The Open University.

Job, D., Day, C. and Smyth, A. (1999) *Beyond the Bike sheds: Fresh approaches to fieldwork in the school locality*, Sheffield: Geographical Association.

Kent, M., Gilbertson, D. and Hunt, C. (1997) 'Fieldwork in geography teaching: A critical review of the literature and approaches', *Journal of Geography in Higher Education*, 21 (3), 313–32.

Kent, A. and Foskett, N. (2002) 'Fieldwork in the school Geography curriculum: Pedagogical issues and development', in M.Smith (ed.), Teaching Geography in Secondary Schools, London: Routledge/Falmer.

Lenon, B. and Cleves, P. (1994) *Fieldwork techniques and projects in geography*, London: Collins Educational.

MacKenzie, A.A. and White, R.T. (1982) 'Fieldwork in geography and long term memory structures', *American Educational Research Journal*, 19 (4), 623–32.

May, S. and Richardson, P. (2005) *Managing Safe and Successful Fieldwork*, Sheffield: Geographical Association.

Moss, S. (2012) *Natural Childhood*, Available from: http://www.nationaltrust.org.uk/servlet/file/store5/item789980/version2/natural_childhood.pdf [Accessed 10 April 2012].

Ofsted (2008) *Geography in schools: Changing practice*, Ofsted Ref 070044.

Ofsted (2011) *Geography: Learning to make a world of difference*, Ofsted Ref 090224.

Parkinson, A. (2009) *Fieldwork – an essential part of a geographical education*, Available from http://www.geography.org.uk/download/GA_FieldworkEntitlementGuidancev2.pdf [Accessed 20 February 2012].

Pawson, E. and Teather, E.K. (2002) 'Geographical Expeditions': Assessing the benefits of a student-driven fieldwork method', *Journal of Geography in Higher Education*, 23 (3), 275–89.

Pointon, V. and Wood, P. (2007) 'The new AS/A level specifications', *Teaching Geography*, Autumn 2007, 124–6.

Powell, R. (2002) 'The Sirens' voices? Field practices and dialogue in geography', *Area*, 34 (3), 261–72.

Qualifications and Curriculum Authority (QCA) (2007) *Geography: Programme of study for key stage 3 and attainment target*, Available from: http://media.education.gov.uk/assets/files/pdf/g/geography%202007%20programme%20of%20study%20for%20key%20stage%203.pdf [Accessed 2 October 2011].

Rickinson, M., Dillon, J., Teamey, K., Morris, M., Choi, M.Y., Sanders, D. and Benefield, P. (2004) *A review of research on outdoor learning*, Shrewsbury: National Foundation for Educational Research and King's College London.

Riley, M. (2000) 'Into the KS3 history garden – choosing and planting your enquiry questions', *Teaching History*, 99, 8–13.

Roberts, M. (2003) *Learning through Enquiry*, Sheffield: Geographical Association.

Roberts, M. (2009) 'Investigating Geography', GA Presidential Lecture, 17 April 2009, Geographical Association Annual Conference, University of Manchester 16–18 April 2009, Available from: http://www.geography.org.uk/download/GA_Conf09MargaretRoberts1704.ppt   [Accessed 20 December 2011].

Rynne, E. (1998) 'Utilitarian Approaches to Fieldwork: A Critique', *Geography*, 83 (3), 205–13.

Taylor, L. (2004) *Re-presenting geography*, Cambridge: Chris Kington Publishing.

The Geography Collective (2010) *Mission: Explore*, London: Can of Worms Kids Press.

Van Matre (1979) *Sunship earth – an acclimatization program for outdoor learning*, American Camping Association.

Whittle, J. (2006) 'Journey sticks and affective mapping', *Primary Geographer*, 59, 11–13.

Chapter 14

How has technology impacted on the teaching of geography and geography teachers?

Alan Parkinson

> In the economy of ideas that the web is creating, you are what you share –
> who you are linked to, who you network with.
>
> (Leadbeater, 2008, p. 60)

Introduction

The majority of geography classrooms are connected with the world, via the teacher's laptop, desktop or tablet, by being connected to the internet. Nevertheless, many teachers may still make use of resources written for an audience of some years in the past, and follow a curriculum which has changed little. At the same time, these same teachers feel subject to constant change in an increasingly complex world; however they may have not necessarily changed their practices or assumptions about what it means to teach (Leat, 1999). Thus, teachers as well as students are often uncritical of material sourced online (Bartlett and Miller, 2011).

What this opening paragraph shows is that the balance between the consumption of geographical information, the critical use of new tools, and the extent to which students are involved in constructing their own learning are matters of great uncertainty and flux. This chapter aims to pick a course through such matters and asks questions such as:

- What technology is used in geography classrooms and by geography teachers, and to what effect?
- How is the changing nature of online spaces, and the rapid rise in social media changing the relationship that learners – and teachers – have with each other and the subject?

The chapter also explores another self-evident 'truth': that technology now allows teachers to network and share each other's practice: an important element of professional development. This has come at a time when traditional models of Continuing Professional Development (CPD) are being replaced by more informal ones.

TECHNOLOGY MAKES ITS WAY INTO THE GEOGRAPHY CLASSROOM

By 1980, the few computers that had found their way into schools were often used for programming and monitoring scientific equipment. Computer Assisted Learning (CAL) was a term used to describe this early use of technology. CAL in geography in the 1970s and 1980s often suffered from teachers' misconception of it as only being mechanistic 'programmed learning' (Unwin, 1991), perhaps one reason for its relatively low take-up in schools (Kent, 1983). For geography teachers wanting to know more about CAL in geography, one source for professional development at the time was the Geographical Association's journal *Teaching Geography* where articles such as Hall et al. (1985) researched the use of CAL in schools and provided teachers with a useful overview. In 1986 the journal introduced the 'TG Computer Page', which began by offering software reviews, rather than suggestions for how the use of information and communication technology (ICT) could enhance and support pedagogy. The computers were in the room, but they weren't changing things dramatically. Despite the arrival of the classroom computer the pedagogic practices remained firmly rooted with the teacher as demonstrator and expert, with students passively positioned. Even with the appearance of early 'computer rooms', which meant a number of students could access geography software such as simulations, they remained passive consumers of teacher-selected activities. This continued for the next decade, during which time computers and software became more powerful and adaptable, although Hassell (2002) noted at the time that the use of ICT was often restricted by a 'lack of access to equipment, training and other issues, many ... beyond the gift of the average geography teacher' (p. 150). Small-scale case study research carried out in the early 1990s identified a similar range of reasons where geography teachers did not use ICT; these included the micropolitics of access and professional unease (Watson, 2000).

THE USE OF DIGITAL TECHNOLOGIES IN GEOGRAPHY

The arrival of the internet has of course had significant impact on society and economy – and therefore on schooling and geography classrooms. The subsequent development of the social web or 'Web 2.0' as it became known, changed the nature of the internet from something that was consumed to something that could be altered by the user. The term 'read-write web' was also used: webpages were not just for reading, they could also be produced by students (Murphy and Lebans, 2008).

One valuable use of technology is to draw out the potential that students have to explore beyond the classroom, often virtually. There are some landscapes which the students are unlikely to ever experience in person, but technology can 'take them there'. In May 1994, an article in *Geographical* magazine described a student eager to get home to get started on their homework, who

puts on goggles and control gloves. Thus equipped, he flies across the world to compare average temperatures in Death Valley and the Dead Sea, making notes on his virtual palmtop to use later in an essay.

(Ostler, 1994, p. 12)

With 'virtual reality' came the potential for the 'virtual' fieldwork, which was actually sanctioned by awarding bodies when the Foot and Mouth outbreak of 2001, which closed off large swathes of the countryside, prevented a lot of 'actual' fieldwork taking place.

Into the 21st-century and teachers, and their students, have benefited from discovering and utilising new types of geo-media,[1] particularly digital mapping and imagery, visualisation tools and GIS (geographical information systems). Geo-media and the visualisation of information from digital media sources can open up the geography classroom to the world enabling students to connect remotely with distant places via webcams, or allow them to engage with real people, for example via email, blogs, video conferencing and Voice over Internet Protocol (VOIP) services such as Skype. Students can pose questions which are answered more immediately than through research, and this can lead to further questions. Data which are fresh and contemporary can be introduced and visualised in a way that makes them more accessible to a wider range of learners. Hans Rosling's work with Gapminder (Rosling, 2006) and Sheffield University's Worldmapper project (Barford and Dorling, 2006) have found enthusiastic advocates in the classroom. Many then cascade the benefits of these and other new technologies to other class-room teachers through journal articles (e.g. Lang, 2011), conference presenta-tions (e.g. Parkinson et al., 2012) and perhaps most appropriately via communication online, through social media such as Facebook, Nings and Twitter.

The Ordnance Survey has been supportive of education, distributing free maps to schools, producing magazines and website materials, including a GIS Zone. Maps have always had an important place in the geography classroom, but technology now means they can 'come down from the walls'. Digimap for Schools is an online mapping service which replaced the free paper maps in 2011. It offers scope for exploring maps at different scales and the website provides tools for creating new map layers. The ability to create collaborative online maps means students can take ownership of maps, and add their own data. Maps are a surface on which stories can be told, helping students to 'write the earth'. The age of the citizen cartographer (and journalist) has arrived.

Many of the new mapping tools have sharing built in. This helped lead to the idea of 'neo-geography', which relates to the relationship between mapping and technology (see Turner, 2006). However, there is a tension between the 'real' world and the 'virtual' one. One tool that illustrates this is Google Earth, which offers the potential for personal investigation of familiar and unfamiliar places, and has now been downloaded over 500 million times. It is one of several 'virtual earths' that are used in classrooms, often projected to fill the room as a focal point for lessons. The community of users has shared hundreds of thousands of

resources that have been linked with particular places. For teachers and students alike it can certainly 'capture the magic of experiencing their environment' (Buchanan-Dunlop, 2008, p. 14). However, students may not always realise that what they are looking at is not the 'real world' and neither is it a particular moment in time, but a mosaic of many images and layers.

Teachers have also turned to the internet for resources, just as students turned to it for their homework. Within a 'Ctrl-C, Ctrl-V' Culture, students cutting and pasting work has become a common theme. Online plagiarism services have been one consequence of this, with online essay services for students setting up. Perhaps the parallel impact for teachers is the tempting ready access to 'lessons'. In the first week of the Autumn term, 2010, over a million resources were down-loaded from the *Times Educational Supplement*'s resources area; it predicted over 40 million downloads in 2010 (TES Connect, 2010). How these materials were actually used by teachers would be interesting to know, for although websites such as this clearly satisfy a demand, it is a moot point as to whether they fulfil what excellent classroom practice needs. However, these developments have begun to challenge traditional models of publishing and format of resources that are produced. Apple's launch of iBook Author in January 2012 added another possibility and a further level of sophistication to resource sharing.

With a wealth of resources available at the touch of a button, or increasingly the touch of a screen, 'critical media literacy' is an important concept and one that is still developing. A Demos report in September 2011, *Truth, Lies and the Internet*, examined British young people's ability to critically evaluate what they consumed online; it discussed the need for students to be taught this digital lit-eracy (Bartlett and Miller, 2011). Students should be critical of the information that they are presented with and also of the way it is communicated, consumed and reproduced in the classroom. They need to acquire the skills necessary to 'engage with misrepresentation and underrepresentation' (Kellner and Share, 2005, p. 382). There are a growing number of geography teachers using social media and digital technologies in innovative ways, including using Facebook as a context for learners to improve literacy[2]; using Twitter to connect with farmers in the south of England, and climate scientists in the Arctic Ocean[3] and using Skype to talk to someone living a few miles from the Eyjafjallajokull volcano during the 2010 eruption.[4] Such innovative and interactive geographical activities also pro-vide opportunities for teachers and students discussing together aspects of critical media literacy.

Technology's additional benefit is its 24/7 nature. Learning doesn't have to start at 8.30 am and finish at 3 pm. Some schools have, controversially, experi-mented with the nature of the school day in response to suggestions about the 'body clocks' of teenagers, and there are increasing 'pressures' on teachers to be available outside school hours, and perhaps never 'clocking off'. In this way, technology is seen as a driver of the restless neoliberal 'vibrant city' (Wadley, 2008) in which we all live – and perhaps we should be wary of its capacity to dull 'our ability to think for, or beyond, ourselves' (p. 650). Just because technology enables this or that does not require us to do it!

CHALLENGES OF USING DIGITAL TECHNOLOGIES IN GEOGRAPHY

'The teacher's traditional ally is a piece of chalk, and the closer any modern aid approaches this still indispensable material in some respects the more likely he is to use it' (Page and Kitching, 1981, p. 60). Chalk dust is no longer found in most schools, but the metaphor endures: thus, while ICT has become common in geography classrooms, its physical presence, however, does not guarantee that it will be used effectively. Media technology can facilitate communication, but can potentially also form a barrier (Shirky, 2008).

Has the huge investment in technology in schools, approaching £2 billion between 1998 and 2008 (Ofsted, 2009), made a measurable difference to teaching and learning? Becta, the agency for educational communications technology, carried out research in a number of areas including Interactive whiteboards (Becta, 2003); the full extent of their interactive use has been found to be wanting (Smith et al., 2005; Becta, 2009). In a similar way, the use of PowerPoint® in lesson 'delivery' has reinforced didactic classroom patterns. Whatever the technology, it seems that it needs to remain subservient to pedagogic principles. This debate is also relevant where tablet devices like Apple's iPad are being introduced into schools in large volumes. The full potential of such technologies rests in its capacity to 'give permission' to students to get involved in managing a changing relationship with information – and the teacher. Some schools are developing digital leaders to help with this process. Digital leaders undergo training and are able to support teachers where technology may otherwise be underused.

Teachers have a broad and expanding pedagogic toolkit with which to shape curriculum documents, and turn them into meaningful experiences for all students. This act of 'curriculum-making' is an important element of a teacher's professional role, and this is enhanced by technology. Thus, a downloaded enquiry-led lesson could deviate from the original, with learners following a personalised route. The Geographical Association's 'curriculum-making' model emphasises that teachers and students should both have agency and use the subject discipline as a resource (rather than inert content to be delivered). There is an alchemy that occurs in the classroom which can be improved by the addition of new elements. Technology is one of those elements. Where teachers act as 'gatekeepers' to the technology this can inhibit progress, but gatekeepers can open as well as close the gate.

TEACHERS' PROFESSIONAL DEVELOPMENT AND THE USE OF TECHNOLOGY

The Geographical Association's inaugural journal, called *The Geographical Teacher* was first published in 1901. In the introduction to the very first issue, indeed on the very first page, Douglas Freshfield said:

> In Britain, teachers are for the most part too scattered and too busy to come together frequently for discussion. They require a medium through which

they may readily communicate with one another, exchange experiences and learn the progress that is being made in method or in appliances in our own country and abroad.

(p. 1)

Freshfield's solution was to establish the journal for which he was writing the introduction, but the challenge that he describes still remains. One response has been by geography teachers who have realised the benefits of new technologies for communicating, creating and collaborating online (Richardson, 2008).

Websites were an early visible and accessible form of teachers accessing information and resources. There are some successful free and subscription websites for geography resources. In 1999 Chris Durbin and colleagues at the advisory service for Staffordshire established a forum for geography teachers to chat and exchange ideas, using a 'bulletin board' structure the Staffordshire Learning Network (SLN). This continues to act as a highly visible public site for geography teachers to express themselves, seek advice and share ideas.

Blogging is another form of non face-to-face communication within the geography community. Blogging is a way of creating webpages, which can include text and images, but also embedded video and links through to additional content. Little technical knowledge is required to set up a blog and, importantly, they are free. Teachers began to see the benefit of blogging (Parkinson, 2004; Warlick, 2005) although there are still colleagues 'discovering' blogs today. Teachers use blogs in a number of ways. These include reflecting on practice, sharing resources and classroom practice, completing a project by adding a daily resource (the 365 projects) or collaborating on a study or revision guide co-produced by staff and students. David Lambert and John Morgan's 'Impolite Geography' (started in 2010, and now incorporating GEReCo, the 'geography education research collective') is a fairly recent addition to the canon of educational blog, and forms part of the important task of connecting the worlds of academic and school geography. Wood (2009) described the emergence of a blogging community, and the value that was placed on the opportunity for global feedback. Students are also appreciative of the global audience that this potentially gives them for their work – no longer is it the 'secret exchange' between teacher and student with few people ever seeing the results of their efforts. However, with a more 'pubic exchange', geography teachers need to be alert that while a digital footprint takes time to build up we should remind ourselves what is placed online has a 'permanence' which can be surprising. The Wayback machine can unearth previous iterations of websites as it allows users to trawl 150 billion webpages archived from 1996, so teachers as well as students must understand the power of the medium.

Beyond the sharing of resources and collaborative projects, the benefits of discussing professional development are starting to be realised. Even as little as 75 minutes a month discussing professional practice with colleagues through 'teacher learning communities' can be transformational for one's professional practice, according to Dylan Wiliam, who has researched the benefit of such

professional discourse and has suggested that a regular period of focused conversation with colleagues can improve practice (Stewart, 2008). Where face-to-face opportunities are restricted, the medium that is being increasingly turned to is 'social media', and a range of social networks. Over the last decade a wide range of opportunities for teachers to engage in professional dialogue with colleagues has increased, with Facebook groups, Ning networks and more business-oriented communities like Linked In, all providing what Leadbeater (2009) refers to as 'endless, lateral connections' (p. 5). Exposure to the experimentation of other colleagues, both in the UK and elsewhere, can provide inspiration and also help avoid the pitfalls experienced by others. There is also a longer-term benefit of engaging in online communities and networks in that a professional reputation can be developed which extends beyond the school. Ewan McIntosh of No Tosh consultants, who developed the Teachmeet model,[5] describes the value when 'small passionate communities' form and connect together. The internet enables educators from all over the world to meet virtually and share ideas through short presentations online. Such events also have a 'back-channel' which allows teachers who can't make it physically to follow the conversations and view the presenters. People who have 'hubness', a capacity to network and gather people around them, are important here.

Such networks can be part of the formal geography community such as in the Geographical Association which has moved into these online spaces. The GA's Facebook page was launched in 2009, following the introduction of Ning networks in 2008. Similarly, the RGS-IBG funded networks which are led by Chartered Geographers – a professional status which was developed as part of the Action Plan for Geography (2006–11). The pace of adoption of particular technologies such as Twitter, founded in 2006, has been remarkable. Used both by organisations and individual teachers, there are immediate benefits from using this rapid micro-blogging site such as the regular Thursday night meeting of educators, who debate a theme on the hashtag #ukedchat. It is early days in terms of research into the impact of tools like Twitter but it is already attracting interest (see Watts, 2012).

The significant changes to a teacher's professional network, approaches to networking and the wider opportunities for professional dialogue and collaboration are usefully summarised by two diagrams created by Alec Couros of the University of Regina, Canada (see Figure 14.1a and Figure 14.1b). While continuing to recognise the importance of colleagues and family/local community in a teacher's network, 'The Networked Teacher' (Figure 14.1b) emphasises the increased possibilities for online collaboration and co-creation through a wide range of digital technologies.

HOW WILL TEACHERS' USE OF DIGITAL TECHNOLOGIES DEVELOP IN THE FUTURE?

In the previous section I have outlined how social networking platforms such as Nings and other online tools are increasingly used for CPD and networking.

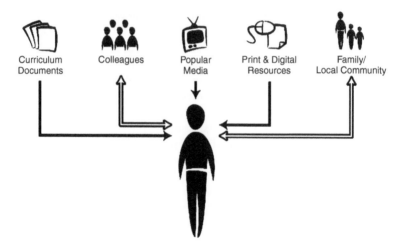

Figure 14.1a Typical teacher network

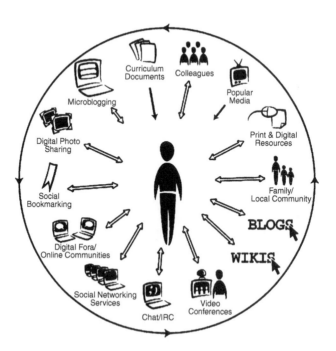

Figure 14.1b The networked teacher

In this section, I raise some important questions on the challenges social media and digital technologies in general can present for schools, teachers and learners.

Does the movement of teachers into another online space mean there are now 'too many rooms'? That is, are we overpowered by choice and the diversity of what's on offer? And how do we prioritise and select? In the past, teachers gave their attention to one room at a time, the majority of their time spent in the classroom. Should geography teachers focus their energies and professional development on this manageable, physical space, or is it important that teachers engage on as many channels as possible? Do we spend too much time connecting and collaborating and passing on materials, with only superficial engagement of the messages and challenges that such material presents? There is a need for mediation by the teacher during this process, plus an element of content-curation and responsible sourcing. Should such skills be written into a teacher's job description, or is this a function performed by a wider community of practice such as the GA?

The increase in social media has been rapid, and education has had a mixed response to it. The banning of 'YouTube' in many local authorities is an example of the 'gatekeeper' model in action. In a Best Practice Research Scholarship[6] focusing on the use of the internet by geography teachers, it was discovered that one early 'bad experience' of being let down would reduce the chances of using technology frequently enough for it to become embedded in practice (Parkinson, 2001). Martin (2006) reminds us that not every teacher needs 'to be an ICT pioneer' (p. 158), however, there may already be a new digital divide opening between those geographers who use social media as part of their professional as well as personal lives, are literally 'connected' 24/7, and those who for various reasons make limited or no use.

Even if many geography teachers want to utilise new technologies with their learners in lessons, do current school cultures and the organisation of schooling enable this? The first decade of the century has seen the rise of the smart-phone and the tablet, which along with the game console are becoming the device of choice of young people. Use of these digital devices outside school and the formal curriculum means the majority of young people's use of digital technologies 'is unmediated by official pedagogy' (Moore, 2012, p. 155). For many young people starting out in primary schools, the touch-screen device is what they are most familiar with, and there can be a frustration with the hardware that they find in the classroom. This echoes David Buckingham's (2003) argument that there is a growing gap between the worlds of young people outside school and their educational experiences in schools.

> While the social and cultural experiences of children have dramatically trans-
> formed over the past 50 years, schools have singularly failed to keep pace
> with the change. The classrooms of today would easily be recognisable to
> [students from] … the mid nineteenth century: the way in which teaching

and learning are organised, the kind of skills and knowledge that are valued in assessment, and in a good deal of curriculum content, have changed only superficially since that time.

(p. 32)

In attempting to 'keep pace' with rapid technological change, many schools have introduced virtual learning environments (VLEs). These vary in usage and quality depending on the platform that was selected for their construction and the enthusiasm of teachers to add content and promote their use. The number of schools successfully operating VLEs has fallen behind the national timescale for implementation (Ofsted, 2009) and by the time all schools get one, technology will have advanced and they may have become 'an expensive irrelevance' (p. 35). Very often the early adopters of new and 'next' technologies are the risk-takers, and at a time of economic uncertainty, schools (and teachers) may well want to 'play it safe'. Will this limit the further adoption of new ideas? Schools and teachers will certainly have to do without the research base, support and advice of Becta[7] in informing their decision making on the future use and development of digital technologies. Whatever hardware schools have now and in the future, it is how teachers and learners utilise it that will remain important. For as Mason and Rennie (2010) have concluded in relation to Web 2.0, it 'is no longer about transmission and consumption; it is about co-creating, sharing, repurposing, and above all, interacting (p. 294).

Conclusion

This chapter has provided a practitioner's perspective on the present and potential uses of technology by geography teachers. In considering different aspects of geography: teaching, learning and professional development, we should continually ask the question: 'is technology always the best tool to use?' Clay Shirky, author of *Here Comes Everybody. The Power of Organizing without Organizations*, writes extensively on ideas relating to our relationship with technology. In an interview he said that: 'the best tool ever invented for improving communication is the table. Online tools aren't better than face-to-face contact, they're just better than nothing' (cited by Staines, 2010, p. 16).

With the speed of technological change faster than schools' responses to the potential that Web 2.0 and social media offer, is the role of the teacher likely to change? Ian Gilbert (2009) argues this question in his provocatively titled book: *Why do I need a teacher when I've got Google?* As more freedom has been given to the learner, there is still a need for the skilled subject practitioner. A report on *Learning about Learning* by the Harris Federation of schools (2009) reinforced the value young people place on the teacher, something echoed in the findings of the GA's Young People's Geographies project. In the school of the future, whatever technologies are being used, these remain 'tools' for the learners and teachers to learn with and through. Whether learning online or face-to-face,

it is teachers who will continue to have the crucial role in helping young people to engage critically with geography and make sense of the different forms of geographical knowledge they are presented with, whatever media this is presented through.

Sir John Jones, speaking at the Scottish Learning Festival in September 2011, summed up the continuing importance of teachers nicely: 'Google can teach you history, but it can't teach you the love of History.' The same is equally true for geography.

Notes

1 The term geo-media forms part of an EU-wide project to engage teachers with technology – read more at http://www.digital-earth.eu
2 T. Cassidy; see his presentation 'What if they had facebook' at http://www.slide-share.net/funkygeography/facebook-and-twitter-profiles.
3 K. O'Donnell – see his blog at http://geodonn.blogspot.co.uk/.
4 V. Vannet on Twitter at https://twitter.com/#!/ValVannet.
5 The Teachmeet started amongst Scottish educators in 2005. In March 2012, creator Ewan McIntosh was present as over 300 educators met in Sydney in the largest Teachmeet at that time.
6 Between 2000 and 2004, the DfES funded the Best Practice Research Scholarship programme (BPRS) to promote teachers' engagement in small-scale classroom-based research.
7 Becta was closed by the coalition government in March 2011 – the website and its research reports have been archived, and can be accessed on the national archives website.

Key readings

1. Jonassen, D.H. (1995). 'Supporting communities of learners with technology: A vision for integrating technology with learning in schools', *Educational Technology*, 35 (4), 60–63.
   When teaching with ICT David Jonassen's seven qualities of meaningful learning with technology are useful to keep in mind. Jonassen and others make a strong case for the value of situated learning, or learning in context, which is exactly what teaching with GIS, for example, can involve.
2. Mason. R. and Rennie, F. (2010) 'Social Networking as an Educational Tool', in J. Arthur and I. Davies (eds.), *The Routledge Education Studies Reader*, London: Routledge.
   The authors provide a very useful overview of students and teachers' engagement with digital learning. Research issues concerning the use of Web 2.0, social networking and course design provide the reader with valuable literature when debating how teachers and schools may respond to the use of digital media.

References

Barford, A. and Dorling, D. (2006) 'Worldmapper: The world as you've never seen it before', *Teaching Geography*, 31 (2), 68–75.

Bartlett, J. and Miller, C. (2011) *Truth, lies and the Internet: a report into young people's digital fluency* [online], Available from: http://www.demos.co.uk/publications/truth-lies-and-the-internet [Accessed 21 March 2012].

Black, P., Harrison, C., Lee, C., Marshall, B. and Wiliam, D. (2003) *Assessment for Learning: Putting it into practice*, Maidenhead: Open University Press.

British Educational Communications and Technology Agency (Becta) (2003) *What the research says about Interactive Whiteboards*, Coventry: Becta.

British Educational Communications and Technology Agency (Becta) (2009) *Evidence on the impact of technology on learning and educational outcomes*, Available from: http://cnp.naace.co.uk/system/files/impact_of_technology_on_outcomes_jul09.pdf [Accessed 2 February 2012].

Buchanan-Dunlop, J. (2008) 'Virtual Fieldwork', in D. Mitchell (ed.), *ICT in Secondary Geography: A short guide for teachers*, Sheffield: Geographical Association.

Buckingham, D. (2003) *Media education: Literacy, learning, and contemporary culture*, Cambridge and Oxford: Polity Press in association with Blackwell Publishing Ltd.

Freshfield, D. (1901) *The Geographical Teacher*, 1 (1), 1.

Gilbert, I. (2010) *Why do I need a teacher when I've got Google*, London: Routledge.

Hall, D., Kent, A. and Wiegand, P. (1985) 'Computer assisted learning in geography: the state of the art', *Teaching Geography*, 10 (2), 73–6.

Harris Federation/NESTA (2009) *Harris Federation Report: Learning about Learning*, Available from http://www.nesta.org.uk/library/documents/Harris-Report.pdf [Accessed 25 March 2012].

Hassell, D. (2002) 'Issues in ICT and Geography', in M. Smith (ed.), *Teaching Geography in Secondary Schools*, London: Routledge/Falmer.

Jones, J. (2011) 'The Future is not what it was' keynote. Scottish Learning Festival September 2011.

Kellner, D. and Share, G. (2005) 'Towards Critical Media Literacy: Core concepts, debates, organizations and policy', *Discourse: Studies in the cultural politics of education*, 26 (3), 369–86.

Kent, A. (ed.) (1983) *Geography Teaching and the Micro*, York: Longman.

Lang, B. (2011) 'Gapminder: Bringing statistics to life', *Teaching Geography*, 36 (1), 17–19.

Leadbeater, C. (2008) *We Think: Mass innovation, not mass production: The Power of Mass Creativity*, London: Profile Books Ltd.

Leadbeater, C. (2009) The Art of With [online], Available from http://www.cornerhouse.org/wp-content/uploads/old_site/media/Learn/The%20Art%20of%20With.pdf [Accessed 25 March 2012].

Leat, D. (1999) 'Rolling the Stone Uphill: Teacher development and the implementation of Thinking Skills programmes', *Oxford Review of Education*, 25 (3), 387–403.

Martin, F. (2006) *E-geography: Using ICT in quality geography*, Sheffield: Geographical Association.

Mason, R. and Rennie, F. (2010) 'Social Networking as an Educational Tool', in J. Arthur and I. Davies (eds.), *The Routledge Education Studies Reader*, London: Routledge.

Moore, A. (2012) *Teaching And Learning: Pedagogy, Curriculum And Culture*, 2nd edn, Abingdon: Routledge.

Murphy, J. and Lebans, R. (2008) 'Unexpected outcomes: Web 2.0 in the secondary school classroom', *International Journal of Technology in Teaching and Learning*, 4 (2), 134–47.

Ofsted (2009) The importance of ICT: Information and communication technology in primary and secondary schools, 2005–2008, Available from: http://www.ofsted.gov.uk/resources/importance-of-ict-information-and-communication-technology-primary-and-secondary-schools-20052008 [Accessed 9 August 2012].

Ostler, T. (1994) 'Revolution in reality: Virtual reality applications in geography', *Geographical Magazine*, 66 (5), 12–13.

Page, C.F. and Kitching, J. (1981) *Technical aids to teaching in higher education*, Guildford: Society for Research into Higher Education.

Parkinson, A. (2001) 'Best Practice scholarship' unpublished.

Parkinson, A. (2004) 'Have you met GeoBlogs', *Teaching Geography*, 29 (3), 161–3.

Parkinson, A., Lyon, J. and Solem, M. (2012) Geomedia in Secondary Education, Lecture at the Geographical Association Annual Conference, University of Manchester, 12–14 April 2012.

Richardson, W. (2008) *Blogs, Wikis, Podcasts, and Other Powerful Web Tools for Classrooms*, California: Corwin Press Inc.

Rosling, H. (2006) 'Debunking myths about the "third world"', TED Conference, Monterey, California, USA, February, 2006 [online], Available from: http://www.gapminder.org/videos/hans-rosling-ted-2006-debunking-myths-about-the-third-world/ [Accessed 31 March 2012].

Shirky, C. (2008) *Here Comes Everybody. The Power of Organizing without Organizations*, New York: The Penguin Press.

Smith, H.J., Higgins, S., Wall, K. and Miller, J. (2005) 'Interactive Whiteboards: Boon or bandwagon', *Journal of Computer Assisted Learning*, 21 (2), 91–101.

Staines, J. (2010) *Excited atoms: an exploration of virtual mobility in the contemporary performing arts*, Available from: http://on-the-move.org/files/news_files/excited_atoms_final.pdf [Accessed 10 April 2012].

Stewart, W. (2008) '75 minutes to up your game', *Times Educational Supplement*, 28 November, 2008, Available from: http://www.tes.co.uk/article.aspx?storycode=6005714 [Accessed 21 March 2012].

TES Connect (2010) 'TES Connect to reach 40 million free resources downloads', Available from: http://www.pressbox.co.uk/detailed/Education/TES_Connect_to_reach_40_million_free_resources_downloads_444201.html [Accessed 1 April 2012].

Turner, A.J. (2006) *Introduction to Neogeography*, Available from: http://pcmlp.socleg.ox.ac.uk/sites/pcmlp.socleg.ox.ac.uk/files/Introduction_to_Neogeography.pdf [Accessed 2 April 2012].

Unwin, D.J. (1991) 'Using Computers to Help Students Learn: Computer Assisted Learning in Geography', *Area*, 23 (1), 25–34.

Wadley, D. (2008) 'The Garden of Peace', *Annals of the Association of American Geographers*, 98 (3), 650–85.

Warlick, D. (2005) *Classroom Blogging: A Teacher's Guide to the Blogosphere*, 2nd edn, Raleigh: Lulu.com.

Watson, D.M. (2000) 'Information and communication technologies: Researching the reality of use', in A. Kent (ed.), *Reflective Practice in Geography Teaching*, London: Paul Chapman Publishing.

Watts, J. (2012) 'The uses of Twitter for geography teachers/students', Reporting Research session at The Geographical Association Annual Conference, University of Manchester, 12–14 April 2012. Available from http://eternalexploration.wordpress.com/2012/04/13/twitter-for-geography-teachers-and-students-ga-conference/ [Accessed 18 April 2012].

Wood, P. (2009) 'Advances in E-learning – the case of blogging in U.K. school geography', *Research in Geographic Education*, 11 (2), 28–46.

Chapter 15

Geographic Information (GI) – how could it be used?

Mary Fargher

Imagine for example, a young child going to a Digital Earth exhibit at a local museum. After donning a head-mounted display, she sees Earth as it appears from space. Using a data glove, she zooms in, using higher and higher levels of resolution, to see continents, then regions, countries, cities, and finally individual houses, trees, and other natural and h(u)man-made objects. Having found an area of the planet she is interested in exploring, she takes the equivalent of a 'magic carpet ride' through a 3-D visualization of the terrain.

(Gore, 1998)

Introduction

In his speech 'Digital Earth: Understanding our planet in the 21st Century', Gore encouraged us to imagine what a geographical education with GIS[1] in the 21st century might involve. According to Gore, Digital Earth[2] would allow us to 'capture' vast amounts of digital information about our planet. Although his speech did not quite herald the new era of geographical knowledge that its rhetoric suggested, it partially predicted the significance of geographic information (GI) and its potential influence on our geographical imaginations. In the time since he made his speech, we have become increasingly familiar with 'Digital Earth' through virtual globes such as Google Earth.[3] Some may also be familiar with more conventional GIS software and applications such as ESRI ArcGIS,[4] Digital Worlds[5] and AEGIS 3 GIS[6] through university degrees or through its use in schools. GIS is a term that can be interpreted in a range of different ways. For some it is the hardware and software that makes up a computerised geographic information system capable of digitally displaying mainly mapped information about on- or near-surface geographical phenomena (Schuurman, 2004). This chapter interprets the acronym more broadly, considering GIS to include the hardware, the software and the user as part of the geographical system, as Elwood (2008) contends when she defines GIS as:

digital systems for storing and representing spatial information; they are complex arrays of social and political practices; *and* they are ways of knowing and making knowledge.

(Elwood, 2008, p. 257)

In schools, the National Curriculum revisions in 2007 highlighted the use of GIS as a central element of study in geography for the first time. It is identified as a key technology that pupils can use to collect data through enquiry learning at Key Stage 3 (KS3) (Fargher and Rayner, 2011). At GCSE and A level students are now required to use and demonstrate both knowledge and understanding of technologies such as GIS and their role in investigation in geography (Geographical Association, 2011a).

This chapter introduces and critically examines a range of key debates about the use of GIS in geography education in terms of the nature of GI, its educational value and the role of teacher knowledge in teaching with GIS.

CONVENTIONAL GIS

Despite the recent mushrooming of Web 2.0 GI, it is worth remembering that GI has been around for a long time. The earliest digital geographic data appeared on the screens of computerised mainframe GIS in land use analysis and census mapping in the 1960s. Since then, GI has gradually become the cornerstone of what is now widely known as the geospatial industries providing digitally referenced geographic information in a vast array of human contexts including industry, government and higher education. This is conventional GIS that uses a specific set of spatial tools to identify, locate and map geographical phenomena.

At the same time, evidence reflecting the educational benefits of using conventional GIS to develop student spatial skills is growing, particularly in American secondary school education (Kerski, 2008; Bednarz and Bednarz, 2008). A number of research studies have considered how GI can be used successfully in enquiry learning (Fargher, 2006; Scheepers, 2009). The cross-curricular benefits of the use of GI, particularly between geography and science, have also been explored (Sinton and Lund, 2007). Supporting teachers in developing their teaching with GIS has also been researched in the United Kingdom (see GA's Spatially Speaking project, GA, 2006).

It is important to remember, however, that a very particular type of spatial thinking lies at the core of conventional GIS. GIS protagonists view it as a rigorous, scientific technical application, one which can be used to solve geographical problems, follow scientific enquiries, predict events such as environmental hazards and locate economic resources (Schuurman, 2004; Bednarz, 2004; National Research Council, 2006).

It is worth considering here the emphasis placed on related spatial thinking in the US education system where GI is used to teach geographical topics mainly within the science curriculum. Sinton and Bednarz (2007) summarise this approach:

> Students in pursuit of a well-rounded education must learn to think spatially [National Research Council, 2006]. Spatial thinking enables us to comprehend and address issues of spatial relationships. As students explore geographical

space, they gain the facility and confidence to grasp and imagine abstract spaces, to solve multi-faceted problems, and to think critically and participate actively in our complex, multidimensional world.

(Sinton and Bednarz, 2007, in Sinton and Lund, 2007, p. 19)

In their study of the Hurricane Katrina disaster, Sinton and Bednarz (2007) discuss how 'spatial data' helped people understand the event, its causes and its aftermath, and how framing this knowledge through GIS helped to build a 'cognitive geographical context'. This is an important point, that framing geographical learning is a key part of using GI. Conventional GIS does indeed provide a framework for fixing GI to specific coordinates and displaying it as a map or satellite image. Because it is digitised, the user viewing a GIS can manipulate the information displayed on the screen, transform it, analyse it. Advocates of GI use provide plenty of examples of its powerful analytical capabilities. For example, Openshaw, a GI scientist makes this bold statement about its potentiality:

> GIS can be used to analyze river networks on Mars on Monday, study cancer in Bristol on Tuesday, map the underclass of London on Wednesday, analyze the groundwater flow in the Amazon basin on Thursday, and end the week by modelling retail shoppers in Los Angeles on Friday.
>
> (Openshaw, 1991, p. 624)

This is a GI Science view of spatial thinking; one that is subject to quite heated debate amongst the broader geography and geography education communities, particularly those involved in human geography.

CRITICAL GIS

Since the 1990s, academic human geographers have been critical of the positivist philosophical underpinnings of GIS; the debatable ethics of military applications of GIS; the arguably non-participatory nature of a technology that only the privileged few can afford (O'Sullivan, 2006) and its potential (in their eyes) to stunt ways of thinking geographically (Schuurman, 2000). In his seminal text: *Ground Truth: The Social Implications of Geographic Information Systems*, Pickles (1995) spelt out a number of burning Critical GIS[7] issues for many in using a technology (GIS) that appeared to be able to quantify but not qualify. *Ground Truth* makes a strong case for the under- or misrepresentation of social phenomena through geographic information systems. One result of critiques of GIS has been the emergence of a more socially aware form of GIS: Critical GIS (cGIS) which aims to represent a broader range of GI than the narrowly scientific ones most often associated with conventional forms (Pavlovskaya, 2006; Dunn, 2007; Schuurman, 2009). One of the most championed movements to emerge within critical GIS

has been public participatory GIS (PPGIS). Though still not short of critical review by some sceptics, public participatory GIS is considered by some to be 'GIS for the people'. PPGIS embraces an approach where local community issues drive the use of technology and where there is a stronger emphasis on community involvement with GIS. Some of the projects that adopt a PPGIS approach have included urban regeneration and sustainable development, for example the Rwandan 'Grounds for Change'[8] project that promotes fair trade coffee. In particular, PPGIS such as these differ from more traditional GIS in that they include more complex geographic information, often including indigenous geographical information. This in itself is an interesting aspect of PPGIS because it attaches importance to deep local knowledge being of value in society. There is an argument to be made that PPGIS could be used to further develop geographical understanding in schools of local issues (Fargher, 2011).

GI THROUGH WEB 2.0

Most recently, the proliferation of device platforms (PC, laptop, network, mobile) on which GI can now be accessed has made digital geographic information more readily available (Elwood, 2008). Web 2.0 is the host platform for the emerging GI technologies that have so radically altered our recent interactions with GI. These include geobrowsers such as Google Earth, Bing Maps and Worldwind, all of which support 'annotating the planet' with volunteered geographic information (VGI). *Neogeography* is the term used to describe these non-conventional GIS media (Schuurman and Goodchild, 2009).

Though research evidence of the influence of easier access to less technical GIS is not yet substantial, there are indications that geography teachers are beginning to make more use of earth viewers[9] (Kerski, 2008; Fargher, 2011). At the same time, young people are becoming increasingly more familiar with engaging with GI in informal settings; it is important that their involvement in using GI in school contribute positively to this wider geographical experience. In particular, internet users have become familiar with interacting with digital maps, scrolling satellite imagery and accessing other georeferenced GI data.[10] Some advocates of GIS[11] actually consider this kind of 'geovisualisation' to be the 'fourth R' in 21st-century education – as important as reading, writing and arithmetic (Goodchild, 2006).

> The idea of GI satellite imagery as powerfully affecting *and* affective both visually and conceptually is an important one to explore. In the past, satellite imagery in particular was mainly used in the military domain to target the enemy, to monitor land-use change and in planning. More recently, however, these types of GI has moved at least partly into the public domain to the extent that virtual globe atlases are becoming the 'default meta-geography of the media'.
>
> (Dodge and Perkins, 2009, p. 497)

Another aspect of using Web 2.0 applications such as Google Earth is the ability to upload 'geographical information' (as kml files) into the virtual globe itself. Some may even argue that this is a new, quite different type of geographical knowledge which has not yet been categorised, a kind of 'neogeography' (Turner, 2006). This type of participatory GIS (for some have defined it thus) requires careful critical consideration by educators. If we are to let students loose on virtual worlds we need to be aware of the origin, validity and value of the various 'wikis',[12] podcasts,[13] vidcasts[14] and other 'geotags'[15] 'that we may be justifying and validating by facilitating their access to them. This more emancipatory, 'bottom-up' approach to using GIS and virtual globes may open up a world of opportunities for geography education. However, caution about the quality of 'geographical information' we may wittingly or unwittingly sanction seems prudent. Whichever way the use of GIS and virtual globes is considered, for many it is in a sense a new way of looking at the world, one in which it is important for us to consider the technology behind it and the reasons for the production of the geographic information that is visible or not visible within it (Fargher, 2009). Whatever their origin or format, it is clear that more complex GI use is evolving at pace. Goodchild (2008) summarises this heterogeneity:

> People are indeed finding uses for the geobrowsers that are very different from typical GIS applications. They have none of the analytic modelling, and inferential power of GIS, and while oriented to visualisation are nevertheless very limited in what can be visualised, because of their insistence on content that is inherently visual. In other ways, however, the uses of geobrowsers go well beyond those of GIS, reaching into a broad and rich domain of spatial concepts that may be very powerful aids to geographical understanding and insight.
>
> (Goodchild, 2008, p. 40)

It could be argued that more significant use of GIS in schools also requires more critical teacher understanding of how GIS frames knowledge (Fargher, 2011). By engaging more meaningfully in the type of critical debate about GIS already well established in universities, teachers might be better placed to decide on a more productive use of GI in school geography. There are a number of related important questions for geography education here. If teachers choose to adopt conventional GI in geography, what are the implications of constructing geographical knowledge through a predominantly quantitative technology? Which elements of geography can/cannot be measured? If teachers opt to use VGI in their lessons, where has that information come from? How trustworthy or reliable is geographic information uploaded on to the web? Several educators argue that these types of technologies will become much more important in education in the future (Kerski, 2008; Fargher, 2011). Although the technologies are emergent, the philosophy behind them ties in with earlier ideas about developing 'spatial intelligence'[16] with GI.

HYBRID GIS

The other emerging GI-related technology that should be considered in this discussion is multi-source hybrid GIS that combines elements of conventional GIS. This idea is not new in either industry or higher education. In her GIS assessment of flood vulnerability of a core tourist area in New Orleans (*three years before the Hurricane Katrina event of 2005*), Koravec (2002) explains such an approach where conventional GIS is supplemented with a wider range of other information which reflects historical, socio-economic and political aspects of geography of New Orleans. Several of the leading companies in GIS industries (including the market leader – ESRI) are now working the hybrid approach to using GI. In a sense this involves using the rigour and structure of the geometry of a GIS but complementing it with the richness of Web 2.0 This could allow for some elements of space within a GIS to be quantifiable but also to bring to it the richness of more qualitative elements such as Koravec has highlighted. The geographical thinking that might lie behind such an holistic, multi-source GIS may present geographic information in ways which seem relevant and accessible to users other than conventional GIS specialists. The possibilities of geotagging (labelling/annotating digital earth representations); geoblogging (writing about places through the web); embedding photographs, video and other media alongside more traditional GIS use is an area of growing debate amongst geographers and geography educators (Goodchild, 2011). However, the need for critical use of volunteered geographic information remains paramount with regards to verifying its authenticity and source on the Internet.

CHALLENGES TO USING GI

Despite the growing body of research indicating the value of using GI in geography, only a small number of UK schools are using it effectively to support geography teaching and learning (Ofsted, 2011). The small uptake continues to be connected with the fact that many teachers associate GI technologies with a steep initial learning curve, costly training and a scarcity of advice on constructing pedagogy with GIS (Fargher and Rayner, 2011). Research evidence also suggests that all ICT-related curriculum development requires teachers to develop their pedagogic strategies in considerably more complex ways than they may have done before. They need to be familiar with a range of areas of knowledge: their own subject content knowledge, knowledge about how students think and learn and increasingly in the twenty-first-century classroom, knowledge about how to use technology make this a complex set of challenges for teachers (Mishra and Koehler, 2006).

Mishra and Koehler's *TPACK framework* is useful to consider here (see Figure 15.1). What kind of knowledge does a geography teacher need to bring into play to use GI in their classroom? *Technological Content Knowledge (TCK)* could involve a teacher developing their understanding of how geographic information

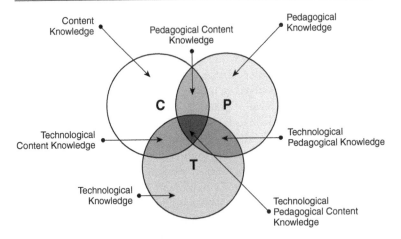

Figure 15.1 Mishra and Koehler's *TPACK framework*.

(GI) is stored in vector or raster IS (each of these are different ways of displaying information digitally. *Technological Pedagogical Knowledge* (*TPK*) could involve their being familiar with the pedagogical benefits of using Google Earth (the web-based earth viewer) for manipulating global images when teaching scale. *Technological Pedagogical Content Knowledge* (*TPACK*) is the amalgam of all of these elements. TPCK requires technological competency, pedagogical skills and firm foundations in subject knowledge:

> TPACK is a form of knowledge that expert teachers bring to play anytime they teach.
>
> (Mishra and Koehler, 2006, p. 15)

It could be argued that effective GI-supported teaching and learning in geography education are more likely to occur through careful consideration of a framework such as Mishra and Koehler's TPCK. However, if we are to develop support for teachers using GIS further, consideration of a theoretical framework is likely to be only the beginning of the process. Even when teachers are trained to use particular software packages, familiarise themselves with the intricacies of new or adapted hardware or painstakingly learn associated terminologies, their training can be difficult to arrange, costly and become swiftly out of date (Mishra and Koehler, 2006). Added to this, several software packages and online GIS currently in use in schools were not designed with education in mind (ArcGIS, Google Earth). This is particularly true of conventional GIS packages (Bednarz and van der Schee, 2006).

There are also significant external and internal factors which may affect teachers' decisions to become involved with GI (Bednarz and van der Schee, 2006).

Authority, manageability and consistency are important external influences. For example, seminal texts may sway teachers' attitudes towards and not away from GI As in the case of the Mapping Our World series of texts produced by the GIS software company dominates the use of GIS in schools in the USA.[17] Decisions can be directly linked to authority too – compulsory inclusion of GIS in schools for use at GCSE level is beginning to have an effect on the uptake of GI use in schools. Manageability is seen by many as a vital factor, with teachers less likely to adopt GI practices that are difficult to master. Consistency is cited as an attractive feature of manageability too – if a GI technology 'fits in' with current practice and systems easily it becomes a more attractive proposition.

GI AND THE NEW GEOGRAPHY CURRICULUM

Recent national political shift and the Coalition government's 2010 White Paper *The Importance of Teaching* (DfE, 2010) offers us another lens with which we can look at the role of GI in geography education. With its emphasis on clarifying and streamlining the curriculum, the sharp focus on core or essential knowledge and academic rigour (Lambert, 2011) makes the use of GI in constructing factual declarative knowledge in geography seem much more justified. Let's explore the idea that GI may be used to develop core or essential knowledge a little further. In their most recent report on geography in UK secondary schools: *Geography – Learning to Make a World of Difference* (2011), Ofsted states:

> Core knowledge for the majority of the students surveyed, but especially for those in the weaker schools, was poor. All but the best students interviewed were spatially naïve. The mental images they held of the world were often confused and they were not able to locate countries, key mountain ranges or other features with any degree of confidence. For example, they understood about development issues in Kenya but had little or no idea of where Kenya was in Africa. Many of them had studied Amazonia and could talk with some conviction about the exploitation of resources and environmental degradation but they knew nothing about the rest of South America. Their study of geography was isolated and not set within a context that they could identify with.

> (Ofsted, 2011, p. 22)

According to Ofsted, core geography knowledge comprises basic factual geographic knowledge, vocabulary about and the ability to locate geographical features accurately. The argument presented in this quotation suggests that core knowledge is only one part of the complex subject of geography and its fundamental role in contributing to young people making sense of the multi-faceted world around them.

The role of GI in promoting geography's position in UK schools could be of considerable relevance, here. As a subject it continues to be rigorously scrutinised and subjected to both positive (Lambert, 2011; Geographical Association, 2011b) and negative critique (Standish, 2007). Negative commentary has focused particularly on poor curriculum planning at KS3 and falling candidate numbers at GCSE and A level (Ofsted, 2011). Whilst it cannot be a panacea to address the range of issues that have led to geography's decline, GI may have a significant role to play in enhancing the subject's kudos and creating a curriculum that is contemporary and relevant to young people (Fargher, 2011) in the ways that the 2007 National Curriculum advocates. Lambert (2011) makes a strong case for the importance of the mutual dependence of core and powerful subject knowledge in geography education.

Other geography educators argue that the critical use of GI in constructing a synthesis of core and powerful geography subject knowledge is of considerable social significance in developing young people's awareness of major contemporary issues of our time (Annoni et al., 2011; Fargher, 2011). It is arguable that school geography could look to views on this from colleagues in the higher education sector. Cosgrove (2008), for example, offers words of warning about trying to pin geography down to distinct categories:

> We need to be vigilant in the face of a constant temptation to leap from inscribing order and pattern into (geo) graphic images to inferring something more universal. Such inference can lead – indeed too often – has led inexorably to the temptations of applied geography: imposing a single vision across the wonderful variety and individuality of geographical actuality and human freedom.
>
> (Cosgrove, 2008, p. 33)

Cosgrove is advocating multi-perspectives and not a narrowed view. Some, like Cosgrove, argue that more critical use of such technologies has much to offer in promoting geographical understanding. There is another element of this argument that perhaps needs reinforcing here. A case can be made for developing strong core geography knowledge through the use of GI but only if that constitutes part of a richer and broader geographical picture which enhances access to more powerful geographical knowledge (Fargher, 2011). For example, on a global level, at a time when climate change is at the top of many agendas some advocates of GIS and virtual globes are beginning to actively promote 'climate literacy through GI for the twenty-first century' (Herring and Leopold, 2007).

Conclusion

In its *Geography Manifesto: A Different View*, the Geographical Association (GA, 2009) encourages us to take a fresh look at how we approach geography education in a way that is relevant to this discussion. By re-engaging with 'discovery' in

our subject and by travelling 'with a different view', the GA's manifesto encourages teachers to invest their knowledge, expertise and energy in stimulating student interests and needs. The type of young people's geography illustrated in the manifesto is dynamic and challenging, inspiring a living geography for change in a changing world. In a broader but significantly related context, many young people are already very adept at using geo-technologies. It is important that their experiences of using GIS and virtual globes in school contribute to this wider understanding of the world. In particular, the burgeoning development of Neogeography and volunteered geographic information (VGI) over the last five years has changed the landscape of web-based geo-technologies and are becoming a part of the metaphor of the 'geographical conversation' that the GA's manifesto encourages. For example, in the flatter digital world that young people experience, geography educators are best placed to explore the implications of this for the central concepts of scale and connection, and proximity and distance. Massey and Clark imply the level of responsibility that this kind of thinking shifts onto the shoulders of geography educators in the 21st-century when they argue that:

> We are often led to believe that the 'big' global changes in the world are inevitable, that there is nothing we can do. Clearly, some things may be impossible – or extremely difficult to change. Yet there is perhaps a need to bring some of these 'big' things down to earth, to see how they are made.
>
> (Massey and Clark, 2008, p. 28)

As Massey and Clark (2008) suggest, whether we wish it or not, we are all implicated in the way worlds are 'made' and as geography educators we need to critically consider these deeper epistemological questions when choosing how to approach teaching with GIS. It could be argued that the recent exponential explosion of GI onto the Web makes our need to be conscious and critical of the language and meanings *behind* the signs and symbols present in Web 2.0 as much as when critical GIS first emerged in the 1990s. As with any semiotic medium, it is important to be aware of the different discourses which are being represented within it. GIS the commercial product comes straight from realist and pragmatic origins, and is often constructed or used to predict events and to problem-solve. Web 2.0 is also commercially driven; appropriate for some types of student enquiry some might argue, but surely worthy of more careful consideration if education is to include ways of thinking about and representing ideas beyond the 'googlization'[18] and geotagging of geography (Fargher, 2011).

The perspectives examined in this short chapter by no means exhaust the debates that could be had about the ways in which GI could or should be used in geography education. My intention has been to introduce and critically analyse a number of key issues about the nature of GI, its educational value, the role of teacher knowledge in teaching with its various conventional, Web 2.0 and hybrid guises. This chapter has argued that teachers using GI thoughtfully, critically

and skilfully in education can support young people to further develop their geographical perspectives of our changing world. As Elwood states:

> GI(S) is tremendously important because it is such a powerful mediator of spatial knowledge, social and political power, and intellectual practice in geography. In short, the answer is the same as it was ten years ago: Because the stakes are high.
>
> (Elwood, 2006, p. 693)

Notes

1 Geographic Information System.
2 Digital Earth is an umbrella term to describe the range of digitally displayed representations of the earth (Gore, 1998).
3 Google Earth was the first widely available 'free' earth viewer – released in 2005.
4 ESRI ArcGIS is an industrial desktop GIS.
5 Digital Worlds is a version of ArcGIS adapted for schools.
6 AEGIS 3 GIS is a GIS designed specifically for schools.
7 Earthviewers are digital globes such as Google Earth.
8 Georeferenced GI data is digitally linked to a specific set of geographical coordinates.
9 Geographic information systems.
10 Wikis are web-based encyclopaedias.
11 Podcasts are downloadable audio recordings.
12 Vidcasts are downloadable video recordings.
13 Geotags are a form of coordinate-referenced post-it notes.
14 Spatial intelligence refers here to spatial thinking with conventional GIS.
15 *Mapping Our World – GIS Lessons for Educators* (Malone, 2005).
16 Spatial intelligence refers here to spatial thinking with conventional GIS.
17 Mapping our World – GIS lessons for Education (ESRI, 2005).
18 Googlization is a phrase by Vaidhyanathan (2010) which casts a critical eye over the world's compulson to 'google'.

Key readings

1. Kerski, J. Milson, A. and Demirci, A. (eds.) *International Perspectives on Teaching and Learning with GIS in Secondary Schools,* London: Springer. Very useful for following up these debates from different international perspectives, the UK chapter is Fargher, M. and Rayner, D. (2011) 'United Kingdom: Realising the Potential of GIS in the School Geography Curriculum'.
2. O'Sullivan, D. (2006). 'Geographical Information science: Critical GIS', *Progress in Human Geography*, 30 (6), 783–91. David O'Sullivan's article offers an interesting and alternative view on the contribution of more critically informed use of GIS which involves an engagement with the technology rather than just criticism of it from the outside.

References

Annoni, A., Craglia, M., Ehlers, M., Georgiadou, Y., Giacomelli, A., Konecny, M., Ostlaender, M., Remetey-Füllöp, G., Rhind, D., Smits, P. and Schade, S. (2011) 'A European Perspective on Digital Earth', *International Journal of Digital Earth*, 4 (4), 271–84.

Bednarz, S.W. (2004) 'Geographic Information Systems: A Tool to Support Geography and Environmental Education?', *GeoJournal*, 60 (2), 191–9.

Bednarz, S.W. and van der Schee, J. (2006) 'Europe and the United States: The implementation of Geographical Information Systems in secondary education in two contexts', *Technology, Pedagogy and Education*, 15 (2), 191–206.

Bednarz, S.W. and Bednarz, R.S. (2008) 'Spatial thinking: The key to success in using geospatial technologies in the social studies classroom', in A.J. Milson and M. Alibrandi (eds.), *Digital geography: Geo-spatial technologies in the social studies classroom*, New York: Information Age Publishing.

Cosgrove, D.E. (2008) *Geography and Vision: Seeing, imagining and representing the world*, London: Palgrave Macmillan.

Department for Education (2010) *The Importance of Teaching: Schools White Paper*, Available from: http://www.education.gov.uk/schools/teachingandlearning/schoolswhitepaper/b0068570/the-importance-of-teaching/ [Accessed 20 February 2012].

Dodge, M. and Perkins, C. (2009) 'The View from Nowhere? Spatial Politics and Cultural Significance of High Resolution Satelite Imagery', *Geoforum*, 40 (4), 497–501.

Dunn, C.E. (2007) 'Participatory GIS—a People's GIS?', *Progress in Human Geography*, 31 (5), 616–37.

Elwood, S. (2006) 'Critical Issues in Participatory GIS: Deconstructions, Reconstructions and New Research Directions', *Transactions in GIS*, 10 (5), 693–708.

Elwood, S. (2008) 'Geographic Information Science: New geovisualization technologies – emerging questions and linkages with GIScience research', *Progress in Human Geography*, 33 (2), 256–63.

Fargher, M. (2006) 'Linking lessons learnt from the classroom with research findings on pedagogies with GIS', *ESRI European Conference Proceedings, Stockholm* (2006). Available online from: <http://gis.esri.com/library/userconf/educ06/papers/educ_1461.pdf.

Fargher, M. (2009) 'Putting place at the centre of digital earth', Paper presented at the Symposium for Digital Earth, Beijing.

Fargher, M. (2011) 'Geography with a different view through GIS' ESRI conference proceedings, Madrid (2011).

Fargher, M. and Rayner, D. (2011) 'United Kingdom: Realising the Potential of GIS in the School Geography Curriculum', in J. Kerski, A. Milson and A. Demirci (eds.), *International Perspectives on Teaching and Learning with GIS in Secondary Schools*, London: Springer.

Geographical Association (2009) *A Different View: A manifesto from the Geographical Association*, Sheffield: Geographical Association.

Geographical Association (2006) *Spatially Speaking* Available from: http://www.geography.org.uk/projects/spatiallyspeaking/ [Accessed 4 February 2012].

Geographical Association (2011a) 'GIS in Secondary School Geography' Available from: http://www.geography.org.uk/download/GA_CPDGISKeyStages.pdf [Accessed 4 February 2012].

Geographical Association (2011b) Curriculum Consultation Full Report [online] Available from: http://www.geography.org.uk/getinvolved/geographycurriculumconsultation/ [Accessed 4 February 2012].

Goodchild, M.F. (2006) 'The Fourth R? Rethinking GIS Education'- ESRI ArcNews. Available from: http://www.esri.com/news/arcnews/fall06articles/the-fourth-r.html [Accessed 4 February 2012].

Goodchild, M.F. (2008) 'Whither VGI?', *GeoJournal*, 72, 239–244.

Goodchild, M.F. (2011) 'Looking forward: Five thoughts on the future of GIS', *ArcWatch* (February). [500] 'Grounds for change' A public participatory GIS project. Available from: http://www.esri.com/news/arcwatch/0811/user-conference.html [Accessed 4 February 2012].

Gore, A. (1998) *The Digital Earth, Understanding our Planet in the 21st Century*, Speech given at the Californian Science Center, Los Angeles, California on 31 January 1998.

Herring, D. and Leopold, A. (2007) 'GIS and Climate Literacy', Paper presented at the Symposium for Digital Earth, Berkeley, California, June 2007.

Kerski, J. (2008) 'The role of GIS in digital earth education', *The International Journal of Digital Earth*, 1 (4), 326–46.

Koravec, N. (2002) 'GIS Assessment of the Vulnerability of a Core Tourist Area in New Orleans to Impacts of Flood Inundation During a Hurricane Event', *Trends in Cultural Geography* GEOG 7011 Cultural Landscapes, Spring 2002.

Lambert, D. (2011) 'Reviewing the Case for Geography, and the 'Knowledge Turn' in the English National Curriculum', *Curriculum Journal*, 22 (2), 243–64.

Malone, L. (2005) *Mapping our world: GIS lessons for educators*, Redlands, CA: ESRI Press.

Massey, D. and Clark, N. (2006) Introduction, in N. Clark, D. Massey and P. Sarre (eds.), *Material Geographies: A World in the Making*, London: Sage.

Mishra, P. and Koehler, M.J. (2006) TPACK model. Available from: http://www.tpck.org/ [Accessed 4 February 2012].

National Research Council (2006) *Learning to think spatially: GIS as a support system in the K-12 Curriculum*, Washington, DC: The National Academies Press.

Ofsted (2011) *Learning to Make a World of Difference*, February 2011, Available from: www.ofsted.gov.uk/publications/090224 [Accessed 10 February 2012].

Openshaw, S. (1991) 'A View on the GIS Crisis in Geography, Or Using GIS to put Humpty-Dumpty back together again', *Environment and Planning Part A*, 23 (5), 621–8.

O'Sullivan, D. (2006) 'Geographical Information science: Critical GIS', *Progress in Human Geography*, 30 (6), 783–91.

Pavlovskaya M. (2006) 'Theorizing with GIS: A tool for critical geographies?', *Environment and Planning Part A*, 38 (11), 2003–2020.

Pickles, J. (ed.) (1995) *Ground truth: The social implications of geographic information systems*, New York: Guildford Press.

Scheepers, D. (2009) 'GIS in the geography curriculum', *Position IT*, July 2009, 40–5.

Schuurman, N. (2000) 'Trouble in the heartland: GIS and its critics in the 1990s', *Progress in Human Geography*, 24 (4), 569–90.

Schuurman, N. (2004) *GIS: A short introduction*, London: Blackwell.

Schuurman, N. (2009) 'Is the Rubric "Critical GIScience" Effective? An Argument for Theoretical GIScience', *Cartographica*, 44 (1), 10–11.

Schuurman, N. and Goodchild, M. (2009) 'The new Brave New World: geography, GIS, and the emergence of ubiquitous mapping and data. An interview with Michael Goodchild', *Environment and Planning Part D*, 27, 571–80.

Sinton, D.S. and Bednarz, S.W. (2007) 'About that G in GIS', in D.S. Sinton, and J. Lund (eds.) (2007) *Understanding place GIS and mapping across the curriculum*, Redlands, CA: ESRI Press.

Sinton, D.S. and Lund, J. (2007) *Understanding place GIS and mapping across the curriculum*, Redlands, CA: ESRI Press.

Turner, A. (2006) An Introduction to Neogeography. Available from: http://pcmlp.socleg.ox.ac.uk/sites/pcmlp.socleg.ox.ac.uk/files/Introduction_to_Neogeography.pdf [Accessed 4 February 2012].

Vaidhyanathan, S. (2010) *The Googlization of everything (and why we should worry)*, Berkeley, CA: University of California Press.

Chapter 16

How does geography contribute to 'employability'?

John Lyon

> There is no point teaching them geography.
>
> (Lord Harris of Peckham, TES, 2011, p. 4)

Introduction

In August 2011, Lord Harris of Peckham unveiled his plans for establishing small school academies in inner-city areas for children who have been excluded from school. In an article in the *Times Educational Supplement* (TES) he emphasised that the academies

> would teach mechanics, hairdressing, plumbing ... teaching pupils a trade. There is no point teaching them geography. We could get them into work rather than being unemployed when they are 16–24. We have got to teach them skills.
>
> (TES, 2011, p. 4)

Lord Harris' quote clearly expresses his views about the value he places on vocational learning as opposed to academic learning for a specific group of young people. This positions teaching a trade versus academic subjects as an 'either or approach' to vocational and academic learning with seemingly no connection or relationship between the two. Furthermore, the juxtaposition of geography with subjects seen as having more relevant skills required for employment presents geography at a deficit in terms of valuable skills required by young people for employment. The argument appears to be that geography is irrelevant to real life.

The relevance of geography to living and working in the 21st-century is not a new discussion (see Stamp, 1960) and at times the very existence of geography as a curriculum entitlement has been questioned (Morgan and Lambert, 2005). With regard to geography's place in the curriculum, the Geographical Association's Manifesto (2009) justifies it in the following terms:

> Geography serves vital educational goals: thinking and decision making with geography helps us to be, and live our lives, as knowledgeable *citizens*, aware of our own local communities in a global setting.

> Geographers are skilful: using maps and mediated images of people and place, numerical data and graphical modes of communication and getting to grips with the geographic information systems that underpin our lives, make geographers *skilful and employable*.
>
> (GA, 2009, p. 5)

To assert that the study of geography can develop knowledgeable citizens who are both skilful and employable is by no means new. In 1902 E.G. Hewlett noted how geography 'provides ... necessary information of a technical character to many vocations of life, such as commerce, politics or war, some provision of which must be made in school' (p. 104). This was geography teaching in part aimed at providing an educated workforce able to support and enhance Britain's position as a world power. Much later, Norman Graves presented the aims and objectives of geographical education as broadly serving a dual purpose 'for the development of mind and for the social, economic and political needs of society' (Graves, 1980, p. 9). However, he doubted whether pupils would fully understand the aims of geographical teaching, since most pupils are 'highly pragmatic in their attitude to school knowledge; they tend to look upon such knowledge as a means to an examination or to a job, even if incidentally they may become interested in what they are studying' (1980, p. 9). One of the challenges facing teachers is to be responsive to pupils' pragmatic attitudes to learning, the future and career paths, whilst also keeping in mind broader educational aims for the subject.

With regard to the value of geography, teachers may face a range of questions from students: Who are geographers? What do they do? Does the geography I am doing now relate to a career I want to pursue? And the question every geography teacher should be ready for is: 'What use is geography to me when I leave school, will it get me a job?'

GEOGRAPHY AND EMPLOYABILITY

A widely used definition of employability is 'the capability to gain initial employment, maintain employment and obtain employment if required' (Hillage and Pollard, 1998, p. 1). More detailed is the definition by ESECT (2003) of 'a set of achievements – skills, understandings and personal attributes – that make graduates more likely to gain employment and be successful in their chosen occupations' (p. 4). So to what extent are young people who have studied geography or have graduated with a geography-related degree more employable that those who have not? According to Darrel Sheinman, founder of the company Polestar, a global GIS satellite tracking company, 'There is no question that the understanding and skills that come from a study of geography are highly valued by employers' (RGS, 2008, p. 12). Several recent studies of graduates have demonstrated the employability of geographers. A survey of university graduates (HESA, 2010) showed the unemployment rates for geographers to be among the lowest

recorded, second only to law. Esri UK, the leading Geographical Information Systems business, commissioned a survey of 200 business leaders across the UK public and private sectors. Also published in 2010, it showed that the graduate skills/knowledge business leaders are looking for in future employees are 'critical thinking (78% of businesses leaders), advanced analytical skills (76%), understanding and interpreting complex data (71%), advanced technology skills (57%) and understanding socio-economic environments (54%) – all of which are gained through the study of geography' (Esri UK, 2010).

However, the Royal Geographical Society with IBG (RGS-IBG) claims that the usefulness of geographical knowledge in the workplace, together with the unusually wide set of transferable skills that people learn through studying geography, is not always understood and that there is a need to make it more explicit to young people. In 2008 Christine Gilbert, Her Majesty's Chief Inspector for Education, reflecting on the state of geography education in schools, commented that 'more needs to be done to make the subject relevant and more engaging for pupils' (Ofsted, 2008).

This orthodox position is not without its critics. For example, the late Rex Walford (2000) was not convinced. For him, geography itself is intrinsically interesting and stimulating and so is worthy of study on its own merits. Ron Johnston also strikes a note of caution. He makes the point that if learning how to learn is increasingly everything in ensuring employability skills in a changing world, and geography is everything, then surely geography must be well placed to respond. However, he notes that geography must continue to maintain the core identity and values of the traditional discipline, continuing to innovate in the curriculum while being wary of wholeheartedly jumping on short-term materialistic bandwagons driven by political decision-makers (Johnston, 1997). He goes on to say, 'Geography is an academic discipline, not a profession, and one of its traditional strengths in British higher education is its use as a vehicle for the development of critical intellectual skills' (1997, p. 245).

The report by the Expert Panel for the National Curriculum review (DfE, 2011) notes that 'the school curriculum should develop pupils' knowledge, understanding skills and attitudes to satisfy economic, cultural social, personal and environmental goals' (p. 16). Satisfying future economic needs for individuals and for the workforce as a whole is only one of five key aims in ensuring a balanced and broadly based curriculum. One key issue for geography teachers then is deciding on the balance and relationship between subject knowledge, values and skills and broader competences such as problem-solving through enquiry and independent learning, increasingly associated with developing capacities for future growth. A second key issue is concerned with decisions about how geography teachers make connections between the subject and the workplace to enable students to more clearly see these opportunities.

We may see the value of learning geography as being of increasing importance as students are entering an employment market that has rapidly changing patterns in an increasingly uncertain world (Jenkins and Healey, 1995). There is an

increased demand for employees to be able to solve environmental and spatial problems, which are essentially geographical issues. However, few of these employees, often drawn from geography graduates, will call themselves 'geographers' at work, which can be problematic, particularly when these are portrayed in the media, for example as Town Planner, Coastal Engineer or Environmental consultant, with the 'geography' effectively hidden. As career opportunities involving working with and solving such environmental and spatial problems are increasing, so raising awareness of these vocational pathways may be a course adopted to raise the perceived value of the subject. This applies to careers that are directly related to geography as well as careers that use skills developed through geographical learning. There is a range of techniques that can be used to promote career pathways, including making direct reference to career opportunities related to the work being done in class, making field visits and the use of adults other than teachers in lessons who employ geographical skills significantly in their work, such as RGS 'Ambassadors'. These graduates may provide inspirational role models, demonstrating the value of geography for them to their further study and careers (see GA and RGS-IBG, 2011).

At the OECD Education Ministerial Meeting in November 2010 it was noted that

> today, education and training need to prepare learners at all levels for more rapid change than ever before, for jobs that have not yet been created, using technologies that have not yet been invented, to solve problems that cannot be foreseen. In fact, at the current rate of growth of knowledge, students can expect significant advances in knowledge during their education.
>
> (OECD, 2010, p. 1)

Ministers highlighted the challenge to countries needing to develop 'flexible educational pathways through initial education; promote skill acquisition and equity of access to learning' (OECD, 2010, p. 6). They further noted that teachers are the key professionals on the front line facing these new demands and expectations.

How explicit might we make connections between the knowledge, skills and capabilities developed through geography with the workplace and the skills needed to live lives as knowledgeable *citizens*? Perhaps the largest and most thorough recent investigation into these issues is the *Nuffield Review, Education for All: The Future of Education and Training for 14–19 Year Olds* (Pring et al., 2009a) led by Richard Pring. The review posed the question: 'What counts as an educated 19 year old in this day and age?' The 'Summary, Implications and Recommendations' to the review argued for an understanding of education *for all* which would provide:

- the knowledge and understanding required for the 'intelligent management of life';

- competence to make decisions about the future in the light of changing economic and social conditions;
- practical capability – including preparation for employment;
- moral seriousness with which to shape future choices and relationships;
- a sense of responsibility for the community. (Pring et al., 2009b, p. 3)

The Review proposes that 'such knowledge, capability and qualities are potentially important for, and (in different degrees) accessible to, all young people' and that 'all learners will have to become more rounded, resilient, creative and social, if they are to help shape an increasingly unpredictable and demanding world' (2009, p. 3). Therefore, what matters, as argued in the Review, is how essential knowledge, capabilities and qualities are translated into the learning experience of young people.

This need for workers to be agile and possess new skills and ways of understanding requires a response from geographers.

GEOGRAPHY AND VOCATIONAL PROGRAMMES

Before looking at how geography and geographers have responded, it is worth briefly exploring what we mean by the term 'vocational education'. The Wolf Report, a comprehensive review of vocational education commissioned by the government, notes there is no formal definition of the term in England and that it is applied to wide-ranging and very different programmes. The report notes that

the many ways in which the term vocational is used, reflect the many different purposes which 14–19 education serves and its large and diverse student body. Some qualifications are highly specific, oriented to a particular occupation. Others are more general, and are referred to sometimes as vocationally-related or pre-vocational.

(Wolf, 2011, p. 23)

Geography's focus on place, space and environment means geography teachers are able to contribute significantly to many of the vocational and pre-vocational courses taught in school and beyond. Over the years geographers have successfully contributed to vocational courses such as the Technical and Vocational Education Initiative (TVEI) and General National Vocational Qualification (GNVQ) courses. TVEI was announced in 1982 and ended in 1997 with GNVQs announced in 1991 and last awarded in 2007. In particular, geography teachers have been involved with Leisure and Tourism in several guises, notably GNVQ Leisure and Tourism and the subsequent Vocational Certificates of Education (VCE) courses in 'Leisure and Recreation' and 'Travel and Tourism'. These were created in September 2000 to replace the Advanced GNVQ and the BTEC Level 3 Extended Diploma in Travel and Tourism. The latter offers

an in-depth knowledge of the travel and tourism industry and is the equivalent of three A level passes.

In September 2002, eight new General Certificate of Secondary Education (GCSE) courses in vocational subjects were introduced designed to have the same rigour and standards as other GCSE subjects but encouraging practical and work-related rather than theoretical types of learning. In many schools geographers became involved with Travel and Tourism, Leisure and Tourism and other vocational GCSEs and GCEs partly because aspects of the specifications covered many of the contemporary issues taught in geography such as environment change, destination management and human mobility. However, geography teachers who contribute to vocational subjects should be aware of some of the challenges these courses present. While geographers have the subject knowledge, particularly in tourism development and impacts of tourism/sustainable tourism, other aspects such as marketing and customer service lie beyond most teachers' experience, and indeed the scope of geography. GNVQ specifications often stressed the tasks without necessarily needing to understand the geographical characteristics of the business. There has been Ofsted criticism of teachers who were delivering on courses such as GNVQs and the Applied GCSEs. These include reports of geographers teaching GCSE Leisure and Tourism who found it challenging to 'teach this very different subject' (Ofsted, 2004, p. 20) and later of schools and colleges not providing enough opportunity for practice in realistic environments such as simulated aircraft cabins or travel shops (Ofsted, 2009). To create conditions on vocational courses for learners to function as realistic practitioners, teachers need to move beyond classroom geography.

In 2008, a new wave of vocational courses known as the 14/19 Diplomas were introduced. They were intended to overcome the division between the academic and the vocational, to the extent that the terms 'vocational' and 'academic' were studiously avoided in the official literature. Geographers have been involved in four of the fourteen diplomas, notably construction and the built environment; environment and land-based studies; travel and tourism; and to a lesser degree sport and active leisure. These appeal to geographers since diplomas such as Environment and land-based studies provide opportunities for students to explore 'vitally important issues such as global warming and gain practical skills, working on real nature conservation projects' (City and Islington College, 2011). In addition, the RGS website lists a wide range of careers linked to this area including Environmental campaign organiser, Conservation worker, Environmental health officer, Pollution analyst, Environmental consultant and Environmental impact officer. All of these are examples of roles which are key players in our economy and which command considerable geographical and spatial expertise.

George MacDonald Ross (2009) asserted that the vocational strand has always been treated as inferior, with the consequence that students avoid training for careers which would be rewarding for themselves, as well as contributing to

the UK economy, in favour of academic study for which they may not be suited, and which may not lead directly to employment. However, the government decision was influenced to some extent by the conclusions of the Wolf Report, which noted that young people's employment patterns imply a need for fairly general, rather than highly specific, vocational qualifications. The report further found that the general pattern in most developed countries' education systems in response to a changed labour market is to delay specialisation to later and later stages. England is an exception with its earlier and more complete specialisation. 'The overwhelming majority of respondents to the Review were in agreement that there should be no substantial degree of specialisation before the end of KS4' (Wolf, 2011, p. 107).

Liz Atkins, who has carried out extensive research with students moving in and out of vocational provision, commented in her submission to the Wolf Report that:

> If young people are disaffected, perhaps schools could explore models of pedagogy rather than subjects – it is difficult to see how a person could be disengaged from the whole of a broad subject curriculum ... I am increasingly of the opinion that vocational education needs to be grounded in a broader, academic education so that young people have the necessary Basic Skills to progress freely.
>
> (Wolf, 2011, p 109)

The report makes ten recommendations of which one was designed to safeguard pupils' access to a common general core as a basis for progression, 'such that they can progress to a wide range of post-16 academic and vocational options; but also to ensure that academically successful pupils are given the chance to take practical courses' (2011, p. 113).

In their Curriculum Proposals and Rationale the Geographical Association (2011) looks at issues of pedagogy noting 'thinking geographically is a distinctive procedure ... (it is) learned through exposure to, and direct experience of, high quality geographical enquiry which might include decision making or problem solving scenarios' (p. 2). This is essentially the approach of applied geography.

APPLIED GEOGRAPHY

Applied geography can be seen as

> the use of geographical knowledge as an aid to making choices from the many alternative courses open to us about how we use the planet and its resources, how we distribute ourselves on the surface and how we relate to fellow men.
>
> (Sant, 1982, p. 1)

As early as 1960, Dudley Stamp, a pioneer in the field of applied geography proposed:

> if the past 50 years have been spent in developing geographical method of survey and analysis, surely the time has now come to apply these methods towards understanding and interpretation of some of the features of the world of today' and use these methods 'in helping towards the solution of some of the great world problems – the increasing pressure of population on space, the development of underdeveloped areas, or the attempt to improve living conditions which is the object of town and country planning'.
>
> (Stamp, 1960, pp. 10–11)

Towards the end of the 1970s and into the 1980s geography needed to respond to governmental pressure, following the then Prime Minister, James Callaghan's speech in 1976 at Ruskin College, Oxford. He emphasised the need to make the curriculum more relevant to young people in preparation for their adult life. He was concerned about a disconnection between industry and education and that the school curriculum did not prepare young people for the demands of employment in a modern industrial society (Jamieson and Lightfoot, 1982). The speech refocused attention on the nature of the curriculum and the relationships between school and work. The Schools Council Industry Project (which became the School Curriculum Industry Partnership (SCIP), identified sets of overlapping pressures. The most relevant to geography were the pressures of the Industrial Society in general which were related to calls for the school curriculum to be broader and less academically orientated, and to prepare young people more adequately for adult life (Corney, 1985, 1992).

One solution was to develop closer links between schools and industry. The Geography Schools Industry Project (GSIP) was one such response, having been established by the Geographical Association with several aims including the desire to forge school–industry links as a strategy in helping geography teachers contribute to their students' economic understanding. Building on the traditions of geographical education established by the Avery Hill, Bristol and Geography 16–19 Projects, GSIP stressed an approach to teaching based on active student learning, assessment for learning and an emphasis on the economic dimension. It focused on issues and questions deemed relevant to students. It employed a meaningful sequence of geographical enquiry through which students gained first-hand experience of workplaces, people at work, local communities. It contrasted environments and allowed scope for the involvement of people from industry and the community in planning and implementing units of work. For many this was a refreshing approach with its rich resources and relevant, topical units of work. Teachers were engaged with making their own curriculum, refreshing the subject matter and changing the way young people see the world.

Others viewed it differently. For Huckle (1985) projects such as GSIP were concerned largely with the management of change as the state sought to restructure in the face of new challenges and with sectional interests of a community of educators rather than being progressive educational developments.

Government influence continued in 1985 when Sir Keith Joseph, the then Secretary of State, returned to this theme and posed the following set of questions to the Geographical Association:

> Is enough attention paid to the impact of political and economic processes and activities in geographical patterns and changes?' and 'is there not more scope for more effective cooperation between geography teachers and their colleagues in other disciplines to foster economic awareness and political understanding?
>
> (see Joseph, 1985, p. 29)

Further emphasis entered the curriculum as Economic Understanding was one of the five major cross-curricular themes of the National Curriculum Council and Geography seemed well placed to contribute. The HMI view expressed in 'Geography from 5–16' was that 'geography can make a significant contribution to ... education in economic understanding ... and preparing young people for the world of work' (Bennetts, 1986, p. 302). For older students, the Geography 16–19 Project was in part an attempt to support this aim. The key to understanding the Project's approach to geography was that it was 'educational rather than strictly academic, enabling students to draw on geographical knowledge and theories in a meaningful way and to develop a wide range of skills and abilities' (Naish and Rawling, 1990, p. 61). In this way it offered a role for geography in the 16–19 curriculum which had appeal and relevance for a large cross-section of students. Such an educational approach was felt to have possibilities in relation to some wider access courses in higher education. The Project recommended that the study of geography at the 16–19 age-level should take place through enquiry-based teaching and learning. The approach to geography focused on questions, issues and problems arising from the interrelationship of people with their varied environments. For example, questions, issues and problems may be investigated in such topics as the management of coastal landforms, responses to natural hazards, the quality of life in cities and approaches to Third World development. An important emphasis in the enquiry-based work was the development of students as responsible and competent individuals capable of playing a participatory role in society which incorporated the development of economic understanding and political literacy. Furthermore, it encouraged independent thinking at A level and in many ways preceded the later underlying educational philosophy of the diploma. However, the 16–19 Project was not overtly vocational in its approach, offering no real direct reference to specific vocations, but it certainly offered a wide set of transferable techniques and skills

of value in a vocational context , could easily complement geography's presence in vocational courses such as Travel and Tourism and could be seen as an example of effective applied geography.

For Pacione (1999), applied geography involves problem-orientated research in both human and physical geography, and encompasses 'the fundamental philosophy of relevance or usefulness to society' (p. 4). An applied geographical approach therefore has the potential to illuminate the nature and causes of problems such as extreme natural events, for example floods and drought; environmental concerns such as deforestation and disease; human issues such as crime and poverty; as well as inform the formulation of appropriate responses. Sant (1982) notes that such an approach is not, however, neutral in its application or in choices that are made about reaping some personal or social advantage. These choices and decisions are made by someone, somewhere. Who makes these choices? Do they make these choices in a professional capacity? Are they geographers? And does it matter if they are not?

Of course, Stamp gave greater emphasis to land classification and evaluation and land-use planning than other forms of applied geography, reflecting as it does his interests drawn from the First Land Use Survey of Britain which he set up and organised in the 1930s. Nevertheless, it moved some way towards making explicit some of the careers involved in this approach to geography. By 1960 he noted that 'natural geographical factors are more important than they have ever been in the past. Man (*sic*) has not emancipated himself from these factors' (p. 194). It would be interesting to see how Stamp would have developed his thinking in response to new global challenges. Paul Crutzen, an atmospheric chemist, has begun to develop the idea that we now exist in the *Anthropocene* where human activities are having an impact on the Earth's ecosystems so significant as to constitute a new geological era. Applied geography is well placed to address some of the issues this idea raises.

Conclusion

So, as the nature and value of vocational and applied dimensions to the curriculum are discussed by the Coalition government, what are the choices and decisions to be faced by geography curriculum makers?

One important choice concerns the potential for geography students to apply their knowledge and skills to causes and concerns of global importance. If we return to the GA *Manifesto*, we understand that Geography

> *deepens understanding:* many contemporary challenges – climate change, food security, energy choices – cannot be understood without a geographical perspective which includes sound locational knowledge and understanding.
>
> (GA, 2009, p. 5).

Such matters concerning the future of the planet and its peoples have been taken up by John Morgan who argues

> We live in a time where there are serious questions about the ability of the planet to sustain current levels of economic development. Future generations are likely to face a bleaker environmental future and will need to learn how to mitigate and adapt to the effects of climate change. However despite the obvious importance of these issues most schooling continues with little direct engagement with questions of environmental change.
>
> (Morgan, 2011, p. ii)

These are big issues involving some significant choices. The set of skills, knowledge and pedagogy that geography promotes offers significant opportunities for young people to explore how societal, economic and environmental change is likely to impact on all our futures and can enable them to better understand the world and their place in it. Geography itself is not a vocational subject but when taught thoughtfully it offers powerful specialist knowledge, a skills set and an ability to understand issues from multiple perspectives that ensure geographers are highly sought after in the workplace. Within an applied context, geography teaching also has the potential to include detailed information about the people and jobs that will be involved in responding to crucial economic, social and environmental issues such as effective resource management or climate change.

I have tried to show in this chapter the long-standing debates over not only the nature of geography as an applied subject but also its role in relation to employability and vocational preparation. In the final analysis these are debates about geography, but also geography in a vocational setting. The value of geography would appear to be its contribution to a broad base of knowledge, perspectives on the world and the development of practical and cognitive skills.

Key readings

1. Naish, M., Rawling, E. and Hart, C. (1987) *Geography 16–19: The contribution of a curriculum development project to 16–19 education*, London: Longman for School Curriculum Development Committee. This book explores a complete philosophy about geography and applied approaches.
2. Rawling, E. (2001) *Changing the Subject The Impact of National Policy on School Geography 1980–2000*, Sheffield: Geographical Association. In Eleanor Rawling's excellent account of school geography between 1980 and 2000, Chapter 7 covers the debate about the 14–19 curriculum and academic vocational divide.

References

Bennetts, T. (1986) 'Geography from 5 to 16: A View from the Inspectorate', *Geography*, 70 (4), 299–314.

City and Islington College (2011) [online] Available from: http://www.candi.ac.uk/school-leavers/environmental-and-land-based-studies/ [Accessed 22 February 2012].

Corney, G. (ed.) (1985) *Geography Schools and Industry*, Sheffield: The Geographical Association.

Corney, G. (ed.) (1992) *Teaching Economic Understanding Through Geography*, Sheffield: The Geographical Association.

Department for Education (DfE) (2011) *The Framework for the National Curriculum. A report by the Expert Panel for the National Curriculum review*, London: Department for Education.

Enhancing Student Employability Co-ordination Team (ESECT) (2003) *Briefings on Employability 2, Are your students employable?* Report from HEFCE's Enhancing Student Employability Co-ordination Team (ESECT) [online] Available from: www.qualityresearchinternational.com/esecttools/esectpubs/B0E2%20Are%20your%20students%20employable.pdf [Accessed 24 February 2012].

Esri UK (2010) Press release: UK Businesses Call For Advanced Technology Skills To Boost Economy. 17 November 2010. Available from: http://www.esriuk.com/aboutesriuk/pressreleases.asp?pid=647 [Accessed 25 February 2012].

Geographical Association (GA). (2009) *A Different View: A manifesto from the Geographical Association*, Sheffield: Geographical Association.

Geographical Association (2011) *The Geography National Curriculum, GA Curriculum Proposals and Rationale* [online] Available from http://geography.org.uk/getinvolved/geographycurriculumconsultation/ [Accessed 24 February 2012].

Geographical Association and Royal Geographical Society (with IBG) (2011) *The Action Plan for Geography 2006–2011 Final Report and Evaluation.* [online] Available from: http://www.geography.org.uk/download/GA_APGFinalReport.pdf [Accessed 24 February 2012].

Graves, N. (1980) *Geography Education in Secondary Schools*, Sheffield: The Geographical Association.

Hewlett, E.G. (1902) 'Aims and difficulties in the teaching of geography', *The Geographical Teacher*, 2, 104–107. London: Geographical Association/London Geographical Institute.

Hillage, J. and Pollard, E. (1998) *Employability: Developing a frame work for policy analysis*, London: Department for Education and Employment.

Huckle, J. (1985) 'Geography and Schooling', in R. Johnson (ed.), *The Future of Geography*, London: Methuen.

Jamieson, I. and Lightfoot, M. (1982) *Schools and Industry. Schools Council Working Paper*, No.3, London: Methuen.

Jenkins, A. and Healey, M. (1995) 'Linking the Geography Curriculum to the Worlds of Industry, Commerce and Public Authorities', *Journal of Geography in Higher Education*, 19 (2), 177–81.

Johnston, R.J. (1997) '"Graduateness" and a Core Curriculum for Geographers', *Journal of Geography in Higher Education*, 21 (2), 245–59.

Joseph, K. (1985) 'Geography in the School Curriculum', *Geography*, 70 (4), 290–97.

MacDonald Ross, G. (2009) 'The 14–19 Diploma in Humanities and Social Sciences', *Discourse*, 9 (1), 127–42.

Morgan, J. (2011) *Teaching Geography as if the Planet Matters*, London: Routledge.

Morgan, J. and Lambert, D. (2005) *Geography: Teaching school subjects 11–19*, London: Routledge.

Naish, M. and Rawling, E. (1990) 'Geography 16–19: Some implications for higher education', *Journal of Geography in Higher Education*, 14 (1), 55–75.

Naish, M., Rawling, E. and Hart, C. (1987) *Geography 16–19: The contribution of a curriculum development project to 16–19 education*, London: Longman for School Curriculum Development Committee.

Ofsted (2004) *Developing new vocational pathways: Final report on the introduction of new GCSEs*, London: HMI.

Ofsted (2008) Press release: *Geography in schools – changing practice*. 17 January 2008. Available from: http://www.ofsted.gov.uk/news/geography-schools-changing-practice [Accessed 25 February, 2012].

Ofsted (2009) *Identifying good practice: A survey of college provision in leisure, travel and tourism*, London: Ofsted.

Organisation of Economic Co-operation and Development (OECD) 'Investing in Human and Social Capital: New Challenges', OECD Educational Ministerial Meeting, Paris, 4–5 November 2010 [online] Available from: http://www.oecd.org/dataoecd/59/13/46253090.pdf [Accessed 24 February 2012].

Pacione, M. (ed.) (1999) *Applied Geography: Principles and Practice: An Introduction to Useful Research in Physical, Environmental and Human Geography*, London: Routledge.

Pring, R., Hayward, G., Hodgson, A., Johnson, J., Keep, E., Oancea, A., Rees, G., Spours, K. and Wilde, S. (2009a) *Education for All: The Future of Education and Training for 14–19 Year Olds in England and Wales*, London: Routledge.

Pring, R., Hayward, G., Hodgson, A., Johnson, J., Keep, E., Oancea, A., Rees, G., Spours, K. and Wilde, S. (2009b) *Education for All: The Future of Education and Training for 14–19 Year Olds in England and Wales: Summary, Implications and Recommendations*, Available from: http://www.nuffieldfoundation.org/14-19review [Accessed 10 August 2012].

Rawling, E. (2001) *Changing the Subject The Impact of National policy on School Geography*, Sheffield: The Geographical Association.

Royal Geographic Society with Institute of British Geographers (RGS-IBG) (2008) *Going Places with Geography*, London: RGS-IBG.

Sant, M. (1982) *Applied Geography – Practice Problems and Prospects*, Harlow: Longman.

Stamp, L.D. (1960) *Applied Geography*, Harmondsworth: Penguin.

Times Educational Supplement (TES) (2011) *Academy sponsor hit by riots plans skills schools for excluded*, [online] Available from: http://www.tes.co.uk/article.aspx?storycode=6109267 [Accessed 24 February 2012].

Walford, R. (2000) *Geography in British Schools 1850–2000*, London: Woburn Press.

Wolf, A. (2011) *Review of Vocational Education, The Wolf Report* [online] Available from: https://www.education.gov.uk/publications/eOrderingDownload/The%20Wolf%20Report.pdf [Accessed 3 November 2011].

Chapter 17

How do we deal with controversial issues in a 'relevant' school geography?

David Mitchell

> The more contemporary the issue the greater the problems for the teacher ....
>
> (Stradling, 1984, p. 3)

Introduction

In August 2011 the news reported youth riots in English cities, famine in East Africa, debt crisis in the EU, and the potential legacy of the London 2012 Olympics. Geography teachers take pride in their ability to teach current topics like these, 'geographically'. Such events or issues seem 'relevant' to pupils by being current and newsworthy, and having resonance with pupils' lives (be that through their material lives, or thoughts and feelings). Stradling's quote reminds us that the more current the issue the more controversial it is likely to be, making the teacher's role more difficult. Stradling points out the lack of hindsight, that primary sources of evidence are likely to be incomplete and biased, and that the criteria for valid 'evidence' may not yet be established. When dealing with the future, uncertainty is particularly great. Geography, we often claim, is 'relevant' to the present and has something to say about the future. Bonnett (2008) suggests that geography is a project with two purposes for humanity – first for survival and secondly for the understanding of one another. But, in undertaking such bold work, we deal in uncertainty and opinion about how the world is, how it ought to be and what part education should play. School geography is therefore 'shot through' with values (Slater, 1996) and, as Hopwood (2007) puts it, where values arise, controversy follows.

If we consider schooling and geography together, it emerges that school geography is not a neutral vehicle for the teacher to use as he or she wishes. Literature in the field of curriculum studies such as Apple (2004), Kelly (2009) and Fielding (2011) argues that the school curriculum has become dominated by a discourse of 'effectiveness' making it difficult for the teacher to tackle (or raise) controversy through deep engagement with the subject. J. Morgan (2011, 2012), through a historical analysis of the curriculum, argues that *school* geography has served a project, not so much for human survival and understanding, as for the interests of the corporate capitalist state.

Amidst such uncertainty, how should geography teachers handle controversial issues? And how does *geography*, the subject itself, help us to do so? This chapter discusses these questions, and the tensions and problems within literature which emerge. It can be argued, rather than seeking to diffuse or avoid controversy, pupils are better served by a school geography which raises controversy and poses problems.

WHAT ARE CONTROVERSIAL ISSUES IN GEOGRAPHY EDUCATION?

The 'Crick Report' (1998) defines a controversial issue as:

> … an issue about which there is no one fixed or universally held point of view. Such issues are those which commonly divide society and for which significant groups offer conflicting explanations and solutions.
>
> (Advisory Group on Citizenship, 1998, p. 56)

Using this definition, geography is awash with controversial issues. Geography tends to deal with issues of super-complexity which defy clear 'proof' and definite 'clear-cut' answers (Lambert, 1999; Lambert and Morgan, 2005). Morgan (2006) uses the notion of 'wicked problems' to show how geographical issues become controversial. Wicked problems are difficult to define, are contested and have no clear cut answers. 'Answers' are value laden with 'better or worse' rather than 'right or wrong' solutions – climate change is a good example. A. Morgan (2011) argues that, unlike many non-humanities subjects, geography raises complex ethical and moral questions. It therefore becomes important for the geography teacher to develop 'ethical knowledge' to tackle the many 'geo-ethical' issues (such as environmental decay, terrorism, conflict and poverty). Coupled to this notion of super-complexity is that of instability. Barnett (2011) calls the world the student encounters 'radically unstable', radical, in that not only does the world change, but the very frameworks by which we understand the world (including subjects like geography, and institutions, such as schools) change too. This is a bewildering problem for the teacher. Not only does the world change, but the discipline of geography changes. Not only does the discipline change, but curriculum frameworks (like the National Curriculum and examination specifications) change, and simultaneously, schools change and young people change.

Making sense of controversial issues requires value judgement by learners and teachers – objective reasoning alone cannot result in certainty. Stradling (1984) made this link between values and controversy. Tackling controversy in geography teaching is closely linked to how we approach values. Halstead and Taylor (1996) define values as deep or fundamental convictions, stances, ideals or standards which guide or influence behaviour and are used as reference points in evaluating particular issues. Slater (1982) draws on Rokeach (1973) to

emphasise the enduring nature of values over attitudes. Attitudes and opinions, however, are useful indicators. They can be expressive of the more deep-seated values (Slater, 1982). To use the example of migration, an opinion might be that all asylum seekers should be given shelter by the British state and legal representation. The attitude here is one of concern for the well-being of asylum seekers, but the deeper value is of social justice for all people.

Values become an important concern for geographers, encountered alongside the objective 'facts' of the world. But complicating matters further, there is doubt about whether there is any objective reality (the 'facts') at all. Depending on one's beliefs, the world (i.e. all geographical knowledge) is either more or less a social construct. So, for social constructivists who reject a realist view of knowledge, geography is constructed by people, and a matter of value judgement and interpretation, as well as power and control.[1] This makes all geography potentially controversial. A tension within the subject is reflected in different opinions in literature over how school geography should position itself in terms of fact versus value. Standish (2007, 2009) calls for a return to 'the facts', arguing that school geography has been diminished by the 'global dimension'. Marsden (1995) was wary of geography being used to promote 'good causes' and Lidstone and Gerber (1998) are concerned that geography is used to promote an environmental ethic. Such arguments have to be considered in light of critiques of the notion that school geography (and schooling itself) can be neutral. Teaching is always a political act, whether the political stance is open or hidden (Huckle, 1985; Apple, 2004; J. Morgan, 2011). Furthermore, Lambert (2008) argues that geographical knowledge cannot be reduced to 'facts' but is dynamic and changing and better understood as a conceptual framework.

Most geography educators accept some objective reality – that there are some objective 'facts' about the world, whilst recognising that some knowledge is socially constructed. This is as social-realist theory of knowledge (Wheelahan, 2010; Young and Muller, 2010).

The literature thus gives geography teachers two concerns to recognise in relation to controversial issues in geography. First, the curriculum is itself controversial by the selection of content. What is to be included and excluded is a value judgement and exposes the purposes of school geography as controversial. Secondly, school geography encounters issues which arouse strong emotion, personal differences of opinion and uncertainty. I now go on to explore these two concerns and the tensions in the literature relating to them.

CONTROVERSIAL PURPOSES OF SCHOOL GEOGRAPHY

The view of school geography as neutral knowledge about the world has been discredited. Recognition that the purposes of school geography are controversial helps teachers take a critical and morally careful approach to curriculum. In the

1970s, the 'new sociology of education' (Young, 1971) exposed knowledge and curriculum as matters of power and control. Claims to the possibility of 'rational curriculum planning' (Marsden, 1976), independent of political power, are therefore problematic. Drawing on the new sociology of education and Foucault's notion of the political economy of knowledge, radical geography educators, such as Huckle (1985) and J. Morgan (2011, 2012), give historical accounts to argue that school geography is not neutral, but serves the corporate capitalist state. An example of how value laden geography can be presented as 'fact' is through textbooks. The printed page carries an authority that can belie controversial views. From a right-wing perspective, Aldrich-Moodie and Kwong (1997) reported that textbooks in the UK and USA presented opinions about environmental value positions, for example, giving a message that recycling is good, before pupils understand what resources are and how recycling fits into the economics of scarce resource use. Lambert and Balderstone (2000) argue that the 'morally careful' teacher is one who is conscious to help pupils distinguish values and opinions from facts.

Apple argues that schooling tends to see controversy as a bad thing, as it leads to conflict, and conflict is to be avoided, or quickly resolved. Yet, as Apple points out, controversy and conflict are the vital life blood of change and progress (in science and in society). Schools are teaching pupils to avoid conflict in order to reproduce human capital – willing workers and consumers, accepting of hierarchy, who will serve the economy and ensure profits and wealth for the elite. Schooling therefore is not neutral, but *ideological*. Controversy and conflict are essential to human progress, and a part of being human. They should therefore be welcomed, not diffused, if education aims to give hope, equal opportunity and the possibility of social change, Apple (2004) argues.

Radical school geography (seeking action and change) was losing ground by the 1990s. Neoliberal ideology has since been immersed in school geography, Morgan (2012) argues. This can be seen in the ways environment and environmentalism is handled. 'Ecological modernisation' has become accepted as 'common sense' (i.e. that sustainable development can be achieved within capitalist economic growth – alternatives are not given serious consideration, nor is capitalism itself seen as controversial). Lessons teaching children to behave in more 'green' ways, and to see the benefits of technological solutions, without challenging the system that creates the problem, exemplify 'ecological modernisation'. Thus apparently well-meaning attempts to deal with issues such as fair trade in geography become more about helping the consumer construct their identity (as idealised 'ethical' consumer) than looking at possibilities for social justice. Thus children are being taught to accept neoliberal consumerism as the only way to proceed (see Pykett, 2011). *Problem-solving* tends to validate and bolster the social and economic system, whereas *problem-posing* tends to expose and challenge its failures. Morgan (2012) suggests the former has become the focus of the handling of 'controversial' school geography, rather than the latter.

The political and economic landscape changed again in 2008 as global capitalism entered a crisis on a similar scale to that of the 1970s. Education and geography are now operating in a climate of increased scarcity in all aspects of life. The Coalition government of 2010 have heralded something of a 'knowledge turn'. The National Curriculum review is exploring a return to 'core knowledge' likely to reflect Hirsch's (1987) notion of 'cultural literacy' or a view that there can be transmission of 'the facts' of geography, and an avoidance of 'controversial' and value-laden geography. This may represent an elitist turn to school geography, which Young and Muller (2010) call 'knowledge of the powerful'. However, this moment also provides opportunities for school geography to become more 'problem-posing' using the subject to challenge the underlying causes and connections behind the problems of human–nature relations.

Historical analyses show that the geography curriculum is always controversial. It is ideological and linked to the social, economic and political agendas of the powerful. The 'morally careful' geography teacher must choose what and how to teach with critical consideration of underlying purposes. They must ask: *what is this geography for?*

ENCOUNTERING CONTROVERSIAL ISSUES IN THE GEOGRAPHY CLASSROOM

Earlier, in this chapter, I discussed the challenge of the 'super-complex' and 'radically unstable' world that students grapple with. Amidst such uncertainty, Barnett (2011) suggests that students may be inclined to give up on learning. In dealing with controversy and uncertainty about the future, he argues that students must have 'willingness to be changed as a result of one's learning' (p. 11). The will to learn is thus essential. Students must be open to being changed or 'becoming' who they are (Barnett, 2011).

Some aspects of geography are likely to arouse strong emotions and at the same time bring different opinions to light, based on different personal values. Issues such as race, cultural difference, immigration, housing, poverty, inequality and questions about futures are examples which every geography teacher will encounter. The disagreement resulting may lead to debate, or argument. This can be a threat, with the risk of disorder in the classroom, anger or resentment amongst pupils. But it can also be an opportunity for values education through geography. There is substantial disagreement and tension in the literature over how values education and controversial issues should be handled.

VALUES EDUCATION IN GEOGRAPHY – NEUTRALITY, BALANCE OR COMMITMENT?

Much of the literature of teaching of controversial issues deals with the question of how the teacher should present a value position or positions. Stenhouse (1975) emphasises the teacher's role as one of 'procedural neutrality', arguing that if the

teacher had a personal value position they should not reveal it to the class. Each pupil should work out their own value position, rather than be influenced by the authority of the teacher. The pupil's values would therefore be more authentic and they would place more importance on that value, or opinion, than if it was passed on to them by the teacher (Halstead and Taylor, 1996).

Stradling (1984) suggests that complete neutrality is unrealistic and 'committed impartiality' is preferable, meaning that the teacher reveals their opinion without imposing it on others. The teacher's main role is to ensure fairness for debate, discussion and reasoning in a democratic setting. Oulton et al. (2004) and Cotton (2006) emphasise the need for the teacher to take a *balanced* position, whilst they also recognise the difficulty of remaining neutral. Another position is that of 'devil's advocate', which can enliven discussion. Each teaching approach (neutral, stated commitment, balanced and devil's advocate) can support the geography teacher, when used in the appropriate context, Stradling (1984) suggests.

The commitment to a democratic classroom, placing trust in the class to develop and clarify their own values, draws from Freire's (1970) critical pedagogy. This rejects the teacher as holder of authority and giver of knowledge, and encourages an emancipatory approach by which the learners can find their own voice and realise their own authority. Freire's ideas were grounded in the context of Brazil in the 1960s and 70s, in which most lived in inescapable poverty and were taught obedience to religion and state, but Freire has influenced ideas about democratic, critical and emancipatory pedagogy elsewhere. The democratic classroom also draws from the child-centred tradition of education. Dewey (1916) emphasised the importance of the learner making sense through experience and activity. (Recent interest in young people's geographies reflects the child-centred tradition.) In the context of values, the child-centred approach gives weight to pupil voice and individual difference.

Socratic dialogue is an important principle to recognise in democratic approaches which use discussion. Ideas and opinions are tested with questions. Logic and reasoning lead to the development of robust, defensible value positions. Citizenship education particularly, argues for the power of debate, discussion and dialogue (Hayward, 2007; Hess, 2009). Ultimately, though, there must be a moral judgement underlying the reasoning. When two or more values conflict, for example a conflict between individual freedom and an equal society, the relative strength of values comes into play again relying on judgement and what A. Morgan (2011) calls 'ethical knowledge' of the subject.

The notion of the neutral teacher, child-centred education, the democratic classroom and a strong 'pupil voice' is opposed by proponents of adult authority. The titles of work by these educationalists are evocative: *Wasted – why education isn't educating* (Furedi, 2009); *The dangerous rise of therapeutic education* (Ecclestone and Hayes, 2009); and *The corruption of the curriculum* (Whelan, 2007). The theme amongst these (drawn upon by the right-wing think-tank, Civitas) is that the curriculum must pass on the best adult knowledge, culture

and values. Teaching must model adult authority. Failure to do so, they argue, is leading to education as 'therapy'. This is the result of a diminished view of children and a crisis of confidence in society, such that adults are not asserting their authority.

At the time of writing, the aftermath of the youth riots in 2011 have given fresh impetus to a debate about how best to approach values, education and (a perceived) 'moral decay'. It can seem like a straight choice between either pupil voice (democratic debate) or adult authority (transmission of values). But human rights education offers a perspective which may be able to reconcile the two. Basic human rights are universal; they apply to everyone, equally, adults and children alike. The protection of human rights is a collective responsibility, so the state has an important role in this. But human rights (as stated in the Universal Declaration of Human Rights, which all nations signed in 1948) are sometimes confused with the way human rights are applied. So, for example, everyone has the right to work (article 23), but this does not mean everyone has the right to an equal share of wealth. The political right sometimes portrays human rights education as part of a culture of entitlement and individualism. This misunderstands human rights education, which actively challenges such a destructive culture (Amnesty UK, 2009). Human rights education is as much about learning the importance of protecting other people's rights as it is realising one's individual rights. It is also noteworthy that human rights are deeply geographical in two ways. First, they are universal. Whilst cultural and political difference and national sovereignty are recognised, the Universal Declaration of Human Rights gives an integrating, global perspective to the governance of all people. Second, they are place-based, playing out locally by changing the environment and communities in which we live. Human rights, therefore, are a lens for geographers to tackle controversial issues, particularly when they arise across different cultural, political and national contexts (Mitchell, 2009b).

Hopwood (2007) raises an important point with respect to pupil voice. In reviewing literature in geography education, he finds that, in dealing with controversial issues, much attention has been given to the teacher's role, but little to the pupil. Hopwood's own research into pupils' engagement with values education in geography shows that pupils generally feel the subject allows them to express a different view to others and that it teaches them to respect different viewpoints. However, they also feel that geography promotes a 'green' political position (Hopwood, 2004). Hopwood (2007) notes that there is a research gap in how *pupils* engage with values in their geography education. Literature on controversial issues in education is skewed towards the teacher's role.

There is an important difference between the teaching of values and teaching through values, which affects the question of how far the teacher should or can be neutral. The former suggests predetermined values to be transmitted to the pupil, the latter suggests more openness to a range of value positions which the pupil may develop. Lambert and Balderstone (2000) differentiate between five types of values education (see Figure 17.1).

The five approaches show that values education can take place within different ideologies and discourses of education. So, for example, values clarification sits easily with a child-centred ideology, values inculcation within a discourse of adult authority, and action learning with an ideology of education for social change. This does not mean such values approaches can only happen within those ideologies. But this shows that the processes of values education can themselves indicate the educational values and beliefs of the teacher or values embedded in the school subject.

Deep in human value systems lie beliefs of what is morally right and wrong. Issues which raise questions of values usually raise moral questions too. Lambert and Balderstone (2000) see the geography teachers' role as a moral one. It is 'morally careless', they claim, to teach without helping pupils consider what is right and wrong. Sometimes, they suggest, it is unhelpful to tell pupils that there are 'no right or wrong answers', as this implies a vagueness to geography and moral ambivalence. There are occasions when something is clearly (in moral terms) either right or wrong. 'No clear-cut answers' is a better way to phrase the challenge of understanding the 'super-complex' world, they suggest. Marsden (1995) advocates 'moral reasoning' through discussion and debate. The view here is that moral questions can be dealt with *rationally* through appeal to reason and evidence. Fien and Slater (1981) advocate a similar process of rationality leading to defensible value judgements in their approach to values analysis. Purported 'facts' are assembled and tested against value principles. Pupils thus can both clarify their own values and understand the value principles behind the planning and decision-making process. Huckle (1981), however, argues that it is inappropriate to apply a diminished form of rationality and balance to values. This leads to acceptance of situations, he argues, and that powerful emotions should be embraced. This might encourage conflict, and thus lead to change.

Values inculcation	Has the objective that students will adopt a predetermined set of values.
Values analysis	Uses structured discussion and logical analysis of evidence to investigate values issues.
Moral reasoning	Provides opportunities to discuss reasons for value positions and choices with the aim of encouraging growth of moral reasoning ability.
Values clarification	Has the objective of helping students become aware of their own values in relation to their behaviour and that of others.
Action learning	Encourages students to see themselves as interacting members of social and environmental systems through having them analyse and clarify values with the intention of enabling them to act in relation to social and environmental issues according to their value choices.

Figure 17.1 Approaches to values education (from Lambert and Balderstone, 2000, p. 293).

Conclusion – using the subject

Controversy arises both in the purpose and practice of school geography, and much of the literature deals with how best to handle or cope with controversial issues when they arise. However, geography offers a subject framework which can help us to make sense of (and even to seek out) controversial issues.

School geography offers a balanced approach to investigation of a subject grounded in both humanity and science. Thus, Maye (1984) provides a values-based framework for problem-solving and decision-making and Roberts (2003) shows how geographical enquiry provides a broad framework for making sense of the complexity world, which can be applied to both values and factual enquiry. Both Maye and Roberts take a 'rational' approach to the learning process, offering a framework for pupils based on logic and analysis of data, to draw conclusions. (Though as noted earlier, a rational approach to values issues is contested.)

Place, space and scale, concepts at the heart of geography, encourage a distinctive way of thinking about the world. Geographers thus have a distinctive way of approaching controversial issues, through a geographical lens. Jackson's (2006) 'thinking geographically' and Massey's (1991) 'global sense of the local' express this unique perspective, which can provide particular insight into controversial issues. The notion of 'living geography' (Mitchell, 2009a) helps to express the relationship between the subject, controversial issues and relevance to everyday life. To give three examples from pupils' own localities; violations of human rights and loss of community can be examined through the concept of place and place-making; sustainability through the lens of integration (of society, economy and environment); and the injustice of poverty through the lens of scale and connection of local to global.

Morgan (2011, 2012) draws on the concept of integration (social, economic and environmental) arguing that pupils can be helped to see through superficial causes and consequences to deeper, often hidden structures which reproduce life in the world. Thus, Morgan and Lambert (2001, 2003) suggest, school geography can challenge racism by showing how race and racism are constructed. There are opportunities, they argue, to deconstruct common and ideological representations of urban and rural, insider and outsider, established residents and newcomers. Morgan (2011, 2012) applies the same critical deconstruction to the controversy of the environment and sustainability. By helping pupils see that political economy produces and reproduces life in all respects, he argues that school geography can provide a deeper understanding of the world than the dominant neoliberal world view. This brings more hope for action and change. Morgan follows a radical tradition of school geography such as Huckle (1985) and Fien and Gerber (1988), and radical curriculum critique more widely, such as Apple (2004). Radical school geography seeks to awaken pupils to social injustice and how the capitalist world fails people and nature. School geography makes full use of the powerful concept of integration (and interconnectedness) when it accepts that this will pose problems for young people, rather than reassure with solutions. Geography thus offers teachers a conceptual framework to embrace controversy.

However, not all teachers will take such a radical position. There are different educational traditions (sometimes described as philosophies, beliefs or ideologies) in school geography and no tradition can claim superiority over another (because the purposes of education are a matter of values).[2] Radical geography (seeking to change the world, or 'social reconstruction') is one tradition, but others include child-centred education, academic scholarship, cultural heritage and for social/economic 'efficiency'. Teachers tend to hold a mix of these traditions and beliefs about education. But geography teachers (and departments) can vary substantially in their views over the purpose of geographic education. This affects the approach to controversial issues in geography. So, for example, a child-centred focus may use geography to support pupils clarifying their own values, a social/economic efficiency focus might use problem-solving geography a great deal, and an academic scholarship focus might be expected to make strong use of knowledge-based reasoning. School geography therefore presents much opportunity for teacher and pupil to engage with controversial issues, though the 'educational' outcomes of the engagement may be very different depending on the department. This makes controversial issues a matter worthy of the geography teacher's planning, reflection and research.

Notes

1 For an account of the controversial nature of geographical knowledge and challenges to the authority of science, see Unwin (1992). For theories of the relationship between curriculum, knowledge and power see (Young 1971) and Young and Muller (2010).
2 For a discussion of educational traditions and 'ideologies' in geography, see Walford (1981) and Rawling (2001). For more general analysis of different educational ideologies, see Schiro (2008) and Taylor and Richards (1985).

Key readings

1. Stradling, R., Noctor, M. and Baines B. (eds.) (1984) *Teaching controversial issues*, London: Edward Arnold. The introductory chapter by Stradling, 'Controversial Issues in the Classroom' provides an excellent argument for why controversial issues are educationally important, and considers the strategies for the teacher handling controversial issues.
2. Slater, F. (1982) *Learning through Geography*, London: Heinemann. In this book, chapter 4, 'Interpreting and analysing values and attitudes' is very helpful in illuminating how values arise from geographical learning.

References

Advisory Group on Citizenship (1998) *Education for citizenship and the teaching of democracy in schools: Final report of the advisory group on citizenship*, [online] Available from: http://www.teachingcitizenship.org.uk/dnloads/crickreport1998.pdf [Accessed 18 August 2011].
Aldrich-Moodie, B. and Kwong, J. (1997) *Environmental Education*, London: Institute of Economic Affairs.

Amnesty UK (2009) *Making Human Rights Real: Teaching Citizenship through Human Rights*, London: Amnesty. [online] Available from: http://www.amnesty.org.uk/uploads/documents/doc_20103.pdf [Accessed 18 August 2011].

Apple, M. (2004) *Ideology and Curriculum* 3rd edn, New York: RoutledgeFalmer.

Barnett, R. (2011) 'Learning about learning: A conundrum and a possible resolution', *London Review of Education*, 9 (1), 5–13.

Bonnett, A. (2008) *What is Geography?* London: Sage.

Cotton, D. (2006) 'Teaching controversial environmental issues: Neutrality and balance in the reality of the classroom', *Educational Research*, 48 (2), 223–41.

Dewey, J. (1916) *Democracy and Education: An Introduction to the Philosophy of Education*, New York: Macmillan.

Ecclestone, K. and Hayes, D. (2009) *The Dangerous rise of Therapeutic Education*, Abingdon: Routledge.

Fielding, M. (2011) *Radical education and the common school: A democratic alternative*, Abingdon: Routledge.

Fien, J. and Gerber, R. (1988) *Teaching Geography for a Better World*, Edinburgh: Oliver & Boyd.

Fien, J. and Slater, F. (1981) 'Four strategies for values education in Geography,' *Geographical Education*, 4 (1), 39–52.

Freire, P. (1970) *Pedagogy of the Oppressed*, New York: Continuum.

Furedi, F. (2009) *Wasted: Why Education Isn't Educating*, London: Continuum Press.

Halstead, J.M. and Taylor, M.J. (eds.) (1996) *Values in education and education in values*, London: Falmer Press.

Hayward, J. (2007) 'Values, beliefs and the citizenship teacher', in L. Gearon (ed.), *A practical guide to teaching education in the secondary school*, Abingdon: Routledge.

Hess, D. (2009) *Controversy in the classroom: The democratic power of discussion*, Abingdon: Routledge.

Hirsch, E.D. (1987) *Cultural Literacy*, New York: Houghton Mifflin.

Hopwood, N. (2004) Pupils' conceptions of geography: Towards an improved understanding, *International Research in Geographical and Environmental Education*, 13 (4), 348–61.

Hopwood, N. (2007) *Values and controversial Issues. GTIP think piece.* [online] Available from: http://www.geography.org.uk/gtip/thinkpieces/valuesandcontroversialissues/ [Accessed 18 August 2011].

Huckle, J. (1981) 'Geography and values education', in R. Walford (ed.), *Signposts for Geography Teaching*, Harlow: Longman.

Huckle, J. (1985) 'The Future of School Geography', in R. Johnston (ed.), *The Future of Geography*, London: Methuen.

Jackson, P. (2006) 'Thinking Geographically', *Geography*, 91 (3), 199–204.

Kelly, V. (2009) *The Curriculum: Theory and Practice*, 6th edn, London: Sage.

Lambert, D. (1999) 'Geography and Moral Education in a Super Complex World: The Significance of Values Education and Some Remaining Dilemmas', *Philosophy and Geography*, 2 (1), 5–18.

Lambert, D. (2008) 'Review article: The Corruption of the Curriculum', *Geography*, 93 (3), 183–5.

Lambert, D. and Balderstone, D. (2000) *Learning to teach Geography in the Secondary School*, London: RoutledgeFalmer.

Lambert, D. and Morgan, J. (2005) *Geography – Teaching School Subjects 11–19*, Abingdon: Routledge.

Lidstone, J. and Gerber, R. (1998) 'Theoretical underpinnings of geographical and environmental education research: hiding our light under various bushels', *International Research in Geographical and Environmental Education*, 7 (2), 87–9.

Marsden, W.E. (1976) *Evaluating the Geography Curriculum*, Edinburgh: Oliver and Boyd.

Marsden, W.E. (1995) *Geography 11–16: Rekindling good practice*, London: David Fulton.

Massey, D. (1991) 'A Global Sense of Place', *Marxism Today*, June 1991 [online] Available from: http://www.aughty.org/pdf/global_sense_place.pdf [Accessed 18 August 2011].

Maye, B. (1984) 'Developing valuing and decision making skills in the geography classroom', in J. Fien, G. Gerber and P. Wilson (eds.), *The Geography Teacher's Guide to the Classroom*, Melbourne: Macmillan.

Mitchell, D. (ed.) (2009a) *Living Geography*, London: Optimus.

Mitchell, I. (2009b) 'Living with Rights – A human rights approach to geography', in D. Mitchell (ed.), *Living Geography*, London: Optimus.

Morgan, A. (2006) 'Argumentation, Geography, Education and ICT', *Geography*, 91 (2), 126–40.

Morgan, A. (2011) 'Morality and Geography Education', in G. Butt (ed.), *Geography Education and the Future*, London: Continuum.

Morgan, J. (2011) 'What is radical school geography today?' *Forum*, 53 (1), 116–28.

Morgan, J. (2012) *Teaching Secondary Geography as if the planet matters*, London: Routledge.

Morgan, J. and Lambert, D. (2001) 'Geography, 'Race' and Education', in *Geography*, 86, (3), 235–46.

Morgan, J. and Lambert, D. (2003) *Race, Place and Geography Teaching*, Sheffield: Geographical Association.

Oulton, C., Day, V., Dillon, J. and Grace, M. (2004) 'Controversial issues – teachers' attitudes and practices in the context of citizenship education', *Oxford Review of Education*, 30 (4), 489–507.

Pykett, J. (2011) 'Teaching Ethical Citizens' in G. Butt (ed.), *Geography, Education and the Future*, London: Continuum.

Rawling, E.M. (2001) *Changing the subject: The impact of national policy on school geography 1980-2000*, Sheffield: Geographical Association.

Roberts, M. (2003) *Learning through enquiry, making sense of geography in the key stage 3 classroom*, Sheffield: Geographical Association.

Rokeach, M. (1973) *The Nature of Human Values*, London: Free Press.

Schiro, M. (2008) *Curriculum theory: Conflicting visions and enduring concerns*, London: Sage.

Slater, F. (1982) *Learning through Geography*, London: Heinemann.

Slater, F. (1996) 'Values: Towards mapping their locations in a geography education', in A. Kent, D. Lambert, M. Naish and F Slater (eds.), *Geography in education: Viewpoints on teaching and learning*, Cambridge: Cambridge University Press.

Standish, A. (2007) 'Geography used to be about maps', in R. Whelan (ed.), *The Corruption of the Curriculum*, London: Civitas.

Standish, A. (2009) *Global Perspectives in the Geography Curriculum*, London: Routledge.

Stenhouse, L. (1975) *Introduction to curriculum development*, London: Heinemann.

Stradling, R. (1984) 'Controversial Issues in the Classroom', in R. Stradling, M. Noctor, and B. Baines (eds.), *Teaching controversial issues*, London: Edward Arnold.

Taylor, P.H. and Richards, C.M. (1985) *An Introduction to Curriculum Studies* 2nd edn, Windsor: NFER-Nelson

Unwin, A. (1992) *The Place of Geography*, London: Longman.

Walford, R. (1981) *Language, ideologies and geography teaching*, in R. Walford (ed.) *Signposts for Geography Teaching*, London: Longman.

Wheelahan, L. (2010) *Why Knowledge Matters in Curriculum: A Social Realist Argument*, Abingdon: Routledge.

Whelan, R. (ed.) (2007) *The Corruption of the Curriculum*, London: Civitas.

Young, M. (1971) *Knowledge and control: New directions for the sociology of education*, London: Collier-Macmillan.

Young, M. and Muller, J. (2010) 'Three Educational Scenarios for the Future: Lessons from the sociology of knowledge', *European Journal of Education*, 45 (1), 11–27.

Chapter 18

What does geography contribute to global learning?

Alex Standish

> A focus on global connections helps students see the ways in which their daily lives are affected by change and interdependence. They begin to see how their lives are affected by complex systems involving environmental issues, political policies, demographic shifts, international trade, and diverse ideologies and religions.
>
> (Wisconsin Department of Public Instruction, 2002, p. 22)

Introduction

Since the end of the 1980s, education, both in the UK and elsewhere, has been widely discussed in terms of a global framework. This has taken several forms including the global dimension as a cross-curricular theme, global education or global learning as an umbrella term for an array of development education initiatives, international education, global citizenship and skills for the global market. What is common to all is the notion that we have moved past schooling in the context of the nation towards a global approach to education. The above quotation from Wisconsin's influential *Planning Curriculum in International Education* illustrates that the discussion of global learning is as much about what is happening 'here' as the geography 'over there'. In other words, the global dimension seeks to engage children in a discussion about changing values and society (wherever that may be).

Geography, as the subject that teaches about the world, has been seen by policy makers and geographers as an important vehicle for the global dimension. This chapter explores the meaning of the 'global' in educational settings (with a focus on the UK and USA), the origins of global education and the contribution made by geography.

WHAT IS GLOBAL LEARNING?

Explaining the global dimension and global learning is not easy as they mean different things to different people in a range of contexts. According to Walter Parker, a US educationist, the movement for global learning thus 'solves a variety

of problems, serves an array of masters, and expresses diverse and sometimes conflicting values' (Parker, 2008, p. 202). Thus, Parker surmises that global learning is characterised by a lack of coherence and a lack of precise terminology. A few examples will illustrate the different ways in which the terms have been utilised.

The UK government report *Developing a Global Dimension in the School Curriculum* suggests that young people should be given opportunities to:

> [C]ritically examine their own values and attitudes; appreciate the similarities and differences between people everywhere; and value diversity; understand the global context of their local lives; and develop skills that will enable them to combat injustice, prejudice and discrimination. Such knowledge, skills and understanding enables young people to make informed decisions about playing an active role in the global community.
>
> (DfES, 2005, p. 2)

In the secondary national curriculum for England (QCA, 2007) *global learners* are described as:

- Successful learners who enjoy learning, make progress and achieve.
- Confident individuals who are able to live safe, healthy and fulfilling lives.
- Responsible citizens who make a positive contribution to society. (Brown, 2010)

Global learning has also been aligned with the aims of Every Child Matters (ECM). For example:

- Addressing racism, bullying, and their impacts on mental health links to the ECM outcome, 'Be Healthy'.
- Young people can 'Enjoy and achieve' when learning links to their experiences in a globalised world.
- Exploring worker's rights both in the UK and globally can contribute to the 'Achieve economic wellbeing' outcome.
- 'Making a positive contribution' can include actively making a difference on global issues (for example, through fundraising, lobbying or personal action. (Brown, 2010, p. 9)

Reading these examples, one might be tempted to reach the conclusion that global learning can mean almost anything: responsibility, citizenship, good health, personal achievement, participation or making a living. Indeed, in recent years the term *global* has become an umbrella concept under which different educational initiatives have coalesced, notes David Hicks (2007a). Today, the term 'global' is often used in an inclusive sense, encompassing international education, sustainable development education, global citizenship education,

21st-century skills, development education, human rights education, and other such 'big' concepts. At the outset, we must recognise the different meanings of the word global. According to *Oxford Dictionaries* 'global' means 'relating to the whole world, worldwide' or 'relating to or embracing the whole of something, or of a group of things' (2011). While some use the word in its geographical sense, others emphasise the holistic or inclusive meaning of the term (Marshall, 2005; Hicks, 2007a). This latter meaning has become an important part of mainstream thinking on education. A holistic or inclusive approach is often celebrated today as a way of breaking down traditional boundaries (between cultures, nations, everyday/academic knowledge, and education/social reform). Of particular significance, the inclusive approach opens education up to different interpretations blurring the line between education and social causes, training for work or therapy (see Ecclestone and Hayes, 2009).

FROM WHERE DOES GLOBAL LEARNING ORIGINATE?

David Hicks also reports that global education is a field of study that originated in the 1960s and 1970s. This field embraced the themes of interdependence, development, environment, racism, peace and the future, as advocated by social movements and non-governmental organisations (Hicks, 2007a). Global studies became a significant theme in American education during this period. Some of the founders of global education include Lee Anderson, James Becker and Robert Hanvey. Central to the global approach to education was the notion that society had entered a *global age* in which the human condition had become 'globalized'. Coming at a time of vocal anti-establishment movements (anti-war, minority rights, pro-environment), global thinking expressed the view that nations needed a shift in attitude. Anderson (1979) argued that many trends in society were accelerating exponentially and could not be sustained. In his thesis on the global age, Anderson illustrates a number of 'J' curves to demonstrate the exponential growth induced by humanity, including fertiliser use, books published, circulation of money, speed of communication, atmospheric carbon dioxide, life expectancy, energy consumption and population. All of these, argued Anderson, had driven nation states to work together in ways that had not been thought of in previous times; hence, the condition of humanity had become *globalised:* we have been propelled together in time and space to such a degree that our world system becomes interdependent. A sense of discomfort with the present, and past, and hence the need to create an alternative future is a key part of the global outlook.

Becker (1982) suggested that children needed to learn about political, cultural and social themes in order to obtain a 'global perspective' (seeing the world as a whole). In *An Attainable Global Perspective* Hanvey (2004 [1976]) outlined five dimensions that could be used to teach children about the 'global condition of humanity'. These included perspectives consciousness (recognising that others

have different viewpoints), state of planet awareness (the dangers of exponential growth), cross-cultural awareness (recognising diversity of ideas and practices), knowledge of global dynamics (interconnectivity) and awareness of human choices (there are alternative futures) (Hanvey, 2004 [1976]).

In England, early projects for global learning or development education received backing from both governmental and non-governmental sources (see Lambert and Morgan, 2011). The World Studies Project (1973–80) was launched by the One World Trust with financial support from the Department of Education and Science, the Leverhulme Trust and the Ministry for Overseas Development. The project's aim was 'to encourage modification of syllabuses at secondary school level to reflect a world perspective rather than national attitudes' (One World Trust, cited in Heater, 1982, p. 220). This project was followed in the 1980s by World Studies 8–13, produced by the Schools Council and the Joseph Rowntree Trust. This programme offered a multicultural approach to education and aimed to develop international understanding. Lessons in world studies were designed to help pupils cope with global issues, to clarify their own values, study cultures different from their own, and consider how the world could be different. Simon Fisher recalls that world studies necessitated reflecting at different levels: 'How would we like things to be in the world as a whole, in our country, locally, for me?' (Fisher, 1985, p. 31). By the mid 1980s, 'over half the education authorities in the UK were promoting world studies' (Holden, 2000, p. 74) and many more teachers were using resources produced by aid agencies and a growing number of development education centres.

Global learning is sometimes claimed not only by those who want to surpass the national framework, but also by political and corporate elites seeking to promote national interests beyond their borders. In the US, an International Education Act was passed in 1966, the main aim of which was to add international content to the curriculum. This Act was in keeping with America's growing international role and the perceived need for citizens to be more aware of international issues and foreign policy. It was during this period that National Resource Centers for Foreign Language, Area, and International Studies were established. The Act was followed by a Task Force on Global Education. Launched by Commissioner Earnest L. Boyer, its remit was to examine the need for a global perspective in American schools. The task force reported that 'global education contributes to a fundamental competence in a world context, to educational excellence, and to the nation's vital interests' (Office of Education, 1979). Several States published guidelines for global or international education. For example, *Education for a Global Perspective: A Plan for New York State* (1983) required pupils to take two years of 'global studies'. Especially in the US context, the expansion of global and international studies during the 1980s was tied to its growing international role and also the globalisation of markets. In the words of the late Samuel Huntington (2004), this was about 'merging America with the world'.

We can conclude that there are at least three rationales that underpin initiatives for global/international learning: social change (global citizenship/global perspective), economic (skills for the global market) and academic (knowledge about the world).

ADVOCATES FOR GLOBAL LEARNING

From the 1980s onwards there was growing support for global learning from politicians, business leaders, and policy makers who saw education for international awareness as tied to the success of increasingly globally orientated corporations. This was especially the case in the US, where multinational employers were looking for graduates who were comfortable doing business with companies based overseas and sensitive to foreign markets and cultures. Governors, mayors, policy makers and politicians were joining the ranks of those advocating international and global education in schools. For instance, an influential report – *America in Transition: The International Frontier* – asserted that 'international education must become part of the basic education of all students' (National Governors' Association, 1989, p. 1). The report outlined the need for more young people conversant in foreign languages, for teachers to know more about international issues, and for the business community to support international education so that they have access to information about export markets, trade regulations, and overseas cultures.

Since the 1980s, education has become almost synonymous with skills for employability in the minds of many. The movement for a 'global skills curriculum' has gained significant traction over recent years. Formed in 2002, the Partnership for 21st Century Skills is a public–private coalition that aims to 'modernise' education by incorporating '21st century skills' into the curriculum in every US state. The approximately 35 members of the partnership include Cisco Systems, Microsoft, the National Education Association, and the Walt Disney Company. Among the skills the partnership proposes as more 'relevant' for today's children are critical thinking, global awareness, civic literacy, communication skills, and leadership. 'Global skills' have also been promoted in the UK, for instance *Putting the World into World-Class Education* (DfES, 2004).

From the outset, non-governmental organisations (NGOs) have been central to the promotion of global education in the UK and USA. Some of the more influential NGOs are Oxfam, Amnesty International, the Red Cross, Practical Action, the Development Education Association (now Think Global), the Catholic Agency for Overseas Development (CAFOD), Christian Action Research and Education (CARE), ActionAid, Christian Aid, the Council for Education in World Citizenship, the Asia Society, the Longview Foundation, the Council for World Affairs, the Council for Global Education and the American Forum for Global Education. Harriet Marshall (2005) reports that in the 1990s there was increased collaboration among NGOs and consolidation of projects under the heading of 'global education'.

One of the most significant documents published on global learning is Oxfam's *Curriculum for Global Citizenship* (1997). The publication includes Oxfam's vision of a global citizen and eight themes for global citizenship: sustainable development, conflict resolution, values and perceptions, diversity, human rights, social justice, interdependence and citizenship. Oxfam's curriculum has been used far and wide. Its eight themes of global citizenship were adopted for the key government report *Developing a Global Dimension in the School Curriculum* (DfES/(DfID), 2005).

In the UK, there was a more abrupt shift towards the global dimension from the end of the 1990s. While the original national curriculum (DSE, 1991) was influenced by competing views of education, it also reflected a national orientation towards education. By the end of the decade the New Labour government was actively promoting the global dimension and its new citizenship curriculum, complete with references to global citizenship. Other government documents were also written in consultation with representatives from NGOs. These include *A Framework for the International Dimension for Schools in England* produced by The Central Bureau for International Education and Training and the Development Education Association (DEA), and *Citizenship Education: The Global Dimension*, published by the DEA and written by a consortium of government agencies and NGOs. Here, New Labour was utilising multiple bodies to coordinate and implement policy.

In 1997, the role of the DEA (now renamed as Think Global) was expanded with direct funding from the newly formed Department for International Development (DfID). With official backing for the global dimension, its place in schools has grown exponentially. There are some fifty development education centres across the UK working to support global education in schools. Many of these work with schools and universities to supply teaching materials on development or global issues and train teachers in how to teach the global dimension. Many activities are funded by the DfID and coordinated by the DEA/Think Global. Several universities have played a prominent role in the promotion of global learning, both for their students and in relation to schools. For instance, Bournemouth University has a Centre for Global Perspectives and London South Bank University coordinates a Teacher Education Network for Sustainable Development and Global Citizenship.

International organisations have also played a role in the development of global education. Established in 1945, UNESCO was specifically charged with the task of building international education. UNESCO's aim is to 'build peace in the minds of men and women' (UNESCO, 2009). In 1974, UNESCO published *Recommendations Concerning Education for International Understanding, Co-operation and Peace and Education Relating to Human Rights and Fundamental Freedoms*, another key document that endorsed an international approach to learning. More recently, UNICEF has become actively involved in promoting global education and posts teaching materials on its website to promote its work and ideals. In Europe, the North–South Centre of the Council

of Europe recently published *Global Education Guidelines: Concepts and Methodologies on Global Education for Educators and Policy Makers.*

HOW DOES GEOGRAPHY CONTRIBUTE TO GLOBAL LEARNING?

Since its founding, geography has been concerned with exploration and developing knowledge about human and physical phenomena across the surface of the globe. *Geographie* or 'Earth describing' evolved as a quest for gaining knowledge about unknown people and lands, with mapping integral to this endeavour. Even in Ancient Greece it was theorised that the world was a sphere (Guthrie, 1997). The pursuit of global knowledge expanded with the European discovery of the new world. Such exploration took a scientific turn with the voyages of James Cook (1728–79). Cook took a more methodical approach to learning about distant lands and people, keeping detailed records, making observations and measurements, and seeking to understand different cultures. Following Cook, Alexander von Humboldt (1769–1859) advanced geography through his quest to understand the interconnectivity of natural and human phenomena. Humboldt searched for causal relationships, ecological relationships between species and the laws of nature. He saw the world as an interrelated system, a *cosmos*, with geography as the subject best placed to uncover its inner workings.

At the beginning of the 21st-century, global learning is rarely conceived as simply the pursuit of geographical knowledge. Commenting on the release of *Developing a Global Dimension in the School Curriculum*, Bourn and Hunt suggest that the publication 'moved dominant thinking forward from seeing learning about development and global issues as about faraway places to one that recognised the interdependent nature of people's lives and raised the importance of a values-approach with the emphasis on social justice, equity and fairness' (Bourn and Hunt, 2011, p. 9). For many advocates, the purpose of global learning is to encourage children to think about, and possibly change, their own values or lifestyle in response to a global concern. This is illustrated in *Geography: The Global Dimension*, which asks us to 'observe the similarities and differences that exist around our world today and relate these to our own lives' (DEA, 2004, p. 2). The approach taken in this key publication will be briefly summarised.

According to the booklet, the purpose of teaching the global dimension is for pupils to learn to 'think geographically' in a global context and 'to help them understand their own feelings about places and the people who make them' (values education) (DEA, 2004, p. 7). An important part of the global dimension, suggest the authors, is to encourage critical thinking by 'engaging pupils in complex issues such as trading systems in a globalised economy, poverty and inequality; discrimination and social exclusion; and environmental protection at both local and global scales' (2004, p. 7). Here, the aim is to engage children in a 'conversation' about complex global issues rather than 'delivery' of subject content. The authors add that creative thinking is another aim of teaching about

the global dimension since it is hoped that pupils will 'develop imaginative solutions to challenges' (2004, p. 7).

Several activities are included as examples of classroom practice for developing a global dimension in classrooms: developing talk, developing maps, developing sustainable futures, developing empathy and understanding, developing interpretations and developing partnerships. With all, the purpose is to make connections between geographical phenomena and pupils' lives. For example, with the activity 'Developing Maps' pupils are asked to begin with a Multiple Identities exercise by answering the question: 'What places do I connect with?' (DEA, 2004, p. 20). They complete a graphic describing their different identities: 'personally, as a member of a family, within my local community, for my nation(s), internationally, globally' (p. 20). The aim is to show pupils that they have formed relationships with places and that this has helped shape their identity. Pupils are then asked to produce an 'affective map' (with symbols plotted for feelings that particular places evoke). The aim of drawing such a map is to help the pupils develop their 'sense of place' (DEA, 2004, p. 21). Finally, it is suggested that the activity is used to reflect on the ways in which maps can be used to transmit a view, a value or perspective.

In the activity 'Developing Empathy and Understanding' pupils learn about the daily experiences of people in faraway places and draw comparisons with their own lives, with the aim of evoking empathetic feelings. Pupils study the story of a named person from the 'South', such as Chemjor Chapkwony, a 60-year-old Kenyan man who cannot read. In this story, Chemjor fell sick and was taken to hospital and given some medicine. Unable to read the label, he took an incorrect dosage, became unconscious and was returned to hospital. Pupils are then asked to again complete the above Multiple Identities exercise, but this time about Chemjor rather than themselves. This helps pupils to 'think about their daily lives, and their similarities and differences with the daily lives of other people' (DEA, 2004, p. 25). A suggested extension to the activity is to explore the consumption habits of pupils themselves. The authors introduce the concept of fair trade to teach about the different actors involved in production and to help pupils 'empathise with the producers of agricultural products' (2004, p. 25). In the final section 'Reflection', the authors describe how the activity helps children to 'grasp some of the ways in which people's lives are shaped by choices – both their own choices and the choices made by others maybe thousands of miles away' (2004, p. 25). Learning to see life through the eyes of others is an important part of a child's education. However, care must be taken not to project western prejudice as a 'global ethic', which may well 'reproduce power relations and violence similar to those in colonial times', cautions Vanessa Andreotti (2006, p. 41).

As noted above, the field of global education grew out of concern with the trajectory of social, economic and political systems in nation states. Advocates present global education as an opportunity to hold 'a conversation' with children so that they may consider alternative paths and futures (Hicks, 2007b). This

helps us to understand the emphasis placed on pupils making personal connections with global issues/distant people and participating in commensurate actions and behaviour. It also accounts for the association of 'futures education' with global learning. For example, in a chapter about teaching geography for a sustainable future, Alun Morgan highlights the importance of sustainability as a concept when planning for the future. Morgan cites a number of possible activities to encourage children to think about sustainable and unsustainable futures. 'Strategy 1: Probable and Preferable Futures' is one of these activities, in which pupils draw time-lines with different branches for alternative paths. The activity begins with pupils considering an issue, which can range from the local (traffic) to the global (climate change). Next pupils:

> [D]raw a single time-line outlining crucial events relating to the issue up to the present, their time-line then forks into two branches. The probable (usually the lower limb) is labelled with the likely events that would occur, given the existing trajectory. The preferable (upper limb) is labelled with the events that the student(s) would like to see happen.
>
> (Morgan, 2006, p. 276)

After the activity is completed, children are asked to discuss the different decisions and actions that could lead society down each branch.

The final section of *Geography: Developing the Global Dimension* is about 'Developing Partnerships' with other schools. This idea can be traced back to the School Journey Association which began running excursions into Europe in the 1920s. However, in recent years the number of schools finding sister schools abroad has grown exponentially with encouragement from government and NGOs. One of the larger schemes is the DfID's 'Global School Partnership' which provides financial and logistical support to schools. Martin (2008) notes that the emphasis of this initiative was on making links between schools rather than curricular development. She suggests that teachers would be better prepared to teach development if there was more training for them on this subject.

There is a parallel emphasis on collaboration with international schools and intercultural exchange in American schools. This can be found in state-wide initiatives to 'internationalise' the curriculum, such as *North Carolina in the World: Preparing North Carolina Teachers for an Interconnected World* (Center for International Understanding, 2006). Another example comes from the 21st-century Geography Skills Map, a collaborative project between the Partnership for 21st Century Skills (P21) and the National Council for Geographic Education, which includes 'social and cross-cultural skills' as part of its 'skills map'. The authors view geography contributing to 21st-century skills through three lenses: scholarship (quest for knowledge), stewardship (concern for the positive relationship between people and the environment) and citizenship (skills needed to be an effective and responsible citizen). The Geography Skills Map is organised

around the following '21st century skills': information literacy, creativity and innovation, media literacy, ICT literacy, flexibility and adaptability, initiative and self-direction, social and cross-cultural skills, productivity and accountability, leadership and responsibility, critical thinking and problem solving, communication and collaboration. For example, the twelfth-grade pupils 'outcome', 'Works effectively in a climate of ambiguity', can be achieved by the following activity:

> Students use blogs to engage in dialogue about an issue of importance to them, such as sustainability efforts at a local university campus, health problems in their local community (such as asthma or diabetes), or immigration policies in their state, demonstrating understanding, tolerance, and respect for the points of view of others.
>
> (P21/NCGE, 2009, p. 12)

Another example is the Association of American Geographers' Center for Global Geography Education. Designed for undergraduates the centre was launched in 2003. The website includes teaching modules on climate change, the global economy, migration, national identity, population and natural resources, and water resources (see Association of American Geographers, 2011). The approach to global learning here places more emphasis on theoretical knowledge and less on values education. In order to comprehend each of the topics, the module is introduced with an extensive conceptual framework. For example, the global climate change module begins with a conceptual framework explaining theories of climate change and cycles. This is followed by several case studies in which students can learn to apply this knowledge and consider policy responses. There are also opportunities for collaborative study made available through the website.

By no means does this imply that the rationale for global learning as social change is absent in the USA. It is certainly ingrained in schools, but takes a different form from its counterpart in the UK. For instance, Pearson's *World Geography: Building a Global Perspective* includes references to 'global issues' and 'global connections' (Baerwald and Fraser, 1995). In the USA, a global perspective places greater emphasis on cultural tolerance and accepting different points of view.

Conclusion

Geography has supported global dimension curricular initiatives by adding international content to the curriculum and engaging children in a dialogue about significant contemporary problems. Particularly in the US context, where geography has weaker curricular standing, this has encouraged teachers to bring a much-needed international dimension to education. It has also enhanced the role of geography. A strength of global learning is that it brings the experiences of people in distant places into the classroom. It can encourage children to see things from the perspective of others and challenge them to think about how the world could be different.

Nevertheless, by emphasising a holistic approach that erodes boundaries, *global learning* blurs the line between education and other activities and blurs the boundaries of disciplinary knowledge itself (see Standish, 2012). When education is global it is opened up to different interpretations allowing different social actors to put forward their different agendas for geography: training for work, social change, values education or academic learning. Yet, without clarity as to the distinctive quality of education it is difficult to establish its meaning and purpose; hence it has become confused with political activism or other endeavours. 'The acquisition of knowledge is the key purpose that distinguishes education ... from other activities', suggests Michael Young (2008, p. 81).

Making distinctions and drawing boundaries are also an essential part of education itself. Such distinctions are the very basis of knowledge, notes Johan Muller (2000), since it is through distinctions that we learn new and more complex concepts as well as identify the unique contribution of different disciplines. Again, an incautious application of the term global can confuse rather than clarify. For example, development education's use of the term *global issues* often fails to address the local context. Instead of exploring the problems and challenges people face in their own geographical, cultural and political settings, global issues have been abstracted from this context and tend to be treated the same the world over (often from a western perspective) (see Standish, 2009). To make sense of the predicaments faced by people in different localities necessitates sensitivity to different contexts and making judgments about people's different needs. Thus, global learning may well circumvent the essential geographical distinctions pupils need to make the intellectual and ethical judgements that advocates of the global dimension so desire.

Key readings

1. Development Education Association (2004) *Geography: The Global Dimension* (Key Stage 3), Available online from: http://www.think-global.org.uk/resources/item. asp?d=888 This joint Geographical Association/Development Education Association publication reflects its combined understanding of the global dimension at that point in time. It draws from Oxfam's *Curriculum for Global Citizenship* and illustrates the ways in which geography can contribute to each of its aims, and includes lesson outlines.
2. Andreotti, V. (2006) 'Soft Versus Critical Global Citizenship Education', *Policy and Practice – A Development Education Review*, 3, 40–50. Andreotti analyses the different ways in which global citizenship education can be interpreted. She highlights the western-centricity of the way the term is often applied and the neocolonial implications of this practice.

References

Anderson, L. (1979) *Schooling and Citizenship in a Global Age: An Exploration of the Meaning and Significance of Global Education*, Bloomington, IN: Mid-American Program for Global Perspectives', in Education.

Andreotti, V. (2006) 'Soft Versus Critical Global Citizenship Education', *Policy and Practice – A Development Education Review*, 3, 40–50.

Association of American Geographers (2011) Center for Global Geography Education. Available from: http://globalgeography.aag.org/ [Accessed 2 February 2012].

Baerwald, T. and Fraser, C. (1995) *World Geography: Building a Global Perspective*, Upper Saddle River, NJ: Prentice Hall.

Becker, J. (1982) 'Goals for Global Education', *Theory into Practice*, 21 (3), 228–33.

Bourn, D. and Hunt, F. (2011) *Global Dimension in Secondary Schools*. London: Development Education Research Center: Research Paper #1. Available from: http://www.oecd.org/dataoecd/56/53/47522080.pdf [Accessed 2 February 2012].

Brown, K. (2010) 'The Benefits of Global Learning', *SecEd*, Available from: http://content.yudu.com/A1lzp7/SecEd04Feb2010/resources/index.htm [Accessed 4 February, 2012].

Center for International Understanding (2006) *North Carolina in the World: Preparing North Carolina Teachers for an Interconnected World*: Available from: http://ciu.northcarolina.edu/wp-content/uploads/2010/06/Preservice.Teacher.Final_.Report.pdf [Accessed 4 February 2012].

DES (1991) *Geography in the National Curriculum (England)*, London: HMSO.

Department for Education and Skills (DfES) (2004) *Putting the World into World-Class Education: An International Strategy for Education, Skills and Children's Services*, London: DfES.

Department for Education and Skills (DfES)/Department for International Development (DfID) (2005) *Developing a Global Dimension in the School Curriculum*, London: DfES.

Development Education Association (2004) *Geography: The Global Dimension* (Key Stage 3), London: DEA.

Ecclestone, K. and Hayes, D. (2009) *The Dangerous Rise of Therapeutic Education*, London: Routledge.

Fisher, S. (1985) *World Studies 8–13: A Teacher's Handbook*, Edinburgh: Oliver & Boyd.

Guthrie, W.K.C. (1997[1950]) *The Greek Philosophers from Thales to Aristotle*, Oxon: Routledge.

Hanvey, R. (2004 [1976]) *An Attainable Global Perspective, republished by the American Forum for Global Education*. Available from: http://www.globaled.org/an_att_glob_persp_04_11_29.pdf [Accessed 4 February 2012].

Heater, D. (1982) 'Education for International Understanding: A View from Britain', *Theory into Practice*, 21 (3), 218–23.

Hicks, D. (2007a) 'Responding to the World', in D. Hicks and C. Holden (eds.), *Teaching the Global Dimension: Key Principles and Effective Practices*, London: Routledge, 3–13.

Hicks, D. (2007b) 'Lessons for the Future: A Geographical Contribution', *Geography*, 92 (3), 179–88.

Holden, C. (2000) 'Learning for Democracy: From World Studies to Global Citizenship', *Theory into Practice*, 39 (2), 74–80.

Huntington, S. (2004) *Who Are We? Challenges to America's National Identity*, New York: Simon and Schuster.

Lambert, D. and Morgan, J. (2011) *Geography and Development: Development education in schools and the part played by geography teachers (Research Paper 3)*, London: Development Education Research Centre.

Marshall, H. (2005) 'Developing the Global Gaze in Citizenship Education: Exploring the Perspective of Global Education NGO Workers in England', *International Journal of Citizenship and Teacher Education*, 1 (2), 76–92.

Martin, F. (2008) 'Mutual Learning: The impact of a study visit course on teachers' knowledge and understanding of global partnerships', *Critical Literacy: Theories and Practice*, 2 (1), 60–75.

Morgan, A. (2006) 'Teaching geography for a sustainable future' in D. Balderstone (ed.), *Secondary Geography Handbook*, Sheffield: Geographical Association.

Muller, J. (2000) *Reclaiming Knowledge: Social Theory*, Curriculum and Education Policy, London: Routledge/Falmer.

National Governors' Association (NGA) (1989) *America in Transition: The International Frontier. Report of the Task Force on International Education*, Washington, DC: NGA.

Office of Education (1979) *US Commissioner of Education Task Force on Global Education: Report with Recommendations*, Washington, DC: Office of Education.

Oxfam (1997) *Curriculum for Global Citizenship, Oxfam Development Educational Programme*, Oxford: Oxfam.

Oxford Dictionaries (2011) [online] Available from: http://oxforddictionaries.com/ [Accessed 4 February 2012].

Parker W. (2008) 'International Education: What's in a Name?', *Phi Delta Kappa*, 90 (3), 196–202.

Partnership for 21st Century Skills (P21)/National Council for Geography Education (NCGE) (2009) *21st Century Skills Map: Geography*. Available from: http://www.p21.org/storage/documents/21stcskillsmap_geog.pdf [Accessed 4 February 2012].

Qualifications and Curriculum Authority (2007) *Secondary National Curriculum*, London: QCA.

Standish, A. (2009) *Global Perspectives in the Geography Curriculum: Reviewing the Moral Case for Geography*, London: Routledge.

Standish, A. (forthcoming 2012) *The False Promise of Global Learning: Why Education Needs Boundaries*, New York: Continuum.

UNESCO (2009) 'Introducing UNESCO: What We Are'. Available from: http://www.unesco.org/new/en/unesco/about-us/who-we-are/introducing-unesco/ [Accessed 4 February 2012].

Wisconsin Department of Public Instruction (2002) *Planning Curriculum in International Education*, Madison, Wisconsin: Wisconsin Department of Public Instruction.

Young, M. (2008) *Bring Knowledge Back In: From Social Constructivism to Social Realism in the Sociology of Education*, Abingdon: Routledge.

Chapter 19

How does education for sustainable development relate to geography education?

Maggie Smith

> As I see it, we have five imperatives ... The first and greatest of these is sustainable development – the imperative of the 21st century. Saving our planet, lifting people out of poverty, advancing economic growth – these are one and the same fight.
>
> (Ban Ki-moon, 2011)

Introduction

Sustainable development is an issue of global concern and as such it is rarely out of the news. Ban Ki-moon, Secretary-General of the United Nations, in his statement (above) calls it the most urgent issue facing us in the 21st-century. Concerns about sustainable development have spilled over into education, raising questions about how education might best prepare learners for life in the future. In trying to address these concerns, it is the geography subject area within the school curriculum that is often given major responsibility for teaching and learning about sustainable development.

Sustainable development, however, is a complex and contested concept. It means different things to different people. This chapter therefore seeks to clarify what people mean by 'sustainable development' and 'education for sustainable development', examine the way that education for sustainable development has evolved in schools, and explore the relationships between education for sustainable development and geography education.

WHAT IS SUSTAINABLE DEVELOPMENT?

The term 'sustainable development' grew out of the work of the United Nations – particularly the work of the World Commission on Environment and Development (WCED) set up in 1983, whose report *Our Common Future* (1987), often called the Brundtland Report, defined sustainable development as:

> ... development that meets the needs of the present without compromising the ability of future generations to meet their own needs.
>
> (WCED, 1987, p. 43)

However, this definition itself is open to different interpretations and hides a number of tensions. A wealth of literature sets this out. For example there are those who see a logical inconsistency in juxtaposing 'sustainable' against 'development' (Jickling, 1992). Others see sustainable development as representing a predominantly western model of economic development (Cross, 1998; Bonnett, 2002). Some prefer to use the term 'sustainability' – although sustainability is usually seen as the goal while sustainable development is the process by which the goal is achieved. Natural scientists disagree about what should be sustained and at what scale while social scientists may use the concept to maintain economic growth (Huckle, 1991). The meaning of sustainable development takes on different forms within different political ideologies, and within different forms of knowledge, values and philosophies, and within different cultures. For instance, a technocentrist viewpoint, such as might be held by liberal and social democratic reformers, would support weak sustainability, whereas, at the other end of the spectrum, ecocentrists such as green socialists and those holding postmodern holistic views would support strong sustainability (Williams and Millington, 2004; Huckle, 2005). Each of these viewpoints is valid within its own context. The problem is that sustainable development is dealing with the future – which is uncertain – so we can never see the whole picture (Stables and Scott, 2001) and there can be no 'right' answers.

The existence of multiple definitions and interpretations of the concept of sustainable development can create confusion, especially to those people who are new to the ideas. However, it can also be argued that multiple definitions and interpretations mean sustainable development can be regarded as a broad set of complex ideas which can evolve and adapt to suit local situations (Fien, 2000; Alsop et al., 2007). Its looseness means that many people can relate to it, whatever their personal viewpoint. Its strength therefore is in being an umbrella term under which people can work together even if they do not necessarily agree on the ways forward (Alsop et al., 2007).

However, today there is more general agreement that a study of sustainable development must involve a consideration not only of what was traditionally perceived as environmental matters (such as degradation of habitats), but also social issues (e.g. poverty and health), economic issues (such as trade, production and consumption) and cultural issues (such as the media) – as well as the moral, political, ecological and personal issues that accompany them.

WHAT IS EDUCATION FOR SUSTAINABLE DEVELOPMENT?

If sustainable development is a problematic term, then it follows that what constitutes education in relation to sustainable development is equally troublesome. It was the United Nations Conference on the Environment and Development (UNCED) at Rio de Janeiro in 1992, and particularly the global action plan for sustainable development in the 21st-century, Agenda 21, which emerged from it,

that first made explicit the essential links between education and sustainable development:

> Education ... should be recognised as a process by which human beings and societies can reach their fullest potential. Education is critical for promoting sustainable development and improving the capacity of the people to address environment and development issues.
>
> (United Nations, 1992, para. 36.3)

There is a range of interpretations of education and sustainable development, and a range of labels that can be applied to learning about sustainable development. Education for sustainable development (ESD) is one of these, but so is education for sustainability (EfS), sustainability education, education for sustainable futures, and sustainability literacy, to name but a few. ESD, however, seems to be the label which has gained greatest acceptance in organisations, in government departments in the UK and globally, and in educational circles. It has provided a 'common banner' (Selby, 2006, p. 354) under which a number of educational groups, such as those concerned with environment, development, and human rights, can work together.

However, as was recognised by the United Nations Educational, Scientific and Cultural Organisation (UNESCO) at the launch of the Decade of Education for Sustainable Development which started in 2005, there is no agreement on a single model for ESD:

> While there will be overall agreement on the concept, there will be nuanced differences according to local contexts, priorities and approaches. Each country has to define its own priorities and actions ....
>
> (UNESCO, 2003, p. 2)

This is not necessarily a problem. There needs to be adequate scope and flexibility in the term ESD so that educators can take into account the local economic, environmental, social and cultural conditions when trying to determine what sort of ESD is appropriate for their particular situation.

Implementing ESD in schools, however, may be more difficult than the rhetoric suggests. How exactly can teachers orientate pupils' thinking towards sustainable development? Probably most of the ESD seen in schools at the present time reflects a modernist orientation to education (Littledyke, 2008). This involves a transmissive type of teaching and learning (Vare and Scott, 2007) which focuses on developing knowledge and understanding of the issues related to ESD, on increasing pupils' awareness of the need for behaviour change (i.e. developing positive attitudes towards ESD), and encouraging those changes to take place by promoting appropriate behaviour.

Some argue, however, that ESD should move on from focusing on the shallow learning of information and facts about issues that inform what might

be only a short-term behaviour change, towards a phase of socially critical education which is concerned with ongoing learning and permanent lifestyle change (Fien, 2003). This represents a constructivist postmodern approach to ESD in which cognitive and affective elements are bonded together in order to promote positive views of ESD. However, making ESD a learning process for social change is not easy for teachers to engage with. It requires the teaching and learning of ESD to take a more transformative stance (see, for instance, Sterling, 2001), so that it focuses on developing a socially reflective and critical approach to learning (e.g. Huckle, 1991; Fien, 2000), in which pupils are encouraged to recognise and question vested- and self-interest in order to develop their own thinking about the sort of society they want to be part of, and to reflect on alternative solutions and lifestyles that can achieve that state. Educational outcomes are more difficult to measure in this sort of approach, but on the other hand it is more likely to produce meaningful outcomes to the individual learner in terms of their personal understanding of sustainable development and their capacity to deal with an uncertain future. Probably a mix of both of these approaches is needed (Vare and Scott, 2007): transmissive learning needs to go hand in hand with transformative learning. However, as Vare and Scott stress, it is vital that sustainable development is seen as a learning process – rather than a rolling out of a set of predetermined behaviours.

Recently there has appeared in the literature a new strand of thinking about ESD (Rickinson, 2001). These alternative conceptualisations focus on promoting an understanding of the meanings of sustainable development for the individual. They stress the importance of engaging the affective domain in the learning of ESD (Littledyke, 2008). They explore the question of what the relationship between people and the environment (nature) should be (Bonnett, 2002), and they emphasise the experiencing of nature itself (Payne, 2006). Bonnett, for instance, talks about 'Education for sustainability as a frame of mind'. This is not to be confused with the current concern about a 'therapeutic turn' in education (as set out, e.g. by Ecclestone and Hayes, 2009). Rather, as Bonnett argues, ESD is based on experience of, respect for and a sense of harmony with nature and, from that initial and first-hand understanding, learners can develop their own values and move on to explore the political, social and economic motives underpinning decisions about the environment.

However, we still do not fully understand the nature and dynamics of learning in relation to ESD, and the sort of pedagogies that most effectively support pupils' learning in relation to ESD. Many pedagogical practices that are already widely used in schools – those used to promote enquiry, decision making and critical thinking, for instance, encourage effective ESD. However, it is likely that pupils will also need to be supported in developing skills for envisioning the future (Hicks, 2001), and creating partnerships. A key focus must be to help learners develop the ability to make sound choices and learn the way forward (Reid and Scott, 2006). In addition, teachers will need to develop appropriate pedagogies that enable them to:

... understand the need for students to develop skills to question the embedded cultural values of our everyday choices, and to organise their students to actively identify and assess, communicate about and resolve real environmental problems ... it cannot be assumed that teachers share this understanding or are prepared for this role.

(Kennelly et al., 2008, p. 55)

This is technically challenging teaching (Lambert and Balderstone, 2000). It requires teachers to be equipped, personally and professionally, to recognise and acknowledge cognitive, affective and existential responses on the part of the pupils (Hicks and Bord, 2001). It requires teachers to encourage pupils to participate in a culture of argument (Myerson and Rydin, 1996) – something that would seem not to be encouraged in many current school practices, and it requires teachers to grapple with complexity, uncertainty and risk analysis – areas in which teachers may not have had specific training.

WHAT IS THE PLACE OF ESD IN THE SCHOOL CURRICULUM?

Although ESD has relatively recently appeared in the school curriculum, its roots, environmental education and development education, have an earlier history. Environmental education had appeared in the curriculum by the 1970s, often in the form of discrete subjects such as Rural or Environmental Studies; and development education, which is concerned with the quality of life of people across the world, appeared by the 1980s and was located particularly within the geography subject area.

The term 'sustainable' was first introduced into the National Curriculum in England in 1995, within the geography subject orders (DfE, 1995). However, the status of ESD was significantly raised in the 2000 and 2007 curriculum revisions. In the current National Curriculum in England, sustainable development is one of the overall aims of the curriculum and ESD is a statutory requirement in the geography subject area as well as in citizenship, science, and design and technology. While the raising of the status of ESD in this way was welcomed by many as being a significant step forward, others noted that it represented only one perspective on ESD. It did not address the deeper and more complex questions underlying ESD so that it has appeared in the curriculum as something nearer a mindset, a worldview, or set of accepted values (Ashley, 2001).

Despite support from a number of government publications including a specialist Ofsted report (2003), the creation of an ESD website[1] providing information and guidance for teachers and school managers (QCA, 2003), and a national framework for Sustainable Schools (DfES, 2006), as well as other ESD initiatives such as Eco-Schools, little action for ESD has been seen in schools (Ofsted, 2008). A number of reasons have been put forward to try to explain this. The pressure within schools to meet these requirements has meant

that curriculum and professional development for ESD has been regarded as a low priority for both classroom teachers and school managers (Ofsted, 2008). Alternatively, the positioning of ESD in the curriculum might be the cause of the lack of action. Much of the ESD in the curriculum is non-statutory and cross-curricular and in a subject-based National Curriculum, cross-curricular work tends to be given a low priority.

In many secondary schools therefore it seems to have been left to interested teachers in a small number of subject areas to develop ESD within their subject (Ashley, 2001). Primary schools on the other hand have tended to have been more successful in moving towards becoming sustainable schools (Ofsted, 2008). However, it is a piecemeal and uncoordinated picture: there are individual examples of good practice in ESD, but on the whole it seems that engagement with ESD is taking place only very slowly within education so that ESD still remains marginalised in schools. Only rarely does thought and direction seem to have been given at a management level in schools to the way ESD is implemented, how ESD within the curriculum might be joined up with ESD across the whole school and, indeed, how ESD might be spread across the wider school community.

WHAT IS THE RELATIONSHIP BETWEEN GEOGRAPHY EDUCATION AND ESD?

As an overarching approach or learning process rather than a subject, ESD can be taught and learnt through all subjects of the school curriculum. Geography, however, has a particularly close relationship with ESD: geography 'encourages a critical understanding of big ideas such as sustainable development' (GA, 2009, p. 13). In the 2007 version of the national curriculum in England (QCA, 2007), considerable responsibility for ESD was directed towards the geography subject area. 'Environmental interaction and sustainable development' took its place as one of the seven key concepts underpinning the geography curriculum. Similar situations can be seen in the curriculums in Wales, Northern Ireland and Scotland. Beyond Key Stage 3 (KS3), study of sustainable development and sustainability is a requirement in the awarding body specifications for geography at both GCSE and GCE level. The result is that most, if not all, geography teachers in the UK today will find themselves teaching ESD within their subject area.

Geography overlaps with ESD in a number of ways. As Ron Johnston has remarked, 'Geography emerged as an academic discipline in the late 19th and early 20th centuries as a subject bridging the physical and social sciences by studying the interactions between people and their environments' (Johnston, 2005, p. 10). Thus geography, like ESD, is characterised by its integrative and holistic perspective, and its interest in people's relationship with the environment: Geography's wide breadth, its global perspective, and its focus on scales – both spatial and temporal (Chalkley et al., 2010) all match the require-ment of ESD to view the planet as a whole and consider the interconnections

between places. One of the distinctive characteristics of geography is its particular emphasis on synthesis and holistic thinking (Chalkley et al., 2010). ESD too requires the drawing together of a wide range of considerations, including economic, social, political, ecological and physical factors, in order to arrive at informed conclusions.

In addition, school geography has built up a distinctive pedagogy. Many aspects of this, for example approaches that are learner-centred, that develop autonomous and critical thinking, and that develop skills of enquiry, creativity, imagination and collective decision making, are all highly relevant to the teaching and learning of ESD (Reid, 2000). So too is the use of a wide range of text and media resources to support teaching and learning, and an emphasis on fieldwork, particularly locally based fieldwork, to help pupils look critically at their everyday lives and surroundings. They contribute to developing in pupils an ability to envision the sort of future they want for themselves and for society. Geography therefore 'offers us a lens for viewing and making sense of the world around us in all its complexities and connections; it is an essential discipline to engage with when teaching for, about and through sustainable issues' (GA, 2010).

However, despite the overlaps in content and pedagogy, several commentators note that geography has not yet fully engaged with ESD. In higher education, geographers 'are only partially exploiting their natural advantage in the ESD arena' (Chalkley et al., 2010, p. 97). In schools, Ofsted reported that a consideration of 'issues relating to sustainable development should be at the heart of geography teaching but this rarely was the case in the schools visited' (Ofsted, 2008, p. 10). The reasons for this lack of engagement are not entirely clear. At university level, it might be a consequence of the drifting apart and fragmenting of the physical and human sides of the subject in the latter part of the 20th-century (O'Riordan, 1996). This made it difficult to find a place in the subject for the study of sustainable development which requires the study of physical and human geography in an integrated way. In school geography, tight prescription of the curriculum, and the strength of the accountability agenda in schools since the 1990s have undoubtedly had a negative role in depressing 'the dissenting tradition in school geography which really pushed against the boundaries and aimed to create a better world' (Hicks, 2011b, p. 9).

HOW DO WE MOVE FORWARD?

Sustainable development is undoubtedly one of the big questions of the twenty-first century. So what is needed if we are to reunite and re-inspire geographers around a focus on ESD? Two key issues seem to present themselves as barriers to progress in teaching and learning ESD through geography. The first of these is how to support geography teachers in teaching ESD more effectively. A useful framework to guide the effective teaching of ESD was developed by Fien, Scott

and Tilbury in 2001 and is set out below. It identifies five crucial factors that underpin effective teaching of ESD. These require teachers to:

1   have a full history of sustainable development in order to appreciate the relevance and see the application within their own subject;
2   understand why they need to include ESD in their practice;
3   be aware of the pedagogy for teaching about sustainable development;
4   understand how their practice might have to be reviewed or changed in order to do this; and
5   understand the resources available to support their students' learning adapted from Fien, Scott and Tilbury (2001, p. 392).

The first two points in the framework emphasise the importance of teachers developing their own conceptions of ESD. Effective teaching of ESD requires teachers to engage with ESD at a deep level. This engagement needs to be rooted in a secure understanding and awareness of the subject matter of ESD and the theoretical base that underpins it, so that teachers can recognise their own values in relation to those theories. At present the evidence suggests 'that few teachers have a deep enough understanding of sustainability – of the challenges and obstacles ... to teach it well' (Curren, 2009, p. 35). Addressing these shortcomings in knowledge and understanding is not easy. Perhaps there is a need to bring academic geography and school geography closer together (Firth, 2011) in order to achieve this.

Similar shortfalls can be identified in terms of developing pedagogy and reflective practice in relation to ESD, see the third and fourth points in the framework above. The raised status of ESD in the geography national curriculum from 2000 onwards should have provided opportunities to expand the ways that geography teachers identified and met the ESD learning needs of their pupils. However, there is only limited evidence that teachers took advantage of these opportunities and developed new ways of thinking about and planning for the teaching of ESD. In a survey of teachers in 2004, for instance, it was noted that teachers:

> ... acknowledged that there was a lot of opportunity to introduce the concept (ESD) in the syllabus [*the geography national curriculum 2000*] but there was very little progression and understanding of how to link learning from year to year.
>
> (Cheadle et al., 2004, p. 13)

The final point in the framework above refers to the resources available to support pupils' learning of ESD. There is a wide range of resources available to support ESD. However, in a recent survey of newly qualified geography teachers in Scotland, 52 per cent of those interviewed were not aware of what these were (Fenwick and Munro, 2010). It is recognised that ESD is not well represented on

already crowded Initial Teacher Education courses. Time and financial support to attend professional development courses in less mainstream aspects of education such as ESD are hard to find. Creating networks for sharing good practice and engaging in discussion about ESD might be one way to offset this.

The second issue that needs to be considered in order to move the teaching of ESD through geography forward relates to what, and whose, views of ESD are being represented in geography teaching and learning. The ESD presented in much geography education still reflects a largely modernist orientation to teaching and learning, so that although skills such as enquiry learning, decision making and experiential learning are promoted, there is less emphasis on the need for a critically reflective edge that considers new ways of doing things, is transformative in nature, and is better suited to a postmodern society (Huckle, 2005). The current curriculum requirements, for instance, present ESD knowledge:

> ... in the form of straightforward definitions and accounts of what should be taught and learned ... that teachers should, presumably, accept and adopt unquestioningly. Some texts are ... written in a tone that appears to be politically neutral and unproblematic. Consideration of the numerous and very serious moral and political issues at the heart of ESD knowledge seems to be stifled beneath a sanitised 'front' which gives the appearance of an objective science conveyed within an objectives-led curriculum planning framework.
>
> (Winter and Firth, 2007, p. 345)

Particular examples can be found in geography lessons that focus on development issues. We might usefully ask, for instance, whose values are being promoted in the teaching of 'sustainable tourism', or in encouraging pupils to think that buying Fair Trade products will solve poverty (Lambert and Morgan, 2011). Similarly, Hicks (2011b) points to geography lessons in which economic growth, as measured by GDP, is equated with progress and well-being, rather than exploring what other socially based indicators might reveal about the effects of economic growth. Unthinking delivery of what Hicks calls 'neat' case studies leaves the teaching of ESD in geography open to criticism of irresponsible 'green-washing'. Neat case studies tend to be surrounded by clear boundaries that can sometimes make the issue being studied remote and unproblematic to pupils. Adopting a transformative approach to teaching and learning ESD issues would open up the reality and complexity of the issues. It would encourage pupils to develop 'a critical awareness of both self and society and an understanding of what needs to change' (Hicks, 2011a, p. 7). However, at school level challenges may be encountered when it comes to introducing transformative approaches to ESD within geography (Sterling, 2001). Research shows tensions between schools' practices in terms of ESD and their curriculum aims. It is difficult to teach about sustainable development if a school is not itself working

towards becoming a sustainable environment; and it is even harder to promote ESD if a school reflects the norms of society rather than challenging them (Corney, 2006).

ESD and geography education are not the same. However, few geographers would argue that geography is not an important vehicle for teaching and learning ESD. As we approach the end of 'the Decade of ESD', it is timely to think about how ESD might be best developed within geography in the future. Further research will be key here. We need to know more for instance about:

- how to link transmissive with transformative learning;
- the ways in which geography teachers build up their own conceptions of ESD;
- how to connect whole school approaches to ESD with curriculum-based approaches to ESD;
- the role of leadership in promoting ESD within the geography department and across the school;
- how pupils feel about ESD in geography and what they want to know about ESD; and
- ways of developing ESD as an overarching frame of mind.

Most importantly, however, we still know little about the way that learning impacts on people's lives (Scott, 2009) or ways in which peoples' living affects their learning. Research is crucial here if ESD in geography is to become learning about how we live and how we might change how we live. This sort of thinking is essential if geography is to achieve its promise as a subject that

> ... seeks information about how the world works and helps us think about alternative futures.
>
> (GA, 2009, p. 30)

Note

1 Since the change of government in 2010, some of the government websites relating to ESD referred to in the text are no longer available.

Key readings

1. McKeown, R. (2002) *Education for Sustainable Development Toolkit*. This toolkit can be downloaded free of charge at http://wwww.esdtoolkit.org It provides a comprehensive background to sustainable development and ESD, and it also provides useful ideas for a range of professional development sessions for educators.
2. Sterling, S. (2001) *Sustainable Education. Re-visioning learning and Change, Schumacher Briefing 6*, Dartington: Green Books. This is a relatively short and readable book that develops the idea of sustainable education. It discusses the challenge of what needs to change and how – in schools and beyond – in order to develop an education that supports a sustainable future.

References

Alsop, S., Dippo, D. and Zandvliet, D. (2007) 'Teacher education as or for social and ecological transformation: Place based reflections on local and global participatory methods and collaborative practices', *Journal of Education for Teaching*, 33 (2), 207–23.

Ashley, M. (2001) 'The NAEE Farm Gate: Time for Reappraisal?', *Environmental Education*, 67(summer), 6–8.

Ban Ki-Moon (2011) 'Rio+20: Making it Happen', *Newsletter of the United Nations Conference on Sustainable Development*, 31 October 2011, 2 (20). Available from: www.uncsd2012.org [Accessed 24 January 2012].

Bonnett, M. (2002) 'Education for Sustainability as a Frame of Mind', *Environmental Education Research*, 8 (1), 9–20.

Chalkley, B., Blumhof, J. and Ragnarsdottir, K.V. (2010) 'Geography, Earth and Environmental Sciences: A Suitable Home for ESD?', in P. Jones, D. Selby and S. Sterling (eds.), *Sustainability Education. Perspectives and practice across higher education*, London: Earthscan.

Cheadle, C., Symons, G. and Pitt, J. (2004) *Education for Sustainable Development (ESD). Subject specialist teachers: A needs analysis*, Geographical Association/DfES. Available from: www.geography.org.uk/download/GA_NPOGESDNeedsAnalysis.doc [Accessed 10 August 2012].

Corney, G. (2006) 'Education for Sustainable development: An Empirical Study of the Tensions and Challenges Faced by Geography Student Teachers', *International Research in Geographical and Environmental Education*, 15 (3), 224–40.

Cross, R.T. (1998) 'Teachers' Views about What to do about Sustainable development', *Environmental Education Research*, 4 (1), 41–52.

Curren, R. (2009) *Education for sustainable development: A philosophical assessment*, 'Impact' series, London: PESGB. Republished online: http://onlinelibrary.wiley.com/doi/10.111/imp.2009.2009.issue-18/issuetoc (Wiley Online Library, 2011).

Department for Education (DfE) (1995) *Geography in the National Curriculum (England)*, London: HMSO.

Department for Education and Skills (DfES) (2006) *National framework for sustainable schools*, London: DfES.

Ecclestone, K. and Hayes, D. (2009) *The Dangerous Rise of Therapeutic Education*, Abingdon: Routledge.

Fenwick, A. and Munro, B. (2010) 'Early Career Scottish Geography Teachers Perceptions of Education for Sustainable Development', in T.L.K. Wisely, I.M. Barr, A. Britton and B. King (eds.), *Education in a Global space. Research and Practice in Initial Teacher Education*, Edinburgh: Scotdec.

Fien, J. (2000) 'Listening to the voice of youth: Implications for educational reform', in Y. Fien (ed.), *Environment, education and society in the Asia–Pacific: Local traditions and global discourses*, London: Routledge.

Fien, J. (2003) 'Towards the UN Decade: Looking backwards, looking forwards', *The Development Education Journal*, 9 (3), 3–6.

Fien, J., Scott, W.A.H. and Tilbury, D. (2001) 'Education and Conservation: Lessons from an evaluation', *Environmental Education Research*, 7 (4), 379–96.

Firth, R. (2011) 'The Nature of ESD through geography: Some thoughts and questions', *Teaching Geography*, 36 (1), 14–16.

Geographical Association (GA) (2009) *A Different View: A Manifesto from the Geographical Association*, Sheffield: Geographical Association.

Geographical Association (GA) (2010) *Young Geographers Go Green, Pedagogy and Thinking*, Available from: http://www.geography.org.uk/cpdevents/onlinecpd/younggeographersgogreen/pedagogyandthinking/ [Accessed 9 October 2010].

Hicks, D. (2001) 'Envisioning a better world', *Teaching Geograph*, 26 (2), 57–9.

Hicks, D. (2011a) *Teaching for a Better World: Is it geography?* Presentation to Geography Education Research Seminar at the Institute of Education, London on 10 January 2011.

Hicks, D. (2011b) 'A sustainable future: Four challenges for geographers', *Teaching Geography*, 36 (1), 9–11.

Hicks, D. and Bord, A. (2001) 'Learning about global issues: Why most educators only make things worse', *Environmental Education Research*, 7 (4), 413–25.

Huckle, J. (1991) 'Education for sustainability: assessing pathways to the future', *Australian Journal of Environmental Education*, 7, 43–62.

Huckle, J. (2005) *Education for Sustainable Development. A briefing paper for the Teacher Training Agency.* London: Teacher Training Agency. [Also available online at: http://john.huckle.org.uk]

Jickling, B. (1992) 'Why I Don't Want My Children to be Educated for Sustainable Development', *Journal of Environmental Education*, 23 (4), 5–8.

Johnston, R. (2005) 'Geography – Coming Apart at the Seams?', in N. Castree, A. Roger and D. Sherman (eds.), *Questioning Geography*, Oxford: Blackwell.

Kennelly, J., Taylor, N. and Jenkins, K. (2008) 'Listening to teachers: Teacher and student roles in the New South Wales Sustainable Schools Programme', *Environmental Education Research*, 14 (1), 53–64.

Lambert, D. and Balderstone, D. (2000) *Learning to Teach Geography in the Secondary School*, London: RoutledgeFalmer.

Lambert, D. and Morgan, J. (2011) *Geography and Development: Development education in schools and the part played by geography teachers. Development Education Research Centre. Research Paper No. 3*, London: Development Education Research Centre.

Littledyke, M. (2008) 'Science education for environmental awareness: Approaches to integrating cognitive and affective domains', *Environmental Education Research*, 14 (1), 1–17.

Myerson, G. and Rydin, Y. (1996) *The Language of the Environment*, London: Institute of Economic Affairs.

O'Riordan, T. (1996) 'Environmentalism and geography: a union still to be consummated', in E. Rawling and R. Daugherty (eds.), *Geography into the 21st century*, Wiley: Chichester.

Office for Standards in Education (Ofsted) (2003) *Taking the first step forward ... towards an education for sustainable development. Good practice in primary and secondary schools*, London: Ofsted.

Office for Standards in Education (Ofsted) (2008) *Schools and sustainability. A climate for change?* London: Ofsted.

Payne, P. (2006) 'Environmental Education and Curriculum Theory', *Journal of Environmental Education*, 37 (2), 25–35.

Qualifications and Curriculum Authority (QCA) (2003) The ESD website (online – no longer available).

Qualifications and Curriculum Authority (QCA) (2007) *National Curriculum: Key stages 3 and 4*, London: QCA.

Reid, A. (2000) 'Environmental change and sustainable development', in K. Grimwade, A. Reid and L. Thompson (eds.), *Geography and the New Agenda: Secondary*, Sheffield: Geographical Association.

Reid, A. D. and Scott, W.A.H. (2006) 'Researching Education and the Environment: An introduction', *Environmental Education Research*, 12 (3–4), 571–88.

Rickinson, M. (2001) 'Learners and Learning in Environmental Education: a critical review of the evidence', *Environmental Education Research*, 7 (3), 208–320.

Scott, W.A.H. (2009) 'Environmental education research: 30 years on from Tbilisi', *Environmental Education Research*, 15 (2), 155–64.

Selby, D. (2006) 'The Firm and Shaky Ground of Education for Sustainable Development', *Journal of Geography in Higher Education*, 30 (2), 351–65.

Stables, A. and Scott, W.A.H. (2001) 'Disciplined Environmental Literacies', *Environmental Education*, 68, 14–16.

Sterling, S. (2001) *Sustainable education – re-visioning learning and change*, Schumacher society briefing No.6, Totnes: Green Books.

United Nations Conference on Environment and Development (UNCED) (1992) *Agenda 2: Programme for Action for Sustainable Development*, New York: United Nations Publications.

United Nations Educational, Scientific and Cultural Organisation (UNESCO) (2003) *Decade of Education for Sustainable Development (2005–2014). Framework for the International Implementation Scheme.* Available from: http://unesdoc.unesco.org/images/0013/001311/131163e.pdf [Accessed 23 September 2010].

Vare, P. and Scott, W.A.H. (2007) 'Learning for a Change: Exploring the Relationship Between Education and Sustainable Development', *Journal of Education for Sustainable Development*, 1 (2), 191–8.

Williams, C. and Millington, A. (2004) 'The diverse and contested meanings of sustainable development', *The Geographical Journal*, 170 (2), 99–104.

Winter, C. and Firth, R. (2007) 'Knowledge about Education for Sustainable Development: Four case studies of student teachers in English secondary schools', *Journal of Education for Teaching*, 33 (3), 341–358.

World Commission on Environment and Development (WCED) (1987) *Our Common Future*, Oxford: Oxford University Press.

Part III

Subject Debates

Chapter 20

What do we mean by thinking geographically?

John Morgan

Geography is what geographers do …

(anon)

Introduction

One of the perennial questions that geography teachers seem to be duty bound to address is the question: what is geography? One stock response (which is, I think, supposed to be funny) is that 'geography is what geographers do'. Maybe it is my lack of a sense of humour, but I always find that a deeply unhelpful response, an avoidance rather than an answer. In recent years, the same question has tended to be phrased in terms of what it means to 'think geographically'. This move is important because it locates the question within a distinctly educational frame of reference (it gives it a certain gravitas). The idea that geography education is a lesson in how to 'think geographically' is given weight in the Geographical Association's 'manifesto' – *A different view* (GA, 2009). The notion of thinking geographically is also connected to another phrase that is frequently used in discussions about the purposes of geographical education, namely the 'geographical imagination'. This term was popularised with the publication of Derek Gregory's (1994) book of that title, and again, I think, appeals to geography educators because it taps into wider notions of what teaching and learning are for, to create and then to nurture the 'imagination'.

This chapter does not set out to convince readers that there is a single way of thinking geographically or to resolve the issue once and for all. Instead, it sets out a series of examples of what 'thinking geographically' might entail. Its aim is to multiply, and thereby, complicate, the possibilities. My modest hope is that, having read this chapter, readers will recognise the value of some disciplined reflection on the wider purposes of geographical teaching and learning.

GEOGRAPHICAL KNOWLEDGE

Let's begin with some contextual comments about the nature of geographical knowledge. Much teaching in schools proceeds from the position that there is an

objective 'real world' which is studied by geographers to produce 'knowledge' which is then transmitted to students in schools. However, since at least the early 1970s, and influenced by research in the 'sociology of knowledge', it has become possible to argue that geographical knowledge does not innocently reflect the 'real world' but instead reflects the subjective interests of geographers. This is to point out that geographical knowledge is 'socially constructed'. The logical extension of this argument is that, rather than a singular 'Geography', there exist multiple 'geographies'. More recently, the sociologist Michael Young (2008) has argued that whilst knowledge is a social product, the knowledge found in academic disciplines has 'real' features in that it represents the stored and accumulated knowledge and understanding of communities of researchers. It is this powerful knowledge that allows children to transcend and go beyond their 'everyday' experiences. This is a 'social realist' view of knowledge (see Roger Firth's chapter in this volume).

This 'social realist' view of geographical knowledge accords well with David Harvey's (1984) argument that:

> The roles and functions of geographical knowledge, together with the structures of that knowledge, have changed over time in relation to, and in response to, shifting societal configurations and needs. (p. 1)

He argued that the transformation from feudalism to capitalism entailed a revolution in the structures of geographic thought and practice, and the discipline has been concerned with the following set of practices:

> The concern for accuracy of navigation and the definition of territorial rights meant that mapping and survey became basic tools of the geographer's art.
> The creation of the world market meant the exploration of the earth in all directions and the systematic description of the earth's surface as the repository of use values.
> Close observation of geographical variations in ways of life, forms of economy and social reproduction.
> Geographical knowledge has been closely concerned with geopolitical issues. Concern with the use of natural and human resources and spatial distributions led geographers to consider the question of 'rational' configurations of both.
> Geographical thought in the bourgeois era has always preserved a strong ideological content.

This is a comprehensive list of the roles and functions of geographical knowledge and one which allows us to recognise important shifts of emphasis and how these are associated with the purposes of geography teaching. It is important to remember that Harvey here is talking about the role that geographical knowledge plays

in a wider academic division of labour. School geography, whilst informed by the subject discipline, has a degree of autonomy which means that the relationship varies in its intensity, in the degree of direct translation, in emphasis. If we seek to understand what it means to think geographically, we have to do some thinking about that relationship. With this in mind, we can turn to specific instances of what it means to 'think geographically'.

A WAY OF SEEING

The first instance of what it means to 'think geographically' considered here comes from the writings of Sir Halford Mackinder, one of the so-called 'founding fathers' of geography as an academic discipline. Mackinder stressed that geography was not the collection of useless information about places but a 'trained capacity' for thought. This trained capacity was to be able to picture world as a dramatic spectacle on a stage:

> If I have been properly trained in geography, the word Punjab will … probably connote to me many things. I shall see Lahore in the northern angle of India. I shall picture it in a great plain, at the foot of a snowy range, in the midst of the rivers of the Indus system. I shall think of the monsoon and the desert, of the water brought from the mountains by the irrigation canals. I shall know the climate, the seedtime, and the harvest. Kurrachee and the Suez Canal will shine out from my mental map. I shall be able to calculate at what time of year the cargoes will be delivered in England. Moreover, the Punjab will be to me equal in size and population of a great European country, a Spain or an Italy, and I shall appreciate the market which it offers for English exports. This is geographical capacity – the mind which flits easily over the globe, which thinks in terms of the map, which quickly clothes the map in meaning, which correctly and intuitively places the commercial, historical, or political drama on its stage.
>
> (Mackinder, 1890, cited in O Tuathail (1996, p. 87)

This is a remarkable passage. It encapsulates a whole theory of geographical thinking. To think geographically is to have a trained capacity to construct a mental map to see patterns, to recognise relationships, to see movement, to take that map and 'clothe it in meaning'. This is a form of visualisation, and one which is powerful because it is to make informed judgements, intelligent guesses, and to situate itself in human culture. It has resonance still: how many of us as geography educators would still stress one of the aims of our teaching as enabling young people to 'read the newspaper and make sense of the world'? Of course, Mackinder's historical situation was unique. He was clearly an imperialist. His concern was that the future subjects of the British Empire were not adequately trained to imagine the British Empire, and saw this as a problem at a time when British power was threatened by Germany. The newly formed discipline of

geography was to offer a form of integration and wholeness at a time of rapid social and cultural change.

It is useful to compare Mackinder's notion of 'geographical thinking' with a later version, that of A.G. Powell who contributed a chapter on 'Geography' in Denys Thompson and James Reeves' (1947) book *The Quality of Education*. The book as a whole was set in the tradition of 'culture and environment' established by F.R. Leavis and Denys Thompson in the 1930s, and adopted the view that in a world increasingly dominated by urban popular culture (rather than rural folk culture), the role of the school and the teacher was to provide an education against the trappings of mass culture. It represented a call for a 'general', 'liberal' and non-vocational education. The importance of the teacher as a source of authority and the 'initiator' of pupils into the world of objective academic knowledge was paramount.

As befits an essay written at the end of a long and bloody episode of human conflict, Powell's argument about the contribution of geography to such an education stressed the importance of informed knowledge and enlarged humanity or citizenship. He stressed that, 'A vital approach to geography must replace the mechanical deadliness of the past'. He went on to argue that:

> Geography can be made to live only by adopting the Human approach. Man must be the pivot of study and regard will be paid to the physical skeleton only in so far as it directly influences Man or he reacts upon it.
>
> (1947, p. 143)

Powell argues that geography is 'essentially an attitude of mind' and that the teacher must 'concentrate on the development of such an attitude and must train his pupils to 'Think Geographically' upon world affairs':

> Since an ability to think clearly must be one of the main aims of all education, too narrow an interpretation of the foregoing 'end' must be deplored. The geography teacher must secure the full co-operation of allied subjects to ensure clarity of thought on a broadly based approach to the whole realm of the human studies incorporated in 'citizenship'. In this association the aim of the geographer is to establish a comprehensive global viewpoint.
>
> (p. 144)

He stresses that a teacher with an integrated outlook will tend to educate children to have an integrated outlook. In terms of how to do this Powell advocated a judicious mix of 'routine learning' of statistical information relating to relief, climate, population and economic activity and the 'vitalism' which brings home to 'fact of lived experience' in the world's regions and places. Central to this is the need to make connections between the classroom and the outdoor world:

> The living geography we desire cannot come from within the four walls of the classroom ... The geographer must use the open air, the fields, the

woods, the factories, the mines and the towns – the maximum encouragement of personal observation in the individual wanderings of pupils and
students in this present 'Outdoor Age'.

(pp. 147–8)

Once more, in Powell, we see a theory of what it means to 'think geographically'.
It is rooted in a form of 'English empiricism' which assumes that the world exists
independently of the human subject, and whose meanings are revealed through
careful observation and study. There is an assumption that the world can be
known through looking and walking, through 'getting mud on your boots'.

AN INTEGRATED APPROACH

A second feature of what it means to 'think geographically' is associated with
another interpretation of an integrated approach, one in which geography is a
bridge between the human and natural sciences. An excellent example of this way
of thinking is to be found in a little book by John Matthews and David Herbert
(2008) called *Geography: A Very Short Introduction.* Its authors are both professors
of geography within the University of Wales. Their overall argument is that
the original 'Geographical Experiment' was based on an ability to act as a bridge
between nature and society, but that 'the integration of geography as a single
discipline, which was explicit and strong through the earlier decades of the 20th
century, has become less so in modern times'. They seek to advocate the continued value and strength of what they call 'integrated geography'.

The first chapter is entitled 'Geography: the world is our stage' and in it, the
authors make a case for the continuity between earlier traditions of exploration
and the modern discipline. Exploration and travel are seen as the essential characteristics of geography, and that this can be traced through history. The chapter
provides examples of historical examples of exploration, including the Roman
Empire, early explorers and the great explorers sponsored by the Royal
Geographical Society from the 1830s. Through these explorations, the features
of geography as a discipline were identified. These include a practical and empirical approach concerned to collect and present the facts, an understanding of the
meanings and significance that humans attach to places and landscape, and an
understanding of the ways in which human actions can impact on natural environments. These 'echoes of the past' are found in the present where, it is suggested, 'geography is everywhere'. Doing geography today does not necessarily
involve travel because, in an interdependent world, a thoughtful trip to the super-
market can reveal the connections between home and distant worlds.

Having established geography as a subject that is essential to understanding
aspects of the modern world and the challenges humanity faces, the chapter goes
on to focus on the nature of geography as an academic discipline. The authors
provide a brief account of the rise of geography as an academic subject located in
universities and they present figures to support the claim that 'Geography is
now a well-established university discipline'. Having established for readers the

'fundamental importance' of the subject, they suggest that geography possesses three 'core concepts'. These are *space, place* and *environment*. They argue that the 'essence' of geography is the shaded area where the three concepts overlap as 'an integration of spatial variation over the Earth's surface with the distinctiveness of places and interactions between people and their environments'. To support this definition they provide a series of alternative definitions of geography which, they suggest, do not stray far from their own. They assert that geography should be thought of as the nexus where the three core concepts overlap. They suggest that there is no special word to define this nexus, but that 'landscape' comes closest to pinning down what it means.

The final part of their chapter recognises that this nexus of space, place and environment is not stable but has changed over time as geography as a discipline has developed. They identify five developmental phases. These are: exploration, the establishment of the discipline, the dominance of regional geography, the emergence of physical and human geography and systematic approaches, and the current phases of divergent geography characterised by increasing specialisation and fragmentation.

The organisation of the rest of *Geography: a very short introduction* reflects the argument laid out in chapter one. Indeed, the whole book is based on a larger edited volume entitled *Unifying Geography: Common Heritage, Shared Future* (2004). Matthews and Herbert are writing from a very specific location, and this clearly influences how they choose to communicate about geography. They write as experienced and established members of the 'academy' – they are part of the 'professoriat', and have an interest in celebrating, communicating and reproducing the 'geographical tradition' (their list of references and works cited come from learned journals and monographs). Their concern is that this tradition risks being fragmented through runaway specialisation by geographers. However, as the next section suggests, by no means everyone shares this dream of a 'core' geographical discipline.

A MODERN GEOGRAPHY

Alistair Bonnett's book *what is geography?* was published in 2008. Bonnett is Professor of Social Geography at the University of Newcastle, and his voluminous writing ranges from anti-racism and the geographies of Whiteness, through conceptions of 'the West' to radical geography and the place of nostalgia in political thought, interests that in themselves indicate something of the geographical imagination which informs his work. From the start, Bonnett (2008) is honest about his own confusion over the question: what is geography? Though he has spent most of his life in academia, he finds he doesn't have an answer other than to say, it's whatever geographers do. He thinks that geography is 'an attempt to find and impose order on a seemingly chaotic world' (p. 6). This is similar to Matthews and Herbert in that there is almost something 'essential' about this need to know about and understand the world, but different in that Bonnett is clearer that this desire to

know, travel and explore is wrapped up with a broader historical process we call 'modernity'. Thus, for Bonnett 'Industrial modernity shaped geography in its own image. The kind of questions increasingly associated with geography reflected this dominance' (p. 4). These questions were to do with the relationships between nations (us and them) and relationships between people and environment. Another way of putting this is that as the world became increasingly connected though trade and exploration, it brought previous separated communities into contact with each other and begged questions of what and how we can know about them:

> Geography attempts to describe and explain the world and its peoples. There are many pitfalls in such an undertaking.
>
> (Bonnett, 2008, p. 24)

The other set of questions that geography is concerned with is the relationship between humans and the natural world, and this has veered from the idea that the environment determines human activity to the notion that humans can manipulate and control the natural world. In addition to these twin concerns at the heart of the geographical imagination are two other 'geographical obsessions' that have resulted from the development of industrial modernity; these are urbanisation and mobility.

The broad sweep of Bonnett's analysis allows him to place the search for geographical knowledge within a wider set of economic, social and cultural processes. Though he talks of modernity, in practice he recognises the existence of multiple forms of modernity or modernities. This allows him to avoid the ethnocentrism so often found in accounts of geography as an academic discipline. In addition, it allows the argument that the formal, academic geography that has become institutionalised is not the only form of geographical knowledge, and this allows him to 'de-centre' geography as a discipline. An example of this is found in Bonnett's discussion of Doreen Massey's now famous (among human geographers at least) account of Kilburn High Street in North-West London, which is seen as signalling a progressive sense of place based on its openness and interconnectedness, as opposed to the defensive clinging to a bounded or closed place (Massey, 1991). Bonnett (2008) comments that 'If one is in a hyper-mobile, high status, occupation, "place-bound" community may, indeed appear to be an irrelevance, or even a conservative anachronism. The view from less affluent parts of society is likely to be different' (p. 69). He playfully suggests that 'Perhaps academics are not well placed to produce engaged geographical knowledge' (p. 69).

This willingness to go beyond the idea that geography exists simply as an academic discipline allows Bonnett to draw upon a wide range of popular geographical knowledge such as novels, films and travel guides. It also explains his ambivalence around the institutions that have been established to bolster and buttress geography. Whilst these are needed and inevitable in a modern society which favours bureaucracy and form-filling, one of the downsides is that they tend to look to pin down and define what geographical knowledge is. On the other

hand, this institutionalisation is needed because it allows geographical knowledge to reach a 'mass audience'. To put this in terms of school geography: one of the effects of the establishment of geography in schools is perhaps to confine geographical knowledge to the classroom and define closely what 'counts' as valid experience. However, it also has allowed more children to gain access to geographical knowledge.

A DIFFERENT VIEW: THE TURN TO EVERYDAY LIFE

The final take on the theme of 'thinking geographically' is concerned with the turn to 'everyday life'. This work takes its cue from the French Marxist Henry Lefebrve who was particularly concerned with how the spaces of everyday life or what he called 'lived space' were being colonised by the abstract spaces of global forces, as well as the British school of Cultural Studies influenced by Raymond Williams who argue that 'culture is ordinary'. An accessible example of this type of approach is the work of the cultural historian Joe Moran (2005), who seeks to show that 'quotidian spaces – offices, call centres, subway systems, traffic jams, new towns, suburbs, motorways and housing estates – are caught up in global processes while remaining tied to resilient local conditions and histories'. As can be seen from this list, the spaces he studies are mundane and everyday. Moran's argument is that changes in the way we live often appear to us as unimportant and inevitable (indeed we may not even notice them) but are in fact linked to wider political forces.

Given that since the late 1960s human geography has aligned itself closely with the social sciences, it is unsurprising that geographers have also come to take an interest in everyday life. A good example is found in Peter Jackson's article on 'Thinking Geographically' (2006) in which he uses the case of Oxfam encouraging Western consumers to 'give a goat' for Christmas. He demonstrates the complex cultural politics at work in such an act, suggesting how an intention to make a connection with 'distant others' may in fact serve to reproduce and extend the social relations of the market society, and may itself lead to environmentally questionable practices. Jackson provides a model of 'thinking geographically' that takes seriously questions of connection, belonging and morality, and which encourages reflection on the geographical threads that connect people and places. It suggests a particular pedagogical approach, which has a number of features.

First, it allows teachers to start from students' experience of 'everyday life'. Starting from a particular cultural text is a convenient way into more substantive themes. This is in line with Jackson's argument that analysis should proceed from empirical inquiry rather than relying on high theory from the start. This focus on the empirical mapping of cultural texts avoids closed political readings that assume that the task is simply to expose aspects of ideology. In this sense, there is more space for multiple readings and meanings to circulate in classrooms. This is in line with Jackson's commitment to take seriously 'the popular wisdom of everyday life' that children have valid ideas and interpretations, and that academic geographers (and by extension teachers) do not have a 'uniquely critical insight' into the nature and affects of cultural texts.

Conclusion: against manifestos

This chapter has sought to explore various answers to the question of what it means to 'think geographically'. It has drawn on a number of examples in the British literature which span the past 130 years. The point has not been to pin down once and for all the features common to these accounts, but simply to suggest that similar themes recur, refracted through the particular contexts in which they were written. This at least suggests that there is something coherent about the idea of geography. But it also suggests the need to be cautious about rushing to 'define' the subject once and for all, or even its 'core' of essential knowledge concepts and skills. More productive is the need for continued thought and reflection on the aims and purposes of teaching geography in schools.

Key readings

1. Matthews, J. and Herbert, D. (2008) *Geography: A very short introduction*, Cambridge: Cambridge University Press. This book does 'exactly what it says on the tin'. That is, it offers a succinct overview of the concerns of Anglo-American geography, written by two long-established professors of geography. It makes a case for the coherence of the subject as a whole, in opposition to what the authors see as a dangerous fragmentation.
2. Bonnett, A. (2008) *what is geography?* London: Sage. This book, written by another professor of geography, offers a useful contrast to 'a short introduction'. Making the case for geography as 'the world discipline', it portrays a subject more loosely aligned to broader currents of social and cultural theory.

References

Bonnett, A. (2008) *What is geography?* London: Sage.
Geographical Association (2009) *Geography: A different view*, Sheffield: Geographical Association.
Gregory, D. (1994) *Geographical Imaginations*, Oxford: Blackwell.
Harvey, D. (1984) 'On the history and present condition of geography: an historical materialist manifesto', *The Professional Geographer*, 36 (1), 1–11.
Jackson, P. (2006) 'Thinking Geographically', *Geography*, 91, 199–204.
Mackinder, H. (1890) 'On the necessity of thorough teaching in general geography as a preliminary to the teaching of commercial geography', *Journal of the Manchester Geographical Society*, 6 (4).
Massey, D. (1991) 'A global sense of place?' *Marxism Today*, June, 24–29.
Matthews, J. and Herbert, D. (eds.) (2004) *Unifying Geography: Common heritage, shared future*, London: Routledge.
Matthews, J. and Herbert, D. (2008) *Geography: A very short introduction*, Cambridge: Cambridge University Press.
Moran, J. (2005) *Reading the everyday*, London: Routledge.
O Tuathail, G. (1996) *Critical Geopolitics: The politics of writing global space*, London: Routledge.
Powell, A.G. (1947) 'Geography', in D.Thompson and J.Reeves (eds.), *The quality of education: Methods and purposes in the secondary curriculum*, London: Frederick Muller Ltd.
Thompson, D. and Reeves, J. (eds.) (1947) *The quality of education: methods and purposes in the secondary curriculum*, London: Frederick Muller Ltd.
Young, M. (2008) *Bringing Knowledge Back In*, London: Routledge.

Chapter 21

How does geography adapt to changing times?

Charles Rawding

> The one thing I find that nobody wants to talk much about is the nature of the geography that is being taught to pupils in schools.
>
> (Morgan, 2011, p. 125)

Introduction

This chapter discusses the changing nature of geography over the last half century, both in the context of the academy and the school classroom. It hopes to demonstrate that geography has changed, continues to change significantly, and furthermore that continued change to reflect both the developing nature of society and the evolving knowledge base of scientific research is essential. Such sentiments are equally valid for human, physical and environmental geographies (Rawding, 2010a; Suggitt, 2010; Rawding et al., 2010). For the practising teacher, the feelings expressed by Graves in 1972 are ever more pertinent:

> As the length of time grew between the year when we graduated and the present, so we became no doubt more proficient practitioners in the classroom, but what we taught bore less and less resemblance to what current university geographers were doing.
>
> (Graves, 1972, p. 10)

However, as John Morgan's reflections suggest, based on his experience as a teacher educator, it is surprisingly difficult to maintain a productive relationship between the school subject and the wider discipline of geography.

THE CHANGING NATURE OF GEOGRAPHY AND SCHOOL GEOGRAPHY

The changing nature of geography both as an academic discipline and within the school curriculum is well documented (Goodson, 1983; Livingstone, 1992; Agnew et al., 1996; Walford, 2001; Herod, 2011). In the period up until the 1960s, geography adopted a regional approach which, at its best, was able to

evoke vivid and compelling notions of place, often in the context of the historical evolution of regions (Buttimer, 1971). However, too often this produced relatively sterile, atheoretical descriptions which gave idiographic studies a bad name (Sayer, 1985). Since the 1960s, human geography has been subject to many of the intellectual debates which have characterised the other disciplines in the humanities and social sciences (Hamnett, 2001). The so-called 'Quantitative Revolution' (Billinge et al., 1984) arose out of geography's need to keep up to speed with developments in systems theory in biology, and a search for status through the adoption of statistical and positivist approaches from 'hard science'. Thus the study of the unique in geography was replaced by a search for scientific order. Dissatisfaction with these approaches led to a more fragmented approach to the subject during the 1970s and 1980s as humanist (Ley and Samuels, 1978), structuralist (Harvey, 1973) and radical (Peet, 1977) geographies were developed. More recently, post-modern approaches (Harvey, 1989) and the 'cultural turn' (Cloke et al., 2005) have characterised human geography. In physical geography, an emphasis on geomorphology and, in its earliest incarnation, denudation chronology was replaced by scientific method, the study of the physical properties of the earth's surface, including micro-processes, an emphasis on environmental systems and on biogeography (Worsley, 1985). More recently, studies of environmental change and investigating the impacts of humans on the natural environment have become central issues for physical geography, with a significant focus on the nature and effects of global climate change. Throughout this period, regular calls for a more unified approach to the subject have been made by authors cautioning against excessive fragmentation (Matthews and Herbert, 2004; Johnston, 2005; Bonnett, 2008). In this context, the contribution of Doreen Massey, a human geographer arguing for a reunification of geography, offers some thought-provoking insights on physical geography research foci (Massey, 1999).

Up until the dramatic increase in centralised control of the English school curriculum during the late 1980s, it was possible to discern a link between school and academic geography, usually with a time-lag as ideas permeated down from the academy.[1] In general terms, geography in the school classroom moved from regional approaches that reflected the academic geography of the period prior to the mid 1960s, following Vidalian traditions of 'place' (Rawding, 2007) and creating what Graves termed 'explanatory descriptions of landscape' (Graves, 1972, p. 9) towards more scientific and thematic approaches. The activities of academics, such as Chorley and Haggett working with teachers in the 1960s and 70s, acted as a conduit for the latest ideas in universities to be disseminated to schools, and enabled aspects of the Quantitative Revolution to be applied in the classroom (Walford, 1973; Goodson, 1983; Walford, 2001). Such a trend can be identified if one compares one of the best-selling textbook series of the 1960s (Young and Lowry, 1960), with the texts of the 1970s and 80s (Clammer et al., 1987; Farleigh Rice, 1975). This was a period of confident expansion and energetic curriculum and pedagogic advancement – perhaps symbolised by the advent of the home-grown journal *Classroom Geographer* and the introduction of the

Geographical Association's classroom-oriented professional journal *Teaching Geography* in 1974.

In the early 1980s, the work of geography educators such as Huckle (1983, 1985) and the publication of the journal *Contemporary Issues in Geography and Education* (1984–7) gave teachers source materials derived from a range of perspectives related to the new and contemporary geographies. It was not seen as unusual for texts of the time to discuss geographical education from the perspective of academic paradigms within the discipline (see Figure 21.1) (Walford, 1973; Bale, 1983; Huckle, 1983).

However, it would be misleading to overstress these links since Huckle felt compelled to state that: 'a widening communication gap has developed between school and university geographers, and there is some indifference to the subject's claims on the part of those with control over the school curriculum' (Huckle, 1983, p. iv). What is most striking when reviewing the intertwined histories of the academic discipline and the school subject are the similarities between the concerns being expressed, seemingly irrespective of the date. For instance, Goodson's (1983) account of the evolution of the subject from the later years of the nineteenth century through to the 1980s is laced with concerns about the differences between school and university along with appeals for renewed unity in the light of perceived divergence within the subject. It should perhaps be stressed here that there should be differences between school geographies and academic geographies. They serve different audiences and different purposes. Nevertheless, it is essential that some form of relationship exists and develops between the two. Exactly what form this relationship takes is a subject for considerable debate.

The imposition of a more 'traditional' geography curriculum at Key Stage 3 (11–14) in 1991 (Rawling, 2001; Walford, 2001) marked, for some, a distinct backwards step when contrasted with many of the developments that had taken place in the 1980s. The form of school geography was influenced greatly by the dominance of one textbook series in English schools, the 'Key Geography' series (Waugh and Bushell, 1992), which by some estimates was adopted in some 60% of schools (Lambert, 2000). At the same time, geography in universities changed out of all recognition (Rawding, 2010b). Post-modern cultural geography has focused on ideas such as difference, otherness, polyvocality and the notion of multiple discourses, attributes which have only recently found their way into elements of the school curriculum (e.g., the Summer 2011 issue of *Teaching*

3. Behavioural geography	6. Welfare approaches to geography	9. Development education
4. Humanistic geography	7. Radical geography	10. Environmental education
5. Geography through art	8. Political education	11. Urban studies

Figure 21.1 Geographical education: reflection and action: chapter headings. Section B: New perspectives (pp. 29–120). (Source: Huckle, 1983)

Geography has an explicit focus on diversity). It should be stressed here that such approaches are not without their critics in academic geography (Hamnett, 2001). Furthermore, at the time of writing, it seems that the 2010 White Paper, with its insistence on a return to traditional subjects and 'core knowledge', is set to discourage any further development of this trend.

One issue to emerge during this period, especially for teachers new to the profession, was the mismatch between university-educated geographers and what teachers were required to teach in schools. Furthermore we saw a 'pedagogic turn' (Morgan and Lambert, 2011) by the end of the 1990s and the early years of the new millennium marked by the publication of highly influential texts such as *Thinking Through Geography* (Leat, 1998) and *More Thinking Through Geography* (Nichols, 2001). However, what these texts delivered were new approaches to pedagogy rather than content. The two texts provided 16 strategies for developing thinking skills in the geography classroom, encouraging a radical departure from orthodox classroom practice. However, the subject content contained in the exemplars for these strategies was far more conservative in nature.

The point here is to emphasise that the geography being transformed did not represent the latest thinking in the subject. For instance, there is no obvious cultural geography in the texts, while the relatively light focus on physical geography relates to 'traditional' topics. In some instances the topics concerned could be heavily criticised on subject-specific grounds. The Reading Photographs exemplar on urban land use models (Leat, 1998, pp. 144–8) is underpinned by the ancient and largely discredited Burgess model (Rawding, 2006). In many ways, these changes reflect the prevailing political climate of the period. The original National Curriculum has been seen in the context of a 'New Right' emphasis, transmitting traditional cultural values (Ainley and Allen, 2010), while during the years of the Labour government (1997–2010) there was a major change in emphasis towards pedagogy and the teaching of skills. As a consequence, it has been argued that contemporary school geography has become characterised by an unwillingness to focus on the question of what should be taught and is being delivered by teachers who are more concerned with the skills and competences of how to teach than with the subject content itself (Morgan, 2011, p. 113).

However, in the early years of this century, it would be a mistake to characterise the entire government machine as aiming towards a skills-based curriculum. One of the key drivers in moving the subject forward during this period was the Qualification and Curriculum Authority (QCA). Its Schemes of Work, produced in 2000 (Figure 21.2), represented a deliberate attempt to modernise the subject. It undoubtedly had significant success in terms of its influences both on classroom practice and the production of new textbook series which were very different in their content to the previous generation of textbooks. The QCA also encouraged the dissemination of new ideas in geography through the 'Innovating with Geography' section of its website (2004–10) and the introduction of new ideas relating to cultural geography. On the other hand, a new GCSE specification piloted by the QCA in this period has had very limited impact. We can only

1. Making connections	9. Shopping past present and future	17. The changing economic geography of France
2. The restless earth – earthquakes and volcanoes	10. Weather patterns over Europe	18. The global fashion industry
3. People everywhere	11. Investigating Brazil	19. Tourism – good or bad?
4. Flood disaster – how do people cope	12. Images of a country	20. Comparing countries
5. Exploring England	13. Limestone landscapes in England	21. Virtual volcanoes and internet earthquakes
6. World sport	14. Can the earth cope? Ecosystems, populations and resources	22. Mining on the internet
7. Rivers – a fieldwork approach	15. Crime and the local community	23. Local actions, global effects.
8. Coastal environments	16. What is development?	24. Passport to the world

Figure 21.2 Units of study in the QCA scheme of work. (Source: QCA, 2000)

speculate on the reasons for this, but they probably include the inertia that naturally follows raising the stakes of examination results through the introduction of league tables and data-driven performance management.

While it can be argued that the current National Curriculum (September 2008 onwards), with its focus on 'key concepts' rather than content, provides a deliberately open framework to allow teachers to deliver the Geography that they consider to be important, it can be argued that it also risks reducing or diminishing geography to whatever happens in geography lessons. This may be too loose a framework for some, and offer somewhat unnerving autonomy, especially to non-specialists.

CHANGING GEOGRAPHY FOR A CHANGING SOCIETY?

I argue in this section that change in the school curriculum is no less essential than change in the university curriculum if geography is to retain its relevance in the modern world. My personal view is that contemporary geography must be relevant and topical if it is to be worth its place in the school curriculum.

However, the wholesale adoption of the latest research in university geography is neither as straightforward as it might appear nor always particularly desirable. Recent developments in the Academy have seen an increasing fragmentation of the subject and a tendency towards specialism over synthesis. These trends

within the subject have been exacerbated by the modularisation of many degree courses, which in the worst-case scenarios leave graduates with a perception of the subject that is little more than a list of topics which have been covered during their degree. It might also be suggested that some of the quirkier elements of post-modernity may well come to be seen as intellectual fashions that are somewhat short-lived. Such developments leave the classroom geography teacher in something of a predicament when attempting to evaluate which areas of the existing curriculum are in need of revision and what elements of the latest geographical thinking might be incorporated within the school curriculum.

Evaluating the relative merits of 'new' versus 'old' could be carried out using several criteria which might provide an effective framework for making curriculum decisions. First, placing the older geographies within the context in which they were developed should enable us to ascertain the extent to which this content remains valid today. For instance, in human geography many of the key concepts that have become part of the canon of the subject can be traced back to attempts to understand industrial capitalism during its Fordist phase, within a Cold War context where large areas of the world had yet to experience significant industrial and urban development (the Rostow model, the demographic transition model, MEDC/LEDC divide, etc.). Such views of the world often saw development as a linear and relatively uncontested process. Arguably, this world view has become progressively less tenable since the oil crises of the 1970s and subsequent trends towards post-industrialisation in the West which have occurred alongside rapid industrialisation in parts of Asia. In this case, the simple question: 'Is the world still like that?' should suffice in considering whether to retain or discard particular elements of the curriculum.

Having focused on the existing school curriculum, we might consider a second approach through identifying those areas of emerging thought in academic geography that merit consideration for incorporating into the school curriculum where their content/concepts would appear to have greater relevance to contemporary society than existing concepts in the school curriculum. For instance, when studying population geography is it now more appropriate to focus on elements such as global population growth, the implications of aging population structures or notions of hybridity and diasporas rather than studying the demographic transition model (Dorling and Thomas, 2004). Indeed, should the demographic transition model now be the concern of history within the school curriculum?

In physical geography, ideas of landscape evolution through steady change, as characterised by notions such as Davisian cycles of erosion, have been replaced by attempts to understand process–landform relationships linked to catchment hydrology, system inputs, local geology and human management. A major development has been the incorporation of notions of 'tipping points' (Gladwell, 2000; Giddens, 2011) where the focus of study has been on the magnitude and frequency of events, with a recognition that major events such as the 500-year

flood event will lead to 'runoff and erosion thresholds being crossed with dramatic results' (Suggitt, 2010, p. 57). Such approaches suggest a need to actively consider notions of thresholds, trigger points and systems collapse as we grapple with understanding planetary-scale environmental and climate change.

At its best, school geography can be a dynamic, innovative and deeply relevant subject for pupils to study. The burgeoning availability of information via the internet has enabled school departments to update case studies much more easily, for example by following the latest volcanic eruption, tsunami or urban development. However, at a conceptual level change appears much more difficult to embed in curriculum development, and it is here that an awareness of developments within academic geography is crucial to ensure that teachers are aware of the latest thinking on geographical issues. It is important that academic thinking that attempts to deconstruct and analyse the rapidly changing nature of contemporary society is incorporated into classroom approaches to the subject.

Conclusion

Academic geography has moved through a sequence of paradigms, from a focus on regional geography through a range of quantitative, humanist and structuralist approaches. Current approaches to the subject are more diverse, but many are heavily influenced by post-modern cultural thinking. Until the imposition of the National Curriculum in 1991, there were clear links, with variable time-lags, between academic and school geography. Since the introduction of the original National Curriculum, centralised control of subject specifications has had a strong influence on geography in the school classroom, while pressures within the Academy have also resulted in academics disengaging from the school subject. The consequent disconnection of academic and classroom geography has had a range of consequences for the school subject. If geography is to retain a significant position in the school curriculum, then the subject must continue to change in order to reflect and explain the changing nature of society and environment. If teachers are to maintain a relevant, innovative curriculum, it is essential that they endeavour to retain an awareness of the latest thinking within the academic subject.

Note

1   While much of what is written here has wider applications than just the English school system, it is important to mention the increasing divergence of curricula between the countries of the United Kingdom since devolution. It should be pointed out, however, that the relationship between academic and school geography has not always been one of movement down from the universities. Goodson (1988) shows that the early development of the subject was based on pressure from below, ultimately resulting in the establishment of the academic discipline in universities during the early to middle years of the twentieth century.

Key readings

1. Bonnett, A. (2008) *What is geography?* London: Sage. This book provides a succinct and well-argued overview of the importance of the subject. The main argument, potentially very valuable for teachers of geography, is to unify the subject – the world subject – across its popular, school subject and academic manifestations.
2. Lambert, D. and Morgan, J. (2010) *Teaching Geography 11–18: A conceptual approach*, Maidenhead: Open University Press. This book begins by providing an historical and socio-cultural context for understanding changing school geography in England. The main part of the book then concentrates on the changing discipline, providing an over-view of the changing conceptual landscape of geography – written mainly for a reader-ship of school geography teachers. The book aims to extend our professional understanding of some of geography's 'big ideas'.

References

Agnew, J.A., Livingstone, D. and Rogers, A. (eds.), (1996) *Human geography as an essential anthology*, Oxford: Blackwell.

Ainley, P. and Allen, M. (2010) *Lost generation: New strategies for youth and education*, London: Continuum.

Bale, J. (ed.) (1983) *The Third World: Issues and approaches*, Sheffield: Geographical Association.

Billinge, M., Gregory, D. and Martin, R. (eds.) (1984) *Recollections of a revolution: Geography as spatial science*, London: Macmillan.

Bonnett, A. (2008) *What is geography?* London: Sage.

Buttimer, A. (1971) *Society and milieu in the French Geographic Tradition*, Chicago: Rand McNally.

Clammer, R., Greasley, B., McLeod, P. and Nicholls, R. (1987) *Geography Today*, London: Collins.

Cloke, P., Crang, P. and Goodwin, M. (eds.) (2005) *Introducing human geographies* (2nd edn), London: Hodder Arnold.

Dorling, D. and Thomas, B. (2004) *People and places: A 2001 census atlas of the UK*, Bristol: Policy Press.

Farleigh Rice, W. (1975) *Patterns in Geography*, Harlow: Longman.

Giddens, A. (2011) *The politics of climate change* (2nd edn), Cambridge: Polity.

Gladwell, M. (2000) *The tipping point*, London: Little, Brown.

Goodson, I.F. (1983) *School subjects and curriculum change*, London: Croom Helm.

Goodson, I.F. (1988) *The making of curriculum: Collected essays*, London: Falmer Press.

Graves, N. (ed.) (1972) *New movements in the study and teaching of geography*, London: Temple Smith.

Hamnett, C. (2001) 'The emperor's new clothes, or geography without origami', in G. Philo and D. Miller (eds.), *Market killing: What the free market does and what social scientists can do about it*, Harlow: Pearson.

Harvey, D. (1973) *Social justice and the city*, Oxford: Blackwell.

Harvey, D. (1989) *The condition of postmodernity: An enquiry into the origins of cultural change*, Oxford: Blackwell.

Herod, A. (2011) *Scale*, London: Routledge.

Huckle, J. (ed.) (1983) *Geographical education: Reflection and action*, Oxford: Oxford University Press.

Huckle, J. (1985) 'Geography and schooling', in R.J. Johnston (ed.), *The future of Geography*, London: Methuen.

Johnston, R.J. (ed.) (1985) *The future of Geography*, London: Methuen.

Johnston, R.J. (2005) 'Geography – coming apart at the seams?', in N. Castree, A. Rogers and D. Sherman (eds.), *Questioning Geography*, Oxford: Blackwell.

Lambert, D. (2000) 'Textbook Pedagogy: Issues on the use of textbooks in geography classrooms', in C. Fisher and T. Binns (eds.), *Issues in geography teaching*, London: Routledge Falmer.

Lambert, D. and Morgan, J. (2010) *Teaching Geography 11–18: A conceptual approach*, Maidenhead: Open University Press.

Leat, D. (ed.) (1998) *Thinking Through Geography*, Cambridge: Chris Kington.

Ley, D. and Samuels, M. (eds.) (1978) *Humanistic geography*, London: Croom Helm.

Livingstone, D. (1992) *The geographical tradition*, Oxford: Blackwell.

Massey, D. (1999) 'Space-time 'science' and the relationship between physical geography and human geography', *Transactions of the Institute of British Geographers*, 24 (3), 261–76.

Matthews, J.A. and Herbert, D.T. (2004) *Unifying Geography: common heritage, shared future*, London: Routledge.

Morgan, J. (2011) 'What is radical in school geography today?', *Forum*, 53 (1), 113–27.

Morgan, J. and Lambert, D. (2011) Editors' Introduction, *The Curriculum Journal*, 22 (3), 279–87.

Pacione, M. (2009) *Urban Geography* (3rd edn), London: Routledge.

Nichols, A. (ed.) (2001) *More Thinking Through Geography*, Cambridge: Chris Kington.

Peet, R. (ed.) (1977) *Radical Geography*, London: Methuen.

QCA (2000) *Geography: A scheme of work for key stage 3*, London: QCA.

Rawding, C. (2006) 'Putting Burgess in the bin: Reconstructing the urban geographies of Brighton'. Available online at: <http://www.geography.org.uk/download/GA_GTIPGTER awding.doc> [Accessed 2 February 2012].

Rawding, C. (2007) *Theory into practice: Understanding place as a process*, Sheffield: Geographical Association.

Rawding, C. (2010a) *Contemporary approaches to Geography Volume 1: Human Geography*, London: Chris Kington.

Rawding, C. (2010b) 'What are the connections between subject developments in academic and school geography?', *International Research in Geographical and Environmental Education*, 19 (2), 119–25.

Rawding, C., Holden, V. and Worsley, A. (2010) *Contemporary approaches to Geography Volume 3: Environmental Geography*, London: Chris Kington.

Rawling, E. (2001) *Changing the subject: The impact of national policy on school geography 1980–2000*, Sheffield: Geographical Association.

Sayer, A. (1985) 'Realism and Geography', in R.J. Johnston (ed.), *The future of Geography*, London: Methuen.

Suggitt, S. (2010) *Contemporary approaches to Geography Volume 2: Physical Geography*, London: Chris Kington.

Walford, R. (1973) *New directions in geography teaching: Papers from the 1970 Charney Manor conference*, London: Longman.

Walford, R. (2001) *Geography in British schools 1850–2000*, London: Woburn Press.

Waugh, D. and Bushell, T. (1992) *Key Geography*, Cheltenham: Stanley Thornes.

Worsley, P. (1985) 'Physical geography and the natural environmental sciences', in R.J. Johnston (ed.), *The future of Geography*, London: Methuen.

Young, E.W and Lowry, J.H. (1960) *A course in world geography*, London: Edward Arnold.

Chapter 22

Can geography cross 'the divide'?

Graham Butt and Gemma Collins

> A chasm has developed between those who teach at school and those who teach in universities.
>
> (Goudie, 1993, p. 338)

Introduction

The current 'state of play' concerning the health of geography education in English state schools and universities is intriguing. On the one hand, geography remains a popular option in many English schools, experienced positively by large numbers of students who ultimately perform well in public examinations. In these schools standards of teaching on examination courses remain high, with pleasing numbers of students progressing onto geography (or geography-related) courses as undergraduates – where their experiences are also generally positive (Butt, 2008, 2011). The launch of an English Baccalaureate in 2010, in which students are expected to achieve 'good' GCSE grades (at level C or above) in a number of subjects – including either geography or history – has also provided a substantial fillip to the numbers opting for geography. Geography remains a subject of real relevance to many young people in our rapidly changing world, capable of addressing aspects of space, place and environment that will affect their future lives.

On the other hand, geography is under pressure with around 20% fewer candidates entered for public examinations in the subject at the end of the first decade of the 21st-century compared with the beginning (see David Gardner and John Hopkin's chapters in this volume). And just as geography departments in schools have faced pressures, so too have those in universities. Castree (2011) outlines three recent external drivers of change in English universities[1]: the very poor state of Britain's public finances, resulting in massive cuts in public spending on teaching and research in higher education (the disproportionate impact of financial cuts on the humanities and social sciences is also relevant); the raising of undergraduate fees, for many university geography courses to around £9000 per annum; and the National Student Survey (NSS) of graduates' 'satisfaction' with their courses, a determinant of future recruitment.

This constitutes a backdrop to the current shifts in the form and content of geography taught in schools – a consideration when evaluating the potential impact of the recent 'knowledge turn' (Lambert, 2011) in geography education. Any gap between schools and the academy can be considered to be mutually damaging, as Andrew Goudie (1993) noted in his Presidential address to the Geographical Association conference in its centenary year. Here, Goudie bemoaned the lack of involvement of academic geographers both in the Association and in schools, stating: 'A chasm has developed between those who teach in schools and those who teach in universities' (p. 338). However, this begs the question of how best to conceptualise the relation between the school subject and the wider academic discipline. They are different, with different priorities and different purposes. We should perhaps *expect* a 'gap'.

ERODING THE LINKS BETWEEN UNIVERSITY AND SCHOOL GEOGRAPHIES

All school subjects have a 'curriculum story', and probably all subjects experience periods of uncertainty about their status and appeal. For school geography, the rise of humanities teaching in many schools in the 1960s and 1970s, the debate over whether geography would be included in the National Curriculum in the late 1980s (see Bailey and Binns, 1987), and the increased focus on vocational education from the 1990s, all feature as pressure points. Essentially, school geography has always been affected, to a greater or lesser extent, by:

> the prevailing philosophies of education, the existing paradigm of geography in higher education, the economic climate and the political complexion of the government of the day.
>
> (Butt, 2002, p. 17)

The comprehensivisation of state secondary schools from the mid 1960s meant that many secondary school teachers in England found themselves teaching a different student clientele. This led significant numbers of geography educators towards curriculum development, driven primarily by the educational needs of a 'new' student group. Graves (1975) refers to this period as one of 'crisis in geographical education in Britain' (p. 61), a consequence of conceptual shifts in academic geography, advances in education theory and the restructuring of secondary schools. Marsden (1997) echoes these observations, referring to the 'unhealthy stresses' between school and university geography which developed from this time.

For Naish (2000), the period from the late 1960s to the early 1980s was one of 'laissez faire' in geography curriculum development, when considerations of the broader aims, objectives and purposes of education came to the fore. One of the consequences of this increased '*educational* focus' was that many geography

teachers, according to Naish, stepped back from considering the primacy of geography's academic subject content. The Schools Council, founded in 1964, actively supported curriculum reform and development, sponsoring three major geography curriculum development projects in the 1970s: Geography for the Young School Leaver (GYSL); Geography 14–18 (Bristol Project) and the Geography 16–19 Project. Geography curriculum development was also influenced by a project from abroad – the American High Schools Geography Project (HSGP, 1971) – which instructed teachers how to incorporate new ideas, content and techniques from the 'quantitative revolution' in academic geography into their schemes of work. However, most curriculum development projects focused more on how geography could contribute to the fulfilment of the needs of young people, than on considerations of academic subject content. The Geography 16–19 Project, examined at A level from 1982, achieved great popularity, experiencing a near-exponential growth in student numbers during the 1980s. This project had an impact on the teaching of geography within universities – for incoming undergraduates who had studied 16–19 Geography had been taught through a 'route to enquiry' approach, acquiring geographical content, skills, techniques and values very different from those provided by more 'traditional' geography syllabuses. The change was not universally welcomed by university geographers, many of whom criticised the (supposed) superficiality of content covered by the 16–19 syllabus, particularly of physical geography. Although these curriculum development projects offered some connection with academic geographers and their research, the 16–19 Project team stated that there was 'no requirement that all new academic developments necessarily be translated into the school context' (Naish et al., 1987, pp. 26–7).

The geography curriculum development projects were based within higher education institutions (HEIs) – predominantly in departments of education, not geography – with each project team emphasising the need for geography teachers to be involved (Boardman, 1988). The resultant curricula reflected *some* of the changes from the academic frontiers of the subject, often mediated by teacher educators, but also incorporated (and valued highly) the application of innovative curriculum theory. During the late 1970s, university geography departments saw humanistic, behavioural, welfare, and radical geographers reacting against the narrowness of the positivistic, quantitative approaches developed at least a decade earlier. This plurality of approaches may have proved confusing for school geographers, making the application of new ideas in schools problematic. A further, practical issue when considering the connections between schools and universities is the time lag between developments in universities and their adoption in schools, as there is an understandable conservatism about swapping syllabuses.

The 1980s saw increasing centralisation and politicisation of the school curriculum, culminating in the passing of the Education Reform Act (1988) and the establishment of a National Curriculum in English and Welsh schools. The first

iteration of the Geography National Curriculum (GNC) (DES, 1991) has been seen as a 'restorationist' curriculum (Rawling, 2001). As Lambert (2011) succinctly observes:

> The Schools Council projects introduced the idea that subject knowledge was not an end point in education, but a vehicle contributing towards educational ends (geography as a 'medium of education'). The 1991 National Curriculum can be interpreted as an attempt to restore subject knowledge.
>
> (p. 248)

Geography had won the 'status battle' by achieving a secure curriculum place, but arguably at the expense of previous educational, ideological and conceptual gains. It was soon apparent that the 'statutory order' was overloaded with content, making assessment problematic and restricting future curriculum development. Following the Dearing Review (1993–5), a second, slimmer, more pragmatic version of the GNC was published (DfE, 1995). Subsequently the QCA Review (1998–2000), and that of 2007, continued to slim the geography curriculum (DfEE/QCA, 1999; QCA, 2007), eventually shifting its focus from content to 'key concepts'. This may be changing, for the 2012 review of the National Curriculum, under the Conservative-Liberal Democrat administration elected in 2010, appears to signal a shift away from the 'relaxation' of content, towards a more prescriptive and centrally controlled knowledge-based curriculum.

Morgan (2008) has outlined the development of school geography curricula since the 1970s, whilst simultaneously highlighting an uncoupling of school and university geography during this period. He notes the limited involvement of academic geographers in the development of the GNC – just two were chosen to sit on the Geography Working Group, few made significant submissions to the curriculum-making process, whilst only modest numbers engaged in lobbying through their professional associations. This reflects the declining influence of university geographers in shaping the content of geography taught in schools over the past forty years. By the late 1990s, few academic geographers crossed the school–university divide, making limited contributions to the work of awarding bodies, the creation of geography syllabuses, and to the professional development of teachers. From the mid 1980s numbers of geography undergraduates were increasing rapidly, with commensurate pressures on university class sizes, teaching and research quality, funding and research outputs. Just as schools have endured huge changes in policy and practice from the late 1980s onwards, higher education has also been subject to increased bureaucratisation, marketisation and rising accountability. The limited involvement of most academic geographers in debates about the content of public examinations in geography, their general unwillingness to write for school teachers and students, and their lack of engagement in the professional development of teachers may be attributable to their need to publish high-quality research and on preparing high-stakes audits (QAA) (see Castree et al., 2007).

THE 'DIVIDE' BETWEEN SCHOOL AND UNIVERSITY GEOGRAPHY – RETROSPECT AND PROSPECT

The first of the famous Madingley conferences in 1963, creating what Rex Walford called the 'new model army' (Walford, 2001, p. 158), gave academic geographers and (some) teachers opportunities to discuss developments in their subject, under the direction of a couple of exciting and ambitious young Oxbridge geographers, Richard Chorley and Peter Haggett. The tone of these conferences were somewhat paternalistic, given that academic geographers were largely handing down research findings and techniques to those teachers present – who Rawling refers to as 'junior partners in this relationship' (Rawling, 1996, p. 3). Nonetheless, Unwin (1996) comments positively on the influence of Chorley and Haggett's ideas on 'a generation of geography teachers', noting how their emphasis on quantitative approaches, modelling and theory building subsequently 'filtered down into school textbooks and examination syllabuses' (p. 21). Although sceptical about the extent of these impacts across the majority of schools, Unwin (1996) asserts that a minority of geography teachers remained heavily influenced by the research agendas of university geographers in the 1970s and early 1980s.

Whilst it would be a misjudgement to visualise the 1960s and early 1970s as some kind of 'golden age' of interaction between school and university geographers, there is evidence of pockets of influential engagement with regard to examinations and professional development. This gradually changed from the mid 1970s, as the sectors began to grow further apart. One reason for this, according to Bradford (1996), was that:

> during the 1980s and 1990s there has not been one major trend affecting as many areas of the subject as did either the scientific revolution of the 1950s and early 1960s, or the radical geography movement of the early 1970s. The absence of such major changes may partly account for the reduced impact of higher education on the geography taught in secondary education.
>
> (p. 282)

Michael Bradford's view of the school–HE interface as 'presenting a gap or discontinuity in methods and content' (1996, p. 277), has held true for much of the following 15 years, despite attempts to bridge the gap, notably by the Council for British Geography (Cobrig) and its seminars of the mid 1990s (see Daugherty and Rawling, 1996). In fact it seemed like a decision needed to be made about whether 'there should be uniformity or diversity in what is learned' (p. 277) in schools and universities. This is a fundamental issue, at the very heart of our consideration of the connections between the geographies taught within schools and universities. It hints at a basic epistemological divide between the aims, rationale and scope of the work of academic and school geographers, with respect to both teaching and research. Essentially, when considering geography either as an

academic discipline or as a school subject, there will always be differences and divides. Put crudely, geography in the academy is afforded the opportunities to develop in innovative, experimental, tentative and uncertain ways – the very nature of 'cutting edge' academic research work makes this so. Here we are at the forefront of knowledge creation, which is a piecemeal, painful and 'backwards and forwards' process, often leading down blind alleys or at best revealing findings that are contingent and relational. The geography taught in schools probably cannot be of this nature. It is certainly *informed* by the advances in knowledge achieved by academic geographers, but requires more objectivity, stability and certainty about the content it conveys. The selections of geography to be taught in schools have a greater need for endurance than those which may have recently emerged from the frontiers of academic research. Laying aside for one moment the vexed question as to the choice of contents for this enduring school geography, a divide will therefore always exist between academic and school geography; it will not be 'closed' by seeking to align both geographies (an impossible, Sisyphean task) but bridged by achieving a better understanding of their differences.

BRIDGING THE DIVIDE – WAYS FORWARD

We have seen that the issue of a 'chasm', 'gap', 'border' or 'discontinuity' between geography education in schools and universities is persistent (see Goudie, 1993; Machon and Ranger, 1996; Bradford, 1996; Marsden, 1997; Bonnett, 2003; Butt, 2008; Johnston, 2009; Hill and Jones, 2010), although some geographers have recently attempted to build bridges between the two sectors. The need for further dialogue (Jeffrey, 2003; Stannard, 2003), hopefully followed by rapprochement (Yarwood and Davison, 2007; Pykett and Smith, 2009), is generally acknowledged.

We outline below (Table 22.1) ways in which academic geographers, initial teacher educators, professional associations, awarding bodies and geography teachers can connect to develop the content of school geography. There are obvious overlaps between many of the suggested 'activities' and 'agents' – the key is achieving stronger, more frequent and clearer lines of communication between the academy and schools. Often this will occur through the actions of particular 'mediators' and 'ambassadors' interested in the wider development of geography content and pedagogy.

Each year new cohorts of geography graduates train to become geography teachers through programmes of initial teacher education (ITE), be they school or university based. Each trainee must make their own attempt to bridge the 'gap' between university and school geography, striving to translate or transform their recently gained geographical knowledge, understanding and skills to the classroom. This is not an easy process as 'students are recruited to teacher education courses with wildly different concepts of the nature of geography' (Marsden, 1997, p. 250; also see Barratt Hacking, 1996; Walford, 1996; Brooks, 2010).

Table 22.1 Bridging the divide – updating the content of school geography

Activity	Agents
Professional development conferences and events	Professional associations (e.g. GA and GA branches, RGS-IBG and GA conferences)
Academic conferences and events	Academic geographers and initial teacher educators (with some geography teachers) (e.g. COBRIG, Association of American Geographers Conference, IGU, ESRC 'Engaging Geographies' seminar series, RGS-IBG and GA conferences)
Producing textbooks/journal articles for school students/ geography teachers	Geography teachers, academic geographers and/ or initial teacher educators (in schools and universities) (e.g. *Teaching Geography, Geography Review, Geography*)
Producing scholarly/research texts	Academic geographers and/or initial teacher educators (in schools and universities) (e.g. GEReCo, Rawling and Daugherty (1996), Kent (2000), Butt (2011))
Research projects	Geography teachers in association with academic geographers and/or initial teacher educators (in schools and universities) (e.g. Young People's Geographies Project)
Curriculum Development Projects	Notably subject associations (e.g. see under 'projects' on geography.org.uk
'Mediation'	'Mediators' and 'Ambassadors' working in/with geographers in schools (e.g. GA Chief Executive /Professor of Geography Education; RGS-IBG subject officers; key geography academics; initial teacher educators in geography; geography undergraduates in schools; A level geography students attending day 'outreach/widening participation' courses in university geography departments).
Special Interest Groups	As represented in professional associations (IGU, GA, RGS-IBG, etc.)
Political lobbying for government funded initiatives	Professional associations (GA, RGS-IBG) (e.g. Action Plan for Geography); 'mediators'
Award bearing courses/CPD (Masters, Ed D, PhD in geography education)	University Schools of Education
Initial Teacher Education	New geography teachers, with geography educators (e.g. PGCE and PGDipEd courses)
Development and review of examination specifications[1]	Awarding bodies in association with academic geographers, teacher educators and geography teachers

[1] We cannot escape the sustained influence of the awarding bodies on the content of geography taught in schools. Many geography teachers express a desire to include up-to-date research in their teaching and may be encouraged to do so by their choice of syllabus – for example, the GCSE specification AQA B has a theme running throughout its units concerning new ways in which hazards, issues or environments could be managed in the future, giving a valuable opportunity to examine current research. However, most teachers will only teach content which they believe will be credited by the examiners, who may favour 'traditional' (and possibly outdated) answers.

In some sense each ITE student acts as a conduit, bringing aspects of recently acquired geography content from their university courses into schools – a process extended by the growing cohort of geography teachers who go on to study for a Masters degree, Ed D or PhD in geography education.

THE 'KNOWLEDGE TURN'

We have largely focused this discussion on the connections between geography in schools and in Higher Education. We choose to end our deliberations by concentrating on the recent 'knowledge turn' in school geography.

David Lambert (2011) shows that the direction of travel taken by the Schools White Paper, *The Importance of Teaching* (DfE, 2010), encourages (geography) teachers to engage more deeply with the question of 'what to teach?' Here the issue is what constitutes 'essential knowledge'. Whether this is a question solely about 'school geography' or whether the impetus is for geography teachers to engage with developments in their subject discipline is unclear. Lambert welcomes a re-focusing of geography teachers' attention on their subject, arguing that this has been neglected during a period of overemphasis on aspects of pedagogy. David Mitchell (2011) similarly refers to an 'emptying of subject knowledge', and is concerned about the 'weak' geographical content taught in schools – a consequence, according to Alex Standish and others, of the 'ethical turn' in education for social purposes ('education as therapy'), but also of the extent to which pedagogy has come to dominate knowledge. This serves to exacerbate the 'great divide' between university and school geographies as the relevance of the discipline to raising achievement becomes questionable on a practical level. John Morgan (2009), Margaret Roberts (2010, 2012) and Ruth Totterdell (2012) each explore the issue of what makes geography teachers, and their lessons, 'good' – concluding that the focus should be as much on the geography taught (and learned) as on the process of teaching. Mitchell (2011) implies the need to develop a more theorised and sophisticated understanding of perspectives on knowledge, incorporating an appreciation of Young's conceptions of 'powerful knowledge' (Young, 2008), Hirsch's notions of core knowledge and cultural literacy (Hirsch, 1987, 2007), and possibly the 'capability approach' to geography (Lambert and Morgan, 2010).

In these scenarios, geography teachers are visualised as 'independent, autonomous, knowledge workers' (Mitchell, 2011), as well as 'curriculum makers' (Lambert and Morgan, 2010), and of course, this is distinctive and results in a very particular form of geography: that is, geography in education (rather than geography as an independent discipline).The prospects of bridging the gap between schools and universities are not necessarily dimmed by making such a distinction, but we may have to work hard at working out what the links are, or should be. For example, as Peter Jackson (2006) has argued, we could stress that 'thinking geographically', allowing us to apply geographical knowledge and conceptual understanding to different settings, is a uniquely powerful way for

students to see the world and make connections. Conceptualising geography in this way may help us build bridges. But we do not need to unify for, as Noel Castree reminds us, 'students will only come to university to read for a geography degree if they've first been inspired by their geography teachers – teachers who often present a very different sort of geography to that most university academics teach' (Castree, 2011, p. 3). But, we might add, it does need to be geography.

Conclusions

The existence of a 'gap' between school and university geography is increasingly well documented (Clifford, 2002; Thrift, 2002; Bonnett, 2003). It represents a discontinuity keenly felt by many geography graduates who enter initial teacher training, only to discover that the geography syllabuses they teach in schools reflect very little of the themes and content recently studied within the academy.

This is perhaps unsurprising. There will always be significant differences between the two sectors, given their asymmetrical priorities, purposes and concerns: the prime focus of school and university geographers *is* different. But there must always be strong connections between the two if the discipline of geography is to remain healthy, for one important purpose of school is to introduce disciplinary knowledge to young people. More prosaically, universities will continue to supply new geography graduates to be trained as geography teachers and there must be a shared commitment both to, and for, the geographical education of young people. This symbiosis, borne from the mutual needs of both sectors, should encourage the creation of closer ties. Or, if not closer ties, links and connections that are better understood: we do not argue for a 'new model army' – or indeed shock troops of any kind! More modestly we encourage a deeper appreciation of the geography taught in schools and universities, and how collectively this may contribute to 'thinking geographically' (see John Morgan in this volume). This is not to create uniformity, or an overly regimented continuity and progression of geographical themes, but to achieve a mutual, coherent and agreed understanding of the subject, recognisable by both sectors.

Note

1 Castree (2011) estimates that some 80 (of 140) English higher education institutes (HEIs) offer single or joint honours degrees in geography, to around 15,000 students (in 2008–9). Similar numbers are currently studying for degrees in mathematics, and economics.

Key readings

1. Rawling, E. and Daugherty, R. (eds.), (1996) *Geography into the Twenty-First Century*, Chichester: Wiley. Eleanor Rawling and Richard Daugherty's edited work provides a good historical account of how school and university geographies have progressed up to the mid 1990s.

2. Butt, G. (ed.) (2011) *Geography, Education and the Future*, London: Continuum. To take these debates forward, read selected chapters from Graham Butt's (2011) edited work.

References

Bailey, P. and Binns, T. (eds.) (1987) *A Case for Geography*, Sheffield: Geographical Association.

Barratt Hacking, E. (1996) 'Novice teachers and their geographical persuasions', *IRGEE*, 5, 77–86.

Boardman, D. (1988) *The Impact of a Curriculum: Project Geography and the Young School Leaver*, Birmingham: Educational Review Publications.

Bonnett, A. (2003) 'Geography as the world discipline: Connecting popular and academic geographical imaginations', *Area*, 35 (1), 56–63.

Bradford, M. (1996) 'Geography at the secondary/higher education interface: Change through diversity', in E. Rawling, and R. Daugherty (eds.), *Geography into the Twenty-First Century*, Chichester: Wiley.

Brooks, C. (2010) Developing and reflecting on subject expertise', in C. Brooks (ed.), *Studying PGCE Geography at M Level: Reflection, research and writing for professional development*, London: Routledge.

Butt, G. (2002) *Reflective Teaching of Geography 11–18*, London: Continuum.

Butt, G. (2008) 'Is the future secure for geography education?', *Geography*, 93 (3), 158–65.

Butt, G. (ed.) (2011) *Geography, Education and the Future*, London: Continuum.

Castree, N. (2011) 'The future of geography in English universities', *The Geographical Journal*, 136, 4, 512–19.

Castree, N., Fuller, D. and Lambert, D. (2007) 'Geography without borders', *Transactions of the Institute of British Geographers*, 32, 129–32.

Clifford, N. (2002) 'The future of geography: When the whole is less than the sum of its parts', *Geoforum*, 33, 431–6.

Daugherty, R. and Rawling, E. (1996) 'New perspectives for geography: An agenda for action', in E. Rawling, and R. Daugherty (eds.), *Geography into the Twenty-First Century*, Chichester: Wiley.

DES (1991) *Geography in the National Curriculum (England)*, London: HMSO.

DfE (1995) *Geography in the National Curriculum (England)*, London: HMSO.

DfEE/QCA (1999) *The National Curriculum for England: Geography*, London: HMSO.

DfE (2010) *The importance of teaching: The Schools White Paper*, London: The Stationery Office.

Goudie, A. (1993) 'Schools and Universities – the Great Divide', *Geography*, 78 (4), 338–9.

Graves, N. (1975) *Geography in Education*, London: Heinemann.

Gregory, D. (1978) *Ideology, Science and Human Geography*, London: Hutchinson.

Hill, J. and Jones, M. (2010) '"Joined-up geography": Connecting school-level and university-level geographies', *Geography*, 95 (1), 22–32.

Hirsch, E.D. (1987) *Cultural Literacy: What every American needs to know*, Boston, MA: Houghton Mifflin Co.

Hirsch, E.D. (2007) *The knowledge deficit*, Boston, MA: Houghton Mifflin Co.

HSGP (1971) *American High School Geography Project. Geography in an Urban Age*, Toronto, Ont., Canada: Collier-Macmillan.

Jackson, P. (2006) 'Thinking geographically', *Geography*, 91 (3), 199–204.

Jeffrey, C. (2003) 'Bridging the gulf between secondary schools and university-level geography teachers: Reflections on organising a UK teachers' conference', *Journal of Geography in Higher Education*, 27, 201—15.

Johnston, R. (2009) 'On geography, Geography and geographical magazines', *Geography*, 94 (3), 207–14.

Kent, A. (2000) *Reflective Practice in Geography Teaching*, London: Philip Chapman Publishing.

Lambert, D. (2011) 'Reviewing the case for geography, and the 'knowledge turn' in the English National Curriculum', The Curriculum Journal, 22 (2), 243–64.

Lambert, D. and Morgan, J. (2010) Teaching Geography 11–18: A Conceptual Approach, Maidenhead: Open University Press.

Machon, P. and Ranger, G. (1996) 'Change in School Geography', in P. Bailey and P. Fox (eds.), Geography Teacher's Handbook, Sheffield: Geographical Association.

Marsden, W. (1997) 'On taking the Geography out of geographical education – Some historical pointers on geography', Geography, 82 (3), 241–52.

Mitchell, D. (2011) 'A "knowledge turn" – implications for geography initial teacher education (ITE)', Paper presented at the IGU-CGE conference, Institute of Education, University of London, April 2011.

Morgan, J. (2008) Curriculum development in "new times"', Geography, 93 (1), 17–24.

Morgan, J. (2009) 'What makes a "good" geography teacher?', in C. Brooks (ed.), Studying PGCE Geography at M Level, London: Routledge.

Naish, M. (2000) 'The geography curriculum of England and Wales from 1965: A personal view', in D. Lambert and D. Balderstone (eds.), Learning to Teach Geography in the Secondary School, London: RoutledgeFalmer.

Naish, M., Rawling, E. and Hart, C. (1987) Geography 16–19 – the contribution of a curriculum project to 16–19 education, London: Longman.

Pykett, J. and Smith, M. (2009) 'Rediscovering school geographies: Connecting the distant worlds of school and academic geography', Teaching Geography, 34 (1), 35–8.

QCA (2007) The National Curriculum Key Stage 3: Geography, Available from: www.curriculum.qca.org.uk [Accessed 12 December 2011].

Rawling, E. (1996) 'Madingley revisited?', in E. Rawling and R. Daugherty (eds.), Geography into the Twenty-First Century, Chichester: Wiley.

Rawling, E. and Daugherty, R. (eds.) (1996) Geography into the Twenty-First Century, Chichester: Wiley.

Rawling, E. (2001) Changing the Subject. The impact of national policy on school geography 1980–2000, Sheffield: Geographical Association.

Roberts, M. (2010) 'Where's the geography? Reflections on being an external examiner', Teaching Geography, 35 (3), 112–13.

Roberts, M. (2012) What makes a good geography lesson? Available from: www.geography.org.uk/projects/makinggeographyhappen/teachertips [Accessed 12 December 2011].

Stannard, K. (2003) 'Earth to academia: On the need to reconnect university and school geography', Area, 35, 316–32.

Thrift, N. (2002) 'The future of geography', Geoforum, 33, 291–8.

Totterdell, R. (2012) 'What makes a geography lesson "good"'?, Teaching Geography, 37 (1), 35.

Unwin, T. (1996) 'Academic Geography; the key questions for discussion', in E. Rawling and R. Daugherty (eds.), Geography into the Twenty-First Century, Chichester: Wiley.

Walford, R. (1996) '"What is geography?" An analysis of definitions provided by prospective teachers of the subject', IRGEE, 5, 69–76.

Walford, R. (2001) Geography in British Schools 1850–2000, London: Woburn Press.

Yarwood, R. and Davison, T. (2007) '"Bridges or fords?" Geographical Association branches and higher education', Area, 39, 544–550.

Young, M. (2008) Bringing Knowledge Back in: From social constructionism to social realism in the sociology of education, London: Routledge.

Chapter 23

What do we know about concept formation and making progress in learning geography?

Liz Taylor

> if we did not hope that students should progress we would have no founda-
> tion on which to construct a curriculum or embark on the act of teaching.
>
> (Daugherty, 1996, p. 195)

Introduction

A teacher's main task is to create opportunities for their students to progress, but what exactly is progress in learning geography? This is not an easy question to answer. Learning involves change in someone's knowledge, understanding, skills or attitudes (and the meaning of those terms and the relationship between them is complex and contested), but a neutral idea of 'change' is not enough. The change must be seen as valuable, as moving in a positive direction, as progress. This moves the issue into more contentious, political territory – who decides what is positive or valuable? Is this determination to be made by the teacher, the school, the government, or the learner him/herself? Further, in such a broad field of study as geography, a skill or area of content which is valuable to one person may be unimportant to another. Indeed, the subject itself is continually under construction, or in 'progress', so those elements that are valued and promoted change over time.

Not only are different aspects of the subject popular or marginalised at any one time and place, but different levels of emphasis are given within education to knowledge, understanding, skills and values/attitudes. Also, the discourse of 'education' is not unitary: is education concerned with the acquisition of substantive knowledge, gaining skills, or the understanding of key concepts? Of course, most outworkings of these different dimensions are complementary rather than in opposition and the three headings in the 2007 Key Stage 3 curriculum: key concepts, key processes, and range and content, reflect a balance of focus. Even with a broad agreement on the relative importance of these dimensions of learning, there would still be significant discussion over exactly *what* knowledge is valuable (see Roger Firth's chapter in this volume; Lambert, 2011a), or *which* concepts are most powerful for the geographer to deploy in selecting and organising the potential mass of content (see Clare Brooks' chapter in this volume;

Taylor, 2008). In recent years, the dominance of the 'what is geography?' debate has led to attention being focused on what students are expected to make progress in rather than the characteristic ways in which that progress happens. Both debates are important.

It is useful to have theoretically clear and empirically informed work on how children and young people make progress in geography. Research can inform medium- and long-term planning by sharing understanding of the common patterns of progression and problems students encounter in their subject learning. Such understanding might be particularly valuable around break-points between key stages, as maintaining progression across these can be notoriously problematic (Jefferis and Chapman, 2005; Marriott, 2007). Research can also inform meaningful assessment practice, whether this is day-to-day formative practices, or construction of the overarching level descriptors designed for summative assessment at the end of a key stage (Daugherty, 1996; Lambert, 2011b).

WHAT SHOULD STUDENTS BE 'GETTING BETTER AT' IN GEOGRAPHY?

Various 'strands' or 'dimensions' in progression in learning geography have been proposed over time. Since the late 1980s, the production of the National Curriculum, with associated level descriptors designed for assessment at the ends of Key Stages 1–3, has shaped the timescales over which these suggestions operate. For example, the School Curriculum and Assessment Authority (SCAA, 1994, p. 7) proposed that through Key Stage 3 (KS3), pupils in England would increasingly:

- broaden and deepen their knowledge and understanding of places and themes;
- make use of a wide and precise geographical vocabulary;
- analyse, rather than describe, geographical patterns, processes and change;
- appreciate the interactions within and between physical and human processes that operate in any environment;
- appreciate the interdependence of places;
- become proficient at conducting and comparing studies at a widening range of scales and in contrasting places and environments;
- apply their geographical knowledge and understanding to unfamiliar contexts;
- select and make effective use of skills and techniques to support their geographical investigations; and
- appreciate the limitations of geographical evidence and the tentative and incomplete nature of some explanations.

You will notice some similarities between the list above and the table below which formed an appendix to the QCA's schemes of work for KS3 geography, published

to complement the 2000 Geography National Curriculum (QCA, 2000). This suggests 'some aspects of progression in geography at key stage 3' (see Table 23.1).

Table 23.1 Some aspects of progression in geography at Key Stage 3 (QCA, 2000)

	From	To
Vocabulary	• using a limited geographical vocabulary	• precise use of a wider range of vocabulary
Knowledge of places	• geographical knowledge of some places	• understanding of a wider range of areas and links between them
Patterns and processes	• describing geographical patterns and processes	• explaining geographical patterns and processes
Geographical thinking	• participating in practical geographical activities	• building increasingly abstract models of real situations
Geographical explanation	• explaining events and phenomena in terms of their own ideas	• explaining these in terms of accepted ideas or models
Investigation	• unstructured exploration	• more systematic exploration
Map skills	• using simple drawings, maps and diagrams to represent geographical information	• choosing and using a wide range of conventional maps, diagrams and graphs
Fieldwork	• guided practical activities in the field	• working independently outside the classroom

A few writers on geography education have drawn out key elements of progression in geography over a wider timescale than over one key stage. For example, Marsden (1995, p. 81) suggested that progression in geography entailed moving from:

- the familiar to the unfamiliar
- the near to the more distant
- the concrete to the abstract
- the smaller to the larger scale
- the simple to the more complex in terms of:
- breadth of coverage
- depth of coverage
- a more to a less limited range of skills.

More recently, Bennetts (2005a) drew together his thinking on the topic of geographical progression and understanding (Bennetts 1995, 2005a, 2005b), to suggest the following as 'the most significant dimensions of progression in geographical understanding' (2005a, pp. 123–4):

- distance from experience in the sense of the gap between what is required to be understood and what students have experienced or have knowledge of;
- complexity – whether of experience, information, ideas or cognitive tasks;

- abstraction – particularly of ideas about processes, relationships and values, but also forms of presentation;
- precision, in the sense of being more exact and knowing when that is appropriate and useful;
- making connections and developing structures – ranging from applying simple ideas to experience and making simple links between ideas, to the use of sophisticated conceptual models and theories;
- the breadth of context in which explanations are placed, especially spatial contexts, but also temporal and other contexts;
- the association of understanding with cognitive abilities and skills; and
- the association of understanding with affective elements, such as attitudes and values, and the value-laden nature of particular ideas.

These four sets of proposed strands in progression show significant commonality. Each mentions some form of increasing *breadth*, whether in knowledge and understanding of a broader range of places, or in broader contexts for explanations. Breadth is often juxtaposed with *depth*, which presumably refers to greater amounts of detail or complexity for each topic or place studied. There is also a clear association of the move from the *concrete to the abstract* with progress, a move which is often seen as culminating in the understanding or use of models and theories. In addition, the influence of familiar thinking on cognitive stretch, such as that detailed in Bloom's taxonomy (Bloom, 1956; Krathwohl, 2002), can be identified in terms of progress from describing to applying, explaining or analysing. Skills are also mentioned, with the intention that students should be able to use a *wider range of techniques*, increasingly to discern which are appropriate in a given situation and to be able to work independently.

It is significant to note that many of the strands suggested in the above paragraph could apply equally well to education in general, or to other curricular subjects: few are inherently geographical. The mentions of developing understanding of interaction/interdependence and change/process perhaps come closest to this. It is likely that most geography teachers would agree that students who demonstrate such changes in their work over time are making 'progress'. However, Lee and Shemilt, who have undertaken considerable research in this area of history education, suggest that a useful distinction can be made between the more general ideas of progress and 'progression'. They see progression being the more specialised term, referring to 'the way in which pupils' ideas – about history and the past – develop' (2003, p. 13). Lee and Shemilt also counterpose progression and 'aggregation', the latter defined as 'an increase in the amount of information pupils could recall' (2003, p. 13), which perhaps parallels mentions of 'breadth' above. It is not that Lee and Shemilt have a lack of interest in the substantive knowledge base of their subject, or that they do not value this, but their use of 'progression' reflects their desire to see their subject as *more* than accumulation of that substantive knowledge. Their research focuses on analysis of large sets of students' writing, as well as some classroom-based investigation, to

illuminate key ways of thinking associated with the underlying operational structures of history (Lee and Ashby, 2000). They have created progression models in students' understanding of evidence, historical accounts and interpretations, historical explanation and causal reasoning (Lee and Shemilt, 2003, 2004, 2009). Going back to the geography examples above, could the equivalents include the ways in which geographers mobilise ideas of change or interaction in increasingly sophisticated ways?

It is also worth considering the claim to authority of the above lists of strands of progression in geography. None refers directly to empirical research. Instead, their authority is that of their authors' experience of teaching and learning, plus commonsense and logic, whilst their validation is in the mind of the reader – does it 'make sense' for them? As the statements can be seen as aspirational rather than directly descriptive of current patterns, this is not particularly problematic. However, is there any empirical evidence regarding children and young people's progression in geography which we could draw on to flesh out the 'before and after' statements? *In what ways* do children characteristically progress?

WHAT DO WE KNOW ABOUT CHILDREN AND YOUNG PEOPLE'S PROGRESSION IN GEOGRAPHY?

Although it can take some detective skills to locate it, there is a fair volume of empirically based research on children and young people's understandings of topics which come into the purview of geography education. However, not all of this research is 'badged' as geography education. To take one example, there is substantial research on children's understandings of place(s), both local and distant to them. To access this, it is necessary to draw on work originating at the interface with psychology and sociology, as well as geography and geography education. So, one key strand of this work arose from an interest within *environmental psychology*, for example the 'Clark group' in the late 1960s (see special issue of the *Journal of Environmental Psychology*, 7 (4)). The work of Blaut, Stea and Hart also explored the interface between geography and psychology, often with a focus on children's thinking and behaviours, and usually with regard to their local environment (see Blaut, 1987; Hart, 1987). Other environmental cognition research located within, or overlapping with, the discipline of psychology focused on children's mapping of the world (see Matthews, 1992, for a useful summary). For example, Gould and White's classic book *Mental Maps* (1974) explored young people's place knowledge and preferences, using cross-sectional techniques to show how the extent of knowledge was related to age. Young people's knowledge about and attitudes towards other countries has also formed a focus to research over time, from Piaget and Weil's influential study (1951) to more recent work carried out in the context of European integration (Axia et al., 1998; Barrett and Short, 1992; Barrett and Farroni, 1996; Rutland, 1998). These studies tend to be large-scale surveys, highlighting knowledge of location and spatial configuration, or attitudes towards nationalities, rather than in-depth explorations of a broader range of understandings about places.

Another key strand of research is in the field of children's geographies, a branch of geography which tends to be informed by *sociology*. Examples of literature on children's understandings of place from this perspective include Holloway and Valentine's (2000) study, which traced young people's imaginative geographies over sets of emails exchanged in a UK–New Zealand school-linking project, and Vanderbeck and Dunkley's (2003) research which explored young people's understandings of rural–urban difference.

Moving to research on understandings of place generated within a *geography education* context, there is considerable focus on children's world place-knowledge and map drawing (Wiegand, 1991; 1998; Harwood and Rawlings, 2001; Schmeinck, 2006). There is also research on children's understandings of their local area (for example Barratt and Barratt-Hacking, 2000), and distant places. In the 1980s, the latter often tied in with concerns about racism (for example Graham and Lynn, 1989), whilst, more recently, school-linking has been a motivator (Halocha, 1998; Disney, 2005; Pickering, 2008).

Whilst various disciplines have contributed to a substantial literature on children's understandings of place, in other areas of geography, the volume of research evidence varies considerably from topic to topic. Those physical geography topics that border or overlap with science education tend to have attracted more research. These include ecosystems (Strommen, 1995; Dove, 2000), landscape features (Eyres and Garner, 1998; Cin and Yaziki, 2002; Mackintosh, 2004) and weather and climate (Dove, 1998; Alkiş, 2007). Issues of the environment and sustainability have also received attention (for example Cabral and Kaivola, 2005; Walshe, 2008). Human geography has generally received less attention, though there is research on children and young people's understanding of rural and urban environments (e.g. Walker, 2004; Béneker et al., 2007) and globalisation (Picton, 2010). Of course, these published studies are probably the tip of the iceberg – much small-scale research about children's understandings by teachers and trainee teachers is unpublished and therefore not available to the geography education community as a whole.

Insofar as research methods are concerned, most of the studies of children's understandings detailed above describe the oral, written or pictorial representations of young people on a particular geographical topic at *one point in time*. These can be useful to show us the range of different understandings with a group, and if the group is large enough, then these data might be a starting point for identifying and evaluating characteristic ways of thinking about a particular topic. This would be one way in to understanding paths in progression. *Cross-sectional research* (a snapshot of the responses of different age groups at one point in time) is commonly used as a proxy for how children's understandings change over longer periods of time (usually a number of years) and can also be used to inform progression models. However, when trying to understand the processes by which children and young people make progress, *longitudinal research* (following the same children over time) is necessary. Some work on children's understandings of distant place compares their representations at the start and end of a unit of work (Stillwell and Spencer, 1974; Harrington, 1998; Picton, 2008). This is useful in

describing changes at a detailed level, but processes of change may not be evident. In my own research on young people's understanding of distant place, a detailed lesson-by-lesson system of data collection enabled a fine-grained tracking of changes as well as reflections from the students on their experiences of learning. The empirical component of this research consisted of an interpretive case study of one Year 9 class (ages 13–14) who were studying Japan in their geography lessons. Materials resulting from a wide range of methods, including in-depth interviews, visual methods, classroom observation and audio diaries, were used to explore students' representations of Japan and the ways in which these developed over time. The students' initial representations of Japan were found to be diverse and individual in nature, though it was possible to identify common themes (Taylor, 2009). Over the unit of study, some representations of Japan were found to persist, some were modified and new ones emerged. There was evidence for three processes of change taking place: prediction from knowledge of other distant places and personal experience; elicitation of new knowledge; and classification of new knowledge into both familiar and new categories (Taylor, 2011). Different learning activities provided students with distinctive opportunities for understanding and framing diversity, both within Japan and between Japan and other countries. Whilst the work does not involve the explicitly evaluative component needed for constructing a progression model, it does point to some of the learning experiences which seem to have encouraged changes in students' representations.

This leads us to research on conceptual change. This type of detailed, longitudinal work is more common within research in science and mathematics education than in geography, and the processes by which children form and change concepts over time have long been investigated by psychologists. Research on geographical topics that border on science education has given particular prominence to the identification of common 'preconceptions', 'misconceptions' or 'alternative conceptions' (Dove, 1999). These may act as barriers to further learning. Such research can be useful to warn teachers of likely misunderstandings or prior conceptions regarding a particular topic, such as the confusion between global warming and the hole in the ozone layer. However, misconceptions are not necessarily most profitably seen as enemies to be confronted and replaced. Instead, whilst their flaws and limitations of application are acknowledged, it may still be possible for them to be refined and reused in later, more sophisticated reasoning (Smith et al., 1993). Work on conceptual change has sometimes taken a purely cognitive focus, but more recently, affective factors such as motivation and attitudes to learning have interested researchers, the so-called 'warming' trend in conceptual change research (Pintrich et al., 1993). Debate also focuses around whether conceptual change is gradual and cumulative (evolutionary) or more sudden and transformative (revolutionary) (Keiny, 2008). Work in neuroscience suggests that learning is incremental and networks cannot suddenly be restructured (Goswami, 2008). However, 'certain experiences may result in previously distinct parts of the network becoming connected, or inefficient connections that were impeding understanding being pruned away' (Goswami, 2008, p. 388), suggesting an

enticing yet beguiling possibility of research identifying a physical anchor to explain conceptual change.

The work of Meyer and Land (2003) on 'threshold concepts' in economics has sparked interest from some geographers (GEES, 2006; Slinger, 2011). A threshold concept refers to a core learning outcome that involves 'seeing things in a new way' (Meyer and Land, 2003, p. 1). They suggest that a threshold concept is transformative, probably irreversible, integrative, possibly bounded and potentially troublesome, with opportunity cost suggested as an example from economics. This 'troublesome knowledge' is 'conceptually difficult, counter-intuitive or "alien"' (Meyer and Land, 2003, p. 1). A range of possible threshold concepts has been suggested in a geography and earth sciences context, including quantification, time, sustainability and geographical enquiry (GEES, 2006; Slinger, 2011). If we could identify and then research children's understandings of threshold concepts in geography, this would clearly be profitable for informing planning for progression. However, how would such concepts be identified?

Much of the current empirical work in geography education outlined above concerns children and young people's understandings of substantive concepts (rivers, rainforests, cities …) or their knowledge about particular places. There are a great many substantive concepts used in geography, from the concrete (farm) to the abstract (inequality), and complete agreement on which are the most important for a young person's progression in their learning of geography is unlikely. Lee and Shemilt commented of the equivalent work in history education that:

> It is too simple to say that research on substantive concepts failed to find patterns or change in students' ideas, but it ran into problems about whether the concepts were in any clear sense 'historical', why some should be taught rather than others, and how they related to one another.
>
> (2003, p. 14)

Instead, Lee and Shemilt focused their research on looking for characteristic pathways of development in students' understanding of second-order concepts in history, such as evidence or interpretations (Lee, 2005). This follows the interest in the history subject community on identifying Schwab's 'syntactic structures' (Schwab, 1978) within the discipline. Whilst the exact composition of history's set of second-order concepts is still debated, the general move of research focus from substantive to second-order seems to have been profitable:

> Work on pupils' second-order ideas began to provide evidence that it was possible to treat history as progressive in a somewhat analogous way to physics: pupils did not simply add to their information about the past, but acquired understandings that changed in patterned ways as they learnt about history. The concepts of progression began to mean something more specific than progress. It meant that history was not just about aggregation.
>
> (Lee and Shemilt, 2003, p. 14)

The outcome has been a series of progression models showing sets of less to more powerful ideas which students can mobilise when learning about historical topics. Lee and Shemilt are well aware of the potential pitfalls of the ways in which such models can be understood, and their work is well sprinkled with caveats:

> The 'levels' in a progression model are not a sequence of ladder-like rungs that every student must step on as he or she climbs. Indeed, a model of the development of students' ideas does not set out a learning path for individuals at all. Assuming it is well founded, it is valid for groups, not for individuals. That is, it sets out the ideas likely to be found in any reasonably large group of children, the likely distribution of those ideas among students of different ages, and the pattern of developing ideas we might expect.
>
> (2003, p. 16)

Sometimes Lee and Shemilt themselves suggest teaching activities which might help students move on from an understandable, but ultimately unhelpful idea brought from everyday life into their learning of history. At other times practising history teachers have supplied and disseminated such ideas (Lee and Shemilt, 2009). In either case, the combination of rigorous research and innovative practice is very convincing.

Conclusion

Where does this leave this overview of progress in geography education? We have a number of *a priori* descriptors of progress, including the four examples given earlier in this chapter, and of course the various versions of the attainment target in the National Curriculum. We also have a fairly large, though somewhat unsystematic, volume of research on students' understandings of substantive concepts used in geography and somewhat less on their representations of particular places. Some of this research, based on analysis of larger datasets, or on longitudinal work, suggests possible progression pathways for young people's understanding of certain substantive concepts (including some potentially troublesome ones such as 'sustainability') or in deploying geographical skills (such as graphicacy). However, to this point, the geography teaching community in general has had little engagement with the distinction between substantive and second-order concepts in the discipline, so the possible benefits identified by Lee and Shemilt in researching students' progression in the latter have not yet been realised. Perhaps this would be a productive route forward for debate and research in geographical education, although it is noted that the development of this knowledge in history education has resulted from a well-funded Research Council project enabling full-time research endeavour over several years.

Key readings

1. Bennetts, T. (2005a) 'Progression in geographical understanding', *International Research in Geographical and Environmental Education*, *14* (2), 112–32. A good overview of Bennetts' thinking in the area of progression.
2. Daugherty, R. (1996) 'Defining and measuring progression in geographical education', in E. Rawling and R. Daugherty (eds.), *Geography into the Twenty-first century* (pp. 195–215), Chichester, West Sussex: John Wiley and Sons Ltd. A useful overview of thinking on progression in the context of the development of the National Curriculum, including a review of available empirical research at that time; it poses some useful and still unresolved questions.

References

Alkiş, S. (2007) 'An investigation of Grade 5 students' understanding of humidity concept', *Elementary Education Online*, 6 (3), 333–43.

Axia, G., Bremner, J., Deluca, P., and Andreasen, G. (1998) 'Children drawing Europe: The effects of nationality, age and teaching', *British Journal of Developmental Psychology*, 16, 423–37.

Barratt, M. and Barratt-Hacking, E. (2000) 'Changing my locality: conceptions of the future', *Teaching Geography*, 25 (1), 17–21.

Barrett, M. and Farroni, T. (1996) 'English and Italian children's knowledge of European Geography', *British Journal of Developmental Psychology*, 14, 257–73.

Barrett, M. and Short, J. (1992) 'Images of European people in a group of 5–10-year-old English Schoolchildren', *British Journal of Developmental Psychology*, 10, 339–63.

Béneker, T., Sanders, R., Tani, S., Taylor, L. and Van der Vaart, R. (2007) 'Teaching the geographies of urban areas: Views and visions', *International Research in Geographical and Environmental Education*, 16 (3), 250–67.

Bennetts, T. (1995) 'Continuity and progression', *Teaching Geography*, 20 (2), 75–9.

Bennetts, T. (2005a) 'Progression in geographical understanding', *International Research in Geographical and Environmental Education*, 14 (2), 112–32.

Bennetts, T. (2005b) 'The links between understanding, progression and assessment in the secondary geography curriculum', *Geography*, 90 (2), 152–70.

Blaut, J. (1987) 'Place perception in perspective', *Journal of Environmental Psychology*, 7 (4), 297–305.

Bloom, B. (ed.) (1956) *Taxonomy of educational objectives: The classification of educational goals. Handbook 1: Cognitive domain*, New York: David McKay.

Cabral, S. and Kaivola, T. (2005) 'Imagine the world', *Teaching Geography*, 30 (2), 86–90.

Cin, M. and Yazici, H. (2002) 'The Influence of Direct Experience on Children's Ideas about the Formation of the Natural Scenery', *International Research in Geographical and Environmental Education*, 11 (1), 5–14.

Daugherty, R. (1996) 'Defining and measuring progression in geographical education', in E. Rawling and R. Daugherty (eds.), *Geography into the Twenty-first century*, Chichester, West Sussex: John Wiley and Sons Ltd.

Disney, A. (2005) 'Children's images of a distant locality', *International Research in Geographical and Environmental Education*, 14 (4), 330–35.

Dove, J. (1998) 'Alternative conceptions about the weather', *School Science Review*, 79 (289), 65–9.

Dove, J. (1999) *Immaculate Misconceptions*, Sheffield: Geographical Association.

Dove, J. (2000) 'Conceptions of rainforests', *Teaching Geography*, 25 (1), 32–4.

Eyres, M. and Garner, W. (1998) 'Children's ideas about landscapes', in S. Scoffham (ed.), *Primary sources*, Sheffield: Geographical Association.

Geography Earth and Environmental Sciences (GEES) (2006) 'Special issue on threshold concepts and troublesome knowledge', *Planet*, 17. Available from: http://www.gees.ac.uk/pubs/planet/index.htm#P17 [Accessed 12 September 2011].

Goswami, U. (2008) 'Principles of learning, implications for teaching: A cognitive neuroscience Perspective', *Journal of Philosophy of Education*, 42 (3-4), 381–99.

Gould, P. and White, R. (1974) *Mental Maps*, Harmondsworth: Penguin Books Ltd.

Graham, J. and Lynn, S. (1989) 'Mud huts and flints: Children's images of the Third World', *Education 3–13*, 17 (2), 29–32.

Haddon, J. (1960) 'A view of foreign lands', *Geography*, 45, 286–9.

Halocha, J. (1998) 'The European Dimension', in S. Scoffham (ed.), *Primary sources: Research findings in primary geography*, Sheffield: Geographical Association.

Harrington, V. (1998) 'Teaching about distant places', in S. Scoffham (ed.), *Primary Sources: Research findings in primary geography*, Sheffield: Geographical Association.

Hart, R. (1987) 'Environmental psychology or behavioural geography? Either way it was a good start', *Journal of Environmental Psychology*, 7 (4), 321–9.

Harwood, D. and Rawlings, K. (2001) 'Assessing young children's freehand sketch maps of the World', *International Research in Geographical and Environmental Education*, 10 (1), 20–45.

Holloway, S. and Valentine, G. (2000) 'Corked hats and Coronation Street: British and New Zealand children's imaginative geographies of the other', *Childhood*, 7 (3), 335–57.

Jefferis, T. and Chapman, S. (2005) 'Using ICT as a bridging unit', *Teaching Geography*, 30 (2), 108–12.

Keiny, S. (2008) '"Conceptual change' as both revolutionary and evolutionary process', *Teachers and Teaching: Theory and practice*, 14 (1), 61–72.

Krathwohl, D. (2002) 'A revision of Bloom's taxonomy: An overview', *Theory into practice*, 41 (4), 212–18.

Lambert, D. (2011a) 'Reviewing the case for geography, and the 'knowledge turn' in the English National Curriculum', *Curriculum Journal*, 22 (2), 243–64.

Lambert, D. (2011b) 'The lie of the land (revisited)', *Teaching Geography*, 36 (1), 24–5.

Lee, P. (2005) 'Putting principles into practice: Understanding history', in M. Donovan and J. Bransford (eds.), *How students learn: History in the classroom*, Washington, DC: The National Academies Press.

Lee, P. and Ashby, R. (2000) 'Progression in historical understanding among students ages 7–14', in P. Stearns, P. Seixas and S. Wineburg (eds.), *Knowing teaching and learning history: National and international perspectives*, New York: New York University Press.

Lee, P. and Shemilt, D. (2003) 'A scaffold, not a cage: Progression and progression models in History', *Teaching History*, 113, 13–23.

Lee, P. and Shemilt, D. (2004) '"I just wish we could go back in the past and find out what really Happened": Progression in understanding about historical accounts', *Teaching History*, 117, 25–31.

Lee, P. and Shemilt, D. (2009) 'Is any explanation better than none? Over-determined narratives, senseless agencies and one-way streets in students' learning about cause and consequence in history', *Teaching History*, 137, 42–9.

Mackintosh, M. (2004) 'Children's understanding of rivers: Is there need for more constructivist research in primary geography?', in S. Catling and F. Martin (eds.), *Researching primary geography (Register of Researching Primary Geography Special Publication No. 1)*, London: Register of Research in Primary Geography.

Marriott, A. (2007) 'The transition from A level to degree geography', *Teaching Geography*, 31(2), 49–50.

Marsden, W. (1995) *Geography 11–16: Rekindling good practice*, London: David Fulton.

Matthews, M. (1992) *Making sense of place: Children's understanding of large scale environments*, Hemel Hempstead, UK: Harvester Wheatsheaf.

Meyer, J. and Land, R. (2003) *Threshold concepts and troublesome knowledge: linkages to ways of thinking and practising within the disciplines, Enhancing Teaching-Learning Environments in*

Undergraduate Courses Project, Occasional Report 4, Edinburgh: University of Edinburgh. Available from: http://www.etl.tla.ed.ac.uk/docs/ETLreport4.pdf [Accessed 12 September 2011].

Piaget, J. and Weil, A. (1951) 'The development in children of the idea of the homeland and of relations with other countries', *International Social Science Bulletin, UNESCO*, 3, 561–78.

Pickering, S. (2008) 'What do children really learn? A discussion to investigate the effect that school partnerships have on children's understanding, sense of values and perceptions of a distant place', *GeogEd*, 2 (1), Article 3, Available from: http://www.geography.org.uk/download/GA_GeogEdVol2012I2011A2013.pdf [Accessed 12 September 2011].

Picton, O. (2008) 'Teaching and learning about distant places: Conceptualising diversity', *International Research in Geographical and Environmental Education*, 17 (3), 227–49.

Picton, O. (2010) 'Shrinking world? Globalisation at key stage 3', *Teaching Geography*, 35 (1), 10–17.

Pintrich, P., Marx, R. and Boyle, R. (1993) 'Beyond cold conceptual change: The role of motivational beliefs and classroom contextual factors in the process of conceptual change', *Review of Educational Research*, 63 (2), 167–99.

Qualifications and Curriculum Authority (QCA) (2000) *Geography: A scheme of work for key stage 3, Teacher's Guide*, London: QCA/DfEE.

Rutland, A. (1998) 'English children's geo-political knowledge of Europe', *British Journal of Developmental Psychology*, 16, 439–45.

SCAA (1994) *Geography in the National Curriculum, Draft Proposals*, London: SCAA/HMSO.

Schmeinck, D. (2006) 'Images of the world or Do travel experiences and the presence of media influence children's perception of the world?', in D. Schmeinck (ed.), *Research on learning and teaching in primary geography*, Karlsruhe, Germany: Pädagogische Hochschule Karlsruhe.

Schwab, J. (1978) *Science, curriculum and liberal education*, Chicago: University of Chicago Press.

Slinger, J. (2011) *Threshold concepts in secondary geography education*, Paper presented at the Geographical Association Annual Conference, Guildford, University of Surrey April 2011, Available from: http://www.geography.org.uk/cpdevents/annualconference/guildford2011/#13548 [Accessed 12 September 2011].

Smith, J., diSessa, A. and Roschelle, J. (1993) 'Misconceptions reconceived: A constructivist analysis of knowledge in transition', *Journal of the Learning Sciences*, 3 (2), 115–63.

Stillwell, R. and Spencer, C. (1974) 'Children's early preferences for other nations and their subsequent acquisition of knowledge about those nations', *European Journal of Social Psychology*, 3 (3), 345–9.

Strommen, E. (1995) 'Lions and tigers and bears, oh my! Children's conceptions of forests and their inhabitants', *Journal of Research in Science Teaching*, 32 (7), 683–98.

Taylor, L. (2008) 'Key concepts and medium term planning', *Teaching Geography*, 33 (2), 50–54.

Taylor, L. (2009) 'Children constructing Japan: Material practices and relational learning', *Children's Geographies*, 7 (2), 173–89.

Taylor, L. (2011) 'Investigating change in young people's understandings of Japan: A study of learning about a distant place', *British Educational Research Journal*, 37 (6), 1033–54.

Vanderbeck, R. and Dunkley, C. (2003) 'Young people's narratives of rural-urban difference', *Children's Geographies*, 1 (2), 241–59.

Walker, G. (2004) 'Urban children's perceptions of rural villages in England', in S. Catling and F. Martin (eds.), *Researching primary geography*, London: Register of Research in Primary Geography.

Walshe, N. (2008) 'Understanding students' conceptions of sustainability', *Environmental Education Research*, 14 (5), 537–58.

Wiegand, P. (1991) 'The 'known world' of primary school children', *Geography*, 76 (2), 143–9.

Wiegand, P. (1998) 'Children's free recall sketch maps of the world on a spherical surface', *International Research in Geographical and Environmental Education*, 7 (1), 67–83.

Acknowledgements

We are very grateful to the following individuals, groups and organisations for granting permission to reproduce material in the following chapters:

Chapter 5. The Geographical Association for Bennetts' diagram from Bennetts, T. (2005) 'The links between understanding, progression and assessment in the secondary geography curriculum', *Geography*, 90 (2), 152–70.

Chapter 6. A curriculum map of earth science and physical geography in the National Curriculum, based on a document jointly produced by The Geographical Association, The Geological Society, The Earth Science Teachers' Association, The Royal Geographical Society and The Royal Meteorological Society and which was submitted to assist with the review of the National Curriculum for England (December 2011).

Chapter 7. The Geographical Association for Roberts (2003) Enquiry approach from Roberts, M. (2003) *Learning through Enquiry*, Sheffield: Geographical Association.

Chapter 9. Royal Geographical Society with Institute of British Geographers RGS-IBG for Curriculum Making Model from CPD PowerPoint®.

Chapter 13. Royal Geographical Society with Institute of British Geographers for permission to use Table 13.1 and Figure 13.1 from the original publication *Fieldwork Strategies*. Readers will find the schools section of the RGS website particularly helpful. Go to www.rgs.org/schools

Chapter 14. Alec Couros of the University of Regina, Canada for permission to include Figure 14.1a and Figure 14.1b.

Chapter 15. Matthew Koehler and Punya Mishra, of Michigan State University, USA for permission to use the TPACK image from the original source http://tpack.org

Chapter 17. Routledge for permission to include the table 'Approaches to values education' from Lambert, D. and Balderstone, D. (2000) *Learning to teach Geography in the Secondary School*, London: RoutledgeFalmer, p. 293.

Index